Praise for *Bess of Hardwick*
'Utterly absorbing . . . one of those biographies in which the reader really doesn't want the subject to die'
Alexander Waugh, *Independent on Sunday*

'The best account yet of this shrewd, enigmatic and remarkable woman'
Miranda Seymour, *Sunday Times*

Praise for *The Mitford Girls*
'This is an excellent book – calm, dispassionate and respectful of its subjects'
Daily Telegraph

'The remarkable Mitfords have inspired dozens of books but this may well be the best'
Independent on Sunday

'A book that can be heartily recommended'
A. N. Wilson, *New Statesman*

Also by Mary S. Lovell

A Rage to Live: A Biography of Richard and Isabel Burton

The Mitford Girls: The Biography of an Extraordinary Family

Bess of Hardwick: First Lady of Chatsworth

Straight on Till Morning: The Life of Beryl Markham

Cast No Shadow: The Spy Who Changed the Course of World War II

A Scandalous Life: The Biography of Jane Digby

The Splendid Outcast: The African Short Stories of Beryl Markham

Amelia Earhart

The Sound of Wings

MARY S. LOVELL

ABACUS

This edition published in 2009 by Abacus
First published in Great Britain in 1989 by Hutchinson

Copyright © Mary S. Lovell 1989

The moral right of the author has been asserted.

A CIP catalogue record for this book
is available from the British Library.

ISBN 978-0-349-12176-5

Typeset in Garamond by M Rules
Printed and bound in Great Britain by
Clays Ltd, St Ives plc

Papers used by Abacus are natural, renewable and
recyclable products sourced from well-managed forests and certified in
accordance with the rules of the Forest Stewardship Council.

Mixed Sources
Product group from well-managed
forests and other controlled sources
www.fsc.org Cert no. SGS-COC-004081
© 1996 Forest Stewardship Council
FSC

Abacus
An imprint of
Little, Brown Book Group
100 Victoria Embankment
London EC4Y 0DY

An Hachette UK Company
www.hachette.co.uk

www.littlebrown.co.uk

This book is dedicated to the memory of
JOHN A. BELCHER

'He was a verray parfit gentil knight'
(*The Canterbury Tales*)

CONTENTS

MAPS

PREFACE

It is now more than fifty years since Amelia Earhart disappeared whilst attempting to be the first woman to fly around the world. In 1928 she had been the first woman to fly across the Atlantic and four years later became the first woman to fly it solo at a time when only one other person, Charles Lindbergh, had done so. Subsequently she performed any number of 'firsts' in aviation, many of which were also 'first woman' records.

What is it about Amelia Earhart that has kept her name alive? Charles Lindbergh achieved a similar lasting fame, but most of the other early aviators have – for the most part – been forgotten by all except aviation enthusiasts.

Amelia's achievements were remarkable, but some of her reputation rests on the outstanding management skills of her husband, George Palmer Putnam. Putnam was a publicist of such ability that during her life Amelia's name received almost constant media exposure. Indeed, my research indicates that it was largely due to his brilliant management of the name 'Amelia Earhart' that she is still remembered.

Much has already been written about Amelia Earhart. She herself wrote three books, mainly about her flying exploits. Her husband followed these with a biography shortly after her presumed death in 1937, and any number of books have been written since, theorising about what might have happened to Amelia when her plane failed to turn up at its destination on a small island in the Pacific Ocean. But why the abiding interest?

In effect I began to research Amelia's story in 1962, not for a book but out of personal curiosity. I was then (Honorary) Secretary to the Los Angeles Chapter of the Antique Airplane Association, and it was in this connection that I met the famous Hollywood stunt pilot, Paul Mantz. It was common knowledge that Paul had been closely involved with Amelia in her later record-breaking flights. The aviation expert on Amelia's team, he had been her co-pilot when she took part in the National Air Races, and was also a business partner in a Californian flying school. What Paul told me about his involvement with Amelia's departure on her world-circling final flight precipitated my initial interest in her.

Amelia was very much on Paul's mind at that time for he had recently been interviewed by CBS journalist, Fred Goerner. Goerner believed that Amelia had been on a spy mission for the United States government, using the round-the-world flight as a cover. Further he believed that Amelia had made a forced landing near a Japanese-mandated island in the Pacific Ocean, had been captured and had died in captivity.

Paul did not believe that Amelia had been a spy, but what he told me – and others – seemed equally interesting: that Amelia's plane was not ready when she took off on that fatal flight and that he, Paul, anticipated at least another two days' work. He was shocked, he said, to hear that she had gone without even saying goodbye to him. Later his enquiries led him to believe that George Putnam had pressured Amelia into leaving early because he had organised a huge civic welcome for her return to Los Angeles, timed for 4 July. If she delayed any longer, then allowing for contingency delays for weather conditions, spares or engineering faults, she could not make it back in time. Paul also claimed that Putnam used Amelia and her reputation, implying that Amelia was driven to exhaustion because of George's manipulative methods.

This seemed an interesting and plausible story from a man I admired and respected and it never occurred to me to doubt it, or consider that it was simply one side of the story. I had no reason, either, to suspect that Paul Mantz and George Putnam had become enemies after Amelia's disappearance, over a matter concerning her estate. So when, early in 1987, I started full time research on Amelia Earhart for a commissioned biography, I was content to accept the story that George Putnam had used Amelia for his own ends. This has been written about by so many Earhart researchers that I had no cause to question its authenticity.

Gradually, though, as my research progressed, I realised that not only was George Putnam a fascinating person in his own right, but had it not been for him, Amelia would undoubtedly have dropped out of public awareness. Women fliers such as Ruth Law, Louise Thaden, Ruth Elder, Elinor Smith, Ruth Nichols, Katherine Stinson, Bobbi Trout and Phoebe Omlie, are remembered with respect by those interested in American civil aviation, but I suspect few others would recognise their names. Yet all these women were contemporaries of Amelia and all had to their credit great 'firsts' in aviation which at the time made headline news. Without George, Amelia probably would never have performed many of her record-breaking feats, and even if she had it is doubtful that this alone would have been sufficient to keep her name alive for fifty years.

What George did for Amelia's career was threefold. First, he inspired and encouraged her; second, he worked on her behalf to publicise her name and reputation, creating openings for a financially viable career in aviation; third, he introduced her to a wide circle of powerful people and obtained the necessary financial backing for her record attempts. Arguably, without this help Amelia would never have made that final flight with its tragic outcome (for the sponsorship to support the venture would not have been available except to someone of public stature beyond the ordinary); and so Amelia might have lived to a ripe old age.

George himself said of her, after her death, that 'if there had been no George Putnam to lend a hand here and there, some way would have appeared by which the individuality which was A.E. would have secured its freedom to flower, and the wings with which to soar to fame.' But my opinion is that without George Putnam my generation would hardly have heard the name Amelia Earhart outside aviation circles.

Then too, there was the accusation that George 'used' her; that

Amelia recognised and resented George's manipulations of her time and reputation. I found no evidence whatsoever to support this, indeed quite the reverse. There was love between George and Amelia: those closest to them both were aware of it and spoke of it. Surviving correspondence contains loving endearments, and it is only necessary to watch the couple together on old newsreel footage to see the warmth and comfortable rapport that existed between them. If they had disagreements these were no more than the normal everyday ones that occur in any healthy relationship, particularly when the two people involved also work together and both have strong characters.

So this story which started out as a biography of Amelia has become the story of Amelia and George. Their relationship is the real core of the book. But I have also covered their early lives, before they met, so that their characters can be seen developing.

In Amelia's case it has been necessary to cover ground that has already been worked over, some of it often. I have tried to weed out the myths and highlight what I consider to be the essential parts of Amelia's story. This book does not represent all my research; one could fill two volumes with anecdotes and stories, but there is not always evidence to prove that they are not apocryphal.

Fortunately I have uncovered new information which may illustrate some facets of Amelia's character that were previously unknown. And throughout my work I have been aware of Amelia's calm, efficient and, above all, humorous spirit. It is extremely difficult not to like Amelia.

I do not subscribe, however, to the 'Saint Amelia' concept which I often encountered. Amelia, I feel, would have hooted derisively at this canonisation. She could be waspish, intolerant and ill-humoured, just like any of us, and stress often lay at the root of this.

Very little had been previously published about George Putnam, except what he chose to tell in his memoir *Wide Margins*. This is a most frustrating book because it consists largely of portraits of the interesting people he met in his career. As a close friend summed up, 'I told him it was the only autobiography I'd ever read that was about *other* people!' And this is the man who has been accused of gross self-aggrandisement. People either loved or loathed George Putnam, and there is still no middle ground. I find him altogether fascinating with an agile mind and a tremendous drive which also drove and inspired others. But he could not tolerate fools, bores or laziness.

A great injustice has been done to George, though it is fair to say that he was not always entirely blameless. He had an explosive temper and those who suffered the effects of his anger found it hard to forgive him. Also, he had the killer instinct in business; he was savage to anyone who stood between him and success and this earned him many enemies.

Jim Crowell was a student at Bend, Oregon in 1965, when he came across part of George's story whilst searching for the subject for a thesis. George had been editor of the Bend local paper before the First World War, as well as being an all-round colourful character in Bend folklore. I had nearly finished my research when I was put in touch with Mr Crowell by members of the Putnam family; his thesis material, including photographs, which he has kindly allowed me to include here, has been enormously helpful.

This book has brought me into contact with notable people in the world of aviation whom I had greatly admired for many years, but never expected to meet. Elinor Smith and Bobbi Trout for example – fascinating personalities, both still living life to the full. And there was a visit to Muriel Morrissey, Amelia's sister, which really made me feel close to my subject.

Over eighty when I met her in 1987, Muriel was fine-boned and stooped slightly. On the walls of her West Medford apartment were photographs and paintings of Amelia, and there were other memorabilia dotted around on tables and cupboard tops. When Muriel served tea, it was always done formally from an antique tea service of paper-thin china. She would not allow the arthritis in her hands to prevent her pouring the tea with careful precision, handing over the milk jug and sugar bowl in the way easiest for her guest to take.

Apart from the pleasure of meeting Mrs Morrissey, and interviewing her about Amelia, I also gained a clear impression of the upbringing the two Earhart girls had received; for here was a 'lady' in the true sense. Muriel's life was not always an easy one but she had retained an innate grace and soft-spoken charm; I suppose had Amelia lived she would have been similar in many ways.

Many of my informants still sharply recall George and Amelia. Others have only the haziest of recollections – 'you know, all this was a *very* long time ago, my dear . . .' The memories and recollections (the evidence, one might say), differ enormously and so I have tried to bring all shades of opinion into this book in an attempt to paint my portraits of Amelia and George as faithfully as possible.

This book is a biography. It does not set out to add yet another theory to the great 'What happened to Amelia Earhart?' mystery. All the known facts are covered in the appropriate chapters and I hope readers will use them to draw their own conclusion about the most likely explanation. For those not familiar with the various theories – knowledge of which might explain why I have sometimes overstressed certain pieces of information – I have included the best-known ones in an appendix at the end of the text. Some rely on outright sensationalism, others on detailed detective work based on one snippet of information which caught the attention of the researcher. In some one can see the author almost unconsciously manipulating what is known, to match and 'prove' a theory. And undoubtedly there will be yet more theories to come, even if Amelia's plane is located.

My editors feel that I should explain the technical terms of aviation such as 'ground loop' and 'stall speed' etc. Since to explain these within the text would be tedious to the reader and patronising to anyone involved in aviation, I have included a glossary.

Finally, there are several teams of people still working to discover what happened to Amelia's plane when it disappeared on that July day in 1937, most notably Marie and Elgen Long of California. I visited this charming couple in 1988, purely coincidentally on the anniversary of the day Amelia disappeared, and since then we have been in contact by telephone and letter. Their research, conducted over nearly twenty years, is staggeringly detailed and their objective is to locate Amelia's aeroplane which they believe lies some 35 miles west of Howland Island in the Pacific Ocean. If it *is* possible for Amelia's plane to be found by research and deduction, I believe they will find it.

Mary S. Lovell
Lyndhurst, Hampshire
April 1989

INTRODUCTION

It was 19 June 1928. In Southampton, a crowd of several thousand people had gathered on the banks of the River Itchen at its broad mouth into Southampton Water. Despite the unseasonable chill in the damp grey day there was an expectant gaiety in the air.

Shortly after one o'clock in the afternoon the sound of aircraft engines was heard overhead. Nothing could be seen at first because a squall obscured everything above a few hundred feet. Faces craned skywards and at last the misty shape of an orange aeroplane with floats was spotted, accompanied by one of the huge Imperial Airways flying boats acting as escort. There was spasmodic cheering as the float-plane settled on the choppy surface of the water. On her side was the word FRIENDSHIP, in large black letters.

Almost as soon as the engines were switched off a door in the side of the plane opened, and a young woman and two men appeared. One of the men dropped down onto a pontoon and casually lit a cigarette while he waited for a boat to provide a tow. Within minutes two ropes had been attached to the aeroplane and the *Friendship* was on its way to the Imperial Airways landing stage while its former occupants, seated in a launch, were headed towards the waiting crowd on the shore. Crew and workmen lining the decks of ships in the busy port cheered, clapped and whistled as the launch passed by. Ships' sirens and hooters provided an accompanying cacophony.[1]

The aviators had not come far that day, only from Burry Port in South Wales, a flight of some two hours. Once on land the young woman was hugged with proprietorial enthusiasm by a plump matron, although it was their first meeting. 'Well done, my girl!' Mrs Amy Guest said roundly. The crowd cheered wildly and some of the men flung their hats in the air.

It was cold for June, a favourite trick of English weather. Unusually for the period Southampton had a lady Mayor, Mrs Louise M. Foster-Welsh, and she, heading the welcoming committee, wisely wore a dress suit with a fur collar under her impressive chain of office.[2] The young woman wore a weird all-in-one fur-lined suit that was too large by several sizes, and her head was covered by a leather helmet. Her face was thin, her expression one of eager intelligence and she had a ready boyish grin, but her eyes were ringed with dark smudges defining obvious physical tiredness.

The two men accompanying the young woman seemed uncertain of their part in the reception and hung about awkwardly on the fringe of the handshaking and speechmaking centre of the crowd. Reporters and cameramen ignored them. It was clearly the young woman that the crowd had come to see, for as the Mayor was shortly to announce, this young woman had done something no other woman had yet done. 'She is the first woman who can say "I have crossed the ocean by air" . . .'[3]

The two men were Wilmer 'Bill' Stultz, the pilot of the plane, and Louis 'Slim' Gordon, mechanic. The young woman was Amelia Earhart. She was merely a passenger, but she had been the sole reason for the flight of the *Friendship* on 17 and 18 June 1928 from the United States of America to Britain. As a stand-in for Amy Guest (who had wanted to make the flight herself but who had yielded to shocked opposition from her family), Amelia had jumped onto the front page of every newspaper in the world and instantly achieved the status of heroine.

Southampton had been the original destination of the transatlantic flight but after the long crossing the flyers had been uncertain of their exact position and had landed in Burry Port, thinking they were in Ireland. Fuel was so low that there was not enough left for them to take off again. After an overnight rest and refuelling they had flown to Southampton to enable the planned reception to take place.

Amelia was showered with flowers and tributes. She tried hard to ensure that the two men appeared in the hundreds of photographs that were taken of her. She insisted that all technical credit for the flight should be directed at Stultz and Gordon. In this she was largely ignored. These were the days when heroism came in a masculine shape. Only a year earlier Charles Lindbergh had stormed to international fame by virtue of his solo flight across the Atlantic. To have a *woman* transatlantic flyer was a treat for the press and a gift for copywriters and they made the most of it.

Over the next few days reporters examined Amelia's history and wrote tens of thousands of column inches about her. If fact was not available, invention took over. Legends, some of them completely untrue, which were to follow her for the rest of her life – and long after that – were spun.

Back in the United States, manager of the project George Putnam, who had recruited Amelia for the great adventure, was busily drafting the early chapters of an 'autobiographical' version of Amelia's story so that it could be ready for publication shortly after her return to the USA. Despite the fact that Amelia was engaged to be married, and despite his own married state, Putnam had already started to make advances to the young woman he saw as a potential celebrity. Amelia, in turn, was intrigued by Putnam. She had not liked him at first but thought him such an intelligent man that she was soon fascinated.

Putnam exuded confidence, power and success. Although his background was a cultured one, he was an entrepreneur and a wheeler-dealer by nature so that the aura he unintentionally created around himself was one of excitement. Well over six feet in height and with matinee-idol looks, he was forty years of age, looked younger and was at the peak of his career in publishing. Behind him lay enough adventure to fill two lifetimes.

'When I first met Mr Putnam,' Amelia Earhart was fond of saying, 'I just didn't like him . . . [he] seemed brusque.'[4] And George Putnam would explain, 'When she called at my office I was busy, she had to cool her heels – and didn't like it much.'[5]

Notwithstanding this uneasy start to their relationship, the two developed a respect and liking for each other which eventually deepened into love. More unusually for the times, they shared a working relationship that was fulfilling and exciting to them both. Many people, writing about Amelia Earhart, have denigrated George Putnam's role in her life claiming that he 'used' her fame and drove her too hard. In fact Amelia was lucky that she met the one man who could hold her respect and to whom she could be married without feeling she was caged by her marital vows.

At their first meeting Amelia was thirty years old, tall and slim, with her fair curly hair cut short – not in a fashionable bob, but in a style more suited to today than 1928: 'unruly', said some, 'windswept' said others. Her face reflected a natural intelligence and quiet humour lurked in her grey eyes. Amelia had poise, but there was a hint of anxiety about her demeanour for she knew that if she could persuade George Putnam that she was the woman for his project, she would be embarking on the greatest adventure of her life.

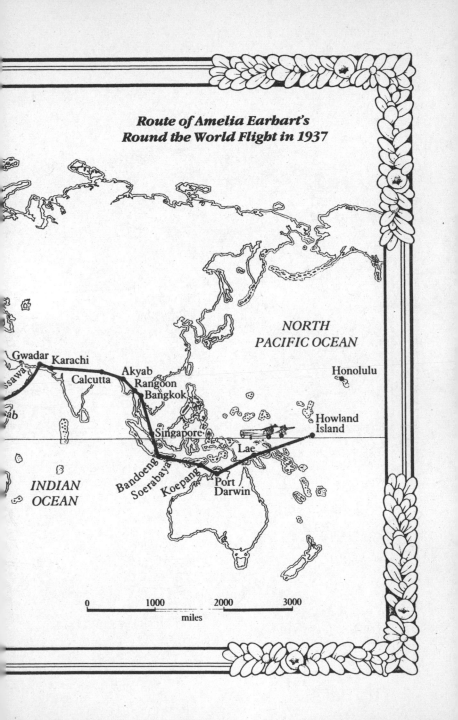

Route of Amelia Earhart's Round the World Flight in 1937

NORTH PACIFIC OCEAN

Gwadar Karachi
        Calcutta   Akyab
                    Rangoon
                    Bangkok

Honolulu

Howland
Island

Singapore

Lae

INDIAN OCEAN

Bandoeng   Soerabaya   Koepang   Port Darwin

0   1000   2000   3000
                    miles

BOOK ONE
Amelia Mary Earhart

COURAGE

Courage is the price that Life exacts for granting peace,
The soul that knows is not, knows no release
From little things;
Knows not the livid loneliness of fear,
Nor mountain heights where bitter joy can hear
The sound of wings.

How can Life grant us boon of living, compensate
For dull grey ugliness and pregnant hate
Unless we dare
The soul's dominion? Each time we make a choice, we pay
With courage to behold the restless day,
And count it fair.

Amelia Earhart (1927)

CHAPTER 1

1897

The small town of Atchison in Kansas seems an unlikely place – or so one might think – to be the birthplace of a woman whose name, fifty years after her death, remains synonymous with adventure, heroism and post-mortem mystery. It is a typical mid-western town, built in the 1860s in the heart of America, and situated alongside the Missouri River. The town owed its survival to the fact that for the huge wagon trains on the trek westwards it was a good place to cross the great river, and for a while Atchison was the last outpost of civilisation before the 'wild west'.

And yet is it so unlikely? Is there a more American heroine than Amelia Earhart? Amelia had that particular brand of questing courage which typified American settlers in the century in which she was born. And although her early years were spent in the safe and sheltered communities of Atchison and nearby Kansas City, almost every adult with whom she came in contact was, to some degree, a pioneer. Perhaps the drive to succeed that she was to display as an adult germinated from these early relationships, fostered by the town itself.

Her distant ancestors were European and although Amelia grew up to be more appreciative of her maternal connections, the Earhart family's lineage was impressive too, with one skein stretching back to Maria Josephs, a Frenchwoman thought to be a niece of Louis XV. Maria is said to have fallen in love with a German officer, Anthony Altman. The pair were married against the wishes of the king and were both subsequently disinherited by their respective families. To avoid royal wrath, the newlyweds fled to America and settled in Pennsylvania.[1]

The Altmans had one son, Philip, who with his wife Louisa moved to Indiana County, Pennsylvania, in 1789,

> . . . when the country was very new and before the Indians had all left the county . . . at one time provisions became so scarce that . . . the family had to cook greens for their daily food for some time, and to insure getting safe plants for their greens, they followed the cows to learn of them the kind of plants that could be used safely. Besides the fear of Indians [who were encamped on the Altman's 102-acre farm] venomous snakes were very numerous, as were the copperhead and rattlesnake.[2]

It must have been very different from life at the French court. Along with the other women, Louisa made all the clothing for their family of nine children, from clipping the sheep to spinning and weaving the wool to making up the clothes. Indeed the lot of women was so hard that in 1897, on reading about their daily life, a descendant enquired of the author of the account, 'What did the men do?'[3] The men did plenty, for the country was rolling and hilly, overgrown with brush and timber. Clearing the land was a backbreaking and endless task and beside that homes had to be built, families kept fed, and farms established.

The Altmans' daughter Catherine married into the Earhart family in 1813 when she took David Earhart as her husband. The third son of this union (there were nine sons and two daughters) was David Earhart, 'a modest and happy man' who became a preacher in the Evangelical Lutheran Church. In 1841 the Reverend David Earhart married Mary Wells Patton, whose family was of English descent through Colonel James Wells of Revolutionary fame. The Earharts had twelve children, three of whom died of scarlet fever and one who was killed in her cradle by a bolt of lightning through an open window. It was their son, Edwin Stanton Earhart, who was to become the father of Amelia Earhart.[4]

In an autobiographical memoir, the Reverend David Earhart recalled:

Kansas was opened for settlement in 1854. But owing to a border ruffian conflict [and] the proslavery and antislavery parties, settlement and improvements in the country were much retarded till 1857. In 1860, the year I moved to Kansas, there was such a severe drought [there] that the farmers' crops almost entirely failed. The people of Kansas had to be assisted by other States to secure the means of a livelihood. The following year, the civil war broke out . . .

The country being new and largely settled by poor people, and having had [for] two or three years a border war, a year's drought, and then the civil war, it was a hard time to gather and organize churches. Not twenty members were in organized Lutheran churches in Kansas when I moved there in 1860. A few years thereafter several plagues of grasshoppers ravaged the country. During the drought in 1860 I received about $100 . . . and during 1861 and 1862 $150 a year, from the Home Missionary Society. By teaching school and other secular labours I managed to live and rear a large family . . .[5]

For thirteen years Reverend Earhart preached twice nearly every Sunday in churches that were anything up to 60 miles from his home. One, 'though 60 miles from the place I lived, I visited and preached [in] for several years, riding mostly on horseback or sulky every four weeks, summer and winter, never failing for heat or cold'.[6] As regent of the State Agricultural College for six years, Reverend Earhart frequently had to make the 100-mile journey to that establishment before the Kansas Pacific Railroad was built.

Such was the stuff of the Earharts, Amelia's paternal relations.

On the maternal side, the family history has been traced back to England in 1581 when John Otis was born in Barnstaple, Devon. He sailed for America in 1635 with his fifteen-year-old son, also John, and drew house lots in the first division of land at Hingham, Massachusetts. The Otis descendants produced leading scholars, politicians, lawyers and physicians. One married into the family from whom Abraham Lincoln descended. Various family members served with distinction in the Revolutionary and Civil Wars.

Amelia's grandfather, Alfred Gideon Otis, was a noted lawyer and, later, judge. Born in 1827, he grew up with his grandparents in New York while his young parents travelled west to the new state of Michigan and settled there. Alfred was followed by ten more children but it was not until he was fourteen that he was to rejoin his parents. Then, as the eldest son, he threw his lot in as a farmer, pursuing classical studies in Greek and Latin each evening after the day's work was done. At the age of twenty-two he decided upon a more cerebral career and, financially unaided by his family, he put himself through college, graduating from the University of Michigan in 1852. He then went south to Mississippi where he taught school and studied law at the same time, graduating in 1854 from the Louisville Law School.[7]

In October 1855, with 'some other young bloods',[8] he moved to Leavenworth, Kansas. Shortly afterwards he transferred to the township of Atchison, then no more than a few timber buildings at a convenient crossing of the vast Missouri River, where he worked for a law practice. He was kept busy with land litigation cases which proliferated in the new territory, and over the next few years he worked hard and prospered.[9]

Before 1854 Kansas was Indian Territory. The Kickapoo Indians were brought in from the East and occupied the land in 1832. Only white men holding the necessary (and rare) permits were allowed to enter the territory until the Kansas Nebraska Act opening the land to settlement was passed by Congress in May 1854. The site that would become Atchison was selected by a resourceful early settler[10] who built a small log cabin at a suitable place on the river, from which he operated a ferry boat across the river for the '48 and '49 gold rush to California, supplementing this income by supplying wood to the steamboats that plied the great river.

The town was named after the famous Missouri Senator, David Atchison, who was pro-tem President of the United States for one day. Just about the same time as Alfred Otis arrived there, the great Mormon wagon train was encamped some three miles to the west, equipping for the trek to Salt Lake. These were exciting days for the young lawyer as his practice grew along with the town. By 1858 the town was served by a steamship and by the daily arrival of the four-horse stage. Then it took 'only four days' for a copy of an address by the President to reach Atchison from Washington, its impressive speed aided by the Hannibal and St Joseph's Railroad. The progress of the railroad and the advantageous location of the town for equipping the wagon trains that constantly streamed west made Atchison's future secure. For two building lots in the business section of the town a Member of Congress from Pennsylvania paid $3,000. On the hills surrounding the town, desirable residential plots fetched up to $350.[11]

> The merchants of Atchison [did] a great trade with the Indians. For several weeks a great number had been in Atchison nearly every day to get their winter supplies. They never left until all the money paid to them by the government disappeared. The Indian men, women and children came to Atchison on beautiful ponies and usually brought along a few to sell. They generally wore nothing on their heads, . . . moccasins ornamented with beads and . . . winter or summer . . . a coarse blanket was thrown over their shoulders. Around their waists, tied in their hair and hanging from their ears were pieces of ornamental tin. Sometimes the Indian men would come to Atchison with painted faces and with Eagle feathers in their hair.[12]

The town's great new asset, The Massasoit House Hotel, opened in September 1858 and was headquarters for the Overland Stage line. It had many famous visitors such as Abraham Lincoln, Kit Carson, Mark Twain, Horace Greeley and even Jesse James. By 1860 there were forty-six freighting firms doing business from Atchison, and in June that year the town celebrated the completion of the Atchison and St Joseph's Railroad.[13]

The gestation of the town was not without its problems. Neighbouring Missouri was fiercely pro-slavery, and Kansas settlers tended, initially, to adopt this policy, but there were a few abolitionists. There were some unpleasant incidents of tarring and feathering, scuffles and gun fights. Alfred, a lifelong Democrat, was known to be an active abolitionist, smuggling runaway slaves to safety in his wagon, covered in grain. Small children were carried in trunks as part of his luggage.[14]

At the age of thirty-five, with his future looking ever more secure, despite the great drought of 1860, Alfred Otis, now a full partner in law practice, decided to put down his roots in the booming little town.[15] Almost certainly he met his future wife Amelia Josephine Harres when she visited her elder sister Mary in Atchison. Mary had recently married Mr W. L. Challiss ('he wore the smallest shoes ever seen on a man').[16] Amelia Josephine was a fine young lady from Philadelphia, handsome and of prosperous Germanic stock. Alfred's attractions must have been great indeed to entice her to Atchison, though the nearness of her sister undoubtedly played some part in her decision to move to the little frontier town. True, she did not find it necessary to travel by covered wagon, for she 'travelled as far as St Louis by train and then came down the river on the steamboat'.[17] Nevertheless, Atchison, Kansas was far different from the civilised society of Philadelphia; at this time it could not even boast a paved sidewalk.

Alfred and Amelia Josephine were married in the Harres home in 1862, after which they returned to Atchison and moved into the fine new house built by the industrious bridegroom on the high bluffs behind the town, which looked down on the fast-flowing Missouri River and the rich, flat farmlands beyond. This pleasant brick and timber-clad home, with its large, high-ceilinged, cool rooms was later to become the birthplace of Amelia Earhart,[18] but this is running ahead of the story.

A period of service in a Kansas regiment during the Civil War hardly interrupted Alfred's career and he was soon regarded as one of the town's leading citizens. In retrospect, the couple's life appears to have been idyllic. They had eight children, six of whom survived childhood. Life was busy but Alfred's success had made him a wealthy man so the traumas of life in the midwest were inevitably cushioned. In 1876 Alfred was elected to the bench and served with distinction.[19]

Amelia Earhart's mother Amy, the couple's eldest surviving daughter, was born in 1869. Hers was a privileged existence. The home on Quality Hill was not typical of a midwestern homestead. Its amenities included crystal chandeliers, a piano in the drawing room, Irish maids and cooks, and men to keep the riding and carriage horses in the large barn and to tend the extensive gardens. Little Amy's grandmother had come from Philadelphia to live with the family and the child was petted and loved by everyone. She and her siblings were all good equestrians. Amy rode her own pony 'sidesaddle and with long skirts'. The whole family 'loved the smell of a book'; the house had a well-stocked library and books formed a great part of the family's lives, as did travel. At least once a year they took a trip;

> father took the whole family. He went with a sense of responsibility, and mother just went because she loved it. We all had to know all of our own country first, before we went to Europe and of course that was very unusual . . . because the first thing you [normally] did upon graduation . . . was to take a trip to Europe. Father and I loved California . . . [He] would often have the coachman stop when we got to the top of the hills and have him turn the carriage around so that we could see the rivers and hills and valleys, and fields of grain waving . . . He wanted us to have seeing eyes, and said 'your eyes were given to you to see things and I want you to see and remember.'[20]

There were other trips to Utah, Oklahoma and Colorado, and Amelia's mother thus saw much of the great continent of America when it was still unsettled and grazed by herds of buffalo.

Amy was not physically strong and her health often gave the family cause for concern. Despite a number of absences from her studies at prep school, her innate intelligence enabled her to fulfil her college entrance requirements, but she was unable to capitalise on her success due to a bout of diphtheria.[21] In any case, she said, 'mother didn't want me to go so far away', so she stayed in Atchison.[22]

Her physical delicacy was however no impediment to her adventurous spirit, for on a trip with her father to Colorado in the summer of 1890, she became the first woman to climb Pike's Peak. For the first 10,000 feet donkeys were used, but then the party had to proceed on foot, some of the men affected by nosebleeds having to turn back. Amy was the only woman to attempt the last hazardous, quarter-mile climb.

That same summer, when Amy was twenty-one, her parents threw a coming-out ball for her in the garden of their home. It was a warm June night and the syringa and heliotrope made the whole bluff top fragrant. Amy's parents had a wooden dance floor built over the grass; they could not move an old wrought-iron Stag-at-Eve so they built flooring around him and Amy put a garland of scarlet roses around his neck and hung a lantern on one of his horns. Wires were strung between the trees and every few feet or so Japanese lanterns were hooked on to be lit at nine o'clock, just as dusk descended.

It was a beautiful evening with very little breeze, which was fortunate as [Amy's father] would not have let us have the lanterns lighted, for fear of the candles tipping and causing fire . . . Seven musicians came down from St Joseph and played music for the Virginia Reel and the Lancers, as well as for waltzing.[23]

One of the guests introduced to Amy by her brother Mark was Edwin Stanton Earhart, a young lawyer. The young couple soon fell deeply in love but when Edwin subsequently petitioned the judge for his daughter's hand, he was told, not unreasonably, that he would have to be earning at least $50 a month. It was fully five years before Edwin's earnings reached the required sum but eventually he was able to reiterate his suit and win Amy's hand. The pair were married on 16 October 1895, whereupon they moved to their own house in nearby Kansas City, which, fully furnished down to its library of books, was a wedding gift from the bride's parents.[24]

Although the railroad company was one of Edwin's clients in his legal work, his means were vastly different from those of Judge Otis. Nevertheless the marriage was, by all accounts, a happy one despite some initial tears on Amy's part. She was unused to housework and was made more miserable by the miscarriage of a baby girl within a year of the marriage, caused when she was thrown against the brake-lever of a cable car. When Amy found she was pregnant again, it was quite natural for her to return to her parents' home in Atchison for the confinement, where she would be pampered and well cared for.[25] The child was born on 24 July 1897 at 11.30 p.m., and was named Amelia Mary after her two grandmothers.[26]

Who could have guessed that the well-behaved and contented baby would blaze a name across the world's headlines? Amy's grandmother died only a year before Amelia's birth and her proudest boast was that she had watched George Washington pass by on his way to meet President Adams.[27] How could parents who had travelled the continent of America in horses and carts possibly imagine that this longed-for child would one day cross the oceans of the world in an aeroplane?

CHAPTER 2

1897–1914

Amelia Earhart was in her early teens when it became obvious to her that her father was a drunkard. This was made all the more painful to her, and to her entire family, by the fact that her father's disgraceful behaviour was equally obvious to everyone in their neighbourhood, and that his job was in jeopardy.[1]

Life in the midwest in the first decade of this century was parochial in the extreme. Although we may look back with fondness on the security of those days, seeing freedom from the problems of life today (there were few instances of rape, muggings and burglary), life then carried its own problems. For example it was almost impossible to maintain one's privacy. In one way this was a good thing. Moral behaviour was exemplary by today's standards because, apart from any other consideration, 'what would folks say?' On the other hand the lack of personal privacy could be very tedious. Amelia's childhood in this tightly knit world may explain much of her seeming 'closeness' about her personal life as an adult. 'What folks said' about Edwin was deeply shaming to Amy and her two daughters, but Amelia, because of her pubescent sensitivity, undoubtedly felt the shame to a greater degree.

Some two and a half years after Amelia was born, Amy had given birth to another child, Muriel. The two little girls – Amelia was known as 'Millie' and Muriel was called 'Pidge' – were very close, as was the entire family. Although there was never much money, domestic problems began to occur only after Edwin attempted to 'make the family's fortune'. There is little doubt that his eagerness to succeed stemmed from Judge Otis's opinion that his son-in-law was a ne'er-do-well and would never amount to anything. Determined to prove himself, and in the best traditions of the nineteenth-century entrepreneur, Edwin invented a device to hold signal flags on trains and spent long hours perfecting it. Unfortunately when he travelled to Washington to patent it he found that a similar item had already been accepted. Worse, he had used money that Amy had set aside to pay their taxes to pay for his trip and the application fee.[2] Edwin's disappointment was touchingly expressed in a letter to his wife:

> My dearest wife,
> For two days I did nothing except tramp from one office to
> another . . . to establish the classification of my poor little flag
> holder as mechanical, semi-mechanical or non-mechanical and
> then as to the area of its usefulness: household, farm, factory
> and so on . . . When I returned to the main office by
> appointment about an hour ago, the clerk handed me back my
> two models with the information that a man from Colorado
> had filed a patent on an identical holder two years ago . . . This
> news is a terrible blow, because I had been counting on
> receiving several hundred dollars from the railroad for my flag
> holder . . . Give love to our small daughters, and as much to
> your sweet self. Ever thine, Edwin.[3]

When the tax bill was presented Edwin had to raise the money quickly to avoid default and quell Amy's panicky fear of prosecution. He called in some outstanding debts and sold a collection of valuable law books which Judge Otis had given him. The immediate problem was resolved but it was not long before the judge heard on the grapevine that his gift had been disposed of in a manner which he thought shameful. It was the beginning of an irreparable rift between Edwin and his father-in-law. From that time, Judge Otis regarded Edwin as totally unable to provide for his family.

In fact the young Earhart family lived in reasonable comfort, even if not at the high level considered by the judge to be suitable for his family. Amelia and Muriel, unaware of any financial constraints whatever, felt secure and happy. Amy may well have had to lower her former living standards but Edwin was a good and faithful husband, a man of great humour and patience. Long afterwards the two girls recalled the trip the family took to the 1904 World's Fair in St Louis. It was a happy holiday which the family enjoyed to the hilt. Edwin paid for the trip from a hundred-dollar fee he had received from the railroad for defending an obscure right-of-way dispute. The judge naturally considered it an appalling waste of money considering the state of the family finances.

On their return from the fair, the seven-year-old Amelia designed and built a roller coaster in the yard with long planks propped against the tool shed roof. An uncle helped in the construction and the children sawed and hammered away with great enthusiasm. Amelia declared it a huge success and her contemporaries thought it great fun but Amy said it was dangerous, so it was demolished after only a few short runs. Such tomboyish games were very much to Amelia's taste, and Amy, while perhaps despairing of this unladylike behaviour, was a practical person. She had two gym suits made for the girls with bloomers, gathered at the knees. 'This was unusual,' Muriel recalled, 'because in those days nice little girls wore long, full-skirted dresses, with ruffled pinafores over them.'[4] The neighbours may have raised eyebrows at this unconventional attire but Amy realised that the girls were happy in their new freedom.[5]

Because Edwin's work often required him to travel away from home and Amy liked to accompany him, the two girls often spent time at the home of their doting, wealthy grandparents. In Atchison, the two girls were 'the judge's granddaughters' and as such enjoyed a certain social cachet. Poor Edwin could never hope to provide his daughters with the advantages that Amy had grown up to take for granted and felt the Otis patronage deeply. He provided his daughters with a great deal besides wealth, however. He took them fishing and played ball-games with them. Despite her grandparents' protests Edwin presented the nine-year-old Amelia with a .22 rifle so that she could 'clear the barn of rats'. 'Oh now, don't worry, Mother Otis,' he said. 'This is really a very small rifle.'

He imbued them with a sense of humour and sang and played the piano with them.[6] Small wonder that they adored him. 'Loving, generous, impractical' was how Muriel summed him up years later.[7]

Over a period of several years Edwin had acted for the Rock Island Line. During that time he had obviously impressed the company's management, for in 1905 he was offered a permanent post in the Claims Department. The opportunity of a regular salary meant freedom from waiting for settlement of small fees by often penurious clients. The job meant that the family would have to move to Des Moines, of course, leaving their happy Kansas City home, but the opportunity was too good to miss. While Amy and Edwin went to Iowa to look for a new house, the two little girls were left with their grandparents for what was intended to be a few weeks. It took longer than Edwin and Amy anticipated to find a suitable home and settle in, and the weeks ran to nearly a year, but although the girls missed their parents, the Otis home was a happy and secure one and the proximity of their two Challiss cousins meant that they never lacked for companionship.

When the Kansas sunshine became too hot for the children to play outside, they stayed in the cool interior of the large house and read books.[8] Books too large to hold comfortably had to be read lying flat on one's stomach on the floor.[9] Classics by Victor Hugo and Alexandre Dumas, housed in grandfather Otis's comprehensive library, were read and loved, and these were backed up by boys' adventure stories in periodical magazines.

A contemporary recalled how Amy encouraged her daughter's love of literature: 'My earliest memories of Amelia and her family are of her mother reading to us as we sat on the floor at the Otis home.'[10] The Earhart family had joined a neighbourhood scheme in which a large number of magazines were subscribed to communally and passed from household to household. Amelia's young, open and impressionable mind fed on stories from *Harper's Weekly* or *The Youth's Companion*. *Peter Rabbit* and *Black Beauty* were favourites from the girls' earliest days, while among Amelia's own collection was a much thumbed copy of *Insect Life*.[11]

Amy also encouraged inquisitiveness into things that might

normally make little girls squeamish; her small daughters kept worms, moths, 'katydids' and a tree toad all collected on nature outings organised by Amy, and the outings were often shared with orphans from a nearby children's home. Once, when Amy prepared a freshly killed chicken, she called her daughters' attention to its anatomy. 'See, girls, how neatly this hen's little lungs fit here, just above her tiny heart.'[12]

There were horses to ride, and there were imaginary horses on which Amelia and her sister and cousins escaped from all sorts of invented perils. Amelia was an excellent horsewoman all her life and many childhood incidents were associated with this love of horses. A friend recalled how she would adjust the tack on horses tied up outside houses to make them 'more comfortable'.[13] Cars were beginning to be seen in Kansas but they were very much rarities.

Amelia and Muriel attended the small private College Preparatory School during 1906 and early 1907 while their parents settled in Des Moines. Amelia's report cards, headed 'Millie Earhart', gave her a gratifying number of Es (Excellent) and VGs (Very Good) across the curriculum of reading, spelling, writing, arithmetic, English, French, geography and sewing.[14]

In 1908 the girls moved to Des Moines to rejoin their parents. In her biography of her sister, *Courage is the Price*, written in 1963, Muriel recalled the radical change in the girls' lives. Here they had no orchard or private park, no barn to play in, no cousins with similar background and interests, and no private school. Altogether they felt most keenly the drop in their social status from that of members of the aristocracy of a small town. Amy considered the public school inadequate when it was suggested that the girls' hair should be cut to discourage the inevitable lice they would pick up. One of the teachers from Atchison's College Preparatory School was sent for and she became the girls' private governess. Geography was now omitted from their studies and the former curriculum was enhanced by more poetry and music lessons.

Before a year had passed the governess returned to Kansas and the girls had to attend the dreaded public school. No lice were acquired, however, and they settled in well despite a certain attitude of superiority in their approach to the other children.

Amelia was ten years old when she saw her first aeroplane in 1908. She was taken to the Iowa State Fair in Des Moines, but when told to look at the contraption because it could fly she was dismissive: 'It was a thing of rusty wire and wood and not at all interesting . . .' she recalled. She was much more interested in a paper hat shaped like a peach basket that she had bought for a few cents. This occurred only five years after the Wright Brothers had made their epic flight and it would be more than a decade before Amelia's interest in aviation was awakened.

Edwin worked hard at his job and in 1909 was promoted to be claims agent, heading a department of five loss adjusters and a small clerical staff. His salary was doubled, his name displayed prominently on the company letterhead, and he received as a perquisite, the use of a private rail car for business and personal purposes.[15] The sudden change in their circumstances enabled the Earharts to move to a larger house in a better part of town and Amy was not slow to advise her parents of Edwin's success.

The happiness of the little family during this period is reflected in Edwin's charming reply (on official Rock Island Line stationery) to his younger daughter's formal claim for compensation after having received an insect bite while en route to visit her grandparents.

August 2 1909

Miss Muriel Earhart,
Atchison, Kansas
I have your claim for $5.00 for having been bitten by a misquito on our train. Before we can pay the same, we would, at least, like to know how big a bite the misquito took and we would like to see the misquito. Of course, we admit that we owe you something and are willing to pay it but you will have to produce the misquito before you could expect us to pay you.

This case will probably have to be referred to the Chicago office as it is so serious a case and I hardly feel like handling it.
Very truly yours
E. S. Earhart[16]

There were two or three years of real contentment including happy family holidays at Lake Worthington, Minnesota. (Many years later a resident wrote to Amelia to tell her that her visits were especially remembered – she had thought Amelia a remarkable child because of 'her preference for celery rather than candy and other sweets').[17] There was also their first – somewhat frightening – ride in an automobile; games of cowboys and Indians when Edwin came home from the office early to play the part of Big Chief Geronimo; and concerts attended by the entire family dressed in their best clothes and rounded off by Millie and Edwin giving a 'by ear' rendering of the arias they'd heard. Amelia liked the opera but criticised the Italian ones: 'The words are so silly!'[18]

'This happy time,' Muriel was to write (Amelia never wrote of these years), 'was unfortunately a prelude to a period which saw the loss of our material prosperity and the beginning of the disintegration of the family . . . when the shadows began to fall on our gifted father and the amenities of life had to be sacrificed for the necessities of existence . . . the hardship and mental suffering that Amelia and I endured as adolescents made an indelible impression upon us and help to explain some of Amelia's actions and attitudes in her later life.' Edwin had begun to drink.[19]

Characteristically, it was nothing at first. The odd drink with his colleagues after work which he couldn't refuse without seeming rude. This extended to lunchtime drinking so that his stenographer often had to secrete letters by Edwin until he was in a 'less belligerent state of intoxication'. Edwin began to lurch home more often than not, and his sunny nature gave way to bad temper when his family remonstrated in anxious concern. His condition became known as 'Dad's sickness' but this euphemism did not fool his employers when his work inevitably suffered.

He overpaid claims and made massive errors which were not picked up by his loyal staff. Head Office warned him about his drop in efficiency, and this was followed by a visit from the claims attorney, Mr George McCaughan. McCaughan found Edwin drunk at his desk and sent him home. A month in a sanatorium to dry out restored Edwin to his anxious family as their 'old dad back again' but to the despair of Amy and the two girls, the cure lasted only days and Edwin began again to drink heavily.[20]

Amy's mother had died in 1911 leaving an estate reputedly valued at a million dollars to be divided equally among the four surviving children. The judge had long ago foreseen Edwin's inadequacy as a provider, and in the last year of Mrs Otis's life she had seen that her late husband's assessment of Edwin had been accurate. She was at least able to make some kind of provision for her daughter and two grandchildren to mitigate Edwin's profligate ways and protect against the possibility of his drinking Amy's fortune away. Amy's share of the inheritance was locked into a trust for twenty years, or until Edwin's death.[21]

This only served to worsen the situation, for Edwin used what he considered to be a studied insult as an excuse to increase his drinking. After he failed to gain reinstatement in his old job in Des Moines he began a fruitless search for work with other railroad companies but it was many months before he was offered anything else.[22] It was a considerable drop in status, a minor clerkship with the Great Northern Railroad in St Paul, Minnesota, but it was work. Meanwhile, Edwin's status within his family fell steadily. Whereas before he had been a hero to his daughters now he was the source of every disappointment.

In St Paul the family rented a large house which had stood empty for two years. Edwin's salary barely covered the rent, let alone the heating, so that in the depths of winter the family were confined to the two rooms they could afford to heat. Here Amelia entered Central High School as a junior. Her mother recalled that Amelia's favourite subjects were Latin and mathematics, and that she preferred geometry to algebra because she had to work at geometry while she could do algebra in her head. She was 'miles above' the other students in her class and regarded the reading matter of her fellow students as 'childish'.[23]

Amelia played in the basketball team and was a good all-round student. To some extent she resented the fact that boys were favoured over girls, a complaint her mother thought was justified. She was, from all accounts, a perfectly normal student apart from her above-average grades. She went to high school dances and summer camps and debated with her parents how late she could be allowed to stay up. 'But she wasn't a rebellious child . . . once in a while she would say "I don't agree with you at all, Mother. This is the way I look at it" . . .'[24]

There was a particularly unpleasant incident when Amelia discovered a bottle of whisky in her father's suitcase as he was packing for a trip. She tipped the bottle down the sink but her father caught her and in his fury would have struck her, had Amy not intervened. Edwin apologised, but the significance of his behaviour, which minutes earlier had been sunny and tolerant, was not lost on the sensitive Amelia.[25]

She maintained an outward confidence in her future and contentment with her lot and relayed this to old friends. But in truth she must have felt far from happy about both. Writing to her friend Virginia (Parks) in Atchison she discusses their mutual plans for attending college in a jocular tone:

March 6th 1914

Blessings on thee little Ginger,
How goes everything mit Ihnen (mit governs the dative)? Of course I'm going to Bryn Mawr if I have to drive a grocery wagon to accumulate the cash . . . You miss a lot by not having a Gym. Last Friday we had a circus. We played basketball, just like you and I did once (remember). No boys tho. I don't know when I've been so tired.

All the girls are so nice it's a joy to be with them don't you know. I am doing my best to get some of them to go to Bryn Mawr with Ginger and Millie. Your letter was scrummy, so long and joysome . . .

Love, Mill[26]

Some wealthy family connections, living in a better part of town, studiously ignored Amy once Edwin's condition became known. It took time for the girls to become friends with their contemporaries and it was a long and cheerless winter, for they were not invited to any of the Christmas parties. There was, however, to be a Twelfth Night party organised by the church and as they had been invited by some boys, the girls especially looked forward to going and dressed early.

Dating, as such, did not yet exist and convention decreed that a girl's father should escort her to a dance and collect her again at an appointed time. Edwin promised to be home by six. The two girls sat dressed in their finery, desolation growing as the clock ticked on through six, seven, and eight o'clock. Edwin came home about nine, drunk and full of bonhomie. Muriel, 'Pidge' to the family, burst into tears and retired to bed. Millie, steely eyed and square-jawed, removed the Christmas decorations and pointedly cleared away the preparations she had made to entertain the boys whom they had intended to ask home for hot cocoa and toasted marsh-mallows.[27] For her, the disillusion of a broken trust was more hurtful than the disappointment of missing the dance.

Throughout the winter the girls helped Amy as much as they could, often walking for miles in the snow to get a bargain that would help the family finances. Amelia even made Easter Parade outfits out of some old curtains. In the summer, after they had at last been accepted by fellow students and had just started receiving invitations, Edwin announced they were moving on because he had been offered a job with the railroad in Springfield, Missouri. It was 1914 and in Europe war had been declared but this all seemed a long way away from their immediate problems.

The family headed for Springfield with packing cases and hand luggage. After a tedious seven-hour journey they arrived to find that the man whom Edwin was to replace had decided not to retire after all. The company, in an attempt to compensate Edwin, gave him a month's work and the cost of the family's train fare back to St Paul. Edwin was righteously indignant and angrily demanded the job he'd been promised, but Amy had had enough. She and the girls left Edwin and went to stay with the Shedds in Chicago, friends from the happy Des Moines period, when Edwin had helped Mr Shedd to a good job in the days when he had influence. Edwin returned alone to Kansas.

CHAPTER 3

1914-1920

Amelia was fifteen when the trio arrived in Chicago. Muriel has written that the Shedds never made them feel that they were a broken family but honoured guests. Nevertheless, it is not difficult to imagine Amelia's feelings at this time.

She had grown up in a happy home where the four family members were close and particularly loving. Until she reached the age of twelve or thirteen, home conditions may have veered between genteel poverty and relative affluence but the stable background of love, support and humour could be taken for granted. In those early days too, the little family had always been confident that Edwin's natural gifts would inevitably be recognised and 'making do' was merely part of the progression of his career. Then, when he was promoted and things were going well they had begun to enjoy the long-anticipated higher standards of living and the respect that success inspires. In addition, there was the wealth and position of her doting grandparents. The social superiority that she had enjoyed when she lived in, and whenever she visited, Atchison as the judge's granddaughter could not help but set her slightly apart from many of her contemporaries, and make her feel that she had a position to live up to.

Until this point Amelia must have felt reasonably happy. She knew exactly what her place in society was and she had the respect of her peers for her own intelligence and qualities of natural leadership. She was confident in herself, her family, her friends, her future. But when her father's drinking had put an end to all their expectations her age alone ensured that she felt, far more than Muriel, the humiliation and even shame of the previous two years. The family's social and financial security had been eroded and from occupying a leading position in society they had become the focus of hushed, pitying gossip. In those days couples stayed together more often than not. Periods of unhappiness were expected to be 'worked out'. Divorce was a stigma in provincial circles, sufficient to invoke side-long glances, and so this separation was always regarded as a breathing space to enable Edwin to regain his self-esteem and for Amy to gather together the shreds of reputation and provide a future for her daughters.

That Amy had some income of her own was the purest luck. She could hardly have adopted such a course of action without that small security behind her. It was only a modest income earned on the capital of the trust fund but it was enough. This created in Edwin great bitterness and helped to assuage, in him, any feeling of guilt that his drinking had been the essential cause of the family's downfall. He was more full of self-pity than remorse and even years later, when Amelia achieved great success, his bitterness over the terms of the Otis bequest showed through his natural parental pride.[1] While Amy and the girls made a temporary home in Chicago, Edwin went to stay with his family in Kansas City where, having realised that he would never again obtain a position with a railroad company, he opened his own law practice and started again.

Their arrival in Chicago was a watershed in Amelia's life. The worst had happened. The trust and respect she had in abundance for her father had been destroyed and disillusionment had taken their place. Her love for him remained, but sometimes it was as though she were the parent and he the child. She hid her distress behind a façade of bravado and quiet determination.

Amy found cheap accommodation in a furnished apartment near the University of Chicago campus and enrolled the girls at Hyde Park High School. The living accommodation left much to be desired. Amy, particular to a fault, was disgusted to find that the landladies draped their bedclothes over the sitting-room furniture during the day.

At school, Amelia's newly found determination and an under-standable intolerance of failure quickly fell foul of the system. She was scathing about the equipment, declaring that the school laboratory consisted of 'no more than a sink!' The level of teaching also fell short of her personal high standards. Her ire became directed at an elderly relative of the mayor who worked as an English teacher at Hyde Park High; the woman was not only deaf but totally unequipped to teach high-school students. Within days Amelia was caught between indignation at the teaching standards and resent-ment that her fellow pupils were happy to taunt the unfortunate and harmless English teacher behind her back.

> She was also accustomed to stimulating discussions on the works of standard authors and was bored by the clowning in the classroom. Amelia spoke to two others in the class who agreed that the situation was terrible. They prepared a petition asking that their teacher be replaced by 'someone who can teach us something'. The morning the petition was ready, one of the girls who had helped prepare it said her parents had forbidden her to sign it. This frightened the second girl so that Amelia's signature stood alone . . . Sitting sideways at her desk near the front of the room Amelia began to speak above the laughing and talking which characterized the silent reading period. She told her classmates that it was a shame the way they were treat-ing their teacher . . .[2]

Her opinion was that the teacher could not help her deafness, but that did not alter the fact that they needed a teacher to teach them, and her subsequent requests to fellow students to back her petition created only noisy opposition. The petition was snatched away from her and torn up. As Muriel points out in her memoir, 'Perhaps she went about her reform campaign in the wrong way. But it is reveal-ing that she dared to undertake it.'[3]

From this point onward Amelia never attended another English class but found ways of continuing her studies to her own exacting standards, alone in the school library. Inevitably she became regarded as odd, 'different' and a loner. When she graduated from high school in 1916, she deliberately boycotted the ceremony and the celebrations: her graduating class photograph was suitably captioned 'The girl in brown who walks alone', and that one line sums up the solitariness of Amelia's adolescent life.

Amelia must have needed some outlet from her depression over her parents, the disintegration of their family life and the general uncertainty over their future. To her credit, her outlet became a driving determination to work her way out of the mess. Despite her unhappiness, Amelia set her sights firmly on attending college, at a time when women did not automatically think of furthering their education.

Muriel records that they hated leaving their friends in Chicago, but it is difficult to feel that Amelia had any such qualms when, in the summer of 1916, Amy decided to return to Edwin in Kansas City. He had managed to stop drinking and persuaded Amy that it was permanent. For Amelia it was intended to be a short stay before she went off to college. In many ways she considered that she had already made the emotional break from the family.

But her stay in Kansas City, where the family were reunited in a small house on Charlotte Street, was to last a year. Pictures of this period show a tall, slim, thoughtful young woman dressed in the confining coverall long-skirted fashion of the day with long hair dressed up, whilst Edwin is gaunt and hollow-cheeked, looking older than his actual years. In an attempt to make the reunion work Amy gave in to Edwin's urgings to break the terms of her mother's will.

The trust had been badly administered by Amy's brother Mark, who had made some foolish investments. The capital was greatly depleted – probably to a far greater extent than if Edwin had been allowed to drink some of it away. Despite her reluctance to air family differences in court, Amy now saw a chance to mollify Edwin's bitterness and to ensure that something was left out of the fast-dwindling inheritance. After a court case based on the incompetence of the administrator together with evidence that Amy's mother was not fully *compos mentis* and did not realise that she was placing her daughter in the same category as her mentally retarded brother Theodore when she put her signature to the trust, the will was broken. Amy's share of the capital which ought to have been around $250,000, was found to amount to only $60,000; Edwin's bad feeling over the will seems in retrospect to have had some foundation.[4]

Now that she had capital on which to draw, Amy was able to send her two daughters to private intermediate schools to prepare them for college. Muriel, who had already decided that she wished to become a teacher, went to St Margaret's in Toronto. Amelia, with her eyes still on Bryn Mawr, went to the Ogontz School, Philadelphia.

Although Amelia now felt that she was again moving in her own social milieu, and the range of subjects across the sciences, arts and humanities was intellectually stimulating, her peripatetic existence and the emotional traumas of the past few years had made her too independent in her thinking to fit neatly into the school society with ease. She clashed with fellow students again when she was invited to join a sorority, this time over the cliquey rules which left some unfortunate girls 'beyond the pale'.[5] Further, she chafed over the confines of subjects then considered to be suitable for young ladies and caused a school-wide debate regarding religious philosophy. Still, she was happy enough, and her letters home told of concerts, and dormitory feasts.

> We had a lovely feast the other night. There were about fifteen of us and several teachers were away so that it was a lovely opportunity. We played the ukuleles at twelve o'clock and sang. Some of the girls had been away and brought back chicken sandwiches and cakes and pastry and we made hot chocolate and put marshmallow on it and had a beautiful time . . .

But in the same letter she strikes a more serious note:

> What do you think of the railroad strike and the abdication of the Tsar? There seems to be no public sentiment back of the

unions as there was in the beginning, which will make their demands harder of attainment. They have gone too far . . .[6]

In the summer of 1917 Amelia spent some time with her parents in Kansas before joining a group of friends at Camp Gray on the eastern shore of Lake Michigan. She hated leaving her father who had travelled part of the way with her, and wrote home 'Poppy was such a lamb last night I came near to coming back with him.'[7] While this indicates an improvement on the domestic front it was only shortly afterwards that Amelia was addressing her letters to her mother care of the Hotel Sutherland, rather than the little house on Charlotte Street. Edwin had started drinking again.

A series of letters to her mother reveals a naivety which would today be surprising in a twenty-year-old. Amelia was still very much the girl, rather than the woman. She was critical of the primitive conditions at Camp Gray – oil lamps instead of electricity, lack of hot water, rather simple food and margarine instead of butter – and she agonised over the fact that her menstrual period obliged her to refrain from swimming in the first week: 'I am in mental torture at not going in swimming and imagine I am thought of as somewhat of a piker . . .' But she thoroughly enjoyed the company of a group of young friends of both sexes: Sarah, Kenneth and Harry – chiefly, one suspects from her letters, Kenneth (Merrill), who was to remain a friend long afterwards. Perhaps Ken was the real reason why Amelia opposed a suggestion that her younger sister Muriel join her at the camp, for she insisted that there were no vacant rooms and it was useless for her mother to enquire. 'Under no circumstances could . . . Muriel come up without you. There is not a place and it is impossible to be alone, Sarah and I would be lost without the Merrills . . . and Ken has toted me around considerably.'[8] Her letters* indicate that she had a schoolgirl crush on Ken, for after two weeks of intense enjoyment the camp quickly lost all its charms for Amelia when he returned home. 'I can't stand it any longer,' she

*Published as *Letters from Amelia*, Beacon Press, Boston, 1982

wrote to her mother '. . . and leave tomorrow . . . Kenneth and Harry left day before yesterday. Kenneth has done so much for me. He is very nice and sensitive and almost brilliant.'[9]

In the fall of 1917 she returned to Ogontz as a senior, and her letters home show a new maturity. She no longer chattered ingenuously, there is a more serious tone in her writing. According to the headmistress, Miss Sutherland, Amelia 'sought out the challenging authors: Shaw, Dreisler, Dostoevsky, since for her, reading was an adventure.'[10]

The marks awarded to her on her report cards were enviable, ranging from good to excellent in a wide range of subjects. But among more conventional items, the bill sent to Amelia's parents for 'extras' included some articles which reflected the sinister overtones of war. Authors such as Wordsworth, Byron, Burns; and Shakespeare's *Hamlet, Othello* and *King Lear*, were interspersed with *What's Wrong with the World?, War Poetry* and *Red Cross Hygiene.* Charges for the supply of surgical dressings and a nursing cap and gown indicate that Amelia was taking some form of first aid training which would later stand her in good stead. As yet, though, Amelia remained largely untouched by the First World War. Occasional notes in her letters home indicate she helped where she could, knitting khaki garments for the boys in the trenches, and she noted in passing that Ken had joined up.[11]

She was delighted when, shortly after school term started she learned that Miss Sutherland had swept away the secret sorority system against which Amelia had spoken out, and instituted an 'honour system' for personal conduct. But she was deeply aware of the ever-widening gulf between her parents and wrote to her mother: 'I have deep twinges of conscience about leaving you to your silent severity (your description). I knew exactly what you were going to have to endure and feel as tho' I could have alleviated some of the loneliness had I remained faithful to my intentions.' Later she begged: 'Dear hen, don't write Miss S. letters of advice and warning. They go through the whole faculty and come to me and I just shrivel. I am not overdoing [things] and all that is needed to [bring me] to bouncing health is plenty to eat and happiness.' Amy clearly did not heed this note and Amelia, obviously suffering some embarrassment, had to write again stressing her plea: 'You won't write any more about me to school dearest Mummy will you?'[12]

Amelia's leadership qualities were evidently recognised by her peers for she was voted vice-president of the class and secretary to the local Red Cross chapter. She also held office in several other organisations. She stood out strongly against some of the girls who were agitating for the reinstatement of sororities, and campaigned fiercely against

> a useless costly [class] ring which is valuable only for the metal in it as there is no artistic and lasting value in a class ring. We others are only asking [that] we turn our money to Red Cross and have only a little gold band for a trifle about four or five dollars instead of the expensive ones – in order to keep its precedent and to have a remembrance of our senior days. Much sweeter to me than a gorgeous one to pass on.

Despite her strongly held opinions she seemed to be respected if not popular, and was known by the sobriquet 'Millie' (occasionally Meelie) or, perhaps as a cynical comment on her over-slim physique 'Butterball', '. . . Butter for short!' she wrote home.[13]

Occasionally, when she wanted to visit someone outside the school or go to a ball-game with friends, she wrote to her mother for permission. And on the 'extras' bill, quaint when one considers the age of the student, is a charge for 'chaperonage'.[14]

For the 1917 Christmas holidays Amelia took the train to Toronto where Muriel was at a college preparatory school working towards her entry requirements for Smith College. Here, for the first time, Amelia came face to face with the grisly effects of war. Although the United States had now joined the conflict, her entry was too recent to give rise to the sights which shocked and saddened Amelia in Toronto.

As a senior member of the Commonwealth of Great Britain, Canada had sent its youth to fight in the trenches from the earliest stages of the war. Toronto, with its Spadina Military Convalescent

Hospital, saw many of the returning wounded. In her book *The Fun of It* Amelia notes her reactions:

> There for the first time I realized what the World War meant. Instead of new uniforms and brass bands, I saw only the results of four years' desperate struggle; men without arms and legs, men who were paralysed and men who were blind. One day I saw four one-legged men at once, walking as best they could down the street together.[15]

After the holidays she returned as planned to Ogontz, but now all ambitions to graduate had vanished and her one goal was to aid the wounded men she had seen and to serve in some useful capacity. Overriding any parental opposition she left Ogontz within weeks and returned to Toronto where she 'took steps to become a nurse's aid' and though she endeavoured to join the American Red Cross in some formal capacity she never quite managed it. Instead she spent the long months as a VAD (Voluntary Aid Detachment nurse), until the Armistice in November 1918, at the Spadina Hospital.[16]

The work of a nursing aid was varied. From 'scrubbing floors to playing tennis with convalescing patients'. Later she was to recall ladling out medicine from buckets, serving meals and massaging cramps. Because she 'knew a little chemistry' she was able to spend some time in the dispensary. In the laboratory she prepared slides, and she fought successfully to improve the general diet of the patients.[17]

Throughout the summer of 1918 she worked long hours six days a week, generally taking only Sunday off. When her free day coincided with her sister's they rode out together on borrowed horses. Both were extremely good horsewomen and fond of riding. Amelia made a great pet of a notably difficult thoroughbred called, aptly, Dynamite. As summer gave way to the Canadian winter she used one of her precious days off to visit former patients at the local airfield and there experienced the first stirrings of what was to become an all-encompassing interest in aeroplanes.

Though I had seen one or two at county fairs before, I now saw
many of them, as the officers were trained at the various fields
around the city. Of course no civilian had a chance of going up.
But I hung around in spare time and absorbed all I could. I
remember the sting of the snow on my face when it was blown
back from the propellers when the training plane took off on
skis.[18]

When the great influenza epidemic struck Amelia worked night
duties on the pneumonia ward as the virus attacked patient and staff
alike, and it was hardly surprising that before long she too fell
victim. She was still recovering when the armistice was signed on 11
November.

                                              December 1918

Kenneth dear,
. . . I am just out of the hospital where the effects of the 'flu
[epidemic] . . . put me. I think working twelve to fourteen
hours at a stretch added to the strain of having carried on all
summer – made me a more than normally easy prey for
influenza, and an infection in my nose at the same time which
later necessitated an operation after which 'flu symptoms
reappeared. Altogether I have had more than a two months
siege and face the awful prospect of doing nothing for two
more.[19]

She took grave offence at the peace celebrations, standing back
and observing:

What a day! All day long whistles kept up a continuous blowing.
No means of transport was available . . . private cars ran the risk
of being stalled in the littered streets and the traction company
just gave up . . . Young men ran round with huge dusters of flour
and blew it on young women . . . Supposedly dignified citizens
snake-danced and knocked each other's hats off. I didn't hear
one serious word of thanksgiving in all the ballyhoo.[20]

Shortly after this letter was written Amelia went to Northampton, Massachusetts to convalesce with her sister. Replying to Ken who had obviously expressed a 'wish you were here' in his letter to her, she told him:

If only I *were* over there instead of gravitating in enforced idleness in the confines of this bally little New England village. My sister is here preparing for Smith and as the Pater is in California on an extended business trip mother and I have taken an apartment for a few months with Muriel . . .

Europe certainly could not have gone madder than this continent on Peace Day. Toronto was simply a riot and the day was an excuse for every possible licence.

What do you think of the President's little flight to France? This country is terribly distrustful of his policies but the other nations don't grasp that and [I] feel objections are to his breaking precedent. Wouldn't it be great to sit at the conference and see people's fate decided for we don't know how long?

I wish after all we could have marched into Berlin as a victorious army and not as the army of occupation. Couldn't the Germans have felt defeat more universally than now, and realized more their inability to trust in arms alone? They are not at all changed as yet. I wonder whether they *will* ever change.[21]

She soon tired of the enforced idleness and, though not able to work officially, found temporary employment working for charity. Her work consisted mainly of stuffing appeal letters into envelopes and addressing them. '. . . The Committee is driving for thirty million and with so large an objective (for now) there must be a correspondingly large amount of work. It is easy to get people to lend the weight of name to a worthy cause but to obtain workers is very different,' she wrote to Ken, adding 'I was sorry to hear of the 'flu attack, I hate and fear it somehow, more than a little. Having seen so much of it I suppose has prejudiced me – with the uncertainty of the treatment adding to the prejudice.'[22] In an attempt to pass the time and rid herself of depression she enrolled in an all-girl class on a course in automobile engine repair.

Together with her mother and sister, Amelia summered at Lake George where she continued her convalescence. She was still markedly low in spirits and her recovery was not helped by news that her father wanted to move permanently to California. Edwin reported that he had ceased drinking by this time but the marriage was held together only painfully. Amy (as well as her daughters) had lost respect for Edwin and though she persevered at keeping the marriage intact it was all a great struggle.

In the fall of 1919 Muriel went to Smith College as a freshman. Amy and Amelia travelled to New York, where Amelia had enrolled as a pre-med student at Columbia University. 'I had acquired a yen for medicine and I planned to fit myself for such a career . . . as usual I had a good time, though I studied hard and didn't have any too much money. But students in New York can get so much with so little if they really wish.'[23] Quirkily, it was from this date onwards that Amelia persisted in knocking a year off her age, always giving her date of birth as 1898 instead of 1897.[24]

Amy's role was again one of chaperone, for having seen her daughter safely installed in a respectable hotel on Morningside Drive, she returned to Muriel in Northampton. Clearly mother and daughter had some discussion of religion, or at least Amelia's attitude towards it. Amy was also worried about Amelia being alone in New York and whether she would eat properly. In a letter to her mother after her first day at college Amelia told her about the domestic arrangements. 'Whittier Hall is some dump and I'm glad I'm not [living] here,' she said outlining her hotel accommodation. 'Don't worry about the meals or mentality . . . Don't think for an instant I would ever become an atheist or even a doubter nor lose faith in the church's teachings as a whole. That is impossible. But you must admit there is a great deal radically wrong in methods and teaching and results today.'[25]

At Columbia Amelia took various courses in chemistry and the biological sciences. And she enjoyed her spare time too. In now well-known feats of daring she climbed to the top of the great dome of the university library and was photographed there in confining bulky clothing complete with ankle-length skirt, buttoned shoes and enveloping black straw hat. She remembered her time at Columbia and the friendships she made there with great pleasure, but it took her only a few months to conclude that she would not make an ideal physician.[26]

In the spring of 1920 she wrote to her mother regarding Edwin's pressing suggestion that the family join him in California and the girls continue their studies there. 'I believe it will be best to all go together out west under the circumstances . . . however, do as you think best.' Amy, recovering from a minor operation, finally joined her husband in California and undoubtedly pressed Amelia to go too to ease the tension between husband and wife, for at the end of the semester Amelia succumbed to the pleas of both her parents to join them.

Ostensibly she was to continue her studies but in fact she appears to have made no attempt to enrol for further education and really acted as a buffer between husband and wife. Muriel, who stayed at Smith College and saw her sister off to California, recalls Amelia's slightly bitter parting shot: 'I'll see what I can do to keep Mother and Dad together, Pidge, but after that I'm going to come back here and live my own life.'[27]

When Amelia set off for California she was twenty-three years old. She had no definite ideas about what shape her life should take. As far as is known she had never even indulged in a serious romance – hedged about as she was, in the main, by the mores of the period and the need for chaperonage for girls of her social class. At Columbia she was regarded as a serious student who, when not working, spent her time at concerts, poetry readings, picnicking with her 'best friend' (Louise de Schweinitz) at the top of the Palisades on the New Jersey side of the Hudson River and joining in naive, slightly dangerous pranks. She rode hired horses in Central Park and she read a lot.[28] She had tried and rejected several possible avenues. College graduation: to what end? Medical degree? Although she had not given up on medicine she could not see herself as a doctor, though when she left New York she still had ambitions to follow a career of some sort in the field of medical research. In short she was still looking for a life of her own.

Neither her books nor her letters indicate that she was troubled by this lack of direction (or that she even recognised it as such). And although her parents were not wealthy by any means, she certainly did not appear to be overly troubled by any requirement to contribute financially toward her own upkeep.

She was always starting and abandoning new projects. She was self-confident in her own social milieu and somewhat reserved outside it. Her humour was still childish but not unpleasantly so, perhaps in the fashion of the time. Though her writing had become more mature than that of the schoolgirl, in reality she had tasted little, outside the time she had spent at Spadina, of real life.

CHAPTER 4

1920–1921

During the time he had been alone in California Edwin had not only set up a legal practice, but had also been befriended by a Christian Scientist neighbour who helped him to overcome his addiction to alcohol completely. The new start gave hope to the entire family and when Amy joined him it seemed the former happy unity might be regained.

The couple rented a house at 1334 West Fourth Street in Los Angeles, not far from Edwin's office. It was a handsome, two-storey timber home with a covered porch, but even after reserving rooms for Amelia and Muriel's use the house was too large, so Amy took in three young male boarders in order to supplement the family's income. As Edwin recovered his business acumen and his practice grew, Amy tried hard to find again the respect and love she had once had for her husband. This was not an easy task given the suffering and hardships the family had undergone because of Edwin's weakness and her feelings consisted of a mixture of duty, guilt and pity for the man that Edwin had become.

Amy obviously felt that the marriage would have a better chance of successful reconciliation if the union were leavened by the presence of the girls, so Amelia and Muriel were both asked to go out to California to continue their education. Muriel wanted to remain at Smith College and, forced to operate on a stringent budget, she was not even inclined to go to the expense of spending the summer in California, so it was left to Amelia to give up her place at Columbia. This seems not to have caused Amelia undue pain, though there was her bitter parting remark to her sister in New York.

By now Amelia was twenty-three years old. Tall, slim and serious with fair, waist-length hair, dressed almost exclusively in her favourite colour, brown, she was not pretty in the sense that she turned heads, but her expressive eyes coupled with a ready boyish grin gave her gamine appeal. When she arrived in Los Angeles she met Sam Chapman, one of her parents' boarders.

Sam was a good-looking man of Amelia's age. Tall and tanned with thick dark hair, he had grown up in Massachusetts and graduated as a chemical engineer from Tufts University before travelling west to carve a career for himself. The two had much in common. Both were well-read and serious-minded. According to Amelia's letters to her sister they spent more and more time together enjoying tennis, swimming and the theatre. A social conscience had long been apparent in Amelia but Sam kindled it into action. Together, dressed in what Amelia called 'slumming clothes', they attended illegal meetings of the socialist organization Industrial Workers of the World (its initials, IWW, were said by its critics to stand for 'I Won't Work').

On at least one occasion the meeting was broken up by the police. The subject under discussion had been pensions for everyone over sixty, in anticipation of the social security laws proposed by Herbert Hoover.[1] An annoyed Amelia told her family, idealistically, 'Pensions are surely better than poorhouse at sixty? I think the government ought to make people save some of their wages and give it back to them when they are old . . . [and] I think we should have had the right to talk it out tonight instead of being sent home like naughty children.'[2]

One day, some months after her arrival in California, Amelia drove with her father to an 'aerial meet' at Daugherty Field, Long Beach. 'The interest aroused in me in Toronto led me to all the air circuses in the vicinity', she wrote[3] and on this occasion she thought she might like to fly. She asked Edwin to enquire about the cost of flying lessons. Her father made enquiries and told her it cost about $1,000 to learn to fly. 'Why do you want to know?' he asked her,[4] but he booked a flight for her on the following day. 'I am sure he thought that one ride would be enough for me,' Amelia wrote.[5] Next morning he accompanied her to the small dirt strip known as Rogers Field, 'no more than an open space on Wilshire Boulevard'[6] and paid ten dollars for his daughter to be taken up as a passenger for a ten-minute flight. Her pilot was Frank Hawks[7] who was destined to become a high-speed flying record breaker.

What must it have been like, the first flight which was to hint to Amelia that here was what she had been seeking; that was to inspire her as she suspected she was capable of being inspired?

Amelia would have been given a helmet and goggles and helped into the deep forward cockpit of the huge open-cockpit biplane; the pilot flew from the rear cockpit. Most aeroplanes used for this purpose were war surplus Canucks or Jennys and with Hawks as pilot it would have been a smooth and uneventful take-off, followed by a climb to a thousand feet or so. A flight over downtown Los Angeles then isolated by citrus groves from the outlying suburbs, was almost de rigueur; Amelia would have been able to gauge their speed by glancing down at the occasional automobile on the highways leading in and out of the city. Perhaps this was followed by a sweep out over the Pacific ocean to give the passenger a glimpse of Catalina Island in the distance, and the beaches and the few big houses in the idyllic setting of the Santa Monica hills. In the month of December the air in the Los Angeles basin can be as clean and clear as crystal, and silky smooth with none of the turbulence of the hot summer months, and Amelia could hardly have chosen a better pilot with whom to take her first flight. A landing amid clouds of dust would have coated her face, leaving two white circles when she took off her goggles, but from her later writings it is clear that Amelia simply loved the sensation of flying from the first moment.

'As soon as we left the ground I knew I myself had to fly.'[8] Here then was the thing for which she had been looking. Lucky indeed that she was able to recognise her destiny in this moment.

'I think I'd like to fly,' I told the family casually that evening, knowing full well I'd die if I didn't. 'Not a bad idea,' said my father equally casually, 'When do you start?'[9]

Her mother raised no opposition either, so Amelia said she'd make the necessary enquiries and let them know the outcome. Unfortunately, her father's reaction had been an attempt at wry humour, rather than casual acceptance. He was astonished when a short time later Amelia advised him that she had not only completed her preliminary investigations but had signed up for lessons for which she expected him to pay. The cost was five hundred dollars for about twelve hours' instruction.

Edwin told her he couldn't afford the lessons and it was not difficult to see his sudden dislike of the entire idea. Amelia would not be put off and said she would get a job in order to pay for the lessons herself. In the meantime she would work at her father's office to repay him. Eventually her determination wore down Edwin's opposition and he agreed to allow her to start learning to fly but the impropriety of his daughter spending time with a male instructor was a real concern. Fortunately Amelia had heard of a woman pilot who gave flying instruction and shortly afterwards Edwin accompanied his daughter when she went to seek out Miss Anita Snook.

It was unusual in December 1920 to find a woman flying instructor. 'Neta' Snook was based at Kinner Field, a small dirt strip in the South Gate area of Los Angeles and, although only a year older than Amelia, had been fascinated by aviation since childhood. She had set out to become a pilot as soon as she left school and when she needed money to pay for lessons she took any job that would provide a wage. Training at the Curtiss School of Aviation she was just about to achieve her ambition, a solo flight, when America entered the war and all civilian flying was prohibited. She caused a stir by her aggressive attempts to enlist in the United States Air Force but was thwarted because of her sex. Instead, she spent the war working as an expeditor for the British War Mission, checking out Curtiss OX5 engines which were being assembled in Canada.

A few months after the war ended Neta bought a wrecked Canuck, a Canadian training plane that was a contemporary of the ubiquitous American JN4 Jenny. It took her a year to rebuild it and in the spring of 1920 she loaded it onto a truck, drove to a nearby pasture, assembled it and took off for her first solo flight. During

that summer she barnstormed her way across the midwest, taking
fare-paying passengers up for 15-minute flights at $15 a ride.
Photographed for publicity posters in the typical flying 'togs' of
riding breeches and boots, with a leather jacket and white silk scarf,
she drew huge crowds. At one point she was earning a thousand dollars a day to make two flights on each of three days, a huge fee at
that time. In the autumn she moved to Los Angeles and started her
own business at Kinner Field, flying passengers, doing aerial advertising and giving instruction to would-be pilots.[10]

Kinner was located on the west side of Long Beach Boulevard
and Tweedy Road, below Huntingdon Park.[11] It was a 50-acre,
bumpy, barren, weed-grown piece of ground on which a small
hangar and a wind-sock had been erected by Bert Kinner a few
weeks before Neta's arrival. Here Kinner was in the process of building a small biplane of his own design, the 'Kinner Airster' which he
confidently expected would one day be owned by every family. It
was a two-seater biplane powered by a three-cylinder Lawrence
model L2 60-hp engine giving a maximum speed of 85 mph and a
design range of 500 miles. In return for the commercial flying rights
on the field, Neta agreed to test-fly all Kinner's aeroplanes.[12]

Neta was only a little over five feet in height, and her personality
matched her bright red hair. One contemporary wrote: 'We were
not quite sure as to whether Snooky was a man or a woman, as few
of us ever saw her except in a pair of dirty coveralls . . .'[13] One hot
afternoon in December 1920, as Neta leaned against her biplane
awaiting her next passenger, she noticed

a tall, slender young lady and an elderly man approaching. She
was wearing a brown suit, plain but of good cut. Her hair was
braided and neatly coiled around her head; there was a light scarf
around her neck and she carried gloves. She would have stood
out in any crowd and she reminded me of the well groomed
and cultured young ladies at the . . . Academy in . . . my childhood home. The gentleman with her was slightly gray at the
temples and wore a blue serge business suit. He walked erect with
a firm step.

'I'm Amelia Earhart and this is my father . . . I want to learn
to fly and I understand you teach students . . . Will you teach
me?'[14]

Amelia and Neta took to each other on sight. Both were mid-
westerners from similar middle-class family backgrounds. Both were
intelligent women but while Neta had already taken destiny into her
own hands, Amelia was still very much the daughter of the family,
still asking permission before she did things or went anywhere.
Whether she actually needed this permission or not is open to
doubt, but she allowed herself to be bound by the conventions.
Muriel has said that Amelia decided to leave Ogontz and go to
Toronto to nurse without waiting for permission to do so;[15] nevertheless she certainly asked parental permission on lesser occasions
long after this incident. Neta's influence on Amelia's life was to
extend beyond her aviation instruction.

From this point on Amelia's life changed. There was no sudden
dramatic alteration, but one detects a new sense of awareness of herself and a new determination in her actions. She had found a
direction and unlike previous interests this one was to last.

Neta advised Amelia that her charges were $1 a minute in the air
and that she expected to be paid each day. Amelia agreed and
arranged to pay with Liberty Bonds – presumably part of Amy's
inheritance. The next day, 3 January 1921, after her work in Edwin's
office, Amelia turned up for her first lesson. She wore her old brown
riding breeches and boots and 'a beautifully tailored brown jacket',
riding clothes being considered the most suitable dress for the aviator, and spent a half hour learning to taxi the Canuck. Amelia had
acquired a book on aerodynamics from the library. 'I soon became
accustomed to seeing her with a book,' Neta recalled. 'She always
carried one.' Amelia's literary interests were extremely varied and
ranged through technical books on aviation to Rossetti's poems,
Fitzgerald's translation of the *Rubaiyyat*, and Carl Sandburg. On one
occasion she brought a history of the Mohammedan religion and
tried, unsuccessfully, to persuade Neta to read it.[16]

For a few weeks all the instruction was ground-based while

Amelia learned about the principles of flight, and over the next two months she logged four hours in the air. By now she had taken her first 'real' job working in the mailroom of the telephone company offices. In addition she continued to work a half day every Saturday for her father.[17]

Neta recalled those days and the primitive conditions in the hangar where the fastidious Amelia and the other students spent most of their spare time:

> We had a few cooking utensils, knives and forks. When we cooked Amelia always washed the dishes *before* we ate. When we bought ice-creams she never ate the part that the handler had touched . . . however she never minded if her hands got dirty helping with plane maintenance . . . [and] she never wanted to dally long at what she called 'frivolous doings', such as eating and joking, if air conditions were right for flying.[18]

Despite her continuing close friendship with Sam Chapman, Amelia was happy to date other boys in company with Neta who recalled that Amelia 'preferred older men' and was disdainful when a picnic in the mountains with two young men was ruined by torrential rain. The boys suggested they should try to find overnight accommodation in a nearby settlement but Amelia insisted that her parents would not allow it and made them drive the 200 miles back to Los Angeles in the rain. She told Neta, 'You see why I don't care for these thoughtless, irresponsible young boys. Mature men wouldn't have put us through such an experience.' It was daylight when they reached the outskirts of Los Angeles. Neta privately didn't think a lot of Amelia's opinion but she held her tongue, even when Amelia later developed a bizarre friendship with 'a slight, emaciated old man'. He wore a small shawl across his shoulders and a light rug across his knees. He used to collect Amelia in his chauffeur-driven car, sitting ramrod straight in the back seat, his hands resting on a gold-topped cane. Once Neta invited Amelia and her unusual man-friend in for a drink but Amelia's companion declined – it was past his bedtime.[19]

There were other male friends, notably Lloyd Royer, a young aeroplane engineer. Amelia and Neta often double-dated to theatres and shows in downtown Los Angeles, and enjoyed dining at ethnic restaurants. Neta recalled that 'Amelia had strict scruples. She didn't feel it was right for a boy to spend time and money on her if she, in turn, had no interest in him. To her it was a form of stealing.' Neta sometimes dined at the Earhart home after a day at the airstrip and noted that Amy had become hard of hearing and quietly disapproved of the two girls being constantly dressed in 'masculine attire':

> She ran her household in a disciplined manner and the food was served formally and in courses. Everyone had his napkin in a ring placed at the top of the plate, and the serving was done from the left . . . After dinner everyone read or played a few hands of cards – flinch or whist. [But] when Amelia and I would retire to the privacy of her bedroom we would giggle and exchange confidences.[20]

One such shared confidence was the fact that Amelia had secretly started to cut her hair, an inch or so at a time. Impressed, Neta asked if her mother had noticed. 'No, I'm keeping it pinned up when I'm home. I only cut off a little every few weeks.'[21] Another and more serious confidence was her request to Neta to help her 'work on Amy' to buy an aeroplane.

> Amelia was trying to persuade her mother to buy it [Bert Kinner's first aeroplane, the Airster] for her. Her father was not financially able to do so nor so inclined . . . All her pilot friends, including myself, advised her against it. I had had the little plane in the air a few times. There weren't many bugs only the engine gave us trouble. It was powered by a three-cylinder Lawrence – 60 horsepower, radial and air cooled [and] the oil system was so designed that the third cylinder periodically became clogged.[22]

By now Amelia had received some six months' instruction in Neta's Canuck. She was a reasonably competent pilot, but she lacked the inherent ability that makes a great pilot. Sometimes she made silly mistakes which provoked Neta into castigating her student. 'Why do you persist in levelling off so high above the ground? Didn't you notice how I had to shove the nose down several times . . . you know the Airster, or any aircraft for that matter can't stand a "pancake".' Amelia would answer ruefully that she 'guessed' she was just daydreamin'.

Years later Neta was to recall Amelia's daydreaming with distress but at the time now she was merely concerned about her friend's insistence on buying the Airster. Her assessment was that it was not a forgiving aeroplane and lacked the stability of the old Canuck. It was under-powered, landed faster, and tended to ground-loop at the merest suggestion of a cross-wind. 'It was not a plane for a beginner,' she said, and in Neta's opinion Amelia was very much a beginner.[23]

This was underlined when one day on a dual instruction flight, Amelia headed for Long Beach without telling Neta of her intention to make what was then regarded as a reasonably long flight. Neta soon suspected Amelia's destination and doubted the plane's ability to make the flight in the existing head-wind unless the fuel tank was full. Cutting back the throttle and yelling to Amelia she queried the fuel situation. 'Did you check it personally?' Amelia shook her head. 'Mr Kinner always keeps it full,' she shouted back. Neta grimly opened the throttle, turned the plane and headed for home. On their return they were met by a worried Bert Kinner who informed them that he had not filled the Kinner the night before as he'd been waiting for the fuel tanker to arrive next day. Not for the first time Neta angrily wondered if she hadn't misjudged her friend's ability.[24]

At this point, Muriel came to join the family. Obviously impressed with her sister's flying activities she was a regular visitor to the airfield, travelling on the electric streetcar from Los Angeles, through Vernon and Huntington Park to the end of the line. From there to Kinner Field was a walk of about a mile, but the occasional passing motorist could easily tell the girls' destination from Amelia and Neta's 'flying clothes' and so they seldom had to walk the entire distance.

There was always something to do at Kinner even when not flying. Small tears in the fabric of an aeroplane had to be patched and doped, wooden struts had to be bound and repaired and flying wires needed to be cleaned and the tension checked. It was a whole new world and though it was populated mainly by men, there seemed to be no restriction on women joining in the fun too, if they wanted to do so. So the two sisters would spend weekends there, carrying a picnic lunch of sandwiches and chocolate cake. When there were no fare-paying passengers for Neta, or Frank Hawks, there was little flying. No one could afford the fuel to fly too often for pleasure alone. As the temperature soared above 100 degrees, pilots, students and mechanics would sit in the shade of a tin-roofed shack, to 'talk aeroplanes' and watch the occasional plane land, causing clouds of dust on the unpaved runway.

At that time, virtually the dawn of civil aviation, the possibilities ahead of them were seemingly limitless. They happily forecast larger aeroplanes that would carry tens of passengers and sports planes with enclosed cabins so that the pilot was not subjected to the extremes of the elements. These things were technically possible already, but technical development had not caught up with practical requirements and all eyes were fixed on what was happening at the Curtiss and Wright companies. There were also the solo operators such as Bert Kinner – the industry would remain fragmented for a long time.

Despite Neta's largely unspoken misgivings, Amelia remained confident in her flying ability and was determined to own the Kinner. Neta was not the only person at the field to advise her against this, but Amelia had made her decision based on her own quiet research. The engine was air-cooled which meant a simplified system and a resultant decrease in weight. Also, because the Kinner was far lighter than the reliable old Canucks or Jennys, Amelia was able to pick the plane up by the tail and move it without help from a man or the use of a dolly.[25]

Shortly before her twenty-fourth birthday in July 1921 she purchased the prototype Kinner, which she promptly named 'the Canary' because it was finished in bright chromate yellow, for two thousand dollars. Initially she had asked her father for the money to buy the plane and finally 'he agreed that I needed the plane and that I should have it, and promised to help out in paying for it. But I'm afraid my salesmanship was faulty for he did not stay sold . . .' Amelia recorded. She had saved a little money from her job at the telephone exchange:

> Perhaps this . . . doesn't seem very convincing, for obviously my salary as playmate of office boys would have to run on a long time before it would wipe out the balance of $2,000. But it did help my credit immensely! I think it made my flying companions believe I was in earnest.[26]

She had already paid her small capital over to Bert Kinner before learning that her father had changed his mind. Having exhausted her slender funds she came to an arrangement with Bert Kinner whereby the plane remained available for sales demonstration work, in return for hangarage and mechanical repairs.[27] Meanwhile, in order to pay the balance of the purchase price, she borrowed all of Muriel's savings and her mother provided the remainder on condition that she give up the job in the backroom at the telephone exchange 'and stay at home a little'. She resigned as backroom girl but stayed with the company as a telephone operator.

Neta continued to instruct Amelia for a while, free of charge, in the Kinner, because Amelia could not afford to pay and she was still not ready to go solo.[28] On 23 July Amelia and Neta flew to the Goodyear Field to look at the huge Cloudster, Donald Douglas's first aircraft.[29]

> A grove of Eucalyptus trees grew at the far end of the runway. On takeoff, the Kinner Airster didn't gain altitude fast enough to quite clear those trees – that pesky oil-clogged third cylinder. There was nothing to do. To nose down for more flying speed meant slamming into the trees. To pull up meant a stall. Amelia pulled up – I would have done the same – the plane stalled [and]

on ground contact the propeller was broken and the landing gear damaged. That was Amelia's first crash. She [had bitten] her tongue but had the presence of mind to cut the switch. When I looked back, she was powdering her nose. 'We have to look nice when the reporters come,' she reminded me.[30]

There were other occasions when Amelia made stupid mistakes that Neta simply couldn't understand. 'You have to learn to fly by feel', she told Amelia who merely replied that she thought Neta was referring to 'flying by the seat of your pants' and that one day there would be instruments to tell you when you were flying level or to show the angle of climb.[31]

More advanced instruction followed but not from Neta. Edwin and Amy, by now obviously reconciled to Amelia's ambitions, raised no objections when their daughter turned to a former World War One pilot, John 'Monte' Montijo, who sometimes demonstrated the Airster and flew it in air races for publicity purposes.

Amelia, according to Neta's records, had four or five hours in the Canuck and some seven hours in the Kinner,[32] but she still felt she needed some 'strenuous' further instruction from 'Monte' before making her first solo flight. While in retrospect this seems an unusually high number of hours to solo, Amelia was later to write she 'refused to fly alone until I knew some stunting. It seemed foolish to try to go up alone without the ability to recognise and recover quickly from any position the plane might assume, a reaction possible with practice.'

On her first attempted solo flight, one of the shock absorbers broke as she was taking off causing the port wing to sag, so that having faced and overcome the mental agony of preparing to take-off she had to abort for on-the-spot repairs. Unlike the average student who is content to fly a circuit or two at low level, when Amelia got off the ground she went up to five thousand feet and stooged about for a while to the alarm of Monte and Neta,[33] returning to make, in her own words, 'a thoroughly rotten landing'.[34] She celebrated by buying a leather flying coat. The obvious newness of this shiny garment caused a certain amount of good-natured teasing by the crowd at the airfield, so Amelia 'aged' it by sleeping in it and staining it appropriately.

But there still remained that serious reservation about her skill as a pilot and her lack of natural ability.[35] This is no disparagement of Amelia, simply the view of many of her contemporaries in the flying world. Indeed, given this apparently significant drawback, it is greatly to her credit that she was subsequently able to achieve so much.

CHAPTER 5

1921–1927

With characteristic enthusiasm Amelia now became more and more obsessed with flying. From earliest childhood days she was capable of bringing spirited exuberance to anything which struck her as adventurous:

> Whether it was considered the thing to do or not was irrelevant. As a little girl I had ridden my buggy in the stable; I had once climbed up on a delivery horse; I had explored the fearsome caves in the cliffs overlooking the Missouri; I had invented a trap and caught a chicken; I had jumped over a fence that no boy my age had dared to jump; and I knew there was more fun and excitement in life than I would have time to enjoy.[1]

In time aviation became, not only a *raison d'être*, but also a means of escape from an increasingly troubled home life – a place where she could be herself.[2]

Despite the financial difficulties involved she kept up her flying instruction, and whenever she could earn enough to pay for fuel she flew solo in her Kinner 'Canary'. There was no easy way for Amelia to earn money but she was not afraid of work. She was still working at the telephone exchange even though this meant she was 'ostracised by right-thinking girls' of her class.[3] She also continued to work for her father part-time and according to her friend Lloyd Royer she 'had several other part-time jobs too'. Some five years later Amelia was to write that she had had 'twenty-eight jobs' among which were 'driving a truck, selling sausages and working in a photographic laboratory'.[4] Allowing for her nursing career and the jobs mentioned above, and three jobs that are known about after she left California, this still leaves some twenty jobs to be accounted for about which nothing is known. But, 'like the rest of us,' her friend, Royer, summed up, 'she never had any money to buy gasoline'.[5]

Neta Snook had sold her aeroplane and left Los Angeles in the fall of 1921 to visit her parents before getting married.[6] Amelia was thus the sole female representative at the Kinner airstrip. Her careful upbringing enabled her to tread the fine line between friendship and over-familiarity. She was always happy to be shown how to strip down an engine or to learn some new mechanical skill, 'to muck in with the boys' and to laugh with them, so to speak, but at the same time she maintained a reserved dignity so that her male contacts treated her with immense respect.

In the summer of 1922 Amelia was pictured in the Los Angeles *Examiner* with her Kinner aeroplane, above an interview in which she explained that she hoped to fly across the continent in the following year with the intention of 'dropping in at Vassar College' where she hoped to take a post-graduate course. 'I don't crave publicity,' she told the reporter, 'but it seems to me it would be the greatest fun . . .'[7] The article went on to advise readers that Miss Earhart was popular in society circles in Los Angeles, being the daughter of Attorney Edwin Earhart.

By October, despite not being able to fly as often as she wished owing to lack of money, Amelia's flying skills must have improved considerably for she startled her family by participating in a record-breaking attempt. Her sister tells the story of how she and her father had gone along to a fly-in at Rogers Field, having been handed tickets by Amelia who told them mysteriously that she wouldn't be able to sit with them. They soon learned why. Amelia took off and was gone for an hour during which time she set a women's altitude record by reaching 14,000 feet. Although her record stood for only a few weeks before being broken by Ruth Nichols, it served to provide Amelia with greater confidence in herself and in the role of aeroplanes. Indeed, had she not encountered engine trouble at

12,000 feet (a fact verified by vibrations recorded by the sealed barograph) she was confident that she could have achieved a much higher altitude.[8]

Some weeks later, Amelia decided to try for the record again. This time weather conditions were not perfect as they had been on the first occasion, and at just over 10,000 feet she flew into thick clouds, encountering snow, sleet and zero visibility. With all her flying being carried out in the Los Angeles basin it is extremely unlikely that she would be prepared to cope with such conditions and she certainly wrote about becoming disorientated and frightened. She also wrote that she deliberately put the plane into a spin 'as the quickest way down my experience would suggest . . . seconds seemed very long, until I saw the clear weather several thousand feet above the world I knew.'[9]

Her friends on the ground were appalled at this course of action and after she had landed safely told her so in no uncertain terms. They had good reason; had conditions deteriorated further – according to her own chronicle of events the ceiling deteriorated from 10,000 feet to 'several thousand feet' in the short time since she entered the clouds – the base could have easily dropped so that she might have emerged from the murk too low to pull out of the spin.

At this distance one is tempted to wonder whether she really spun deliberately, or whether the more likely explanation is that she became disorientated and the plane fell into an involuntary spin, a situation which she hesitated to admit to her peers.

There are more incidents; several times her plane nosed over when the wheels stuck in thick mud or she landed in over-long grass. Once the Kinner stopped so suddenly in tall weeds that it turned over on its back with sufficient force to break the safety belt and throw Amelia out. But despite this seemingly haphazard flying Amelia was no different from the average pilot of the day. Planes were slow and engines unreliable. The occasional crash or bump was nothing to get excited about, although it provided good copy for the newspapers. Amelia applied for, and was granted, a flying certificate (number 6017) by the Federation Aeronautique Internationale on

16 May 1923. Quaintly, it announced that the holder had fulfilled all the conditions required by the organisation for an 'Aviator Pilot' and 'is hereby brevetted as such'. Although it was not, at that time, necessary to have a licence in order to fly, and the FAI certificate was not officially recognised by the federal agency which controlled aviation licences, it was necessary to hold such a certificate in order to make attempts on FAI records.[10]

A further newspaper article appeared in October, in the *New York Times*, with Amelia in flying dress. Certain older family members were not pleased with this publicity and one uncle in particular wrote to Amy to complain that it was simply not done. 'The only time a lady's name should appear in print is at her birth, her marriage and her funeral.'[11] What must he have thought in later years?

By this time Amy's inheritance, having put the girls through various private schools and college courses and, of course, having helped Amelia to buy the aeroplane, had shrunk to twenty thousand dollars. Clearly at the prevailing rate of expenditure it was not going to last long unless it was profitably invested. After much discussion the Earhart family decided to set some aside to complete the girls' education and invest the balance in a small gypsum mining business owned by a young friend of Amelia's, Peter Barnes.

The exact circumstances of what happened to the project are not clear and there are several conflicting versions, but the final outcome was the same no matter who told the story. A flash flood wiped out the mine workings and destroyed most of the plant. Shortly afterwards the firm's remaining truck was hit by a train on a crossing. Very little of Amy's savings could be recovered. Lloyd Royer, one of Amelia's closest male friends at the time, and who worked in the venture, recalled:

We were involved in this business that Amelia had invested in. At that time Boulder Dam was just being built and there was a gypsum mine up there, we used to ship the mineral in big Mack dumper trucks.

Anyway, even before that there was a lot of building going on in the Los Angeles area and there was a big demand for sand and gravel. We used to pick up the material in the hills and come down via Tahuenga, Washington and Cahuenga to Los Feliz to what was then Lankersham across the railroad track just by the San Fernando Road. This was . . . 1923.

The truck got stuck on the railway line and was hit by a train. There had been some floods previously but that wasn't the reason.

. . . After that Amelia bought a Moreland Truck for $7,200 – that was a lot of money in those days – you had to run a truck in quietly. I drove it round carefully for three months . . .[12]

In the archives at the Schlessinger library is a photograph, of Lloyd Royer with a truck, on which he has inscribed, '1923. While I was breaking in the Moreland truck for Amelia that summer, after Pete Barnes wrecked the Mac and was laid up.'

This can be dated to the early summer months of 1923 for in March 1923 Amelia was one of the advertised attractions at an 'Air Rodeo' which took place at Glendale Airport in an item programmed as 'Ladies Sportplane Special: Miss Amelia Earhart flying Kinner Airster and Miss Andree Pyre flying a Sport Farman.'[13] Since, according to Lloyd Royer, it was at this time that Amelia sold her aeroplane, it would appear that she may have done so to help pay for the truck. Sam Chapman was said to be pleased at the sale of the aeroplane but Amelia recorded only that she:

decided to sell it much as I disliked the parting. A young man who had done some flying during the war . . . eventually purchased it. After the new owner took possession the first thing he did was ask a friend to go up with him.[14]

At a few hundred feet the pilot began stunting as Amelia and her friends stood 'rooted to the spot'. Bert Kinner was so concerned that he, practical man that he was, telephoned for an ambulance. It was never needed. The plane slipped off a low-level vertical bank and the occupants were killed instantly.

The following months saw life at home become fraught with rows. Edwin suffered from increasingly poor health while Amelia suffered from extreme guilt about the loss of her mother's money; for according to Lloyd Royer it was she – acting on advice from Sam Chapman – who originally persuaded Edwin and Amy to invest in the venture. The sale of the Kinner was the only thing she had been able to do, personally, to help matters.

The purchase of the Moreland truck was an attempt to keep the original business going, albeit in a reduced form, with a view to recovering some of the losses sustained by the family. But life at home became intolerable. Amy, her financial stability removed, became quarrelsome and bitter. Edwin could do nothing right. Amelia, unable to fly, suffering guilt and having to work even harder (she was trying to run the trucking business in addition to her other jobs), without the same rewards, became tired of it all and moved to a rooming house in Hollywood. Her mother disapproved. She also 'disapproved of the trucking business', just as she had 'disapproved of the aeroplane, but Amelia went ahead anyway'.[15] On occasions Amelia drove the truck.

At about this time Amelia allegedly became engaged to Sam Chapman, but she also had several other boyfriends and at least one of them, Lloyd Royer, was in love with her and proposed marriage. 'But', he said, 'she wasn't interested in marriage.'[16] From June to October she worked for Peter Barnes's brother, Ralph, who owned a commercial photography studio at Ninth and Figueroa Street in Los Angeles. Here she did the backroom work such as printing and developing. When one of the partners sold his shares in the business it nearly went bankrupt and Amelia had to leave.[17] She then set up her own photographic business and although this never prospered she was once in the right place at the right time. She never travelled anywhere without her camera and one day while driving along Wilshire Boulevard an oil well 'came in' just as she was passing. She took a photograph and was immediately accosted by the real estate agent who was selling nearby plots for development. He bought the picture to show prospective buyers what they might expect![18]

To add to her existing problems – and perhaps exacerbate them – a condition which first occurred during her period at Spadina hospital (an abscess in the nasal passages which had created a deep-seated sinus infection causing a great deal of pain), now flared up again. An operation was advised, which she underwent, somewhat nervously.[19] The aftermath was months of further physical discomfort and the ignominy of being harried by a debt collection agency for payment of the $500 medical fees. It took a year for Amelia to pay this sum off but by then she had left California.

The year 1924 found Amelia frustrated and restless; the victim of a self-confessed inertia.[20] Her attempts to revive the family fortunes were proving fruitless. Although she somehow managed to purchase another Kinner plane – piecemeal (she said 'I found I could not buy it altogether') – and eventually flew it, she never achieved the affection for it that she had for the 'Canary'. It was a single-seater with a three-cylinder Lawrence engine.[21] Amelia wrote little about it except to record that on one occasion, as she flew it between the mainland and the Santa Catalina Island, she witnessed the weird darkness of an eclipse of the sun.[22]

By the late spring of 1924 Amelia was thoroughly depressed by family squabbles, lack of money and her mother's continuing disapproval. At this point the Earhart marriage broke down irrevocably. Despite all that had happened in the past, it was Edwin who sued for an uncontested divorce.

In the circumstances Amelia, Muriel and Amy decided that they would return to Massachusetts. For at least a year Amelia had nursed the idea of flying across the continent and returning to further education. Maps, data and charts were already prepared and she asked Amy to accompany her, but Amelia found that the recurring pain in her head whenever she flew made the plan impossible. Muriel, who had been teaching fourth grade classes at Huntingdon Beach,[23] resigned her post and travelled back east immediately, by train, in time for summer classes at Harvard and was living near Boston.

No matter how difficult her mother had become, Amelia loved her and was extremely supportive of both her parents during this difficult period. She sold her second Kinner aeroplane and bought a car – a Kissel, which she referred to as 'The Kizzle' but which later acquired the nickname 'The yellow peril' because of its bright paint job. She decided that if she couldn't fly she would at least drive herself and her mother across America rather than travel ignominiously by train.

Since the divorce Amy had moved into Amelia's Hollywood apartment and in mid-June 1924 they left there to drive to Boston via Sequoia, Yosemite and the Canadian towns of Banff and Lake Louise. It was an enterprising scheme given the stage of development that cars had reached, but Amelia thought it an ideal opportunity to see some of the wonderful scenery of the great northwest.

Lloyd Royer was still driving the Moreland truck and keeping the trucking business going, and wondered what his position was. He wrote to her and received the following reply several weeks later:

Calgary, Alberta
6/26/24

Dear Lloyd,
Our letters crossed. I was glad to hear from you at Seattle.

If you want to cut taitors little O'Malley, do so. There are no outstanding debts other than those I sent check for, but some I owe the Moreland Company. I am repaying them as fast as I can. We never did agree about some of the items.

I suppose I have a lot of mail waiting for me in Los Angeles but I haven't known where to have it sent . . . We have only had one hint of trouble with the motor, the head gasket blew out and every little town has a mechanic who strips all the [unreadable] for me and then they all have to be topped and larger ones put in. I carry two extra gaskets and treat Kizzle like a Ford – shift into low on any little incline.

Can you make expenses? If not let me know by wire at Yellowstone, Montana or later at Chicago, in a week or ten days. Hope your ship was a success. We didn't intend to come into Calgary but found some of the roads better than our awful ones and anyway the scenery is just too grand for words. Heading for Glacier Park in a few minutes . . . Thank you for your care of my affairs.[24]

By the time the two women reached Boston they had travelled 7,000 miles and the car was covered in tourist stickers; wherever Amelia stopped little groups of people gathered to ask how she'd come, what the roads were like and other questions. Cross-continental travel by automobile was still very much a novelty and Amelia thought also 'the fact that my roadster was a cheerful canary colour may have caused some of the excitement. It had been modest enough in California, but was a little outspoken for Boston, I found.'[25]

The pain in her head was, by the end of the journey, insupportable. Within days of her arrival in Boston Amelia entered Massachusetts Memorial Hospital for an operation in which a small piece of bone was removed to allow drainage of the sinuses. It was completely successful and after a short convalescence she was free of pain for the first time in four years. She then returned to Columbia University for the winter of 1924–5. The direction she had found for herself in California had vanished and she recalled that: 'Like a great many other girls at this age I had no special plan for myself.'[26] She was then twenty-seven years old and clearly, from this remark, still thought of herself as a girl.

In May 1925 she returned to the Boston area (the women had an apartment at nearby West Medford)[27] and for a few weeks taught English to foreign students at a Harvard University summer extension programme. From June to October she worked as a companion in a hospital for mental diseases but she found the work 'too confining' and the pay ($70 a month) insufficient.[28]

She still had the hankering to fly but with no regular income her only contact with aviation was limited to visits to local fields and correspondence with Bert Kinner and Lloyd Royer who now wrote to say he was starting his own business in aviation in partnership with John Montijo (Amelia's flying instructor).[29] It was agreed that he should sell the Moreland truck and he would send Amelia her share of the proceeds. She replied on *New York Evening Journal* letterhead.

Dear Lloyd,

. . . Is there any dope on the truck yet? Is that cash supposed to come in a check to you or me or how? I'd just like to know. The letterhead on this paper is deceptive. I have not joined the staff of the *Journal* (tho' I wish I had as I find the newspaper interesting) I am just waiting for a lovely reporter . . . and in the meantime using some of Mr Hearst's paper . . . I have a friend who is a newspaper woman who-knows-the-man-who-owns the *Aeronautic Airway*. She has sworn to lead him to me but as he takes her flying etc., she may prefer to keep him to herself. I would(!) . . . please give me the details on all that happens out there aeronautically.

Amelia[30]

In the autumn of 1925 Amelia answered a newspaper advertisement for the position of 'novice' social worker at Denison House, Boston's second oldest settlement house. The principal, Miss Marion Perkins, liked what she saw in the applicant '. . . a strikingly interesting girl – very unusual vocabulary; is a photographer and wants to write . . .'; and scrawled across the application form, 'Holds a skypilot's licence!' Miss Perkins contacted two of Amelia's referees and received a reply from Amelia's previous employer, Dr Torney, attesting 'Pleasing personality, active, very willing, obliging, an excellent worker, very capable . . . will do well in anything in which she has training and sufficient self-knowledge not to undertake work in which she has no ability.'[31] Sam Chapman, Amelia's fiancé, wrote quaintly that she was 'all right'. He had known her for four years, he said, and paid tribute to her scholarship and general ability.

Sam had followed Amelia back to Massachusetts and was now employed at the Edison Electric Company as an industrial heating engineer. Marriage seemed inevitable, at least to Sam, Amy and Muriel, but one senses there was always a hesitation in Amelia. She obviously cared for Sam a great deal but there was still a questing in her approach to life which she felt would be suppressed by marriage. As a couple, Sam and Amelia joined Muriel and her boyfriend

Albert Morrissey for outings to the beaches at Marblehead. Sam obviously sensed a withdrawal in Amelia and put it down to his unsocial hours (he worked a night shift), which he applied to change in order to spend more time with his fiancée. This merely annoyed Amelia who told her sister, 'He should do whatever makes him happiest . . . I know what I want to do and I expect to do it married or single . . .'[32]

Despite Amelia's lack of experience in social work, Miss Perkins was so impressed with the 'tall slender, boyish-looking woman who walked into my office' that Amelia got the job at Denison, and had she never done anything else in her life it is likely that she would have been perfectly happy with her lot. In the first year she had general direction of the evening classes for foreign-born men and women but as time went on her workload expanded. Socially responsible, she enthusiastically tackled the work of educating the poor, mainly immigrant, families that proliferated in the lower corner of the older Boston. She taught them English and was always eager to learn something of the languages of those she taught; she ferried sick patients to hospital in her car 'the yellow peril', explained Western customs, organised outings, games and plays for classes of children, ran classes on various subjects including citizenship, and found the work totally fulfilling.

Once again she began to look outward. She had little spare time and even less spare money but the situation improved as she received a regular salary of $35 a week. She made contact with local pilots, joined the Boston chapter of the National Aeronautic Association and was able to fly occasionally. In the autumn of 1927 she became a full-time resident staff member at Denison House and was also voted into the position of Secretary to the Board of Directors.

She had kept in touch with Bert Kinner and tried to find a potential sales agent in the Boston area for the Kinner Special. Kinner, however, found one himself, a young architect from Boston, Harold T. Dennison (no connection with Denison House) whom Kinner met while on a trip in California. Their discussions sent him scurrying back to Boston determined to build an airport and market Kinner aeroplanes. On Kinner's recommendation,

Dennison contacted Amelia to ask if she would like to be involved. Amelia hadn't much money but what she had she willingly invested, becoming a director of the company that shortly afterwards built Dennison Airport on the Quincy Shore Reservation Boulevard.[33]

The flying school was equipped with six Waco and Kinner aeroplanes and the original field (known as Harvard Aviation Field) had been, in 1910, the site of the first fly-in in the USA.[34] As well as possessing a flying school and good runways, Dennison operated an air taxi service between the cities of Boston, Chicago and New York, with stops at Hyannis and Boston.[35]

Probably to the distress of her more stuffy relatives, Amelia's name started to appear in the newspapers with a regularity which indicates that Amelia not only recognised the value of publicity but was not averse to it. WOMAN TO FLY FOR CEDAR HILL FETE proclaimed one. MISS AMELIA EARHART FLIES IN A PLANE OVER BOSTON said another, when Amelia 'bombed' the area with leaflets advertising a fund-raising event. The Boston *Globe* interviewed her a few weeks later in June 1927 and she took full advantage of the occasion to promote flying, especially for women. Thereafter she was often in the columns of the *Globe* where she was usually described as 'one of the best women pilots in the United States'.

Feeling that she had a definite role to play in the development of aviation she contacted other women pilots (there were few), to see if they couldn't encourage more women to fly. She wrote a table-thumping, three-page letter to the Boston Chamber of Commerce about the lack of publicity in the area for aviation.

Why aren't we doing something notable here? You know there are two ways to accomplishment – one, through doing exceptional things, and another by sweeping to it by force of numbers. Boston Chapter of NAA has exceptional men in it but not numbers. Aviation needs widespread support.

. . . The Los Angeles Chamber of Commerce expands all over the map, simply by getting so much publicity that it is considered

quite the thing to belong to so well known an organization. So
with the California Automobile Club.

There should be advertising . . . A social worker always thinks
of ways to raise money so I propose a benefit of some sort. There
are various ways from scalping tickets at a popular performance
to putting on one's own. I'd ask Will Rogers to come on, and pay
him a thousand to fill Symphony Hall, for a good profit . . .[36]

Quite what part Sam Chapman played in this busy and fulfilled
life is difficult to assess. Amelia hardly mentioned him in any of her
writing, and he never spoke of her publicly, though the two were to
remain the closest of friends for many years. That they were for
some time formally engaged became apparent only when Amelia
admitted at a later date to reporters that: 'I am no longer engaged.'

It was in April 1927 that Amelia's life changed forever. She was
helping to organise a class play when the telephone rang and she was
sent for. 'I'm too busy to answer just now,' she said. 'Ask whoever it
is calling to try again later.' Pressed, she went to the phone, 'very
unwillingly and heard a masculine voice introduce himself. "Hello.
You don't know me but my name is Railey – Captain H. H.
Railey."' Later that day he asked her if she would like to be the first
woman to fly across the Atlantic.[37]

BOOK TWO
George Palmer Putnam

My father was a publisher, and his father before him. My earliest recollections are of books; and of authors, whom I have never held in proper awe since.

George Palmer Putnam (1945)

CHAPTER 6

1887-1909

George Palmer Putnam was born in Rye, New York on 7 September 1887, into a comfortably well-off, if not wealthy, publishing family. His very earliest recollections were of books[1] and his childhood appears to have been singularly happy. The warm and loving family home created by his parents allowed the extraordinary talents of their son to burgeon freely, and he grew up with an intelligent grasp of what was happening around him, developing a writer's knack of observation.[2]

The atmosphere was a bookish one, and it was generally assumed he would grow up to be a publisher; or, 'at worst, a writer'.[3] Georges's father often took his son to New York to 'the office' on Fifth Avenue, and they would lunch at the Union League Club or the Fifth Avenue Hotel. The small boy enjoyed these trips, but what fascinated him more was a visit to the family's printing press (the Knickerbocker Press) at New Rochelle. George grew up loving the smells of ink in the press room, of glue and paper in the bindery and the special fragrance of leather from the rolls of levant, calfskin and buckram. But, he said, 'the best smells of all, perhaps, were in the foundry . . . where mysterious electrical processes created plates for the presses.'[4]

Despite this dedicated nurturing, George had reached the advanced age of eleven before he entered the world of publishing. At this time he wrote, edited and sold a 'newspaper' under the title *The Will O' the Wisp*; 'to be published semi-occasionally', it proclaimed. The Spanish War had just begun and the already prescient George made it clear from the start that all profits from his paper were to be donated to the Red Cross. By this device he was easily able to sell advertising space to local tradesmen (with the exception of the butcher who would have none of such nonsense), and after the first and only edition was able to deliver 'a net profit of eighty-six dollars to the Red Cross'. Even more satisfying, though, to the youngster, was the fact that his name had been 'at an editorial masthead'.[5]

George was even younger when he first started to exploit his formidable entrepreneurial skills. He had been accustomed to visiting a neighbour, a retired mounted policeman from New York who had a beautiful horse trained to do tricks. The neighbour also kept ducks. 'My [elder] brother, just then, for reasons not clear, wanted ducks . . . Our neighbour agreed to sell me three ducks for 50 cents each. I told him it was a deal. Then I broached the matter to Brother. I told him I had three particularly fine ducks that I could let him have for $2.50. After bargaining he agreed to pay $2.25 if the ducks suited him.' Scampering over to the neighbour, George collected the ducks 'on approval', sold the ducks to his brother and after paying costs found himself with a clear profit of 75 cents. 'When Brother found out the facts, he both thrashed me and told Father . . . Father suspended sentence. Possibly he was pleased.'[6]

In his mid-teens George attended the Gunnery School in Washington, Connecticut. A 'fair' scholar, he spent his spare time trout fishing (much fishing and few trout, he said), climbing alone in the hills, and rabbit and partridge hunting. Although well-built he was poor at athletics and sensitive, 'a group of sturdy football players who headed up school life regarded me with no warmth . . . I was not popular.' It was his own fault, he claimed, recognising in retrospect that because of his lonely preoccupations he probably appeared priggish.[7]

The few friends he had during these years were unusual people themselves – 'daffy', George was to reflect in his autobiography written forty years later. There were Gerald and Gladys Thayer, the children of an artist who lived an unconventional life (thus shocking the neighours, but of whom George was totally uncritical), whom he had met while on vacation in New Hampshire. Rockwell

Kent the artist and writer, some five years older than George, was another friend and seems to have been a sort of ringleader. Franklin D. Roosevelt, also friends with the Thayers, came into this small milieu as someone at 'bitter loggerheads' with Abbott Thayer and his notions of art. 'They had a splendid time firing broadsides at each other', George commented, but the young Putnam was content to accept Thayer's theories on colouring and the portrayal of fauna, for the artist was a noted naturalist. Although George never elaborated on this youthful friendship with Roosevelt it marked the start of a relationship which would play a larger part in George's life in later years.

When he was seventeen years old George fell in love with Gladys Thayer, 'Galla' as he called her, 'a fragrant girl with a special beauty all of her own'. The young couple contemplated marriage but George's parents foiled the romantic plans and sent him to Scandinavia for the summer. There he had 'an experience' with a girl named Helga – 'she had eyes the colour of cornflowers and fair hair more the shade of honey than buttercups'[8] – who helped him to the conclusion that he was not yet ready to be tied down in wedlock.

The winter months seemed to hold the promise of fun when he returned from Scandinavia, for he was invited to join Gerald Thayer and Rockwell Kent in what turned out to be a winter-long bachelor party. George was not disappointed. The natives of the hamlet of Dublin, New Hampshire hastily lowered their blinds when on one occasion Rockwell and Gerald skied naked (except for shoes and socks), pulled along by galloping horses. One typical Rockwell Kent prank involved laying the tracks of a 'wildcat' in the snow with the aid of some paws filched from a museum. This, abetted by some realistic wildcat yowling at night, together with the normal countryside predations on chickens and small livestock, created a full-scale 'wildcat scare' and terrorised the countryside. Before the joke was through it had even reached the columns of a Boston newspaper.[9] The credulity with which the newspapers took this story on trust made a deep impression on George.

The three young men slept, cooked, ate and argued, and on

occasion worked. The outside temperature seldom rose above zero but there were Schopenhauer, Walt Whitman, Milton, Landor, Swinburne and Coventry Patmore to read and endlessly discuss. George said in his memoir:

> With the way of youth, we discoursed interminably about life and love and death, economics, politics and the welfare of man . . . there was socialism of course, single tax and vegetarianism, and a dash of free love. Communism was not yet in vogue.[10]

Doubtless the afterthought referred to Rockwell Kent's subsequent political affiliations.

Later, George was to spend some time at Kent's house on Monhegan Island off the coast of Maine, the subject of many of the artist's best paintings.[11] It was locally held that any young man who had gone to the trouble of building a home must be in search of a wife and so Kent and George decided it would be uncivil to disappoint the locals. A plot was concocted and on the next occasion that Rockwell Kent visited the mainland on business, George 'happened' to look in at the Dublin post office where he received a letter from his friend which he opened and partially read aloud in apparent astonishment. He later recalled:

> I dare say by evening there was not a person on the island unacquainted with the letter's contents. In that letter Kent (pledging me to secrecy) had unfolded his intimate plans. He was bringing back his bride.
>
> A couple of days later I disappeared, ostensibly to go on a fishing trip, which I often did. Instead I met Kent . . . he had brought from Boston a costume to delight a peripatetic bride, complete with fittings that included a picture hat with veil, a frilly dress, gay shoes and stockings. Also the wherewithal to change my figure so that it would swell at those places where, under the circumstances, it should. Also Kent had with him a gorgeous auburn wig and a make-up box . . . I was a couple of

hands taller than my groom and doubt if I appeared ravishing. But I was rigged out like nobody's business.[12]

The happy couple were transported to the island in the time-honoured fashion, in a boat with an evergreen tree lashed to the masthead. At the landing wharf, 'an impromptu orchestra of white-clad summer folks played the wedding march on combs, horns and sundry other instruments'. A girlfriend and her mother, who had been let in on the secret, shielded the helpless bride from the gaze of the over-curious and helped her into the decorated wedding chariot. Back at Kent's home, 'eager hands had cleaned [the house] as it had never been cleaned before. They positively polished it and filled it with flowers. I remember that even the pins were arranged in heart-shaped designs in the pine wall over an improvised dressing table. There were too, the usual pranks about the bed.'[13]

But there were doubts voiced about the bride's authenticity and the couple had barely reached home when a crowd, angry at what they suspected was a gross deception, approached the house. George quickly donned a pink nightdress, hopped into bed and, turning his face to the wall, sobbed softly. Kent arranged the bride's hair appealingly across the sheets and when he opened the door he was a desperate man. Indicating the piteous figure on the bed he whispered:

'She's collapsed . . . It's been too much. I don't know what to do. Won't you . . . won't you *please* Tom, get me some liquor . . . a little stimulant may revive her.'

Tom Spinney's anger melted away and so did he, pellmell for the village to do his good deed. Shortly he was back with a pint bottle.[14]

This prep-school brand of humour stayed with George all his life. He had a well-developed sense of fun and was always ready for a practical joke. Sometimes, though, it must be said that the subject upon whom the joke was perpetrated found it hard to laugh. George spent the winter of 1906–7 at Harvard reading German,

English, Greek, fine arts, and politics, but left in February 'on account of illness'.[15] College records show that his work until that time was satisfactory and on the strength of his good record the administrative board voted to allow him to return and take up the courses he had dropped, should he wish to do so. He apparently did not wish to do so, for on recovering his health he worked for several months in the educational department of G. P. Putnam's Sons, before travelling to California in the spring of 1908. There he spent the summer on the fringes of the desert south of Los Angeles (now Palm Springs), where he acquired a few gold-mine claims[16] and with the aid of a favourable letter from the Assistant Dean of Harvard enrolled at the University of California at Berkeley for the fall semester, reading French, literature and economics. His time at Berkeley was as undistinguished as his previous educational career, but by now he had met Dorothy Binney.

Dorothy was the daughter of a wealthy industrialist who (among his other interests), was head of the Binney & Smith 'Crayola crayon' company. She was a socialite, but a strong-minded, gifted and attractive young woman. Fair-haired, tall and with an outgoing personality she had a ready sense of humour which George found particularly attractive. Dorothy was spending a holiday in California prior to the new college term at Wellesley and met George 'on a Sierra Club outing,'.[17] 'Six feet two inches, dark and *very* handsome, and a confirmed woman hater' – she mischievously described him to her classmates.[18] Not so much a misogynist as all that, apparently, for within a matter of weeks George had fallen in love and proposed. Shortly afterwards Dorothy returned to her parents' home in Old Greenwich, Connecticut, to finish her education. The courtship continued by mail and with at least two visits by George to Connecticut.

Dorothy having accepted his proposal of marriage, George realised that he needed to make enough money to support a wife and in time-honoured fashion set out to make his fortune. At the beginning of 1909, aged twenty-one and having left college, he travelled north from California to Oregon.

It would be as well, at this point, to reflect that although George was a member of the Putnam family he was a younger son. George may well have had all the attributes of a publisher bred in him, but his elder brother Robert was destined to inherit the role of publisher. George's father had three brothers (Haven, Herbert and Irving), and between them they owned the publishing firm, G. P. Putnam's Sons. Each brother had several sons and probably there was not room for two sons of each partner in the firm.

George had therefore to make his own way in life, and his own destiny. As a child, George had been an avid reader of adventure books, particularly those about the wild north-western United States. Indeed, the first book he had discovered for himself, and to which he was very attached, was *Canoe and Saddle* by John Winthrop,[19] which fired the boy's imagination about the adventures to be had in the great unsettled tracts of country.

In 1909 the sage advice 'Go west young man' was still relevant to anyone wishing to make a fortune starting from nothing but enthusiasm and hard work. George decided to look for adventure and success, and the best place to do this, he concluded, 'was Bend . . . geographically at the centre of Oregon . . . it was one hundred miles from a railroad . . . [in] what the come-hither literature of the Northwest euphemistically called virgin territory.'[20]

'There I was, an easterner in the far reaches of the roaring west,' he wrote. 'I wanted to hear it roar.'[21]

CHAPTER 7

1909-1915

George spent the next six years of his life in Bend, Oregon. These years marked the beginning of a life-long love affair with the mountains and wilderness, for he was never happier than when living in rugged isolation, although he was adaptable enough to translate, with great elan, to a Fifth Avenue office, a New England drawing room or even the White House. For the moment, though, George's chosen land – the 'largest railroadless area in the United States' – was

> a country where a son of the East could dwell on the wonders of both young and old mountains covered with snow almost the whole year; a country where lava flowed, where volcanic cinder cones, once guides for immigrant trains, stood on the lines of future city limits; where centuries before running lava had trapped and made moulds of timber stands; where beautiful blue lakes had been created when mountain tops exploded; where a vast desert stretched a hundred miles north, south and east; and where billions of board feet of pine covered thousands of acres of land.[1]

Though George came to love the rugged terrain, his immediate attention during that first journey to his chosen objective was more probably riveted upon his personal discomfort. From Portland he travelled by train, via Shaniko, the gateway to central Oregon:

> From this dismal jumping off place freighters hauled merchandise to towns as far distant as two hundred miles, and stages

radiated to the south. The sheep of a sheepman's empire congregated there. With streets of mud or dust, according to the season, a score of raw frame shacks, warehouses, livery barns, shipping pens, and hotels Shaniko in its prime was a busy, boisterous town of freighters and sheep herders.[2]

From Shaniko he continued by stagecoach to Bend where many a vehicle was upset on the villainous grades of Cow Canyon, or bogged down in the adobe mud of Shaniko Flats. He recalled his own journey on

a January night when two-day rain had turned to snow, when the air was freezing but the mud was soft, and the up-stage met the down-stage where there was no turning out. Drivers and passengers worked and swore in the murk and the mud, until one stage had been shunted out of the way on a hand-made shelf so to speak; the clothing and the dispositions of all concerned were ruined. But the passing was effected.

There were one hundred miles of road between Shaniko and Bend 528,000 feet of dust, mud, chuck holes, hills, rocks, ruts and bumps.[3]

Nor was there any respite for the weary young man when he arrived at his destination, for there was only one hotel in the little frontier town and it was full. George had to bed down for the night in a room over the saloon and noted before he slept that there was a hole in the floor through which he could look down upon the bar if he wished.[4]

Upon waking, however, he knew that the tiresome journey had been worth the effort, for the clear, clean beauty of the scenery glimpsed through a small grimy window, enchanted him. Located in a great curve on the Deschutes River, Bend looked out upon the panorama of the heavily forested Cascade Mountains, with the snow-covered Three Sisters as a focal point. 'In those mountains,' he decided on the spot, 'I knew I would like to live.'[5] The town boasted a population of 536 persons, although there were as many again in the outlying areas,[6] and his appearance in the town did not go unnoticed for the *Bend Bulletin* noted on 12 May 1909 that George was there for some weeks. 'Mr Putnam has spent about a year on the Pacific Coast representing Putnam and Sons, Publishers, of which his father is the head.'

George was now twenty-one years of age. He dressed well, radiated an air of great confidence, possessed a forceful personal manner and, according to his autobiography, he stepped off the stage coach in Bend with $300 and a considerable curiosity. 'His strong, well-formed face was at the same time sensitive and almost delicate, especially the mouth. [His] uncommonly handsome profile was complemented by an abundance of well-kept, black curly hair and dark, intense eyes . . . and while [he] was in some ways the epitome of the reserved, cool New Englander, he nevertheless fed upon companionship and soon set about seeking new friends.'[7] Unmarried young ladies casting a hopeful eye in the direction of this promising newcomer, were to be disappointed however, for residents recalled later that he remained faithful to his fiancée, Dorothy, and kept a life-size photograph of her on his closet door.[8]

The early days of his time in Bend were notable only for his fishing trips up the Deschutes. But within weeks he had acquired a typewriter and by July was acting as a freelance reporter for *The Oregonian* of Portland, his first published article being a full-page report of Independence Day celebrations in Bend.

Greater things were in store for him. It has been said of Putnam that 'he was the right man, in the right place, at the right time',[9] for the factors that had drawn him to the town, its frontier conditions and lack of railroad, were also the reasons why, without some positive action, it could easily have become a ghost town like so many other hopeful settlements in the north-west. In fact, the residents of Bend had been agitating to bring the railroad to Bend for a decade and more, but success still eluded them in 1909, though the need for a method of transporting goods, materials and people in and out of central Oregon was obvious. The chief hindrance to the scheme was competition between two railroad magnates, E. H. Harriman and James J. Hill, who were fighting for control of the state's railroad system.

By late July 1909 rumours flew that after all the years of fighting, not one but two railroad crews were at work in the area. George, in his role as freelance correspondent for *The Oregonian*, set off into the country to investigate. It was the first of two nearly 100-mile walks that George would make through the Deschutes gorge.

For 10 days Putnam walked along the canyon's bottom, talking to the many Porter Brothers crews and receiving nothing but denials that they were working for Hill. Finally he ascended the walls of the canyon, made his way across the plateau to a telephone and called *The Oregonian* to report on his fruitless efforts. He then put up at the farmhouse of a man and his wife.

There the talk soon got around to the railroads, and the couple casually mentioned that the survey party had been through the area just days before, seeking a right-of-way for a water power project. The men had stopped and purchased some buttermilk from the lady of the house and had paid her with a voucher instead of cash. She asked George Putnam if it was worth anything. One look at the voucher and George Putnam high-tailed it to the nearest telephone 19 miles away. It was a Great Northern voucher. Here at last was solid proof of Hill's link with the Porter Brothers crews.[10]

The story, which George recognised as a sizeable 'scoop', had unfortunately broken earlier that morning in a rival paper. His work, however, gained him the reputation of being the local expert on the railway's progress, and the *Bulletin* readily published his articles on the subject, one of which ended with the ringing conclusion: 'Unless the courts interfere, the Deschutes canyon will see the greatest railroad war in Northwestern history.'[11] Nor was he far out in his predictions for eventually the courts had to step in when physical confrontation between the rival construction groups led to riots.

Meanwhile George had secured for himself an important job. With two railroads racing towards Bend, the little town looked set for a boom. The full-time salaried position of Secretary to the Bend Board of Trade, itself a newly created body, has the stamp of George

Putnam all over it. It is a safe assumption that he suggested the creation of the post to the Board and probably wrote his own job description. Today he would be described as the Town Publicity Officer, for the job specifically required George to 'attend to the Advertising Features and Correspondence' and to publicise the virtues and possibilities of Bend. Reporting the new appointment, the *Bulletin* described George as having been involved in publicity work in California, possibly referring to some job he had undertaken for G. P. Putnam's Sons, and stated that he was to devote most of his time to writing articles for newspapers and magazines.

One of his first moves was the printing and distribution of 5,000 leaflets, extolling the brilliant promise and the inevitable prosperity of Bend, and he took pains to ensure that fellow citizens were made aware that he was succeeding in his task. 'Have you noticed the frequency with which Bend appears in the Portland newspapers lately? This town and section are receiving a world of good advertising these days. It pays to boost . . .' he proclaimed in the *Bulletin*, a month after taking office. He was never modest, but he was effective and over the next months the *Bulletin* carried regular stories on exactly what George was doing to publicise the town. His many articles and features were accompanied by photographs, taken by himself with his ever-present Kodak.[12] Each month he published a newsletter which was vigorously distributed to all north-western newspapers and this was backed up with advertisements.

George returned home to New England for Christmas, but a family reunion was not the only thing on his mind. There was, of course, Dorothy Binney, whom he had not seen since May, and with whom his only point of contact had been a series of letters. He also hoped to gain wider exposure for his articles on Bend in *Putnam's Magazine*, which enjoyed national circulation. But more importantly he needed to discuss with his father a project which fuelled his ambition.

The *Bend Bulletin* was a typical small-town newspaper. Powerful in its monopoly, if not in circulation, it had been established some six years earlier. Perhaps George was faintly irritated by its parochial style and sensed that he could improve its content. Certainly he must have been aware of its potential when the prosperity he was constantly predicting and publicising for the town, arrived. But probably, in the fall of 1909, it was making a loss for the current owner, Don Steffa, for it seems that he and George had already started negotiations before George left to travel east, and George later indicated that Steffa was very anxious to dispose of it.[13]

The trip was obviously successful. The January cover of *Putnam's Magazine* was an engraving of Bend and the lead article was George's 'Opening Up Central Oregon'.[14] Immediately following his return to Bend he left for a trip through central Oregon with a representative of the Great Northern Railroad. In February he impressed the Board of Trade meeting with news of a pamphlet 'designed to be distributed by the millions'[15] upon which he was working in tandem with the Great Northern. He then set off on foot for his second journey through the Deschutes Canyon and the railroad construction camps, which he used as a basis for more articles.[16]

In March the news broke that George had purchased the *Bulletin*.[17] In his autobiography he stated that he acquired it

> for a very modest consideration and mostly on credit . . . and while I was editor wrote blistering editorials . . . A few were published but most of them went into the lower right-hand drawer of my desk. Writing them was almost as satisfactory as seeing them in print. It relieved blood pressure and hurt nobody. There still is a special place where I put certain letters I write, to stay there during a period of incubation. Usually at the end of the probation it seems best not to send them. I'm increasingly inclined to think the things one does not do make less trouble than the things done.[18]

In fact he became the archetypal, battling frontier newspaperman, declaring war on unnecessary bureaucracy, tackling important local issues with gleeful panache, and attacking local corruption with intelligent use of the power his position as editor provided. When he suspected a local judge of dishonesty he wrote one of his blistering editorials under the headline, 'The Courthouse Stench'. When the judge protested that he could not get a fair hearing in the newspaper, George provided his protagonist with a blank column 'to use as he liked'. The paper appeared with the column blank for several issues, bearing only the memorandum to Judge Springer: 'You said you can get no hearing . . . in this space we will print anything you want. There is absolutely no restriction; the space is yours gratis.'[19] The judge was subsequently ridiculed out of office. It has been said that 'the longer George Palmer Putnam remained in the Bend community, the wider the range of his boosting activities became',[20] and his campaigns ranged from cleaning up the town saloons, to a drive to build an automobile road to Burns, 150 miles to the east. Meanwhile his publicity campaign for Bend continued and new settlers began to flow in. 'Never has the future held more brilliant promise for Bend than it does today', the *Bulletin* proclaimed in April 1911, gloating over the sawmills, flour mills, woollen mills and distributing houses then looking at Bend as an ideal location with its double railroad terminus, unlimited water power and endless stands of timber

George was twenty-four years old, an obvious success as promoter of his chosen town and editor of its newspaper, full of confidence and ambition. But he had not forgotten Dorothy Binney, his fiancée back east, and despite all his work to get the railroads into the town he missed the great moment when the final 'golden spike' was hammered into place. When that great event took place, accompanied by 'Railroad Day festivities' consisting of log-rolling, a canoe war, a grand parade, boxing contests, horse and foot races, a baby show, pillow fights and bronco busting, and finishing off with a dance in Linster Hall, George was in Connecticut making arrangements for his marriage.

Dorothy graduated from Wellesley in June 1910. Her fiancé had not been able to escort her at the graduation ceremonies but she had understood that he was busy building his empire in the west. The marriage took place at the bride's home in Sound Beach, Connecticut, on 26 October 1911 and the newlyweds spent four months honeymooning in Panama, Costa Rica, Nicaragua, Honduras, Guatemala, Salvador and Mexico.[21] As usual, George's talent for making important connections surfaced, and they were known to have met and dined with Don Pablo Arosemena, President of Panama, Dr Belisario Porras (who subsequently became President of Panama) and Don Ricardo Jiminez, President of Costa Rica. It was February before they returned to Pinelyn, George's home in Bend,[22] and it was very quickly evident that George had not been idle on his long vacation. He managed to produce his first book (*In the Southland of North America*)[23] compiled from his notes and photographs of the trip, as well as numerous articles in newspapers and magazines about the engineering miracle of the Panama Canal. The book was dedicated to Dorothy, 'the best of travel partners'.

The *Bulletin* had run a front-page piece on the Putnams' honeymoon, but this was totally eclipsed by George's two-column headline announcing that he had purchased 'A MACHINE THAT WILL SET ITS TYPE'. 'The new Model 10 Meganthaler . . . is the finest typesetting machine made and will be the only one of its kind in Oregon or Washington.'[24]

Mr and Mrs Putnam started their married life in February 1912: their home, built in the previous year by George, was a large six-bedroom building boasting its own tennis courts (Dorothy was a keen and excellent tennis player).[25]

George's return to work heralded yet more modern equipment and a new building for the *Bulletin*. Soon the newspaper was capable of producing 1,600 pages an hour on its new presses and the enterprising young owner turned the loss-making concern into a very profitable one.[26] George worked hard and long hours during this period and in his autobiography he claimed that he had done the work of three men.

Seven o'clock saw me in the shop, and by eight everything was cleaned, from floors to ink rollers, and, if it were winter, the fires blazing in the big sheet metal stove beside the foot-power hand press and in the little pot-bellied firebox in the front office.[27]

He wrote the editorials and articles for the *Bulletin*, and under several different pen names, such as Palmer Bend, he acted as stringer for five big-city newspapers. A stringer was paid by space rates, so each month he would paste-up (string) his copy and add up the inches before, submitting his bill. The best remuneration was from *The Oregonian* whose rate was $8 a column. When the *Bulletin* needed advertisements, George would take stock of local business, decide what they needed to advertise, write and paste up the copy, and pull a proof. Then he would take it round to the proprietor and sell the space. He did the same with business cards, letterheads and brochures. He even provided imaginative letters for the correspondence column.

If there were no stories the enterprising Putnam wrote articles – once 'for three weeks there was a prosperous sequence of interviews with a mythical character called Know Joles who went into the mountains clad only in his birthday suit, and had preposterous adventures'. These satirical pieces were aimed at a series of back-to-nature articles appearing in the Portland newspapers, written by Joe Knowles whose 'adventures became pitifully tame compared with what befell my hero'. In one piece 'Joles' delighted city readers with the story of his pet trout, Lucy:

> I kept [her] in a shallow gold pan until she slopped all the water out and developed a knack of getting on comfortably in air. Sometimes I'd take her to town to do tricks for the boys on the bar at Hugh O'Kanes. But once I forgot to shut the door of my cabin when I'd left Lucy there, and halfway across the foot log over the Deschutes River I looked back, and there was Lucy scuffling along after me. I ran back but before I reached her, Lucy lost her balance on the log and fell into the river and was drowned.[28]

As if his editorial duties were not enough, George acquired, through a bad debt, the town movie house. It was converted from a long, narrow shop and seated sixty people. In the winter moviegoers froze and in the summer they baked. George and his assistant ran it after they had completed their day's work at the *Bulletin* and

George stood at the door until he had sold thirty-six tickets, enough to cover the evening's costs. At this point he could leave the job to a high-school girl who doubled as pianist. This lasted only six months for George could never make it consistently profitable.[29]

Besides, he had other and more important duties to attend to. In June 1912, at the age of twenty-four George was elected mayor. Writing about the incident later George explained how, when the incumbent mayor resigned, and in the absence of a replacement, the solid citizens could only fume impotently, while the saloons and gambling joints and bawdy houses ran riot. Finally, a bloody gunfight, involving a woman, her ex-lover and a current lover, which resulted in the death of the lady (who was no better than she ought to be) and the serious injury of one of the men, brought matters to a head. The citizens acted, presenting an anti-gambling, anti-prostitution petition to the council and demanding the election of a new mayor immediately or they would elect one themselves.[30]

There were initially two candidates – one in favour of a wide-open, free-and-easy frontier town, the other a virtuous citizen who sought the path of righteousness and sobriety – and for a month there was a deadlock between the six city councillors over whom to elect. When at last the County Sheriff instructed Bend to 'get its house in order or else', a compromise candidate was quickly found who seemed to upset neither the 'wide-opens' nor the 'tight-shuts'; George said:

> He gambled a bit, drank decently, and was no prude; he was young, and youth is liberal. On the other hand he was married and respectable; being young he'd not had time to be too con-taminated by disreputable influences. So one night, all six harried councilmen voted for this paragon.
> I was it.[31]

In fact George had already served for a very short period as 'Mayor pro-tem' in August 1910 in the absence of the incumbent mayor, so the duties of office were not exactly new to him. Now, he was elected 'six votes to nothing' and became the town's 'boy mayor'.

The little community, for the moment, was in my lap. I tried to do right by it. A reasonably thorough house-cleaning was had. We presented a shining face to the outer world, though perhaps the back of the civic neck had not been scrubbed too thoroughly. Mostly, the dubious ladies went. What gambling remained became orderly and unobtrusive. The saloons found wisdom in keeping strict hours and discouraging drunkenness. Rough stuff was frowned upon. Toughs who wanted to fight were beaten up and sent on their way.[32]

George's term of office lasted a year and a half and included several brushes with Oregon's governor who, when he formally complained to George about Bend's unruly reputation was tartly reminded, in print, that there was far more rottenness in Portland and even under the governor's own nose in Salem, than in Bend.[33]

Another opponent, according to George's autobiography, was one Jack Culpepper, a saloon proprietor possessed of wide blue eyes, 'that were too guileless, and a dashing swagger'. When George and Culpepper clashed over the licensing law, Culpepper spread the word that if George were to appear in the Main Street he would be shot full of holes. George recognised that he either had 'to show up, or be shown up . . . [for] once the town got to laughing at its boy mayor, he'd be through.'[34]

George called Culpepper's bluff. Conspicuously unarmed and with both hands in full view (but, he confessed, with knees shaking), he walked along the Main Street sidewalk. The chief of police, a man with a reputation as an excellent shot, followed a short distance behind with hands in pockets. Nothing happened. But the matter did not end there. George somehow discovered that Culpepper had spent a term in a Montana penitentiary due to a 'slight case of homicide'. Having obtained an official mugshot of Culpepper in prison garb, he reproduced the picture over a two-column article telling the unembroidered story. Then he locked up the type, pulled a proof, and went round to Culpepper to see if he was interested. From that moment Culpepper became George's stoutest supporter and 'friend'. The article never ran.

After six months George's first term of office expired and he was voted back by a healthy majority, polling 208 votes to his nearest opponent's ninety-six. He assumed this signified approval and continued to run the town with 'a middle-of-the-road approach'. He limited the saloons to five in number and issued them with licences at $1,200 a year. He started a civic project for a main sewer and was soon able to report in the *Bulletin:* CITY FINANCES SHOW UP WELL. 'Council Sets Work Record . . . Realty Dealers Licenced . . . $4,500 in Street Improvements . . . Pest House and Hitching Place Authorized, among other municipal triumphs.'

In all this work George was supported by Dorothy. Far from feeling neglected when George drove himself to the limit she encouraged him and even helped at the newspaper office when necessary. When George could be spared from 'the office', sometimes the two would go off on horseback to camp in the mountains. Dorothy, too, was an organiser. She founded and directed the town's glee club, and also (less acceptable to some of George's colleagues) a women's suffrage club which she later claimed 'materially aided the State of Oregon to become a suffrage state'.[35]

On 20 May 1913, a son, David Binney Putnam, was born to George and Dorothy. He was a fine, healthy boy with blue eyes and blond hair. 'It was all done with a couple of pots of hot water and very little fuss in our house that faced the snowy peaks of the Three Sisters. The lad himself was spanked by [the doctor's] huge hand, washed up on the dining table and then, nested in blankets, set to toast before the open fire.'[36]

The little boy's birth almost coincided with the *Bulletin*'s tenth birthday, and George was proudly able to reflect on the success he had wrought during his period as editor. In three years he had taken the paper's circulation from 450 copies to 1650, every copy either sold to a subscriber, over the counter in the office or on the street. When he took the paper over it was a four-page production. By 1913 it contained sixteen pages; he had just cause to feel pleased with himself.[37]

In addition he served on the Fire Brigade and as all the buildings were wooden, fires were frequent. On one occasion when the Opera House was ablaze, George sited himself on the roof of a neighbouring building in order to play the hose on the seat of the fire. He later discovered that the building beneath him housed huge drums of gasoline.[38]

In December George decided not to stand for re-election but to concentrate instead on the *Bulletin,* summing up his term of office with the simple comment that he was 'too tough for the virtuous and too virtuous for the tough'.[39] Physically tired, George decided to take Dorothy and little David for an extended trip back east. For three months they visited relations and cruised the inland waterway through Florida before returning to Bend via New Orleans and San Francisco in March 1914.[40] For the next year George occupied his time running a fierce and, eventually, successful campaign for irrigation, on behalf of settlers. But the pressure was beginning to tell. He was twenty-seven years old but was to write in the following spring that 'editing a newspaper in a small town is a wearying pursuit, full of petty trials and tribulations, hedged by irritating routine and woefully limited by the tools one had to work with.'[41]

By then, though, George's life had already moved on to the next phase when, in December 1914, he was selected from a field of twenty candidates to become private secretary to Oregon's Governor Withycombe, who stated of him:

In many respects, the appointment was one of the most important at my disposal – if not the most important. I looked into the qualifications and desirability of each of the candidates, and while many of them were acceptable, yet I reached the conclusion that Mr Putnam was perhaps the best equipped from every point of view . . .[42]

George left Bend in January 1915, after writing an emotional farewell editorial stating that his removal to Salem was merely temporary. His interest in the town, he said, would not lessen and all his personal wealth would still continue to be invested in Bend. He appointed a managing editor for the *Bulletin* and instructed him only 'to turn out the best paper' he could 'and to work for Bend, first last and all the time'. A civic banquet was held in George's honour.

Despite his intentions however, George's departure from the little town was not a temporary removal, for although over the years he paid the occasional visit, his links with Bend were cut on the day he moved to Salem. The years which he was later to describe with such gusto were behind him. He had arrived six years earlier as a wet-behind-the-ears eastern 'tenderfoot' and had matured in the hurly-burly of frontier life. Certainly George heard the west roar. Several times.

So what manner of man was George Putnam at twenty-seven years old? He was a family man whose family, though it often seemed a mere backcloth to his business schemes, was important to him. His ability to give his undivided attention to the matter in hand meant his wife and son felt no neglect. His family readily attest to the fact that he was a loving husband and father. He had always displayed an air of confidence. Earlier this had merely been a veneer over his self-confessed sensitivity; but with success behind him he was genuinely self-assured and assertive. Physically attractive and naturally energetic, he was a hard worker and had earned the respect of the citizens of Bend, particularly the farmers on whose behalf he had fought. He was capable of great kindness and according the Bend tradition many of his good works on behalf of others at his own request never became known.[43]

His various campaigns had made him many friends but he was never afraid to make implacable enemies by speaking his mind. His mind was agile and once a train of thought had been started he was difficult to stop. He did not suffer fools gladly and, though a cultured man possessed of great charm and grace, was capable of exploding into frightening displays of anger as a result of some minor irritation.

Throughout his life George was never without some current literary potboiler, his own or someone else's. His second book *Oregon Country* was published as he left to take up office in Salem. He loved the outdoors extravagantly, and he experienced this through horse-riding and fishing. It was said of him that he possessed 'ambition, kindness, intelligence, impatience, [and] of such things leaders are made.[44]

CHAPTER 8

1915–1922

Oregon had no lieutenant-governor, so George's position held the promise of great influence. As secretary to Governor James Withycombe he looked forward both to making a contribution to the rapidly growing state, and to his own self-advancement.[1]

Unfortunately, Withycombe had appointed George against the advice of the GOP state leaders who would have preferred an appointee with some political influence. This unknown young man came from 'east of the mountains, where votes were few . . .' George was later to recall, 'the political organization howled, and thenceforward made matters as uncomfortable for me as they could, which was considerable.'[2]

The 'political bushwackers' (as George called them),[3] managed to limit his scope to representing the governor at trade fairs, visiting prisons, operating a publicity machine and roles of a similar nature. George continued to feed articles to western newspapers, and did not forget the *Bulletin*. In April 1916 a feature article called 'Interesting Westerners' in *Sunset Magazine* noted that George had recently been offered a position in New York at more than twice his current salary. Possibly the offer was from G. P. Putnam's Sons. The article must have upset some of George's political opponents by pronouncing that Secretary Putnam was 'largely responsible today for [the] governor's popularity'.[4]

This small puff may have salved George's pride but he was still frustrated and restless. A man of action by nature, he was relieved when in 1916, with World War I at its height, President Wilson issued orders for the immediate mobilisation of the National Guard, subject to call for service on the Mexican border. Oregon 'led the nation with a volunteer enlistment of 92 per cent of its manpower'[5] and George, who had enlisted in the state militia in March, was ordered into active service in June with only one hour's notice.[6]

If he craved action, he was disappointed again. His main activity while serving in Mexico was to provide feature stories for Oregon newspapers. His disillusionment was apparent in an article published in the *Bulletin* in September 1916 in which he describes his activities as 'half police work and half training camp'.[7]

A few weeks after this was written George was honourably discharged from the National Guard and recalled to Salem to continue his duties as secretary to the governor where he remained for six months. He had enlisted for a three-year period, however, and though unassigned, was still technically in the army. In late June 1917 he was assigned to 'special work with the Department of Justice in Washington DC',[8] where he remained for eighteen months prior to entry into the field artillery officers' training school at Camp Taylor Kentucky, where he received his commission in December 1918.[9] During this time George suffered the loss of two members of his family. In 1917 his father died[10] and George grieved:

At heart Father was beautifully gentle. Like many really affectionate people, it was difficult for him to let his feelings show. He was deeply fond of me. Only towards the very end of his life did I understand at all and offer a return half-way decent. And then for the most part I was far away and letters were all we had between us.

. . . in his last fishing trip he was with me in Oregon. I can see him resting at the foot of a tawny pine at the edge of the Deschutes River with a meadow of blue lupin all about, weary and happy. Jaunty flies festooned his battered hat, and his beard, white then, was jaunty too. Though I remember with a pang in my heart the trouble he was having, what with his bifocal glasses and hands a trifle unsteady, adjusting a fresh fly to the leader.[11]

Then, while George was in the army in 1918, his elder brother Robert died from influenza in the great epidemic which swept North America. This totally unforeseen event changed the course of George's career for he never returned to Oregon, as planned. Instead, after his discharge from the army in December he went straight into G. P. Putnam's Sons in his brother's place.[12] When he originally enlisted he stated his occupation as 'Newspaperman', but when he applied for discharge he filed as 'Publisher'.[13]

The firm of G. P. Putnam, Broadway, had been formed in New York in 1840 by George's grandfather and namesake. In 1866 it became G. P. Putnam and Son when George's uncle, George Haven Putnam,[14] joined the family firm. John Bishop Putnam (George's father) took up the honourable calling of publisher in 1868, and on the death of the founder the company name became G. P. Putnam's Sons.

George Haven, universally known in the family and publishing world as 'the Major', a title dating from his service in the Civil War, became 'the dominant figure in the firm as author executive and internationally known personality' and ran 'the office'[15] which was now to become George's world. George Haven is chiefly known for his work in helping to secure the law of international copyright (originally proposed by G. P. Putnam I), for which he was awarded the order of the Legion of Honour by the French Government. Another brother, Herbert, who did not enter the publishing world but became Librarian of Congress Emeritus, also played his part in the writing of this important piece of legislation. George's father, John Bishop, spent half his time 'at the office' but his special interest and creation was 'KP', the Knickerbocker Press at New Rochelle which had so engaged his small son's attention. There was, too, a younger brother, Irving, who ran the Putnam book shop in New York.

Putnam's, the publishing house, had been in existence for almost eighty years when George joined it. Irving's two sons Edmund and Sydney were already employed there in minor jobs but George had no intention of taking anything other than the leading role in the company. His two uncles were both touching seventy years of age and were apparently content to give the ambitious young man his head, so George had *carte blanche* to improve and extend the company's lists.

After settling his family into a spacious mansion in Rye, one of George's first tasks was a three-month trip to the European capitals of Paris, Prague and Warsaw in order to secure for Putnam's the memoirs of the great Polish composer, pianist and statesman, Ignace Jan Paderewski. He met and talked with the great man and managed to extract 'a contract of sorts'[16] but despite protracted correspondence nothing ever came of it; Paderewski was too occupied with the affairs of state and his primary musical art to take time to write his autobiography.

George returned to the United States in December 1919. As usual, his travels generated a literary reward in the form of a dozen articles about Poland for popular magazines such as *Collier's* and the *Ladies Home Journal*,[17] and in his autobiography he claims to have written them all, 18,000 words between a Friday midnight and the following Monday morning.[18] His observations were astute and he recognised the serious position of Poland.

On 27 December, a few weeks after his return, he delivered a powerful speech about Poland's plight at Delmonico's in New York. Predicting that another European War was inevitable within ten years 'because Poland was an impediment to Germany's ambitions which were far from squashed by her defeat', he made it clear that he did not subscribe to the belief that the Great War had ended all wars. Such an unpopular theory, in 1919, was radical enough to receive coverage in the *New York Times* of what had been reasonably anticipated by the guests as a light-hearted social gathering.

It was George's enthusiasm and drive which caused him to commission what he liked to call 'fabricated books'. That is, he thought up an idea for a book and then found an author to write it. The method of having books written to order was a comparatively unknown phenomenon in the publishing world in the early twenties and it apparently paid off as G. P. Putnam's Sons produced, printed and sold more books than ever before.

He had many successes, and inevitably, some failures. For

instance, he turned down Ripley's first *Believe It Or Not* book, which later sold in excess of half a million copies, with the comment that 'it was good newspaper stuff, but it wouldn't do for a book'.[19] He also allowed Lowell Thomas to slip through his hands when he offered too small an advance on royalties. On the other hand, in a typical gesture of faith, loyalty and generosity he helped his friend Rockwell Kent to produce his beautiful – and bestselling – book, *Wilderness*.

The artist desperately wanted to travel to Alaska to paint but could not afford to make the trip. At George's suggestion a company was set up to employ Rockwell Kent. Everything the artist produced became the property of the corporation. George and a friend[20] purchased the entire stock and the company then paid Kent a salary and expenses to enable him to make the trip. Within a year the corporation (i.e. George) had sold enough of Kent's work to declare a dividend, and on Kent's return with enough material to produce *Wilderness*, the corporation was dissolved with the two stockholders repaid in full and Kent financially stable.

George did not shirk the sensational. In 1921 Putnam's published a collection of brilliant essays (originally published by the London office of G. P. Putnam's Sons) entitled *The Mirrors of Downing Street*, which was less than complimentary to leading British politicians. It was 'sizzling stuff',[21] exposing the weaknesses of those in power at a time when most biographies were of the devotee variety. George quickly saw that a book based on the inhabitants of Washington DC could be equally, if not more, sensational. The result, *The Mirrors of Washington* was a success, not least because it was written by two authors who remained anonymous for many years, causing much speculation and keeping the book in the public eye.

Another huge success was a spoof, *The Cruise of the Kawa*, an imaginary adventure cruise under the captaincy of one Dr Traprock, which George described as a 'ribald whimsey that sold near to a hundred thousand copies . . . some publishers looked down their noses. There were those, no doubt, who felt that the ancient respectability of the House of Putnam was being outraged. Myself I

always thought that a little laughter was good for any business –
especially if it sold merchandise.'[22] The *Publisher's Weekly* editorialised:

> An instance of imagination, ingenuity and cleverness beyond the
> capabilities of most merchandising wizards . . . With a book,
> which was at the beginning only a brilliant burlesque with an
> author masquerading under a *nom de plume*, George Palmer
> Putnam, practically overnight made Dr Traprock a nationally
> known figure . . .[23]

Also in 1921 George tried to publish an American edition of
Marie Stopes's sensational *Married Love*. Recognising that it would
never pass the censors in its original form, he prepared a revised
edition but the writer, William J. Robinson, was judged to have
violated a section of the New York City Penal Code relating to
obscene literature. A severely bowdlerised version was eventually
published a year later, leaving George bitterly acrimonious.[24] His
response was to publish a collection of essays by leading authors
entitled *Nonsensorship*, and to speak out publicly, in the *New York
Times* against the 'menace of censorship', notably that of John S.
Sumner, secretary of the New York Society for Suppression of Vice.
Censorship as applied, he growled, was 'unworkable, unnecessary
and unwise . . . Publishers are, or a least should be, capable of judging the decency of their own output.'

The censorship battle rumbled on for some years with George in
the vanguard. In 1923, George (together with Alfred Harcourt of
Harcourt, Brace and Co.) resigned from the Censorship Committee
of the National Association of Book Publishers in protest when the
committee refused to oppose the so-called 'Clean Books Bill'.
George's work behinds the scenes helped to quash the bill.

George's stable of successful authors grew: Louis Bromfield,
Sophie Kerr, George Agnew Chamberlain, Alexander Woollcott,
Ben Hecht, Kermit Roosevelt, Frank Craven, Rockwell Kent,
Dorothy Parker. George was never too busy to encourage an aspir-
ing author, and believed that '*everyone* had a book in them'. He must

have been responsible for inspiring hundreds of books, some of which were never finished but many of which achieved publication and success.

He did not limit his efforts to matching ideas with authors. On one notable occasion he wrote the entire plot for a novel and then found nineteen other well-known authors (ten women and nine men – George was the tenth man), to write the book. It was published as *Bobbed Hair* by Twenty Authors.

In 1923 he leased an office on Forty-fifth Street, a many-storeyed 'rabbit warren' of a place to house his business interests outside Putnam's. Here he ran a small literary agency and housed clients who were working on various projects. Writers, illustrators, cartoonists: George took them all on and encouraged them.

Corey Ford, one author who was contracted by George, recalled the initial telephone call. Ford, already under contract to Scribner's, had written a short parody on a best-selling book, which had been published in a magazine. George recognised its potential and telephoned Ford asking bluntly, and without preamble, if Ford could expand it into a book. 'He had already arranged for my release from Scribner's, he said to my surprise (later I learned not to be surprised at anything). Could I deliver my copy in ten days? That's fine then. Click.'

Ford's literary portrait of Putnam at that time is interesting:

wiry and dynamic with . . . an engaging laugh (he was fond of outrageous puns), and a disconcerting habit of accenting his speech now and then with a hollow *clunk* like a stone dropped down a well, that came from somewhere deep in his nasal passages. His friendly manner was offset by the hard calculating glance behind his steely spectacles. A phrase . . . once used in a story kept recurring to me: 'His eye was as cold as an undertaker's night bell.'

. . . he was usually called 'GP', which was sometimes corrupted to 'Gyp' [and] was the past master of literary legerdemain, a skilled conjurer who could palm an author, pull a best seller out of a hat, flourish his wand and transform a channel swimmer or explorer or aviator into a national sensation. With his knack of showmanship he published the memoirs of page-one celebrities who sparkled briefly and then as they began to fizzle, were discarded for the next headline hero . . . his instinct for the spectacular was almost occult. He could sense a newspaper story before it occurred. When another front-page notable popped up his eyes fairly snapped with electricity, his fingers coiled and writhed like live wires, his voice had the hum of a loaded power line. He was always calculating, always figuring out how to make use of people, always with the commercial end in mind. Everything was for sale . . . I think he was the loneliest man I've ever met.[25]

Ford's description of George as a lonely man is a surprising observation for George's circle of friends and acquaintances was huge, often impressive. And what could have turned the friendly and open young mayor of a frontier town into the coldly calculating entrepreneur that Ford speaks of? His home life was happy enough. His 'charming and vivacious wife' Dorothy[26] ran the couple's imposing mansion home in Rye, New York, with flair and a growing reputation as a hostess. The couple's first child David was nearly ten years old by now and Dorothy had given birth to another son, George Palmer Putnam junior, in 1921.

George commuted to the city daily, leaving home shortly after dawn and often returning only shortly before midnight, sometimes to find the last vestiges of a dinner party which he had organised and long since forgotten, and which Dorothy had necessarily hosted in his absence. One can only assume that Dorothy was either very much in love with her husband, or else extremely long-suffering to accept such cavalier treatment while remaining so supportive. Yet although George has sometimes been portrayed as a cold and lonely man by biographers, his family and those closest to him throughout his life insist that the reverse was true, that he was a romantic at heart, and a very loving person who, when he was not working, gave himself to his family without reservation. Clearly, George had one face for public life and another for his private life, and this is the answer to the conflicting portraits of him.

In September 1922 George and Dorothy made a return visit to Oregon, taking with them on the trip a party of authors. The object was to visit the Pendleton Round-up Rodeo, where some of the broncos were named after Putnam and his entourage. *The Oregonian* carried a report in which it referred to George as 'Lord High Publisher Putnam' and later a book was inevitably written about the trip as well as an eight-page pamphlet written by George and published by the Union Pacific, entitled *The Rough Riders Go West.*[27]

In his autobiography George stated that it was in these days that he acquired the habit of 'always being in a hurry . . . anyway the saddest people I know are those with nothing to do and too much time to do it in.' Certainly he was involved in a multitude of projects, including publicity 'scams' which occasionally backfired. On one occasion, one of his agency clients, a cartoonist, had a comic strip accepted by a leading newspaper in Boston. George conceived the idea of swamping the newspaper with letters from delighted readers and consequently had many of his and the cartoonist's friends write to the editor in glowing appreciation:

> Tied in a neat package, the feature editor of the paper sent those letters on to us. Through a change in plans, the new comic had not started on Monday and had not appeared at all when the letters started to arrive.[28]

Later George was to admit that perhaps he never took his activities as publisher 'quite seriously enough'. Certainly he made many nonsensical forays into what he termed 'extra-curricular' activities. These ranged from practical jokes, aided and abetted by his great friend Rockwell Kent, to large house parties of *literati* and other celebrities at Rye. He had a knack of knowing anyone worth knowing – musicians, politicians, comedians, actors, explorers – and the guest list at Rye was impressive with names such as Leopold Stokowski, Franklin D. Roosevelt, Charlie Chaplin, and Admiral 'Dick' Byrd to name a few. He had dozens of books ghosted for well-known names. He continued his habit of 'thinking up books that needed to be written and finding an author to do it'. Putnam's were turning out more books than ever before, many of them extremely successful. Each year George made several trips to Europe to look for books and to oversee operations at the company's London offices.

He continued, however, needling and wheedling and skilfully extracting books from the great as well as the unknown. To his chagrin he failed to get the memoirs of Calvin Coolidge. He had an appointment for breakfast with the great man at the Vanderbilt Hotel in New York and a friend of George's, who also knew Coolidge well, told George, 'I'll bet you ten dollars I can predict what Coolidge will say either the second or third time he opens his mouth.'

Thinking the boast absurd, George took the bet, asking what Coolidge would say. 'First he'll say "Good morning". His next speech, or the one after it will be substantially, "What advance royalty do you offer?"'

George lost the bet. The conversation apparently went thus:

Coolidge: 'Good morning.'
Putnam: 'Good morning, sir.'
Coolidge: 'Let's get at this book matter.'
Putnam: 'Fine by me.'
Coolidge: 'What royalties and how much in cash?'[29]

CHAPTER 9

1922–1928

By early 1926 George had identified a market need for adventure books. This he translated to true life adventure written in the first person, and his stable of authors included Martin and Osa Johnson, Knud Rasmussen and William Beebe. For George this was hardly enough. A close friend said of him, 'If he went to a dog fight he'd have to be one of the dogs.'[1] It was therefore predictable and probably only a matter of time before he too became an adventurer/ explorer. 'It seemed inappropriate to promote books about exploration without doing a bit of exploration myself. So I did,' he said.[2]

It was while walking through a bad New England snowstorm with Bob Bartlett, Admiral Peary's skipper on his 1909 conquest of the North Pole, that Bartlett commented how the weather in Westchester was puny compared with that he had observed in Greenland. Bartlett spoke, siren-like, to George of his time with Peary, and how he had been nearer to the North Pole on his own two feet than any white man living. Indeed he had spent most of his life north of the Arctic Circle. George was thirty-eight. He had been in harness throughout his twenties and thirties, and suddenly, listening to Bartlett, nothing would do for him but to experience adventure and hardship for himself. Given to sudden, violent enthusiasms which swept all opposition aside, George immediately proposed that he and Bartlett should organise an expedition to Greenland. He was under no illusions about his motives. Although he would endeavour to contribute to the sum of scientific knowledge (and would ultimately succeed in doing so), he fully recognised that 'it was a swell chance to have a very good time'.[3] Besides, he could always write a book about it. Within days an article appeared in the *New York Times*, announcing the expedition headed by George and naming a backer.[4]

Bartlett departed for his home in Newfoundland to collect his two-masted schooner *Morrissey*,[5] 100 feet in length and built of oak in Massachusetts in 1882. George, meanwhile, approached the American Museum of Natural History who had recently completed a magnificent new Hall of Ocean Life. They were short of specimens and with prompting from George, the museum's president, Henry Fairfield Osborn, agreed to back the expedition if financial sponsorship could be obtained.[6]

George knew exactly where to look for backing. A year earlier William Beebe's expedition to the Sargasso sea and the Galapagos islands had been backed by Harrison Williams, a wealthy financier and trustee of the museum. Accordingly, George was later able to report '. . . then, at once, Harrison Williams came forward with a gift that really launched the undertaking.'[7]

How George recruited his team is described by Dan Streeter, official historian to the expedition:

> George was a business man – even worse he was a Publisher with a chronic wanderlust. His was a triple personality. One may expect anything in a case like this and rarely be disappointed. His sanctuary successfully combined a deep monastic calm with the brazen atmosphere of a boiler factory. Yet the only bait that had been needed to lure [me] into it was a telephone call. He sat against a desk in an attitude at once expressive of deep abstraction and alert interest. There was no prologue.
>
> 'I'm organizing an expedition to Greenland,' he said. 'There are to be fourteen of us . . . our object is to collect for the American Museum a few narwhales, white whales . . . local sharks, artifacts, odds and ends –'
>
> The telephone bell rang. He took up the instrument, speaking into it with meticulous accuracy.
>
> 'Yes – yes – yes! No!' That concluded the telephone conversation.

'Where was I? . . . The Arctic? Oh! Yes! We'll touch at
Sydney, then make for Greenland, follow the coast north to
Cape York and Etah, call on the Smith Sound Eskimo – the last
of the world's aborigines. We're making the trip on a hundred-
foot "Banker" owned by Bob Bartlett and manned by a crew
of those silent men from Newfoundland one reads about –
six of them.

'Now a word as to the personnel of the expedition. Besides
myself and Captain Bartlett, there will be a Radio Operator,
Pathe News representative, Montana Cowboy, How and Arrow
expert, Engineer, Cabin Boy, Zoologist, Taxidermist and Famous
Danish Explorer . . .

'. . . Now here's the point. I was taking an artist to paint
Northern backgrounds. He's blown up on me. Will you take his
place?'

'Certainly,' [I] answered, 'but not as a painter because [I] don't
paint and someone might notice.'[8]

The cabin boy, incidentally, was George's thirteen-year-old son
David, who a year earlier had been a member of Beebe's Galapagos
expedition. He was not George's son for nothing; a book came out
of the trip, *David Goes Voyaging*,[9] the first in a series of best-selling
adventure books for boys written by young David.[10]

In his memoir George claimed it took him only six weeks to
organise financial backing, men, stores and logistics before the
Morrissey set off from Rye for her six month voyage,[11] but in fact he
announced the project in February and it was 21 June 1926 when
they left, a hectic six months after his conversation with Bartlett.
From the lawns of the American Yacht Club at Milton Point hundreds of well-wishers waved the expedition off into Long Island
Sound.[12]

A month before the departure of the *Morrissey*, Richard 'Dick'
Byrd had made history by captaining the first flight over the North
Pole. George had become a friend of Byrd's and had negotiated
book rights on his story prior to the record attempt. The two men
had also made an arrangement that should Byrd's flight come to

grief, the *Morrissey* would sail to Cape Columbia where Byrd and his crew would trek overland with hand sleds. When news of the successful flight came through, George was able to pass on his congratulations live to Byrd from the *New York Times* offices, on a specially installed transmitter boosted by 'the most powerful short-wave broadcasting plant in the country: "Dick, I hope this reaches you. We are hoping to meet you soon. Bob Bartlett and I are glad that there is no cause to meet up with you at Cape Columbia . . ."[13] What a story George could have written about *that* rescue!

The *New York Times* carried regular reports from George of the progress of the expedition, including the odd mishaps and near misses, blown up in true journalistic style. On one occasion the ship ran aground and listed at a 45-degree angle for days until she was finally floated off. George fired off a story to the *New York Times*, but Streeter, the official historian, later observed that while some 5,493 gallons of water had been pumped out of the schooner,

> the only wreck worth talking about was the man who did the pumping. But when one is sensitive to 'news value' and intimately connected with the profession, anything may be expected. George would have stopped in the middle of a rotten plank over a chasm a hundred feet deep to broadcast his reaction to a waiting world.[14]

George's story of a 'battle' between a walrus and himself and Bartlett made the front page in those far-off days. The two men were in a dory attempting to harpoon a large bull when the animal threw his flippers around the small boat and drove his two-foot long tusks up through the bottom, missing Bartlett by inches. The dory sank and the two adventurers had to be rescued from the icy waters.[15]

Readers of the *Times* were fascinated by George's adventures, and letters to the editor flowed in. Congratulatory telegrams from Byrd and Roosevelt winged their way to the *Morrissey* via the paper's columns. On 25 August the *New York Times* played its part in a domestic conspiracy and hauled Dorothy into the editorial office for a two-way radio conversation with her husband. In those days voice contact was still not possible, but at least it was direct two-way transmission and a considerable thrill for all concerned. George described his surroundings:

David and I wish you could share with us this unsultry night as we parade up and down Jones Bay in fog . . . Just now on deck [we are] clearing ice off insulators. Fog freezing icy coating over all. Temperature twenty-seven . . . just then we crashed against ice-pan . . . convey *New York Times* . . . greetings and gratitude for transmitting congratulatory messages . . . we are having bully time involving nothing remotely heroic. Just some healthy discomfort and normal perseverence . . . I'd like a swim at the American Yacht Club . . .
> George

Reportedly 'very moved', Dorothy replied:

Heavenly full moon; hot night. A hug for David. My love to the whole crowd. I share your thrills and hope for you good hunting but long to have you all home again.
> Dolly.

Everything was going exceptionally well, but it was nothing compared with the story George came up with on 25 September. For then, with his newspaperman's instinct for a really big story, despite being in one of the world's most isolated places, George came up with a major newspaper scoop.

The front page banner headline screamed:

ESKIMO KILLED PROF. MARVIN, PEARY AIDE; CONFESSES ARCTIC
CRIME OF 17 YEARS AGO; VICTIM REPORTED DROWNED, WAS SHOT

and 'Grim Tragedy of North . . . Kudlooktoo says explorer went mad and left other eskimo to die . . .' sub-headlined over George's sensational revelations that the history books were wrong. 'The

Arctic has given up another secret . . .' George's article began grimly. The *New York Times* gave it three columns on page one, all of page two and ran over onto page three.[16] Birchall, the managing editor, was so impressed that he wired back: QUIT PUBLISHING AND BECOME A REAL REPORTER.[17] George had nursed the story for three weeks for although there was hardly any likelihood of a rival reporter scooping him, given the remoteness of the drama, he was concerned that his radio signals might be intercepted or misinterpreted so he waited until they reached Nova Scotia on the return journey to wire the story through with just enough time to make the next edition.

The Putnam expedition arrived back in Rye on 1 October 1926, to general acclaim and a page one welcome by the *New York Times*. Three books immediately resulted from the pens of Knud Rasmussen, Bob Bartlett and David Binney Putnam and the expedition was also adjudged successful from a scientific point of view.[18] So when George, with his appetite for adventure truly whetted, decided to form another expedition to Baffin Island the following spring, he found no shortage of backers.[19]

It was to be a similar saga, with regular page one reports in the *Times*, near misses, adventures with polar bears, icy swims and the inevitable 'big story' when the expedition discovered that contemporary maps were in error on the area of Baffin Island by some 5,000 square miles.[20]

But before he could leave for Baffin, George found he had a publishing sensation on his hands, and it says much for his desire to seek physical adventure that he was able to leave in June 1927 to lead this second expedition. Indeed, in the weeks and months that followed he must have many times queried his judgement in doing so.

In May 1927, while George was in the final stages of preparation for the new expedition, Charles Augustus Lindbergh, a young man of twenty-five, was finalising his plans to attempt a solo flight over the Atlantic. Atlantic Fever was in the air. There had been numerous attempts to fly the Atlantic, many fatal but only two (discounting airships) had been successful. One was a crossing in stages to Lisbon via the Azores in May 1919[21] and the other was the first non-stop crossing by Alcock and Brown less than a month afterwards. Since then no crossing of the North Atlantic had been made and a solo non-stop flight between the USA and France, for which a prize of $25,000 had been offered by French hotelier Raymond Orteig, had still to be accomplished.

In May 1927 there were three significant contenders: Charles Lindbergh with his *Spirit of St Louis*, Richard Byrd with *America*, and Clarence Chamberlin with *Columbia* (all of whom subsequently made successful crossings). Such was public interest in the contest between them that reporters swarmed around the airport and each time any of the airmen took off for a test flight they were reported as having 'left secretly'.

Even before he left New York Lindbergh had been inundated with offers for books and films should his attempt be successful.[22] Despite the stress of pre-flight preparation, upon which his life depended, Lindbergh remained cool enough to fend off these distractions. George may even have been introduced to Lindbergh at this time, or more likely had marked the event down as something to monitor, for his subsequent shrewdness in approaching Lindbergh indicates either forward planning or a certain knowledge of the flyer's character.

On 20 May 1927, in his modified Ryan, the *Spirit of St Louis*, Lindbergh took off from Roosevelt Field, Long Island, New York. After a flight of 33 hours 30 minutes he landed at Le Bourget Aerodrome in Paris, becoming the first person to complete a solo flight across the Atlantic.[23]

Unprecedented hysteria surrounded the young aviator in those hectic days immediately after his arrival in Paris. If he had been pestered by would-be promoters before the flight he was now besieged, but he resolutely refused to see or talk to anyone except representatives of the *New York Times*, which had exclusive rights to his story. The *Times* had retained journalists Carlisle MacDonald and Edwin James who interviewed the flyer and wrote stories over Lindbergh's name which were cabled back to the States. Often he did not have time to edit or even read them and subsequently he was deeply unhappy about some of the things that had appeared.

The *Times*, in fact, treated Lindbergh with uncharacteristic generosity – uncharacteristic of newspapers that is – for they decided not to make any profit from the young man's heroic feat. They cabled that they would not hold him to the original $5,000 contract but would turn over all receipts from his stories (mainly deriving from world syndication rights) after direct expenses had been met. Lindbergh eventually received around $60,000 from the *Times*, so his initial trust in them seemed to be justified.

On 21 May, George Putnam was deeply involved in last-minute preparations for his forthcoming expedition. But not too deeply involved to want to secure Lindbergh's story for G. P. Putnam's Sons.

George's relationship with the *New York Times* editor, Fred Birchall, was of long standing, both personally and professionally. Now, he traded upon it. Recognising that if he approached Lindbergh direct he would simply be another of the many publishers seeking an audience; and possibly already having knowledge of Lindbergh's intransigence, George went to Birchall, one of the few people Lindbergh felt he could trust.

'We'd like to get Lindbergh's book,' I said.

The stocky little Englishman's near-sighted eyes crinkled in a grin as he peered at me over his glasses.

'Indeed,' he chuckled, 'you – and who else?' . . . I suppose every publisher in America wanted the book.

Anyway Birchall did what he properly could to help. What I needed was [assistance] in getting word promptly into the hands of the harassed flyer, and the Paris office of the *Times* could help with that.

So I pencilled out a message on a page of copy paper and Birchall edited it. I remember how he lowered his short-sighted eyes to within inches of the paper on his desk, changing some words, inserting others, in that meticulous way he had, vastly improving my handiwork. Then he swung round at me. 'At least you ought to know how to spell Lindbergh's name!' he barked. I'd left off the final 'h'.[24]

Lindbergh 'adopted the suggestion'[25] made through Birchall, under the impression that he would tell his story to a journalist who would write it in the third person. He had already developed a rapport with Carlisle MacDonald and so had no objection to working with him on a biography. As George tells it, by the time Lindbergh sailed for the United States aboard the US cruiser *Memphis* on 5 June, a verbal contract had been made that 'Lindbergh would write the book and we [Putnam's] would publish it'. Unfortunately, there was a serious misunderstanding on both sides as to what had actually been agreed.

MacDonald sailed with Lindbergh and used the voyage to interview him in great depth about his background.[26] Almost certainly George delayed the start of the Putnam Baffin Expedition in order to discuss with MacDonald personally the strategy for the rapid production of the book. Lindbergh arrived back in New York on 11 June, and as soon as the *Memphis* docked, MacDonald was whisked to George's home at Rye where a team of secretaries worked to rush the book out while the story was at its height. Using his interview notes and the *New York Times* stories as sources, MacDonald set to work with a deadline of days rather than weeks. The book was announced in a flurry of publicity.

Because of the short Arctic summer, George could not delay his expedition a day longer and the *Morrissey* departed on 12 June. Young David, gathering material for another book, was again part of the expedition, and Dorothy joined them for the first leg of the voyage to Brigus, Newfoundland, which they reached on 20 June.[27] From there George was able to communicate by radio with MacDonald who was already putting the finishing touches to his work. The manuscript was edited, rushed over to the Knickerbocker Press in New Rochelle and by 22 June, only ten days after MacDonald started work, typeset galley proofs were available for Lindbergh's approval.[28] Secure in the knowledge that everything was going according to plan, and that G. P. Putnam's Sons had already received orders for 100,000 copies for immediate delivery,[29] George set off on the next stage of his voyage.[30]

The misunderstanding now came to light. MacDonald had ghosted the book in the true sense, having written it in the first person in Lindbergh's name. Lindbergh would not approve it. It is difficult to believe that MacDonald's impressions could have been so far removed from Lindbergh's understanding of the terms of the agreement. More probably, George realised that what the public wanted was Lindbergh's experiences in his own words and instructed MacDonald to write the book in the first person assuming Lindbergh would accept it as *un fait accompli* once he was shown the completed work in print. Quite uncharacteristically, on this occasion, George misread his man.

Lindbergh refused with a simple but definite 'No'. He raised no specific objections to what MacDonald had written, but – as he later stated – at the time he accepted the contract:

> I was then under the impression that the account would be written in the third person, through interviews, over someone else's name, and that I would confirm its authenticity and contribute a foreword. Instead, a 'ghost-written' manuscript, in the first person, was submitted to me for approval, and rejected.[31]

When it was pointed out to Lindbergh that he'd accepted the contract, that the announcement had been made and that orders were already flooding in, Lindbergh acknowledged that he was under obligation to produce a book. But he insisted that if it was to appear over his own name he would have to write it himself. How much of this was known to George at the time is not clear, though obviously some was, since he was later to write that high blood pressure nearly overcame him. With scarcely concealed impatience on the part of the publishers, Lindbergh was asked when his book would be completed, and was told that a month's delay would be annoying but bearable.

At first Lindbergh predicted a delivery 'in the autumn'. This was in late June, and with the pressure of the hundreds of demands on his time he might have been congratulated at attempting to produce a book in such a short time. Instead George, when advised of this, was apoplectic; the demand was *now*. Ignoring Lindbergh's daunting schedule of public appearances George sent messages to remind the flier that Putman's had a contract based on his verbal agreement with MacDonald, and that on the strength of that contract Putnam's had promised delivery of the book to their customers. 'The MacDonald manuscript was a good job, complete, dignified, well-written . . . we declared [that] we just *had* to have a book. MacDonald's or his own. But promptly.'[32]

If George was hoping to force Lindbergh's hand, it didn't work. Recognising the validity of the arguments Lindbergh purported to cancel all engagements and retire to the home of his friends, Harry and Carol Guggenheim on Sands Point, Long Island. Actually he interrupted his writing to fly to Ottawa, Canada but an inspection of his diary shows he had only the last week in June, and from 4 to 19 July free of commitments so his claim that he took 'about three weeks' to produce the 40,000 word manuscript was probably accurate.[33] George recalled irritably:

He wrote every word in long-hand, on legal size paper. In the upper right-hand corner of each page, as he completed it, he wrote the number of words on that page. One could almost see him counting and saying to himself as he cast up the total, 'Well, *that* many are out of the way, praise be!'[34]

Fitzhugh Green, under commission from Putnam's, wrote an introduction and the book *We* was rushed out by the end of August. Lindbergh settled privately with MacDonald for $10,000 and his ghost-written manuscript was never published.[35] Sales of Lindbergh's book, however, were all that were hoped for, '. . . more than 635,000 copies,' George said 'which is something of a record for a first book. Or a last one!'[36]

From the restrained twin versions of this story one can derive the primary characteristics of both men. Lindbergh, calm, precise, unflappable; confident that right was on his side and refusing to be

hustled. Pedantically writing his manuscript in longhand and anno-
tating each page to ensure that no further misunderstanding or
misconstruction could occur. Putman, frustrated by the distances
involved, impatient, dynamic, scenting colossal success and fretting
that delay could damage the property. Pushing, cajoling, yet even at
his most persuasive failing to impress or move Lindbergh by either
charm or bullying tactics. George was not used to defeat and he was
anything but graceful on the few occasions he suffered it, but he was
later to write objectively that Lindbergh 'was a very dull demigod
indeed, but neither a fool nor a knave'.[37]

The *Morrissey* arrived back in Rye, Westchester on 6 October
1927. A flurry of feature articles, backing up the despatches which
had appeared regularly during the expedition, were published in the
New York Sunday Times. David's book *David goes to Baffin Land*
appeared in due course and George's paper on the voyage was published by the American Geographical Society.[38]

George dived back into publishing with preparations for another
potential best-seller, Commander Richard E. 'Dick' Byrd's first book
Skyward,[39] an account of his 1926 historic first flight over the North
Pole, in a private expedition with Floyd Bennett as his chief pilot.

There was another foray into the world of aviation when an
author who had been a pilot-instructor during the war came to
George with a book entitled *Wings*. It was a romantic epic of men
who lived for today because they knew that tomorrow they would
probably be dead. George had the brilliant idea of selling the book
as a movie but Jesse Lasky, head of production at Paramount, could
not see how a movie could be made 'just about flying'. At this time
there had never been a feature film based on aviation. George
exerted his customary alternating charm and pressure and at last
Lasky agreed to see George and his author.

They talked from 3 p.m. until midnight; next day the contract
was signed. The film, first of a genre, was shot at Camp Stanley near
San Antonio, Texas, where army engineers created a replica of the
Western Front at a cost of $300,000, big money in those days.
Within the year the Oscar-winning *Wings*, starring Clara Bow,
Buddy Rogers and a very youthful Gary Cooper was playing to

record audiences.[40] George, who had 'assisted in the production'[41] was said to have earned a great deal of money from his connection with this enterprise but almost certainly what he got was stock in a newly formed company Talking Picture Epics Ltd of which he became vice president. The company produced several real-life adventure movies based on books by George's best-selling authors: *Across the World* (Osa and Martin Johnson); *Hunting Tigers in India* (George M. Dymott); and *Bottom of the World* (Robert Cushman Murphy); but none achieved the success of *Wings* which won the first Academy Award for best picture of the year. It was during the making of *Wings* that George first encountered a colourful young stunt pilot named Paul Mantz. George 'collected' people, and seven years later he would contact the young pilot again for help in another venture.

Because of his involvement in *Skyward*, *We* and *Wings*, George was moving in the tight circle of aviation during those early months of 1928. He certainly had many social contacts with Lindbergh, though in the light of their earlier misunderstanding the relationship was almost certainly uneasy. It was not improved when in January 1928 George had the handwritten manuscript of *We* bound in two leather volumes for which a collector offered $30,000. George invited Lindbergh to his office to discuss the matter. He 'explained' to the flyer that 'under the arrangements' made between them, ownership of the manuscript 'possibly' lay with Putnam's. But, he continued, he felt that a fair course would be to split the proceeds equally.[42]

It is highly unlikely that the manuscript could have been owned by Putnam's unless a specific clause to that effect had been inserted in a contract, and this episode is a perfect example of George, the hustler and the dealer, at his most devious. He could hardly bear the fact that he could not reach this man, scarcely more than a boy, whose name was quite literally a licence to print money. When George decided to charm, the subject, in general, was charmed; but Lindbergh was the exception and George's smile must have had a fixed quality whenever the two came into contact.

On this occasion, as on others, Lindbergh bested George. He

considered the matter carefully before answering the publisher's suggestion, fully aware that had the publisher any real title to the manuscript the author would never have been consulted. Finally the young Solomon said, 'If it's yours, you do as you wish. If it isn't, I want it.'[43] Of course it was Lindbergh's property and was later presented to the collection of Lindbergh memorabilia housed in the museum in St Louis.

CHAPTER 10

1928

It was probably in early April of 1928 that George's ever-attentive ear picked up the news that yet another record attempt was to be made on the Atlantic. It had been crossed non-stop several times at that stage, by crews in single- and multi-engined airplanes and by Lindbergh. No woman had so far flown across, though several women were involved in preparations of various degrees of seriousness. One, Ruth Nichols, was a neighbour of George in Rye; another, Mabel Boll, was making plans amid as much publicity as she could attract.

According to George's autobiography, his first inkling that an interesting project was afoot occurred when he went with Bernt Balchen to Miller Field on Staten Island. On the ferry Balchen, former pilot to Dick Byrd on their successful transatlantic crossing, told George that 'Byrd had secretly sold the Fokker trimotor airplane to an English woman who wished to fly the Atlantic'. This was all George could discover from Balchen who had not been given any further information concerning the sale; indeed, he only unearthed this small item because he was organising the logistics for Byrd's South Pole flight and he needed to order skis to replace the landing gear on the replacement aeroplane – a Ford Trimotor. George noted:

> Just then my career as a publisher of exploration and adventure books was in full cry. And here I had stumbled on an adventure-in-the-making which, once completed, certainly should provide a book.[1]

By pure coincidence, later that day George's old friend Hilton Railey – whom George had talked into travelling to Poland as a war correspondent seven years earlier – called in at the Putnam offices on a trip from Boston.

I dropped in to see George – as busy as ever and . . . optimistic. I had always liked G.P. in a mellow mood; on this occasion he was particularly ingratiating . . .

'When are you going back?' he enquired with sudden speculation.

'Five o'clock.'

'Pull that chair over. I heard something today that might be of interest to you.'[2]

George told Railey what he'd heard that day from Balchen. He explained that he did not know the name of the woman or anything about the project except that he believed floats were being fitted to the Fokker at the East Boston airport. Why didn't Railey take a run over there to investigate? Railey was initially unimpressed. 'What if it's true?' he asked. 'What then?'

'If it's true,' said his wily friend, 'we'll crash the gate. It would be amusing to manage a stunt like that, wouldn't it? Find out all you can. Locate the ship. Pump the pilots. Chances are they know all about it. Maybe there's nothing to it . . . telephone me if it's hot.'[3]

Before midnight that night Railey had tracked down Wilmer Stultz, the pilot, and Lou Gordon, the co-pilot and mechanic (aeroplane engineers were always called mechanics in that era), at the Copley Plaza in Boston. Bill Stultz had been drinking hard and Railey found him a talkative companion. Stultz admitted that they were preparing for a transatlantic flight but that his only contact was a New York attorney, Mr David T. Layman, who represented the principal.

Here the two stories diverge somewhat, Putman and Railey both claiming that they were responsible for finding Amelia Earhart. George wrote that having learned David Layman's name from Railey, he went to see him:

I was able to tell that I knew my way around in the business of
expeditions and had considerable experience with aviation projects. He seemed visibly relieved.[4]

Layman explained that his client, Mrs Amy Guest, had wanted to
be the first woman to fly the Atlantic. However, Mrs Guest's family
had discovered the plan and were intent on stopping her from doing
anything so foolhardy:

The project, they said, was all right, if she sent someone in her
place. And reluctantly Mrs Guest had agreed.
    Pretty much at the moment that I dropped from the clouds
and introduced myself, Layman was wondering what to do next.
So, suddenly I found myself entrusted with an odd chore. I was
to find a suitable American woman who wanted to fly the
Atlantic.[5]

Railey states in his memoir:

In New York some days later, I got in touch with him [Layman]
and learned that Mrs Frederick E. Guest of London and New
York . . . was the mysterious sponsor who planned to be the first
of her sex to fly the Atlantic. Her family, Mr Layman said, was
much concerned. Soon it was agreed that if I could find 'the
right sort of girl' to take her place Mrs Guest would yield.[6]

The stories are so similar that it seems likely that both men went
to see Layman in his office. Layman emphasised that by the 'right
sort of girl' his client meant 'a lady'. Both George and Railey were
slightly amused by this description, George professing that he was
hazy as to what the word precisely meant, though he had once
humorously defined it neatly: 'A real lady is the kind you meet with
Mr and Mrs M at their home. Those who are not real ladies are the
kind you may meet with Mr M – when he is out on his own.'[7]
    Mrs Guest had set out general specifications to be met by the
successful candidate. She should be a pilot and well-educated;

preferably a college graduate. She should be physically attractive and have manners that would be acceptable to members of English society who would undoubtedly welcome her on her arrival there. There were several women under consideration at that point.

Miss Ruth Nichols of Rye was an obvious contender. A pilot since 1922, dark-haired, attractive and well-spoken, she met the requirements perfectly. But she had been ill and needed time to recover. Six months earlier, in October 1927, Ruth Elder had made her attempt to be the first woman to fly the Atlantic, in a tri-motored Stinson Detroiter named *American Girl*, piloted by George Haldeman. After engine trouble developed they went down in the Atlantic 360 miles north of the Azores, landing in the sea close to a ship which picked them up. The plane exploded before it could be hoisted aboard. After a trip to Paris Miss Elder returned to the USA for a career in vaudeville and, in doing so, probably ruled herself out of Mrs Guest's search for 'the right sort of American girl'. It is doubtful whether, in any circumstances, Miss Mabel 'Mibs' Boll would have been considered by Amy Guest to be the right sort.

Railey takes up the story:

On the merest hunch, when I returned to Boston, I telephoned my friend, Rear-Admiral Reginald K. Belknap, USN (Ret).

'Why yes,' said he, 'I know a young social worker who flies. I'm not sure how many hours she's had, but I do know that she's deeply interested in aviation – and a thoroughly fine person. Call Denison House and ask for Amelia Earhart.'

while George competes with:

It was the trivial incident of an overheard conversation that started me. It was the accident of an Admiral being in the Boston office of my friend Hilton Railey when I telephoned him, that brought our quest to the door of Amelia Earhart. For Admiral Belknap had heard of a girl who worked in a settlement house and also did a bit of flying.[8]

At least both agree that it was Hilton Railey who first contacted Miss Earhart. At first, guardedly, he simply asked the young woman if she would come to his office for an interview. Amelia replied that she would not, until he stated the nature of the project. Railey reluctantly told her that he was organising an exciting but hazardous flying venture and asked if she was interested. Amelia replied, equally guardedly, that she might be. 'There was a pause and she asked for references – personal references. That afternoon, accompanied by Miss Marion Perkins, head worker at Denison House, she appeared at my office.' Railey was convinced on sight that he had found the right woman to make the flight and asked almost immediately, 'How would you like to be the first woman to fly the Atlantic?'[9]

Amelia betrayed no unseemly excitement but he detected a flicker in her cool eyes while she asked for details. He told her all that he was at liberty to tell, and that he had been asked by George Palmer Putnam, the New York publisher, to find the woman who would make the flight. She gave him details on her background, all acceptable.

Railey claims to have been struck by a strong resemblance in Amelia's appearance to Lindbergh and immediately coined the sobriquet 'Lady Lindy' in his mind. At the very moment he thought of it he instinctively knew Amelia would loathe it but he was also aware of the effect it would have on the newspapers! He was deeply impressed by the poise of the young woman who was both warm and dignified in her manner.[10]

On 2 May, probably about a week after their meeting in Boston, Amelia wrote to Railey:

It is very kind of you to keep me informed, as far as you are able, concerning developments of the contemplated flight. As you may imagine my suspense is very great indeed.

Please do not think that I hold you responsible, in any way, for my own uncertainty. I realize that you are . . . only the medium of communication between me and the person, or persons, who are financing the enterprise. For your own satisfaction may I add, here, that you have done nothing more than present the facts of the case to me. I appreciate your forbearance in not trying to 'sell' the idea, and should like you to know that I assume all responsibility for any risks involved.

At our next interview – if there is one – I shall have all the details you asked for.[11]

A week later Amelia was invited to an interview by Layman and Mr John S. Phipps in New York. She was very much aware of being weighed up at that meeting.

It should have been slightly embarrassing, for if I were found wanting on too many counts I should be deprived of a trip. On the other hand, if I were too fascinating the gallant gentlemen might be loath to drown me. Anyone can see the meeting was a crisis.[12]

The details Amelia was given concerning the flight were that Mrs Amy Guest, an American by birth and married to the Hon. Frederick Guest of London, had purchased the aeroplane from Byrd who had originally commissioned it for his planned expedition to the Antarctic. The plane, delivered new from the factory in February, had been test-flown by Bernt Balchen and Floyd Bennett both of whom pronounced it satisfactory. Mrs Guest had already given a name to the aeroplane: it was to be called the *Friendship*, representing Anglo-American relationships. Fitted as standard with two 95-gallon fuel tanks in the wings, an additional pair of extra 95-gallon tanks had been installed, also in the wings, and two 245-gallon tanks fixed in the fuselage – providing a total capacity of 870 gallons – so she had the range for a transatlantic flight. The power source was three Wright Whirlwind J-5 engines each of 220 horsepower. The plane had already been fitted with Duralumin floats at Detroit, Michigan at the time of the sale but these were found to be subject to leaks so a certain amount of welding was needed to make them sound.[13]

Amelia was told that she would be accompanied by Stultz and

Gordon, both sound and experienced for their roles as pilot/navigator and flight mechanic. Stultz, in fact, had already made one attempt to fly 'the first woman across' in the previous autumn in a twin-engined Sikorsky, but had turned back when he thought he sensed (rather than heard) one of the engines 'splutter' 500 miles out. Despite the commands, followed by the pleas, of his passenger, Mrs Frances Grayson, he made for the coast and was vindicated when 30 miles out the port engine died and he limped in on one engine to make a forced landing on the beach.[14] Lewes Gower, another well-known pilot, was to go along as understudy in case Stultz became ill or had an accident, at least as far as Newfoundland where he could help in final preparations. The names of these men would have been well known to Amelia and she could not have felt other than confident in their ability and reputation.

In fact the information given to Amelia was not entirely accurate. Mrs Guest had not purchased the Fokker. It was purchased by Jell-O millionaire Donald Woodward on 9 April for the sum of $62,000 and registered to his Mechanical Science Corporation of Le Roy, New York.[15] Woodward had already backed Byrd's forthcoming expedition substantially and when Byrd decided that the Fokker was not ideal for his project because of the fixed one-piece wing – he eventually took a Ford Trimotor 'donated' by the Ford Corporation who were his chief backers on the venture – Woodward obviously stepped in on a business footing. Mrs Guest leased the plane from Woodward for the flight with some offer of insurance should the flight be unsuccessful, and the *Friendship* was flown to Boston. Plans for the transatlantic flight were already well advanced.[16]

It must have been a tremendous disappointment for Amy Phipps Guest that she was not able to undertake the flight herself. Although photographs of the period show her to be a plump society matron her record reveals that she spent her life looking for adventure. As a young woman she was a forceful and fearless rider to hounds, earning an enviable reputation by riding side-saddle over jumps that were eschewed by other members of the field.[17]

A niece remembered being told that:

Poor Amy had always been thwarted in her attempts to be of help to mankind. During the Spanish–American War she wanted to go to Mexico to nurse the wounded. Grandpa asked her, 'Do you really want to help our soldiers or do you just want to go out there personally, because if you really want to help the wounded, your mother and I will pay for two trained nurses to work at the army hospital for the duration of the war.' What could she say?[18]

In common with a number of other extremely rich young American girls (her fortune was rumoured to be $1.9 billion), Amy married into the British aristocracy, taking as her husband the Right Honourable Frederick Guest, third son of Lord Wimborne.[19] Frederick was not only a keen aviator but a first-class shot and the couple undertook many trips to Kenya where Amy's cool courage on safari impressed even the great white hunter, Baron Bror Blixen.[20]

It was when Amy heard soon after Lindbergh's triumph that a nightclub hostess was planning to be the first woman to fly the Atlantic that she decided to make her move for personal fame. Her niece explains:

There are several versions of the story, but the one I heard was that she did not tell the family about the trip, with the exception of her youngest brother, Howard [Phipps], and she swore him to secrecy. As time for the flight neared, Howard became more and more worried and finally he broke down, called [Amy's son] Winston and spilled the beans. Winston then phoned his mother from Yale and said definitely 'No – the day you get on the plane I will leave college.' So again Aunt Amy had to give up her plans.[21]

Amelia never met Amy on that trip to New York but she did meet George Palmer Putnam. George was busy that day and sent his friend, Dr George McCracken, by taxi to collect Amelia and bring her to his office.[22] When she arrived George was in a meeting and Amelia was asked to wait. The wait was lengthy and his cavalier squandering of her time annoyed her so that when she was finally shown into his presence she was fully prepared to dislike him con-siderably.[23] 'She was as sore as a wet hen!' George was to relate later. 'She didn't like me one little bit and she didn't take much pains to conceal her dislike . . .'[24]

Railey had undoubtedly already mentioned to George Amelia's physical resemblance to Lindbergh. George, busy as usual, was pre-pared to be patronising.[25] Instead he was intrigued, recognising at once her personality and potential. He disguised his true feelings behind a brusque manner and this is what she later recalled. But although Amelia remembered 'no special feelings about Mr Putman at first – I was too absorbed in the prospects of the trip and of my being the one to make it, to notice any one person at that time, she also related that, 'before I had talked to him for very long I was con-scious of the brilliant mind and the keen insight of the man. I recognized his tremendous power of accomplishments and imme-diately respected his judgement . . .'[26]

George was so impressed that he decided at that meeting that Amelia should be the woman to make the flight.[27] However, all too soon Amelia had to leave to catch a train to Boston. George accom-panied her to Pennsylvania Station and later Amelia confided to her sister that 'she wished the ride had been longer because he was so interesting', but she also noted that he had hurried her aboard her train and departed without offering to pay her fare home![28]

BOOK THREE
George and Amelia

Amelia Earhart knew me better, probably, than anyone else ever can. With her discernment, why she married the man she did was often a matter of wonder to me. And to some others.

George Palmer Putnam (1945)

How does 'being in business' (for flying is a business) affect marriage? Obviously I can offer only my own answers – from a woman's viewpoint. It seems to me that the effect of having other interests beyond those exclusively domestic works well. The more one does and sees and feels, the more one is able to do, and the more genuine may be one's appreciation of fundamental things like home, and love, and understanding companionship.

Amelia Earhart (1933)

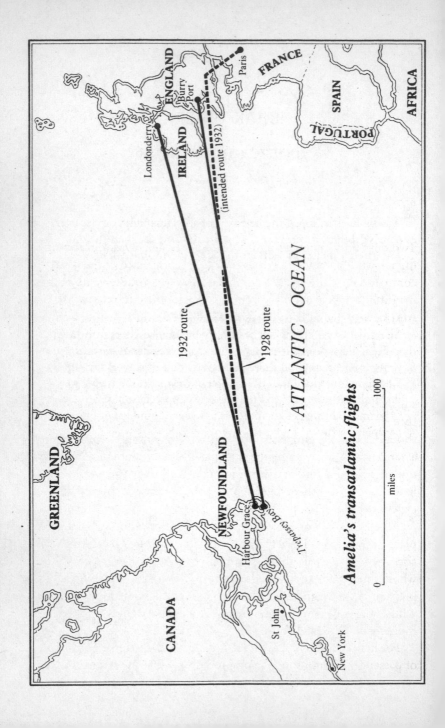

Amelia's transatlantic flights

CHAPTER 11

1928

Two days after the meeting in New York Amelia was told that the flight would be made and that she had been selected as the woman commander, 'if she wished'.[1] She was, however, to receive no remuneration for her part in the venture. 'Under the circumstances . . .' Amelia wrote later, 'I couldn't say no.'[2]

She would not have been slow to recognise the opportunities that the flight offered her. Immediate fame, of course, if the attempt were successful, and George, or GP as she quickly came to call him, would not have been slow in pointing out the potential for earning substantial amounts of money from personal appearances and lecture tours, etc. But Amelia would also have been tempted by the thought of the flight itself. She was already wholly committed to aviation and its development and though she was practical enough not to pass up fame and fortune, it is likely that she would have made the flight if there had been no obvious rewards, purely for the experience.

Amelia having formally accepted the offer, another meeting took place in Boston on 18 May 1928, with Layman and George. For the time being, she was told, it would be better for everyone if the whole thing were kept secret, mainly to avoid press attention while preparations were under way, but also to avoid alerting any competitor whose preparations might be more advanced. No announcements would be made until they had actually taken off.

For her part Amelia had made it clear from the start that the role of passenger did not much appeal to her and that she wished to take her turn at the controls.[3] She had no experience of multi-engine flying, however, nor of instrument flying, so it was agreed that if weather permitted she would be allowed to fly for some of the time. All the same, those present recognised that it was important that Amelia was seen to be in charge of the flight, since its entire purpose was to promote the concept of a woman flying the ocean. Her role as 'commander' was therefore covered by a document drawn up at that meeting. There was no other formal contract:

Boston Massachusetts
May 18th 1928

WILMER STULTZ
LOUIS E. GORDON
J.H. LEWES GOWNER [sic]
AND ANYONE ELSE CONCERNED:

This is to say that on arrival at Treppassy [sic] of the tri-motor Fokker plane 'FRIENDSHIP' if any questions of policy, procedure, personnel or any other question arises the decision of Miss Amelia M. Earhart is to be final. That she is to have control of the plane and of the disposal of the services of all employees as fully as if she were the owner. And further, that on arrival of the plane in London full control of the disposition of the plane and of the time and services of employees shall be hers to the same extent until and unless the owner directs other wise.

David T Layman
Attorney in fact for the owner
A specimen of Miss Earhart's signature appears below[4]

Amelia had already been to see the *Friendship* where it was jacked up in the rear of a large hangar at East Boston airport, awaiting the fitting of the pontoons that were being worked on by welders nearby. Just under 50 feet in length and with a wing span of 71 feet 2 inches it was by far larger than any aeroplane Amelia had yet flown in. The plane had been registered by Byrd under an experimental licence, NX4204 (the experimental status being designated by the 'X'), and was painted international orange (a red-orange) with gold wings, 'the latter described as a warm amber from many coats of spar varnish over birch veneer.'[5] The colour, originally specified by Byrd to make the plane easier to find should he come down in the sea or on ice, would serve the same purpose for the oceanic flight. Amelia saw the *Friendship* only once more prior to the departure from Boston on the flight, and she never got the opportunity to fly in it until then. She was too well known at local airfields to risk even being involved in the preparations. If she were seen taking too close an interest it would precipitate the type of rumours they were all anxious to avoid.

It had been hoped that the *Friendship* would leave Boston for Trepassey Bay, Newfoundland, during mid-May, exactly a year after Lindbergh's flight. Hilton Railey, at Amelia's request, sailed for Europe to organise things at that end. Like Lindbergh's flight though, the *Friendship* enterprise was frustrated by poor weather. Long grey days through to the end of the month kept them in Boston. George was there all the time. His relationship with Byrd was known and accepted and his presence excited no comment. Mr and Mrs Layman came sometimes, as did Dorothy Putnam. Amy Guest's sons Winston and Raymond cautiously made an appearance, not wishing to give anything away.[6]

To help pass the time Amelia took George, and sometimes Stultz, Gordon and Gower, sightseeing in her Kissel roadster. 'On rainy days the top leaked too much for comfort, so we walked.'[7] They experimented, going to different ethnic restaurants each evening, and also to all the theatres.

George and Amelia discovered that they shared a well-developed sense of the ridiculous and one particular show that they attended especially amused them. It was a tragedy in which all the characters save one drowned, and a recurring line, 'The fish are dearly paid for', struck them as hilarious in the circumstances; the crew of *Friendship* instantly adopted it as a motto, 'emblazoned under a goldfish rampant'.[8]

Perhaps it was this shared sense of humour which formed the initial attraction between George and Amelia. But George was naturally drawn towards intelligent people and the cool poise of Amelia in the face of the Atlantic flight, together with her obvious ambition and dedication to her work and her enthusiasm for the future of aviation must all have played their part.

Her personal preparations had been minimal and were completed quickly. Her clothes would consist of those she wore as she climbed aboard: high laced boots, brown broadcloth breeches, white silk blouse with red necktie and her by-now genuinely aged leather coat; a brown sweater, flying helmet and goggles; a white and brown silk scarf (for elegance), and a very necessary heavy fur-lined flying suit borrowed from a friend, Major Charles H. Wooley of Boston who was unaware of the true reason for Amelia's borrowing it.

Her small knapsack contained a toothbrush and comb, two handkerchiefs and a tube of cold cream; Layman lent his camera and George lent his ex-Arctic binoculars; besides that a small log book, an autographed copy of *Skyward* that Amelia had promised to deliver by hand to Amy Guest, and some personal messages to be delivered by hand from those associated with the mission, comprised all her luggage.[9]

Amelia made a will listing her possessions. Her car, a US Treasury Bond and some shares in the Kinner Airplane and Denison Airport Companies would, if sold, pay off some of her debts – which totalled about two thousand dollars – and provide a small sum for her mother. The accompanying letter was wistful in tone:

> This is hardly a will, for I leave no appreciable estate . . . my regret is that I leave just now. In a few years I feel I could have laid by something substantial for so many new things were opening for me . . . *Selah*[10]

To GP she entrusted letters addressed to her parents to be given to them in the event that she did not return:

May 20, 1928

Dearest Dad
Hooray for the last grand adventure! I wish I had won but it was worth while anyway. You know that.

I have no faith that we'll meet anywhere again, but I wish we might.

>   Anyway, goodbye, and good luck to you.
>   Affectionately, your doter
>   Mill[11]

and to her mother:

> ... Even though I have lost, the adventure was worth while. Our family tends to be too secure. My life has really been very happy, and I don't mind contemplating its end in the midst of it ...[12]

Apart from her fiancé, Sam, and her employer Marion Perkins, Amelia confided in almost no one from her immediate circle. Even her mother and sister were excluded from the secret, though there were also two unnamed friends who were invited to attend the *Friendship*'s departure.[13] It was to be Sam's job to tell the family personally, the moment the *Friendship* left Boston.

George tried to get preparations for Amelia's story of the trip under way but in Amelia he had met his match. Fitzhugh Green, then working as George's staff ghost-writer, recalls a meeting between the two:

> I thought I had Lindbergh in my office, but it was Earhart. The likeness was astonishing. Tall slimness, fresh colouring. Blue eyes flashed a Lindbergh grin of white teeth [and the] resemblance did not stop at being physical. 'Now', said businessman George P. Putnam, 'we'd better line up the film people don't you think?'
> 'No.' said Amelia.
> 'Then why not let's get the book into focus?'
> 'Because I haven't made the flight yet.'
> 'But heavens woman, don't you want to arrange the business end of this now?'
> 'No.'
> It wasn't a 'NO!', or a 'no, no'; nor even a 'nope'.

'No.' Just that smiling sort of 'no' that Lindbergh followers know so well.[14]

In fairness to George Putnam and his team, who have been accused of manufacturing this supposed likeness of Amelia to Charles Lindbergh, the comments of Lindbergh's wife, Ann, in a letter to her family after meeting Amelia in 1930, are illuminating:

> The biggest surprise, though, was Amelia Earhart, who was here the first four days. She is the most amazing person – just as tremendous as C, I think. It startles me how much alike they are . . . C doesn't realize it, but he hasn't talked to her as much. She has the clarity of mind, impersonal eye, coolness of temperament, balance of a scientist.[15]

It had been agreed that Hilton Railey would leave almost immediately for London to make preparations to welcome Amelia upon her arrival, and Amelia spent some time at the Railey home working on a biographical sketch that Railey could give to reporters there. Railey's wife Julia found herself in sympathy with Amelia's frustrated cry: 'But I don't know *how* to make myself interesting to order! School – college – war nursing – social work – a couple of planes of my own and a little flying – what more can I say? what is there to say?'

Julia and Amelia (both were social workers and felt they had something in common) went off to dinner together:

> At the curb we climbed into the worst-looking automobile I ever saw, bar none. Its rear end was cigar-shaped and its ground colour a sick canary. She said she had it in California, it was secondhand to begin with and five years old. People got out of the way of it I noticed. [We] scudded through the traffic like a car possessed [and] with something like a flourish drew up at last at 'The Old France' restaurant.[16]

Over dinner Julia told Amelia something of George's impressive history which could only have enhanced the attraction Amelia already felt for him.

The weather continued unsuitable until early June and during this time Stultz and Gordon had managed to make a few test hops in Boston. When the weather was clear in Boston fog surrounded their destination in Newfoundland; when it was clear in Newfoundland they could not take off from Boston. Amelia fretted about the use of floats, receiving conflicting advice as to their usefulness. While they might enable them to make a forced landing at sea, they would make the original take-off considerably more difficult.

Virtually all record-breaking aviators have written with emotion about the waiting period before take-off. Many found it the most difficult part of their enterprise. It was certainly so for the crew of the *Friendship*. To kill time, George and Amelia often visited Richard Byrd's Boston home where Amelia took a great interest in the preparations for the Antarctic venture. In contrast to Amelia's own meagre supplies the house was filled with provisions and equipment. She would not, she said, have been surprised to see a team of huskies harnessed to a sled. Sometimes she met with Stultz and Gordon to go over flight plans and charts.[17]

Her friendship with George grew daily. By now she had started calling him by a nickname, 'Simpkin', in their private moments together (it was to be many years before he discovered the reason). It was already obvious to her that George's attentions were somewhat more than were necessary for the sake of the project and, despite her own attraction to him, Amelia clearly fielded any passes by saying that she had Sam to consider. For his part George was very attracted to Amelia but perhaps even more than any romantic reason he saw the challenge of real fame. 'It wasn't so much that he was romancing her,' said a friend, 'as that he was romancing a property.'[18]

On Sunday 3 June the weather was ideal; enough wind to lift them off the water and reports of clear skies all the way to Newfoundland. A small party consisting of the crew, George, Robert Elmer (technical adviser), some cameramen and sundry others left the Copley Plaza Hotel at 4.30 a.m. and boarded the tug

Sadie Ross on 'T-Wharf' for 'a fishing trip'.[19] Actually, they headed across the harbour towards the Jeffrey Yacht Club in East Boston where the *Friendship* was moored.

Sam Chapman, Marion Perkins and two other close friends of Amelia's joined the party, aboard another tug. It was the third such trip in as many days and the mood was relaxed rather than tense. Who knew if the whole thing would simply be another rehearsal? They loaded vacuum flasks of coffee and sandwiches aboard the aeroplane, and George had 'carefully provided' a small supply of oranges.[20]

The wind created a light ripple on the water as Stultz held the aeroplane into the wind and opened the throttles but, as Amelia wrote in her log, 'the drag of the pontoons held us down'. In fact the plane hardly got up onto the steps of the pontoons. They off-loaded six five-gallon cans of gasoline – of the eight they carried for emergency – and tried again, unsuccessfully. The 180 lbs they had gained in dumping the fuel was not enough. They tried two further runs of greater distance without unsticking. Without saying a word Lou Gower, knowing what was necessary, quietly collected his flying suit and the small personal package that was the sum of his luggage. George and Elmer came alongside in a launch and took Gower off. That made the difference. It took 67 seconds to lift the *Friendship* off the water and head north.

Although there was no fog, a light haze and blinding sun made visibility poor. By the time they reached Halifax, a flight of 410 miles, they ran into thick fog and were forced to land. They took off an hour later planning to follow the coastline but the fog was too thick so they returned to spend the night.

In her personal diary for that night Amelia wrote, '12 pm. Two reporters and camera men are in the next room trying to persuade Stultz and G. to dress and have a flashlight picture taken. I am displeased with their thortlessness [sic] in keeping the men awake and am dropping things in my room to make the men realize I am still awake and disapproving. I don't know whether the newspaper men know I'm here so I am not shouting my sentiments . . .'

News of their flight had preceded them and when they sat down to breakfast they read about themselves. Reading the quotes from her mother, Amelia realised how hurt Amy must have been and how worried she must be now. She sent her a telegram explaining why she couldn't tell her and asking her not to worry. Next day – despite attentions from local pressmen – they were able to get away reasonably early and reached Trepassey by mid-afternoon on 4 June.

As soon as they left Boston the story had broken. Sam had not even reached the Earhart home at Medford before reporters laid siege to Mrs Earhart and Muriel. They knew nothing of the flight, of course, but were able to provide pictures of Amelia as a child and tell of her history. They must have felt bewildered, perhaps even cheated, until Sam arrived to give them Amelia's personal message.

It would be unreasonable to suppose that George had not broken the story, given his record in publicity. Now that the crew were – to all intents and purposes – beyond the reach of newspapermen, he wanted as much hype as he could muster as part of his overall strategy. Lindbergh had been beyond his grasp but with Amelia he must have thought he could control one of the most important news stories – and its aftermath – this century. Some were unkind enough to suggest that this wasn't so much of a story after all. George paid scant attention; if necessary, he knew he could *make* it the most important story. Not all newspapers received the story with unalloyed pleasure, nor fell for the 'Miss Lindy' tag in his press releases, and one editorialised bitchily:

> By manipulation of pictures and publicity, Amelia Earhart, the Boston girl who is crossing the Atlantic with Wilmer Stultz, is to be made a feminine Lindbergh, unless plans go awry. The stunt is financed by George Palmer Putnam, publisher of *We* who now plans a similar book, it is understood, called *She* . . . Amelia Earhart has been in training, coached by the promoters, to emulate Lindbergh in every respect, in attitude, pictures and behaviour.[21]

Unfortunately, far from 'crossing the Atlantic', once at Trepassey the flyers were effectively trapped. Successive days of gales or fog meant they could not attempt to take off. At first they were only mildly disappointed and Gordon used the time to make repairs to the oil tank, which had developed a crack, while Stultz tinkered with the radio. On the fourth day of frustration they attempted a take-off but the wind increased and the water became too rough. In the days that followed they passed the time by playing cards and looking around Trepassey. It was cold and uninviting and all three became dispirited.

They had only one aviation map with them, Bill Stultz's chart of the North Atlantic and on this map, each day, they outlined the series of fronts and storms cabled to them from the Met Office via George. Amelia called in at the local convent school and persuaded the nuns to lend her some geography books with maps and a large globe and she pored over these in an attempt to help pass the time.[22]

Her mood was lifted briefly by a telegram from GP who, knowing she had no change of clothes with her, wired SUGGEST YOU GO INTO RETIREMENT TEMPORARILY WITH NUNS AND HAVE THEM WASH SHIRT ETC.[23] to which she replied THANKS FATHERLY TELEGRAM NO WASHING NECESSARY SOCKS WORN OUT SHORT LOST TO SLIM AT RUMMY CHEERIO A.E.[24] As a matter of fact, personal hygiene was becoming a problem to all three crew members who had to borrow clothes while their own were washed. Amelia did spend 35 cents on a pair of hose, and a khaki shirt was another purchase. It was far too big but she took a tuck in at the back with a safety pin.[25]

Amelia continued to make faithful entries each night in the diary that George had given her. Written in pencil in her untidy scrawl she recorded after a week:

I got a wire from M.P. [Marion Perkins] asking permission to publish one of my poems . . . as the subject was 'courage'. I refused as I know the luck it would bring forth. Anyway I can't remember whether I liked it. [Note: despite Amelia's refusal the poem was published in an article by Marion Perkins.]

After a week of waiting there seemed, on the evening of 11 June, to be favourable conditions. Stultz wired George advising an attempted take-off next morning and asking for full Atlantic weather conditions. Next morning he confirmed their intentions and received from George a reasonable weather report. But the wire also carried bad news: MABEL STARTED SEVEN AM ALLEGEDLY FOR HARBOUR GRACE STOP BYRD BELIEVES 900 GALLONS AMPLE FOR FRIENDSHIP . . .

Mabel Boll, also known variously as the 'Queen of Diamonds' and Senora Hernando Rocha-Schioos, was making a strong challenge to be the first woman across the ocean, in the single-engined *Columbia* (now suitably renamed *Miss Columbia*) which had formerly carried Clarence Chamberlain and his crew safely across the Atlantic (to Germany), setting a distance record.[26] In March Stultz had piloted her and showman Charles A. Levine on the first nonstop flight from New York to Havana, Cuba. Already planning her transatlantic attempt she claimed to have hired Stultz for her project for a reputed sum of $25,000 and thought he had accepted.[27] What becomes clear, however, is that Dick Byrd had talked Stultz into accepting that the Earhart flight was the more likely to succeed. The fee offered was the same in both cases. Before making up his mind, and without telling the Guest–Putnam consortium of his plan, Stultz met Mabel Boll in New York. What happened at that meeting is unknown, though Stultz obviously revealed nothing of the alternative project despite the great pressure placed on him to contract to the Mabel Boll camp. Later he declared he had opted out because the entire enterprise smacked of the circus and unprofessionalism (Chamberlain had much the same to say about Levine's participation in the successful flight to Europe).

The thwarted Miss Boll signed World War I flying aces Oliver C. Le Boutillier and Captain Arthur Argles as her crew, and the publicity-conscious Levine backed the venture. Mabel Boll allegedly wore sweaters woven of pure gold and, with her dark eyes, vividly blonde hair and tempestuous Latin temperament, she made good newspaper copy.[28] She was undoubtedly a threat to the *Friendship*'s more sober venture, and her flight could only have increased the frustration and sense of entrapment felt by the three crew members.

In all their minds must have been the fact that, with *Miss Columbia's* conventional undercarriage, Miss Boll could take off in any fine weather, whereas they had also to contend with sea conditions.

On the morning of 12 June George sent three detailed weather forecasts spaced an hour apart, and with these in mind Stultz tried for four hours to take the *Friendship* off. Unfortunately, as Amelia recorded in her daily log:

> This has been the worst day . . . the receding tide made the sea so heavy that the spray was thrown so high that it drowned the outboard motors. As we gathered speed, the motors would cut and we'd lose the precious pull necessary . . . we unloaded every ounce of stuff from the plane – camera, my coat, bags, cushions etc. She would have gone but for the motors. There was salt water above the prop. hubs.
>
> I received some letters today and . . . 'day after the take-off' paper in Boston. I couldn't read them under the circumstances of this day. We are all too disappointed to talk. The boys are in bed and I am going soon. We rise at six.[29]

With the letters and papers came a further cable from George advising that Mabel Boll was due imminently at Harbour Grace, Newfoundland, and had announced that she would start for London early next morning; commenting on Stultz's intention to try again on the following day he said: HOPE YOU MAKE IT AT DAYLIGHT . . . BYRD AFTER CAREFUL RECKONING BELIEVES EIGHT HUNDRED SEVENTY GALLONS AMPLE IF TAKEOFF WEIGHT ESSENTIAL.[30]

Stultz wired back querying Byrd's calculations on fuel and received back a startled: WIRE RECEIVED STOP IT SAID SIX HUNDRED GALLONS PRESUME SHOULD READ EIGHT HUNDRED WHICH BYRD SAYS PROBABLY SAFE ALTHOUGH 830 PREFERABLE . . . More advice from non-pilot Byrd followed regarding take-off time and landing points.[31]

Given that Stultz would have taken off in the middle of the night if he could have lifted *Friendship* off the water, this advice must have made him grind his teeth, but he wired Byrd in a friendly manner and received back THANKS MESSAGE HARD LUCK IF NOT TOO ROUGH SUGGEST MIGHT GO OUTSIDE FOR TAKEOFF STOP YOUR SUCCESS MEANS MUCH TO ME STAY WITH IT COOPERATING PUTNAM HER REGARDS ALL HANDS BYRD.[32]

Amelia, meanwhile, had her own problems. On reading the 'day after take-off from Boston' papers she found her private telegram to her mother openly, and widely, quoted. Furious at the breach of privacy and no doubt over-reacting due to frustration and disappointment she fired off a 'blistering' letter to her sister before joining the men for another take-off attempt. Even worse, she suspected that Bill Stultz had turned to drinking heavily, his answer to the frustration and boredom.

The boys went after bad booze and got it last night. They had to push the [automobile] for eight miles because the belt broke. They arrived home about six o'clock tired but with happy memories. I could choke Frazer. It doesn't matter whether he drinks but it certainly does whether my gang do . . . I am not easy now as the men are all together in [the landlord's] room and have been for more than an hour. It is so important that Stultz's judgement be good in the crisis . . .

That evening, Wednesday 13 June 1928, it was a thoroughly disheartened crew who returned from yet another day of fruitless effort. 'The days grow worse,' Amelia wrote in her log. 'I think each time we have reached the low, but find we haven't . . . Today Bill and Slim tried to take her off after she had been degassed by 300 lbs. The left motor cut and they couldn't get her off light . . .'[33] They arrived back to find a cable from George suggesting they consider the Azores as a possible destination. This would enable them to lighten the load yet more.

The evening cable from George read . . . IF IN MORNING YOU CAN POSSIBLY TAKE OFF EVEN MINIMUM GAS IRELAND FAR BEST BET STOP SUGGEST TRY TAKEOFF AWAY FROM HILLS . . . IF THIS FAILS REDUCE [GAS] AND GO FOR AZORES STOP IF AZORES SURELY NOTIFY

ME SO ARRANGE GAS WEATHER REPORTS . . . STOPS PROBLEM THERE NAVIGATION DANGER MISSING ISLANDS HOPE YOU HAVE SEXTANT FOR OBSERVATION SENDING RADIO POSITION IF FORCED DOWN STOP MABEL SENDS WORD HERE NO START TOMORROW STOP WEATHER REPORT BOTH FOR IRELAND AND AZORES TEN PM DARN SORRY BUT YOU WILL EMERGE ON TOP WE ALL KNOW YOU ARE DOING YOUR BEST.[34] All cables had so far been between Stultz and various members of the management team. Mrs Guest was obviously worried about this for that evening a wire arrived for Amelia from Layman asking for her personal confidential report on the situation particularly as to the fuel capacity and a possible change of destination. Amelia's reply is lost but Putnam subsequently wired Railey in London BEG CHIEF NOT WORRY SHIP OK DECREASING LOAD HAVE ANNOUNCED OUR PLANS UNINFLUENCED COMPETITION MUST PROCEED PATIENTLY.[35] And, a day or so later, to Stultz: CONFIDENTIAL GUEST SAYS ACCOUNT WEIGHT DIFFICULTY TAKEOFF IF YOU COULD CONSIDER LEAVING SLIM WHO WOULD BE PAID AS AGREED EYE IMAGINE IMPRACTICAL ACCEPT YOUR JUDGEMENT . . .[36]

Since Stultz would be fully occupied flying the *Friendship* and Amelia had not the necessary ability or experience to navigate the Atlantic this was a specious suggestion, to say the least. Perhaps to convince himself that it was possible to fly from Trepassey at all, Stultz pumped out 135 gallons of fuel (810 lbs) and made a 34-minute test flight.[37] Then, bad weather kept the plane moored at the buoy for another three days and in that time the only good news was word that the *Southern Cross* had successfully crossed the Pacific Ocean from San Francisco to Australia via Hawaii. This was an identical airplane to the *Friendship*, except that she had a conventional undercarriage instead of pontoons.

In a confidential cable to Amelia (the date of which is not decipherable) George suggested: . . . FOR OCCUPATION MIGHT WRITE SKELETON THOUSAND WORD STORY FLIGHT THUS FAR HALIFAX TREPASSEY WITH NAMES DETAILS TO ENLARGE HERE AFTER YOU UNDER WAY JUST SAVE PRESSURE CABLE TOLLS OTHER END ADDRESS QUOTE NIGHT PRESS COLLECT TIMES FOR PUTNAM . . . MRS GUEST

SENDS LOVE EYE DITTO SAM PERMITTING OR OTHERWISE THINK OF
FRESH WARDROBE IN LONDON AND GRIN. SIMKIN [*sic*].[38]

In truth there was precious little to grin about. Apart from the
frustrations and tedium Amelia was concerned by Stultz's increasing
drinking. At one point she considered wiring George to send Gower
as a replacement pilot, but as George was later to write, 'AE was a
scrupulously fair person and she knew that she could not do that
without great damage to Stultz; knew also that any such last-minute
switch might well bring the whole project tumbling down about
her.'[39] Stultz was quite simply the best there was and although
barely twenty-eight, his experience was vast. In Amelia's mind, too,
may have been the suspicion that if she appealed to Putnam and
Layman to replace Stultz, they might have thought she was merely
looking for a way out, having lost her nerve.

Nothing could have been further from reality. For days she had
been trying to persuade Stultz to take a chance and set off for
Ireland or the Azores. She pleaded with both men but Stultz would
not make an attempt to take off with unfavourable conditions forecast. She pointed out the competition and the fact that 'thousands
[of dollars] were tied up in the project'. But Stultz would not be
moved and Amelia turned to lecturing them about drinking less and
sleeping more.

On 16 June her nightly diary entry is despairing: 'Just now the
boys are at Paddy Mortons and I know liquor flows . . . they went
on a walk this afternoon and had some then. I shall get them home
at nine or know the reason. I loathe watching men. Why can't they
be more responsible? . . . There is a madness about Bill which is not
in keeping with a pilot who has to fly.'

On the following morning, 17 June, after more than twelve days
of waiting, the weather and tide were suddenly all set fair – or reasonably so. Unfortunately, Stultz had drunk heavily the night before
and was hungover. Gordon and Amelia spent some hours pouring
black coffee into their pilot and finally 'she knew the start had to be
made then or probably never. So she simply got hold of her pilot
and all but dragged him to the 'plane'.[40]

At 11.15 a.m. after two abortive attempts to get off in the heavy sea the crew agreed upon a desperate solution. Realising that even with the forecast favourable tailwinds they were leaving no margin for error they pumped out further fuel, and with 700 gallons remaining, taxied out to try again.[41] It is easy to recognise the desperation of Amelia and Lou Gordon which made them continue in the face of these setbacks. Amelia later confided to GP that that hour seemed to her to be the most dangerous of her life, and certainly the most dangerous of the flight. She had simply trusted that Stultz's flying instinct, which was so inherent in him, would take over.[42]

The first run was aborted because the spray-soaked engines were spluttering too badly to give sufficient power. On the second run they were able to reach the required speed of just over 50 miles an hour, and staggered into the air after 'a desperate take-off run of almost three miles'[43] despite the fact that the two wing-mounted engines were still spluttering from a thorough soaking in salt-water spray – one so wet it was an hour into the flight before it achieved full power.[44]

With little optimism Amelia had left a cable to be sent to George 30 minutes after their departure. It said simply VIOLET STOP CHEERIO. This was the coded signal to George that they had, in truth, left. Only a few villagers saw them off for there had been so many unsuccessful attempts that the majority had lost faith in the aviators, as had many American newspapers who criticised the crew, particularly Amelia, for a seeming reluctance to get going.

CHAPTER 12

1928

EARHART PLANE SOARING OVER ATLANTIC; REPORTED NEARLY HALF WAY TO IRELAND EIGHT HOURS AFTER LEAVING TREPASSEY was how the readers of the *New York Times* learned, on the morning of 18 June 1928, that Amelia and her two companions had departed at last. Take-off was at 2.51 p.m. British Summer Time (Amelia's log recorded 10.51 a.m. Boston time).

As the *Friendship* passed Cape Race at 5.20 p.m. (BST), Lou Gordon transmitted two radio messages, one for George Putnam: OUT OF FOG NOW CLEAR WEATHER and the other to Bill Stultz's wife . . . EVERYTHING GOING FINE.[1] Reports of satisfactory progress filtered in from ships' radios en route; the *Friendship*'s call sign WOX and transmission wavelength of 600 metres had been well publicised for two weeks. Some ships had made radio contact without seeing the aeroplane, some had heard the engines but had been unable to make contact on the radio.[2]

Back at Harbour Grace, Mabel Boll protested that she had not been given the same weather reports as Amelia and thus had been unable to make the decision to get away. In fact she was correct. Although her reports were issued from the same source she was receiving merely the standard transatlantic weather reports put out by 'Doc' Kimball at the Met Office and aimed at shipping. But George, alert to the fact that the weather was such a key factor in the success or failure of the venture, had arranged to pay for special reports tailored to the flyers' needs. Miss Boll wisely decided to sit and wait. If the *Friendship* was unsuccessful, the *Miss Columbia* would have a clear field free of other contestants.

The clear spell of weather did not last and Amelia and her companions were soon in thick cloud again. While the two men occupied the cockpit seats, Amelia sat in the empty main cabin, squeezed between two large fuel tanks to take advantage of any warm air blown back from the cockpit and perched on the three flying suits, since all extraneous items such as cushions had been left behind. Immediately, she started making entries in an informal log book, her often untidy quick scrawl made worse on this occasion by vibration. There was, in truth, little to write about beyond her observations of clouds and fog but she recorded items she thought might later be of interest. '. . . We have only the small Thermos filled with coffee for the boys. I shan't drink anything probably,' she wrote with irony, 'unless we come down'. And later: '4000 feet. More than three tons of us are hurtling through the air. We are in the storm now. Three tons is shaken considerably.'[3]

They made contact with a British ship, the *Rexmore*, towards the evening which gave them a bearing and promised to inform N.Y. of their position; and Bill managed to get several fixes through the patchy fog before the sun went down. After that, all Amelia could see through the one cabin window was 'glowing meteors' from the exhausts. 'I think I am happy,' she wrote at this point, '[a] sad admission of scant intellectual equipment.'[4]

Amelia continued to make log-book entries after dark, using her left thumb to mark the starting point of each line. They were never entirely clear of fog, but now and again they were able to catch glimpses of the sea and at last, as the fuel was used up and the load lightened, they were able to gain sufficient height to climb to 5,000 feet; 6,000 feet; and finally at 10,000 feet they were over the massed, lumpy cumulus that made flying so uncomfortable. It was extremely cold at that height, and all three donned fur-lined flying suits and, striving to keep alert, watched for the first welcome sight of dawn. Amelia spent a short time in the cockpit when Slim went aft to the chart table; but conditions were always too rough for her to take the controls and she spent most of the time in her cabin, sometimes with her nose pressed against the small window, ear-plugs in place to prevent being deafened. As the night wore on she developed a bad headache and slept for half an hour to relieve it.

When light came Stultz decided to lose some height. He hoped that the favourable tail winds might mean a fast passage and in that case they ought to be able to see Ireland before too long. Amelia's log book entry read:

> We are going down, probably . . . going through. Fog is lower here too, haven't hit it yet but will so far as I can see from the back window . . . Everything shut out. Instrument Flying. Slow descent, first. It takes a lot to make my ears hurt. 5000 feet now. Awfully wet. Water dripping in window. Port motor coughing. Sounds as if all motors are cutting. Bill opens her wide to try to clear. Sounds rotten on the right . . . [5]

In her book, *20 Hrs. 40 Min.*, Amelia frankly admitted that she was afraid at this point. At 3,000 feet they broke into patchy clouds and could see the sea again, but the radio appeared to be dead and they could not raise an answer. The port engine continued to give trouble and they were all quietly aware that only two hours of fuel remained. At any time they expected to see land and lines of dark cloud lying on the horizon several times deceived their straining eyesight into thinking they *could* see it. By all calculations the coast of Ireland ought to have been in sight anytime within the last hour.

By accident Amelia discovered a bottle of spirits, smuggled aboard by Stultz and hidden in the tool bag. She agonised at first about what to do, finally moving it to a new hiding place. Perhaps the memory of her father's violent reaction when she had emptied *his* bottle down the drain, all those years ago, came back to her. But Stultz never came looking for the bottle – he was fully occupied and had no need of artificial stimuli.

Just before 8 a.m. (BST) and in a state of grave anxiety about their position, the three flyers saw several ships cutting across their course which, though a welcome sight, perplexed them. Surely the ships should be steaming a course parallel to their own? The radio was still useless. After discussion they decided to stay on course, though by now they were down to an hour's fuel supply.

Another ship, the ocean-going liner SS *America* (though they were unable to identify it at the time), passed some miles away and they detoured, using up precious fuel, to circle over it while Amelia scribbled a note, tied it around one of the 'Boston bought' oranges and bombed the ship. The missile missed, as did a subsequent attempt. The ship made no obvious attempt to signal the aeroplane. Amelia and her companions discussed whether they should land alongside then, while they could be certain of rescue and/or refuelling, but abandoned the idea because the sea was so rough they knew they would never get off again. At last they decided to fly on.

Unknown to the flyers the captain had just given an instruction to paint the ship's position on the deck in large white letters but the *Friendship* flew off before this could be done. Amelia took a photograph of the liner and they retraced the twelve miles to the original course. The ceiling dropped to below 500 feet and all they could see was grey mist as the *Friendship* droned on with its crew in a state of silent, mounting anxiety.

After half an hour, what must have seemed to them an interminable period of time, they saw a fishing boat; and then several more; a fleet of them! And all going in the same direction as the *Friendship*.

Another hour passed before, out of the mists, a shadow – hardly darker at first than the mist, but gradually becoming bluer – claimed their riveted attention. It was land. Slim, who had nervously started to nibble a sandwich yelled with relief and tossed his snack out of the window. Even Bill permitted himself a smile.

They flew over several small islands and followed the coastline in an easterly direction trying to match the coastline to their charts. They were over a huge bay which narrowed into an estuary offering sheltered landing conditions from the big seas running in the bay. The tide was out and large sandbanks were exposed but there was a smooth patch of water beside a small town and, knowing that their fuel was almost exhausted, Stultz decided to land.

They had no idea where they were. They assumed it was Ireland,[6] but in the relief and delight at having made a landfall their chief concern was to taxi to a buoy and tie up. They opened the door in the side of the aeroplane and peered out through thin veils of rain. Slim dropped down onto a pontoon and made the plane fast to a mooring buoy. They could see houses and factories behind the muddy beach. There were three men working on a railroad track and to them they waved and yelled:

Finally they noticed us, straightened up and even went so far as to walk down to the shore and look us over. Then their animation died out and they went back to their work. The *Friendship* simply wasn't interesting. An itinerant trans-Atlantic plane meant nothing.[7]

After a while a few people gathered on the beach but the aviators' shouts raised no answer. Amelia tried waving a towel, and one 'friendly soul' took off his coat and waved back. It was almost an hour before the first boats came out. At low tide it is a long row from the dock where the nearest available rowing boat was kept. At this stage the crew of the *Friendship* were still anticipating refuelling in order to fly on to their intended destination, Southampton.[8] A check of their fuel tanks while they waited revealed that there was nearly 50 gallons remaining which for practical purposes meant the supply was exhausted because of the gravity feed fuel supply; indeed Stultz later told reporters that fuel had already ceased to flow to the carburetters on the landing run. Amelia recorded:

I wish now I had cheered the first boat that came alongside. It was a most ordinary greeting that they gave us. One man in the boat [called out] 'Ship Ahoy!' He asked what we needed. Stultz leaned out of the window and said we had flown across the Atlantic.[9]

The fliers learned to their surprise that they had landed at Burry Port, a small town in South Wales, and not Ireland as they had assumed.

This accounted for the ships crossing their track; at that point they had been flying over the Irish Sea, having flown south of Ireland. Bill Stultz went ashore in a dory to contact Railey, send radio messages to George Putnam and organise refuelling so that they could carry on to their original destination, Southampton. Amelia, meanwhile, exchanged greetings with the occupants of the small fleet of boats which had begun to swarm around the aeroplane. But to all requests for information about the flight she said nothing.

After a few hours, Railey arrived by seaplane from Southampton accompanied by *New York Times* journalist Allen Raymond and they were taken out to the *Friendship*. Stultz decided that it was too dangerous to attempt a take-off against the flooding riptide so the *Friendship* was moved to a sheltered mooring in the town's harbour while Amelia and Lou Gordon were taken ashore.

The inhabitants of Burry Port made up for the slow reaction to the arrival of the aviators. All through the afternoon, word had passed from mouth to mouth and now, determined to make up for their lack of welcome, a huge crowd gathered, its numbers swollen to 2,000 or more by visitors from nearby Llanelli.

Amelia had tied her silk scarf bandana-style over her head and as she climbed the steps of the harbour a hand reached out and pulled it off. She looked around in surprise but could not see who had taken it. It was to be the first of many such incidents. Enthusiasm was such that the police escort were hard pressed to keep their charges on their feet and the High Sheriff of Carmarthen joined with the town's three policemen and a few friends to form a ring with locked arms to escort Amelia from the harbour to the Ashburnham Hotel.

After welcome hot baths came the first interviews by squads of reporters who 'gleefully' informed Amelia that she was being called 'Lady Lindy'. Amelia had her revenge, to some extent. Railey told them all that her story had been sold in advance to the *New York Times* and she was prepared to answer only the most general questions. Consequently many stories were filed describing her likes and dislikes in clothes and make-up. 'She would rather read than eat, rather sit on the floor than on a chair, rather fence[10] than play bridge, rather drive her car than any of these . . . When asked if she ever thought of giving up the flight she replied: Never! I thought all this out in the first five minutes and I knew I wanted to go . . . because I love life and all it has to offer. I want every opportunity and adventure it can give, and I could never welch on one of them.'[11]

Later she spent some hours with Allen Raymond, recounting her story and showing him her log of the flight. Then while Amelia went off to her hotel Raymond occupied a typewriter at the office of a local factory for most of the night. 'As he finished each sheet the local policeman was waiting to take it by car to be wired by the General Post Office at Llanelli.'[12]

The three flyers managed to get five or six hours sleep before awakening to a sackful of congratulatory telegrams, one from President Coolidge expressing: TO YOU THE FIRST WOMAN SUCCESS-FULLY TO SPAN THE NORTH ATLANTIC BY AIR THE GREAT ADMIRATION OF MYSELF AND THE UNITED STATES . . .

At eleven o'clock they took off in the light rain and skeins of mist for Southampton. Stultz had hoped for the escort of an Imperial Airways flying boat to Southampton but engine trouble had prevented it taking off, so he decided to fly to Southampton accompanied by the seaplane chartered by Railey and Allen Raymond. It was unfortunate that they could not have waited 15 minutes longer. Unknown to them Sir Arthur Whitten-Brown, famous for his part in the first successful non-stop crossing of the Atlantic Ocean with Sir John Alcock, was being rowed out to the *Friendship*. The plane took off almost as he reached it and a dramatic moment was lost.

Burry Port, its brief period of fame over, subsided once again into comfortable obscurity. Two years later its citizens subscribed to a commemorative monument celebrating the day when *Friendship* put the name of their town on the front pages of newspapers in cities across the world. The plaque, unveiled by Sir Arthur Whitten-Brown, reveals a small mystery for it cites the duration of the flight as being '20 Hrs 49 Min'. Yet the official time was later given as 20 hours 40 minutes; it is recorded as such in the record books and Amelia subsequently named her book *20 Hrs. 40 Mins*. Amelia's log book, however, recorded that the *Friendship* took off from Trepassey at 10.51 a.m., EST (2.51 p.m. Sunday, BST) and landed at 7.40 a.m., (12.40 p.m. Monday BST) and therefore 20 hours 49 minutes would seem to be the correct figure. The plaque is still in place today in Burry Port's leafy Felindan Square, showing that time.[13]

As the *Friendship* approached Southampton, an Imperial Airways Sea Eagle flew out to meet the flyers and guide them in through the low cloud over Southampton Water. A green light from a Very pistol signalled the *Friendship*'s landing run and this time she had hardly finished taxiing when the launches were snapping at her heels. First to greet the aviators were Amy Guest and her son Raymond.

Meanwhile the story of the successful crossing had been flashed around the world. George had syndicated the stories cabled 'in Amelia's own words', and they made front pages throughout the USA, generating an enormous interest in the fact that a woman had flown the Atlantic. Amelia told how delighted she was to have made the crossing, and explained that most of the journey had been flown blind . . .

> I was a passenger on the journey – just a passenger. Everything that was done to bring us across was done by Wilmer Stultz and Slim Gordon. Any praise I can give them they ought to have. You can't pile it on too thick . . . I did not handle the controls once, although I have had more than 500 hours solo flying and once held the women's altitude record. I do not believe that women lack the stamina to do a solo trip across the Atlantic, but it would be a matter of learning the arts of flying by instruments only, an art which few men pilots know perfectly now . . .[14]

Edwin Earhart had been tracked down in Los Angeles and, interviewed at great length, he unwittingly revealed his hurt at being left out of his daughter's plans: 'When I first discovered she was [learning to fly] I told her I was strongly against it, but that was all I could do in the circumstances. That was about 1921 . . .' 'Amelia,' he continued, 'had had every advantage that money could provide for a person . . . she had a remarkable mind but her remarkable scholastic ability was not due so much to an unusually brilliant mentality as to the fact that she had never had any financial worries or other such distractions. Why she is making the trip I am at a loss to explain . . . I can't see that it will aid the science of flying . . .' He went on to talk more generously about Amelia's love of adventure, however. 'She has ridden horses all her life and once in Toronto she won a prize to any man or woman who could ride a certain outlaw horse at a fair. She rode it even though she was almost killed in the process . . .'[15]

George Putnam had spent the past 20-odd hours in a state of anxiety. He tried unsuccessfully to work and instead paced the floor at his home in Rye, jumping each time the telephone rang. Often it was a reporter seeking the latest news. There were six ships' radio reports in the first five hours followed by silence for more than four hours before the British steamer *Elmworth* heard 'barely audible wireless signals' on 600 metres. This was followed by another five hours' radio silence until just after midnight when Mr Battison of Cambridge, Massachusetts heard a fragmentary message that they 'were about half way across'. A further seven hours were to drift by with no further word.

When at last George could stand the waiting no longer he went to the *New York Times* offices to await any news of the *Friendship*'s arrival. The SS *America*'s sighting of the aeroplane some 75 miles south-east of Queenstown, Ireland, was the first news to come through on the tickertape. The relief at knowing that the flyers had made it safely across the ocean and were within striking distance of land must have been enormous, but George was suddenly too busy to record his own reactions. He started by drafting a cable to Railey, instructing him what to do on Amelia's arrival, and went to work with a reporter to draft the headline story for the next edition of the *Times*. It was nearly two hours later that the news of the safe landing was transmitted and one of his first actions was to send word to Amelia's family.

It genuinely distressed Amelia to see Stultz and Gordon ignored by the reporters and she continually attempted to bring them forward into the limelight, to no avail. It was the woman they had come to see; or rather 'the girl' as they insisted on calling her. She insisted that Raymond send back a story in Stultz's own words. This was published in the *New York Times* underneath Amelia's story, but it changed nothing. It was Amelia the press wanted to talk to, wanted to write about, and whom the crowds came to see. Even President Coolidge had cabled his personal congratulations addressed to Amelia, to which she replied THE CREW OF THE FRIENDSHIP DESIRE TO EXPRESS THEIR DEEP APPRECIATION OF YOUR EXCELLENCY'S GRA-CIOUS MESSAGE STOP SUCCESS ENTIRELY DUE GREAT SKILL OF MR STULTZ STOP HE WAS ONLY ONE MILE OFF VALENCIA AFTER FLYING BLIND FOR TWO THOUSAND FORTY SIX MILES AT AVERAGE SPEED ONE HUNDRED THIRTEEN MPH AMELIA EARHART.[16] George was later to write that in his opinion Amelia had persistently attributed the credit to Stultz so much because she was moved that he had accomplished 'a perfect job in the face of personal, as well as aeronautical odds'.[17] She had personal knowledge of the devastating effect of alcoholism.

A triumphal procession took place to Southampton's South Western Hotel, known to countless sea-going transatlantic passengers, where, dressed in the only clothes she had with her – a beige sweater, white shirt and red tie with dark breeches and black boots – she took tea and tried, a little shyly, to cope with the multitude of questions from the press.[18] Over the next few days hundreds of thousands of column inches would be written about her, a lot of it pure invention; that she had undertaken the flight to redeem a mortgage on her family home; that she had been racing Mabel Boll, etc. Hilton Railey was always at her side and she looked to him constantly for help when things got out of hand.

From Southampton Amelia and her party travelled to London (stopping briefly en route at Winchester to enable Amelia to see the cathedral), where the flyers had been checked in at the Hyde Park Hotel. Amelia was immediately engulfed in a whirl of engagements organised by the Guests; Stultz and Gordon were 'completely ignored . . .' Both were well content to be left alone. 'All we want to do is sleep,' said Stultz.[19] After a few days it was decided to move

Amelia out of the hotel. It was too public and she was too easily exposed to the crowds and publicity. She looked tired and pale, despite the constant smile, and Amy Guest insisted that Amelia move into the Guests' Park Lane home to recover from 'the strain of the trip'. For the remainder of their stay Stultz and Gordon became the forgotten men and drifted about London virtually unrecognised, sightseeing and visiting airports such as Croydon, headquarters of the London–Paris Air Service, to look at the latest in European airliners. Undoubtedly, Amy Guest considered that the two men had been hired as 'crew' and had been well recompensed for their work. They had done their job, and done it well. And that was that.

But for Amelia there were lunches, dinner parties, tea dances; visits to Ascot on Gold Cup day and to Lady Astor's home, Cliveden; to the Olympia Horse Show with Lord Lonsdale; an evening visit to Aldershot to watch an Air Tattoo. Cables and letters (Railey hired a team of four secretaries to answer them all) flooded in and there was always the constant barrage of reporters and other callers. She managed a few shopping trips to buy some clothes, for initially she had to borrow from her hostess and appear in dresses which the newspapers were quick to note were 'several sizes too large'. For Amelia the crowded days passed quickly. A letter from George came by the first ship,[20] and received the simple reply THANKS CHEERING LETTER WILL TRY BE GOOD SIMPKIN SWELL GUY. EARHART.

Not all press reports were kind to Amelia. Some pointed out that she had been merely luggage and contributed nothing towards the success of the flight. An especially sniffy one came, somewhat predictably, from the irascible founder and editor of *Flight*, the prestigious British aviation magazine:

Well, the first lady passenger has crossed the Atlantic by air, although what special merit there is in that is not altogether easy to see. In these days of sex-equality, such a feat should not arouse any particular comment. Compared with the solo flights of such lady *pilots* as Lady Bailey and Lady Heath, the crossing of the

Atlantic as *a passenger* does not seem to us to prove anything in particular. If it were intended to demonstrate that a machine can now cross the Atlantic carrying a full crew and even a passenger then that was proved by Commander Byrd's flight last year and very much more convincingly . . .

The machine itself was in some ways . . . a curiosity: a high winged monoplane, with three engines and twin floats. But it got across, even though the margin was uncomfortably narrow. On alighting at Barrow [*sic*], the pilot is reported to have said he had not enough petrol to take off again.[21]

Such reports hurt Amelia but she was only too aware of the truth in them. The point was that in those early days of flight *any* transatlantic venture was a heroic feat. No one could simply take off and be sure that they would make it. It was an adventurous – if somewhat foolhardy – thing to have done, but the fact remained, luggage or not, she *was* the first woman to have crossed the ocean by air. Airminded women were more generous and Lady Heath, in particular, was kind and supportive:

> 318 St James Court
>
> Dear Miss Earhart,
> I did not go on to dance after I found you weren't going to stay but I've come home to tell you my address and phone number and to tell you that if you phone me I'll throw down whatever I'm doing to come and fly with you or talk – unless I'm on business connected with your luncheon . . . Ring me!
>> Yours
>> S. Mary Heath[22]

Lady Heath was to become a friend and a week later arranged a 'secret' rendezvous at Croydon to enable Amelia to fly the Avro Avian in which Lady Heath had flown solo from South Africa to England, in what was arguably the most impressive flight made by any woman to date. Amelia told no one about this plan, slipping out of the Guests' home just after dawn into a car sent by her conspirator. Mrs Guest was woken and told and, after collecting Hilton Railey, pursued Amelia, arriving at Croydon in time to see Amelia landing a Gipsy Moth in which she had flown with Captain A. H. White to Northolt. Later she flew a few circuits in Mary Heath's famous Avian.

Amelia had not been able to fly solo, having not been checked out in either the Moth or the Avian, but once in the air she took the controls and had flown both aeroplanes part of the time. Probably well aware, now that the reporters had arrived, that her flight in the Avian would be reported, and still smarting from the innuendo that she was a passenger rather than a pilot, she indulged in a mild display of aerobatics and landed grinning enthusiastically, declaring that she was so impressed with the Avian that she would like to buy one and take it home.[23]

Perhaps carried away by the moment, Mary Heath offered to sell that very plane to Amelia who bought it without hesitation. Subsequently she arranged for it to be crated up and shipped back to the USA with the *Friendship*.[24] Quite where Amelia got the money for this transaction is not known. Most likely George had told her before departure what she was likely to receive by way of payment for syndication rights to her story should the trip be successful. Amelia must have anticipated that this income would cover the cost of purchase and transport.

French aviation leaders had wanted Amelia and her two male companions to fly to Paris for a reception and air carnival but after some discussion and cables with George it was decided that they would sail home within a week. Putnam had been able to arrange a civic parade in New York and wanted them back home to capitalise on the immense public interest. Amelia drove to Sheffield to visit a former Denison House colleague who was living there, motored back and spent a day visiting Toynbee Hall in London's East End, the Settlement House that was the model for Denison House.

At the luncheon given by the Women's Committee of the British Empire, Amelia sat between Lady Astor, who appears to have been totally captivated by the young aviatrix, and Winston Churchill.

Amelia delivered a short, serious speech on the future of aviation in the USA. Wherever she went she put over her theories on aviation in general, and woman in aviation in particular, convincingly:

> Just now with aviation in its most fluid state, there is every chance for women; perhaps almost as many chances as there are for men. The woman who can create her own job is the woman who will win fame and fortune . . . there are many possible openings in aviation for women; some of these are as saleswomen, as founders of flying schools for women, as developers of flying fields, as pilots, as organizers of 'air taxi' companies as designers, perfecting or inventing in the field of many needs of a profession still in its infancy . . . The field is clear for the pioneer and if the pioneer has good ideas nobody will ask whether the pioneer is man or woman . . .
> . . . Here is where Atlantic flights by women, or any other good flight helps – it starts other women to think. In our country a man may learn to fly at government expense, if he passes the requirements of the United States Army schools. I do not know of any such instruction for women. So, until some pioneer woman has arranged better chances for young women fliers [they] must learn to fly in some private flying school.[25]

On the eve of her return Amelia dined at Lord Lonsdale's home and next day she attended Wimbledon and watched Helen Wills win a match before driving to Southampton. Stultz and Gordon had gone on quietly ahead of Amelia and were already on board the liner the SS *President Roosevelt* when she arrived at Ocean Terminal. When Amelia boarded she met the Captain, Harry Manning; little did either know what an important role he was to play in her life some years later. Manning, understanding Amelia's need for privacy after the hectic days in London allowed her free access to the bridge deck. Of that return voyage Amelia wrote:

> It was then we came to realize how much water we had passed over in the Friendship. Eastbound the mileage had been meas-

ured in clouds, not water. There never had been adequate comprehension of the Atlantic below us.[26]

A cable from George Putnam advised that thirty-two cities had invited the flyers to civic welcomes. How did Amelia feel about accepting? he asked.[27] Amelia felt it was too much but agreed to accept invitations from New York, Boston and Chicago.

New York welcomed the flyers as only New York can. They were taken off the *President Roosevelt* in Mayor Walker's private barge, then, in a convertible roadster, rode smiling and waving through a storm of tickertape and torn paper, to a civic reception at City Hall where Amelia received the key to the city from Mayor Jimmy Walker. In the background throughout was George Putnam, watching, working, smiling, missing nothing and instantly materialising at Amelia's side at a single glance from her. When the city's token key was presented, for example, she looked over her shoulder at George, who came forward and took it from her.[28]

On the following day Amelia returned 'home' to Boston where she received a similar reception from cheering crowds. Never again for the rest of her life would Amelia enjoy the ability to go about freely, unrecognised. She had become a public figure and she frankly enjoyed the attention, the fame and the publicity. For her, the obvious inconveniences were outweighed by the success which meant freedom from worry about finance, for, despite her father's remarks to the *Los Angeles Times*[29] it is obvious that Amelia had never been free of such concern from the moment Edwin had lost his job.

Waiting quietly at Medford was Sam Chapman, Amelia's fiancé. After yet another welcoming reception there, attended by Amelia's mother and sister, Sam took Amelia off to Marblehead for the day. So little has been written of Sam, of what his reactions to Amelia's adventure might have been, of what he thought of the amount of time she was spending with George Putnam. The truth is that the only two people who knew – Amelia and Sam – never spoke of it. One can only guess at the uncertainty and anxiety he must have felt in addition to pride in her accomplishment. Possibly he realised on that day in Marblehead that he could not hope to keep Amelia, for even in her conversation she would have started to grow away from him.

Next day Amelia went to Chicago, and then returned to New York. According to Muriel, Amelia never saw either Stultz or Gordon again after this period; both men resumed their careers and their paths did not cross. George saw no reason to involve them in the ongoing publicity campaign he had planned for Amelia. In fact, Stultz had 'disappeared just before starting the drive to City Hall' in Chicago and George, worried that Amelia's reputation would suffer if the parade was cancelled, donned Stultz's flying helmet and impersonated him in the parade, afterwards sending his apologies to the mayor that a stomach upset prevented him (Stultz) from attending the luncheon. No one ever guessed.[30]

Initially Amelia assumed that she would write the book George had been pressing her for, collect what rewards she might be able to reap from public appearances and lecture tours and then go back to work at Denison House. But there must have been, at the back of her mind, the hope that her new fame would enable her to play a more constructive part in the future of aviation.

George and Dorothy Putnam gave a grand private party at the Westchester Biltmore at Rye; among the guests were leading American women pilots Thea Rasche and Ruth Nichols. Amelia was determined to further the cause of women in the field of aviation and even before she left on the Atlantic venture she had been at work with Ruth Nichols in an attempt to organise an association for women pilots. The problem was, she thought, that at that time there were only about twenty-five licensed women pilots in the USA.

Indeed, her own 'licence' was actually an FAI certificate[31] issued in 1923 – Amelia claimed incorrectly that it was the first issued to any American woman – but under the laws in force in July 1928 this did not entitle her to a federal licence without examination. Further, her attempts to arrange US registration for the Avian (G-EBUG under its British identification) were complicated by legal difficulties. 'She has two courses of procedure,' a representative of the Department of Commerce wrote to Porter Adams who was agitating on Amelia's behalf at George's behest:

> One is to merely identify [the airplane] and fly it non-commercial as an unlicenced ship. The other is to submit complete engineering data in accordance with the Air Commerce Regulations and in that manner get it approved for licence. The latter is somewhat complicated and inconvenient so perhaps she would prefer the former and operate it as an unlicenced aircraft.
>
> Her decision in the foregoing would determine the necessity of a licence for herself. In the event she merely identifies the ship then she herself would be obliged to operate as an unlicenced pilot. If she adopts the alternative then we would indeed be pleased to facilitate the issuance of a licence for her without publicity. This is somewhat hard to control, however, because the newspaper people, as you know, keep rather close track of such things. You may assure her of our good intentions . . .[32]

Amelia decided to take the more difficult route applying for a full licence for the Avian, and herself. She took the Federal examination in total secrecy, flying from the Bowman Clarke polo ground at Rye, and the press were not informed.[33] The wily dyed-in-the-wool journalist, George Putnam, knew a thing or two about when to call in the media and when not to.

For example, when the manufacturers of 'Lucky Strike' cigarettes offered $1,500 each to Stultz, Gordon and Amelia to endorse their product, Amelia – who did not smoke – turned the offer down. It was George who persuaded her not to on the grounds that this would disqualify the two men, who needed the money, and who did smoke. If she felt so strongly, he argued, why could she not present the money to a good cause – Dick Byrd's Antarctic venture? Amelia agreed, signing a endorsement which read factually: 'Lucky Strike were the cigarettes carried on the *Friendship* when I crossed the Atlantic.'

It made good reading when the letters exchanged were published in full in the *New York Times*.

Dear Commander Byrd,
I have wondered if you know how much your help meant in
connection with the *Friendship*'s flight to England. You not
only aided with your sympathetic interest, but your technical
pioneering and vision largely made success possible. Perhaps
you noticed my 'endorsement' of the cigarettes which were
carried by the men in the plane. I made this deliberately. It
made possible my offering a modest contribution to your
Antarctic expedition which otherwise I could not have done. I
enclose the $1,500 received to help you reach the South
Pole . . .[34]

The reply was an equally carefully worded epistle, thanking
Amelia for 'an act of astonishing generosity'. Indeed $1,500 *was* a
great deal of money in 1928 – after all, only weeks earlier, Amelia
had been a $35-a-week social worker. The letters were calculated –
and almost certainly drafted by George – to secure public approba-
tion and impressive publicity for both clients.[35]

Unfortunately, although the plan achieved the primary objective,
it backfired, for George had been in the final stages of arranging a
contract for Amelia with *McCall's* magazine, where she had been
offered the position of Aviation Editor. This association of the
nation's heroine with smoking – still considered 'fast' in a woman
caused *McCall's* to withdraw the offer. Months later, following rep-
resentations by George, *McCall's* renewed their offer, but by then
Amelia had been offered the job of Associate Editor with
Cosmopolitan magazine.

CHAPTER 13

1928–1929

In the aftermath of Amelia's return, George maximised every opportunity and exploited every possibility of obtaining publicity for her and, although she never earned the enormous amounts of money credited to her by the newspapers, she was in great demand on the lecture circuit and there were several career offers under consideration. Her immediate future was financially 'comfortable' from lecture fees and from her share of syndicated articles about the flight. This, and her full schedule, led inevitably to the conclusion that a return to work at Denison House was unlikely. Her career and her enthusiasms now lay elsewhere.

She was pictured frequently in the newspapers, often among an elite circle of famous men and women pilots: Wilkins; Byrd; Chamberlin; Lindbergh; Rasche; Balchen; Nichols, Landis; and through George's wide-ranging connections she met hostesses of international repute, politicians, and celebrities. She opened buildings, gave public speeches and was interviewed and feted everywhere she went, possibly never realising quite how much of the public's sustained interest was due to George's behind-the-scenes stratagems. Although transatlantic flyers after Lindbergh – Chamberlin and Byrd for example – attracted public and media interest, that interest soon waned unless there was some new achievement in the offing; it took publicity management on a brilliant scale to keep a flyer's name in the forefront of everyone's mind and on the pages of national newspapers.

It is a popular misconception that George 'used' Amelia and

drove her too hard, with the implication that he did this for his own ends, though of course he was earning a management fee from Amelia's earnings (probably the same percentage as he earned from all his clients). But in fact George was simply ensuring that the maximum amount of benefit was reaped from a unique opportunity. He realised that once Amelia's name dropped out of the newspapers she would be just another nine-day wonder. No one would pay to hear her speak once the name of the next record-breaker was on everyone's lips. Amelia was nobody's fool and would also have recognised the sense of this.

She also saw the career George sketched out for her, and she wanted it. She was just as much committed to the property 'Amelia Earhart' as George, and if anything was probably self-driven. Constant publicity would ensure that backers could be found to finance future projects; it was a necessary part of the job and though George's carefully built image of Amelia portrayed her as shy, self-effacing and hating publicity she was – at least in those early days – as keen as he to attract media attention.

George insisted that Amelia stay at Rye while she worked on her book about the Atlantic flight. There she could be assured of privacy and peace; he could help her with advice and, more practically, there were secretaries to transcribe her log book and working notes. Amelia had taken a course in shorthand and typing in California and was a reasonably proficient typist, but the sackful of mail which arrived daily needed answering. Proposals of marriage, invitations of all sorts, pleas for money, offers of jobs, poetry written in her honour, cranks by the score; it amounted to hundreds of letters a day.

As usual, George was in a hurry. There was no question of Amelia being allowed to take months to write her book. He needed it in weeks, agreeing with Amelia how many words she would have to produce each day. Despite the tight schedule she managed to fit in some riding, swimming, dancing, friends and parties 'in tantalizing driblets',[1] as well as several trips to New York. There was a dinner there with the Richard Byrd and Mayor Jimmy Walker,[2] and, on another night, a trip to the theatre accompanied by George. On the

strength of her new income she wrote to her mother, 'If you know
something [Muriel] wants, get it for her and I'll pay. Also you. My
treat, at last.' In the same letter she exhorted Amy not to worry
about her safety: 'I am well protected here . . . if the Hearst reporter
annoys you, wire me and I'll have it stopped.' There is already a new
tone of confidence in her letters to her family.

                                                    Rye, August 26,1928
Dear Mammy,
I got back to Rye with hardly a recognition . . . perhaps you'd
better not talk [about] my intimate details of salary and
business with Pidge. I don't want her to spread the news and
always fear she will. I think I have an apartment, but will let
you know later . . .
    Please throw away rags and get things you need on my
account at Filenes [a large department store in Boston]. I'll
instruct them. I can do it now and the pleasure is mine.
    When and if the reporters come to you please refer them to
Mr Putnam. Don't even say yes or no if you don't want to. Just
say you can add nothing to their tales and ask me or GPP . . .
                            Your doter
                            A.E.[3]

From this point onwards Amelia invariably referred to herself as
'AE' (something which her contemporaries regarded as a piece of
Putnam affectation);[4] she had fallen into the habit of calling George
'GP' almost from the first, as everyone else did. A few days after she
wrote this letter, just as she was putting the finishing touches to her
book, she received word that the Avian, which had been uncrated
and assembled at Curtiss Field, had been flown to Rye. 'Finally the
little book is done . . .' she wrote. 'Tomorrow I am free to fly.'[5]
Amelia dedicated her book, 'To Dorothy Binney Putnam, under
whose rooftree this book was written.'
This done she bought an assortment of air navigation maps and
after a test hop from the nearby polo field she took off on what was
to be a transcontinental 'vacation' flight to California where the

National Air Races were being held. It was the reverse of the trip she had planned some four years earlier.

George, never far from her side, was to accompany her on part of the trip. Although adventurous by nature he was not fond of flying: it was not his element and he was not happy in a situation where he was not in control. He also suffered from air-sickness.[6] They landed and had lunch at Bellefonte Field, and then headed for Pittsburgh, where Amelia ground-looped on landing, claiming to have hit a hidden ditch while taxiing and stating mendaciously (if the reports are accurate) that it was 'her first crash'. The undercarriage and left wing were smashed and the propeller damaged. George took over and faced reporters:

> Miss Earhart had made a perfect landing and was taxiing to a stop when the plane struck an unmarked ditch and went into it The plane made what is called a ground loop and nearly turned over. Miss Earhart feels it is unfortunate that the accident should have happened, particularly as it occurred through no fault of hers.
>
> Miss Earhart had been visiting at my home and while there we decided to take a little jaunt. As she was just 'playing around' with no particular object in view, she headed her ship for Pittsburgh . . . there was no incident of any kind until we ran into the ditch at Pittsburgh.[7]

George telephoned New York for replacement parts but as the aeroplane was not a common type Amelia had to wait a few days for spares. Perhaps it was because of the attendant publicity that George returned to Rye leaving Amelia in Pittsburgh, or perhaps it was because he had work to do, for on his return the proofs of the book *20 Hrs. 40 Min.* were ready. It was rushed into the shops with George's customary aggression.

Within a few days Amelia's intention to fly to California became known, and the media followed her progress across the continent, but the hours of solo flight were balm to her spirit after the tumult of the Atlantic venture and its attendant publicity, the constant pressures of her position as 'a personality' and, not least, by her attraction to George and his continuing attentions to her. All she had to think about as she flew across the continent was each leg of the journey, becoming as she did so the first woman to make the return air flight solo from the Atlantic to Pacific coasts.

That this had not been done before was small wonder. There were few organised airfields. Those few dirt or grass strips that existed were invariably unmarked and difficult to identify. One town looked much like another from the air. 'Oh, for a country-wide campaign of sign painting!' Amelia wrote.

Coming down through a hole in the clouds, any flyer is thankful for a definite check as to his location, even if it is only to check on his navigation . . . imagine automobiling without signs! Imagine trying to recognize a new town the way flyers do – a hundred-mile-an-hour look at a checkerboard of streets and roofs, trees and fields, with highways and railroads radiating and crisscrossing and perhaps a river or two to complicate – or simplify – the geography lesson.[8]

On one occasion her map, which she had pinned to her shirt, tore free and blew away; lost and short of fuel she landed in the wide main street of a small town. She was greatly amused at her appearance in the mirror for the wind and sun had tanned and burned her face to a ruddy glow, except where her goggles covered the area around her eyes, which remained white. In her log book she noted that she would resemble a horned toad by the time she reached her destination.

By mid-September 1928 Amelia was in California where she renewed old acquaintances, visited her father and attended the National Air Races. George kept in constant touch by letter and cable. On one occasion, after having seen an unflattering picture of Amelia in a newspaper report he fired off with his usual verve:

Your hats! They are a public menace. You should do something about them when you must wear them at all! Some of them are cataclysms! But I hasten to add the Pittsburgh bonnet is a peach, as are several of the floppy ones with brims . . .[9]

After this she was hardly ever seen in a hat in public and never again wore the tight-fitting cloches that George loathed. Indeed whenever she was asked about hats she declared that she hated wearing them. The hatless tousled curls became a part of her image.

She set out on the return journey at the end of the month, but engine trouble forced an emergency landing in Utah where the only available space was scrubland, bumpy and littered with tumbleweed and mesquite. The Avian was damaged and had to be shipped to Salt Lake City for repairs[10] and it was 16 October before she reached New York. George was quick to send out a press release stating that the problem had been a mechanical one. Amelia had many forced landings and crashes over the years (as all pilots did in those days) but according to her press statements none was ever due to pilot error. Meanwhile her appointment with *Cosmopolitan* had been made public,[11] the contract calling for eight articles a year on the subject of aviation; this load was considerably increased by the vast amount of correspondence from readers.

A series of lecture tours organised by George to publicise her book took her to as many as thirty different venues in a month and this punishing routine was to be repeated many times over the next years. Whenever possible Amelia flew to her engagements, to publicise the practicality of aviation. She enjoyed speaking in public; her naturally friendly, unaffected and humorous personality was projected into the lectures that she quickly came to know by heart, creating almost instantaneously a bond between her audience and herself. And she was so enthusiastic about her subject that her audience was seldom bored.

Throughout November she travelled as part of the Putnam 'team', consisting of Amelia, George – who lectured on his Arctic explorations – and Dick Douglas, a boy scout who had accompanied Martin and Osa Johnson on safari in East Africa and had produced a book for Putnam's based on his adventures.

George was an old hand at the lecture circuit and prior to the tour had written a memo to advise her:

> . . . you are apt to take less time than you think you will take. Have plenty of spare ammunition on cards to fill the gaps. To this end I suggest you mapping out your talk on the small cards I am having handed to you with your films.
>
> Remember you will be working with a pointer (get a pointer!) with the slides. You will have a tendency to turn your back on the audience. This is a difficult trick. You really have to remember to always talk into your microphone and explain.
>
> Remember too your tendency is to let your voice drop at the end of sentences. And perhaps most vital of all is the necessity of ending matters crisply and definitely. Many a good speech, like a railroad, is ruined by lack of good terminal facilities.[12]

In mid-November Amelia met Sam in Medford. She had probably already reached a decision about him on her 'Gypsy tour' of the continent. Her life had grown dramatically beyond that of the quiet, intellectual young man, for in a way he represented her past, while George was the exciting present. On 23 November 1928, she announced publicly that she had broken off her engagement. 'I am no longer engaged to marry,' she told reporters. And then, with a twinkle, 'But you never can tell. If I was sure of the man I might get married tomorrow . . .'[13] Sam remained a close friend for the rest of her life.

Another incident which intruded into her busy schedule concerned a teenage girl. Elinor Smith, who at the age of sixteen was the youngest licensed woman pilot (her FAI certificate was signed by Orville Wright!), had set an altitude record and made headlines when she flew, illegally, under all four bridges on New York's East River. Now Elinor was practising for an attempt on the endurance record and achieving a significant amount of publicity.

George's intention was to project Amelia to the public as the 'foremost woman pilot'. Women such as Ruth Nichols and Louise Thaden were modest by nature, not headline seekers and while they may have been better pilots, they created no competition for Amelia; indeed they were to become great friends. But this young, attractive girl who had already acquired a full Department of Commerce licence (which AE did not possess), and a hunger for adventurous flying in the fullest sense, was a positive threat to George's plans.

Elinor Smith was thrilled when she received a telephone call from George asking her to meet him in Chicago where she was scheduled to appear at an air show. George and Amelia were in Chicago as part of their tour, the venue probably organised so that Amelia could attend the air show. Amelia flew in, with Louise Thaden as her passenger. Two weeks earlier Louise had given birth to her first child and her doctor was appalled when his patient told him she was going to the air races, forbidding her to 'go jolting along in a train for eleven hours'. He consented, however to a three-hour plane journey.

To Elinor Smith, the call was the answer to her prayers. Her ambition was to make a successful career in aviation and here, it seemed, was the key. She knew that Putnam had put Amelia's name 'into orbit and it was common knowledge that Amelia was earning $500 a week for her public appearances and talks . . . I looked forward to this meeting on two counts.' In Elinor's memoir, *Aviatrix* (written in 1981), she recalled the meeting:

> I was about to meet my personal heroine, and maybe just maybe, Mr Putnam would have some ideas on how to solve my problem . . . With my daily appearance at the show and Amelia's own activities our meeting was delayed, but we finally managed to have breakfast one morning in her suite . . .
>
> My last minute nervousness was dispelled by her friendly warmth. There was nothing cold-fishy about her handshake either. Taller than I, she was slender as a reed. A tracing of tiny freckles across her nose enhanced a perfectly natural complexion. I hadn't realized until that moment that there was a noticeable spacing between her front teeth.
>
> I was able to distinguish . . . the Putnam publicity touch from

the very real and warm individual I was facing. The image of a shy and retiring individual thrust against her will into the public eye was a figment of Putnam's lively imagination. Amelia was about as shy as Muhammad Ali. I do not mean to imply she wasn't modest . . . but she was already a woman of thirty who knew what she wanted and where she wanted to go. She left no doubt in my mind that it was the same direction as I . . .[14]

As a matter of fact Amelia was extremely self-conscious of the gap in her teeth and after a whole series of unflattering pictures taken in the aftermath of the transatlantic flight she was learning to smile with her lips closed. Her slight, boyish figure made her a good camera subject, though there were inevitably some photos which caught her with an unflattering expression; her natural humour enabled her to laugh at these and she even included a selection in early editions of *20 Hrs. 40 Min.* Amelia's other unhappiness was her ankles. Long and slender her legs may have been, but they were somewhat shapeless from knee to ankle and her feet were apt to swell. When she later adopted trousers as her normal mode of dress she told friends it was to hide her 'thick' legs. Elinor continued:

George Palmer Putnam was a handsome man. He was over six feet tall with snapping dark eyes and close cropped hair, and you could feel his electricity across a room. Wiry and dynamic, he exuded the authority of a bank president or millionaire, which he was. If that weren't overwhelming enough, his manners were impeccable. Before I knew it I was agreeing with his implied opinion that our meeting was one of the high points of his long and successful career and wasn't it a shame that our paths hadn't crossed until now.[15]

Overawed by Putnam, but wooed by Amelia's obvious sympathy, Elinor listened while George outlined his suggestion that 'some sort of company' should be set up to manage the affairs of top pilots and provide backing for record flights and arrange appearances. Unaccountably, he seemed angered by her query 'Do you mean something like a literary or theatrical agent?' Brushing it aside brusquely with the comment that what he had in mind was a strictly professional organisation he stressed that he could not, at this time, make any offer but asked her to outline her future plans. She did, and later was to regret it deeply. One thing she said which disturbed George more than anything was in answer to his query, 'What is your ambition?' Her aggressively naive reply, 'To take Amelia's place as number one woman pilot!' raised his hackles.[16]

Both Amelia and George reacted again when Elinor mentioned that thus far no woman had been allowed to fly the big powerful aeroplanes being manufactured by Fokker or Bellanca – at least no more than hold the controls. 'Certainly no female has ever taken one off or landed it,' she informed them. George must have instantly recognised the latent publicity opportunity inherent in this statement.

Elinor returned home, but the call George had promised to make as she bade the couple goodbye never came, and for a long time she was to find constant pinpricks and minor barriers placed in her way by officials and the media, many of which, she was to claim in her memoir, she was subsequently able to trace directly to interference by George. This was particularly apparent in the case of publicity. She found it difficult to get reporters to cover aviation feats that – prior to her meeting with George – would have automatically attracted attention. Sometimes, when reporters had attended some exploit, the story was filed away as a tiny piece at the bottom of a column, or more often never appeared. This was disastrous for Elinor. She had no private income, and without publicity she could not attract the necessary sponsorship to further her career.

George, meanwhile, had decided that he wanted 'a first' of his own, and conceived a first non-stop flight from New York to Bermuda with Bill Lancaster as pilot and Harry Lyon (previously navigator on the successful Pacific crossing by the *Southern Cross*) as a navigator. They took off from Port Washington, Long Island in a characteristic blaze of publicity but, George wrote later, 'our undertaking lost no time in becoming a comedy of errors'.

Midway along the Jersey Coast the engine failed and they made a deadstick landing in a 'gummy mass of mud'. An incoming wave picked the plane up and 'bounced it into the air for a hundred foot or so and nearly broke the plane in pieces'. After a rescue they took off again for Atlantic City where they found that there was water in the fuel tank. Between Atlantic City and Norfolk they got hopelessly lost and George, perhaps not surprisingly, wondered if there was something besides water affecting their navigation. They landed at Norfolk where the station commander, having received a report on the plane's equipment from his engineers, suggested that if it was suicide George was bent on, there were easier ways . . . George took the hint and sheepishly entrained for New York where Amelia met him at Pennsylvania Station. 'She never once said "I told you so." She had, and I should have listened.'[17]

Meanwhile, despite her continuing punishing schedule, Amelia was delighted to accept official invitations to government installations in Washington, DC to see experiments in wind tunnels and to discuss the role of civil aviation. She revelled in this, for it implied that she was playing a constructive role in aviation's future. It also fitted well with George's plans for her so there were constant introductions to politicians and government figures. What he wanted was the name Amelia Earhart synonymous (in the mind of the general public) with the term 'best woman pilot'. At the same time he had booked Amelia into such a tight, non-aviation, public appearance schedule that even when she was offered the chance to accompany Bobbi Trout in an attempt on the world's endurance record she had to turn it down.[18] Bobbi later made the attempt with Elinor Smith and the two set a record (for women) of 42 hours 3.5 minutes using in-flight refuelling to stay aloft. Perhaps, though, George simply did not want Amelia to share her glory with anyone.

When Lady Heath paid a short visit to New York for the purpose of organising her speaking tour in the spring of 1929, Amelia gathered together as many women pilots as she could, to honour her friend. George threw a dinner party for them both and talked to Mary Heath about her plans. Like Elinor Smith, Lady Heath would soon regret sharing her confidences.

George took his family to Havana and Panama in late December

1928,[19] and Amelia spent Christmas in New York in her apartment at the American Women's Association Club at 353 West 57th Street. Amy came to stay with her and during the holiday Amelia and her mother flew over New York City and the Statue of Liberty as paying passengers on a $15 pleasure flight.[20]

As winter gave way to spring the constant workload began to take its toll. Amelia carelessly turned her plane on its nose at Curtiss Field and when, only days later, she was on her way to Los Angeles by train, she wrote to her mother saying how tired she was. Even on the train she could not relax for it was in snatched hours such as this that she wrote her magazine articles.

Often it was necessary for Amelia to fly to an engagement with an entourage of secretary and pressmen. George, too, was a constant companion on these trips. When this happened a larger aeroplane than the two-seater Avian was needed. The British pilot Captain Bill Lancaster, who had flown to Australia a year earlier with a woman passenger (achieving the first two-person flight between England and Australia) was hired as Amelia's 'mechanic', but in fact he was pilot rather than mechanic on these flights. Amelia did not take easily to flying large aircraft and found them difficult to handle, but Lancaster later told Mary Heath that he had been sworn to secrecy over his actual role because 'Putnam wanted Amelia always to be given the credit and publicity for flying the aeroplanes'.[21]

There was a certain amount of talk about Amelia and George in aviation circles. It was hardly surprising, for the two spent a great deal of time together and even when they were accompanied by others on trips they were more often than not apart from their travelling companions – very much a couple. Whether this gossip ever reached the ears of George and Amelia is not known, but there is reason to believe that Dorothy Putnam was increasingly aware of the situation and was less than happy.

In March 1929 Lancaster and Amelia flew into New Castle airport where young Elinor Smith, still suffering (though fighting) the effects of George Putnam's powerful machinations, was working as a demonstration pilot for Bellanca. That Elinor was on the roster of select pilots which included Clarence Chamberlin, Martin Jensen, and Bert Acosta, speaks volumes for the young woman's ability as a tough, precision flyer. It was only two years earlier that Bellanca had refused to allow Lindbergh to fly one of his aeroplanes (Lindbergh's first choice of plane before he went to Ryan) across the Atlantic. Although Elinor did not know it at the time, Amelia had in her pocket a bank draft for $25,000[22] with which she hoped to buy the Bellanca.

Amelia's test flight in the machine appalled Elinor for, as she recalled in her memoir, as Amelia took over the controls 'our big calm bird suddenly lurched out of control and wobbled all over the sky'. After they landed Amelia quietly asked Elinor if they could go up again, alone. The Bellanca flew with the nose well below the horizon, rather than on it, the usual position for small aircraft, and Elinor thought this might have confused Amelia. After guiding Amelia through some gentle banks and turns Elinor handed the controls over: 'Again we slipped and skidded all over the sky. I was baffled, for the ship's flying position had been established, the rest of it should have been like flying a small biplane.'[23] Although she said nothing to Amelia, Elinor privately concluded that Amelia's flying ability was considerably less than she had been led to believe. She had been told as much by Lady Heath but hadn't believed it.[24]

Bellanca, who chose his customers carefully in order to protect the reputation of his product, refused to sell to Amelia, despite a great deal of hassle from George. Elinor thought it just as well. Amelia, she felt, simply hadn't the ability to fly the big ship and for her to enter it in competitive events (which was what George apparently had in mind) would have been highly dangerous.[25]

A few weeks later Amelia hit the headlines again with a forced landing when the Avian's engine stopped near Utica, NY where Amelia had been visiting her sister. When Muriel married Albert Morrissey in late June 1929, Amelia was almost late for the wedding for she was first delayed by fog and then by a damaged propeller. She travelled to the wedding by train and had to suffer the attentions of reporters still trying to make a romantic link between her and Sam Chapman who was an usher at the ceremony. Sam 'begged' the reporters 'to leave me alone', while Amelia, when asked if she had any plans for a wedding of her own, stated: 'I would make a poor wife, running around the country as I am.'

On 29 March 1929 she had been granted her aviation transport licence.[26] One requirement for this was that the pilot, who had to be the holder of a Department of Commerce licence, must have logged a minimum 250 hours of flying time. According to Amelia's second log book she had a 'brought forward total' of 559 hours and 46 minutes flying time. This was the first entry, dated 20 July 1929 in the new log book; but it is frankly difficult to see how, with the financial restrictions she had suffered during her time in Los Angeles and the small amount of flying she had done between 1924 and 1928, she managed to build up this very considerable number of hours.[27] It is also known that Amelia was given private instruction, flying from the Bowman Clarke polo field near Rye, before taking the flying test; this in itself is strange, for any pilot with 500 hours should need little in the way of instruction to take a basic flying examination.[28]

During that summer of 1929 the airline industry was striving to improve its image. Commercial flying remained very much a novelty, not helped by the media who fastened on every crash with almost ghoulish relish. But aviation was growing up. In his book *Wings over America* Harry Bruno stated: 'In the ten years which followed the first flight of the Wright brothers at Kitty Hawk, airplanes changed only a little, but the decade after the Lindbergh flight to Paris saw practically every new plane rendered virtually obsolete within six months of its creation.'[29] Aviation was growing up fast.

Bigger, faster aeroplanes were readily available with more features than even Amelia and her friends sitting on the hangar floor in Los Angeles had been able to predict five or six years earlier. All eyes were fastened hopefully on the experimental work in blind flying being carried out by the Guggenheim Fund for the Promotion of Aviation, under Jimmie Doolittle's direction. Once flight schedules could be made truly independent of normal weather conditions the airlines could truly be said to be providing a regular commercial service. Meanwhile there were numerous local airline services and a few brave attempts at national ones.

In July Amelia was appointed Assistant to the General Traffic Manager of one of these national airlines: Transcontinental Air Transport (more popularly known as TAT and the foundation company of today's TWA) with special responsibility for attracting women passengers onto the airlines.

Amelia's satisfaction and pleasure at her new appointment was marred by the news that Bill Stultz had been killed in an accident at Roosevelt Field. He had taken up two passengers who wanted to experience some aerobatics. After several perfectly executed manoeuvres the Waco performed a loop but at the bottom of the loop the plane went into a tailspin from which it never recovered. Witness testimony makes it obvious that Stultz applied full power in an attempt to recover, seconds before the plane hit the ground killing all three occupants, but it was some time before the cause of the accident was understood. One of the passengers had jammed his feet under the rudder bars to brace himself. With no rudder control Stultz would have found it virtually impossible to recover and at 400 feet he had no chance. The shoes were wedged there so tightly from the pressure that Stultz had applied to try to operate the rudder that when the passenger was pulled out of the wreckage the shoes remained jammed in place.[30]

A few days later Amelia was on the inaugural flight of TAT's 'East to West' passenger service aboard the Ford Trimotor *City of Washington* for the outward journey to Los Angeles. Simultaneously Charles Lindbergh was flying a similar aeroplane from Los Angeles on the eastbound inaugural flight. The two planes landed in Arizona where Lindbergh changed aeroplanes and flew the *City of Washington* on to California. Amelia was quick to point out to her colleagues that 'luxuries' such as refreshments might attract more women to the airlines, and once women were happy to fly they would persuade their men to fly also. She felt very strongly that if the newspapers would only take a different attitude towards reporting 'incidents' her campaign would stand a better chance of success. While Amelia had a point, and the media did fasten on to even the most trivial bump involving an aeroplane, it is fair to point out that serious crashes were still far from few; Wilmer Stultz's crash, for example, was the third fatal accident *that week* at Roosevelt Field alone.

Dorothy Binney Putnam attempted to aid Amelia's campaign to get women into the air by travelling to Los Angeles and back in seven days, becoming 'the first woman passenger to use Transcontinental Air Transport for a round trip'. George's publicity machine never slept![31]

Amelia felt a responsibility to educate women on the practicality of flying, and to dissociate the dangers and informality of so-called 'sport flying' from those of the strictly regulated civil commercial aviation. Her articles from this point become harder-edged and concentrate not only on trying to attract women into aviation but also on making them aware of their equality with men.[32] She advocated the setting up of a formal separate classification for women's aeronautical records, just as there was for athletic and sports records, and qualified her stance: 'Of course such regulation does not mean that when a woman is capable she cannot compete with men on equal terms. I'd like to see men's and women's records, and [also] a sexless thing called a World Record . . .'[33]

In other articles Amelia pointed out the track record of passenger-carrying airlines in the USA:

> Though everyone knows that regularly scheduled planes fly from London to Paris across the Channel, not many are aware that about fifty-three thousand passengers were carried in 1928 on similar lines in the United States. As I write there are forty-four operators who carry passengers or mail or express, or both, flying more than sixty-two thousand miles every twenty-four hours *on schedule*.[34]

On her return to New York Amelia found George had fixed up an unusual item, guaranteed to attract newspaper coverage. With George and Dorothy, in a Loening amphibian piloted by its designer/builder Grover Loening, she flew to Block Island. There, with the submarine *Defender* (described as the smallest submarine in the world and the only privately owned one) on the surface, she was

Amelia Earhart in 1937

Amelia's parents, Edwin and Amy Earhart

Amelia's first crash in 1921, south of Los Angeles. Crashes were a frequent hazard in the early days of flying

George Putnam aged twenty-three, taken at Bend, Oregon

'There I was . . . in the roaring west,' George wrote, 'I wanted to hear it roar.'
Bend, Oregon, in 1910

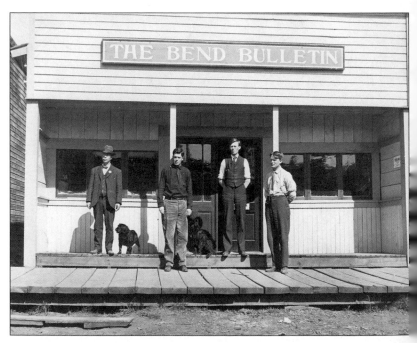

George Putnam, newspaperman (second from left), outside the offices of the
Bend Bulletin, c. 1911

Amelia and George in Boston, May 1928, a few weeks after they first met

Poster for Amelia's first lecture tour, October 1928

Miss Amelia Earhart
"Lady Lindy"—the First Woman to Fly the Atlantic

AND

George Palmer Putnam

Arctic Explorer, Boy Scout Enthusiast and Publisher

Tomorrow at 2:30

Horne Auditorium, Seventh Floor

Miss Earhart, the first woman to cross the Atlantic by aeroplane, will tell of her thrilling flight about which she has written the book, "20 Hours and 40 Minutes."

Mr. Putnam will give a talk on his Arctic explorations which he will illustrate by moving pictures. He will also present and tell the story of Robert Dick Douglass, Jr., Boy Scout who was his guest on a safari with Martin Johnson into British East Africa.

At the conclusion of the talks, Miss Earhart, Mr. Putnam and Scout Douglass will autograph books purchased.

Extraordinary arrangements have been made to accommodate the great crowd that will be here to meet and hear these celebrities.

Boy Scout, Girl Scout and Campfire Girls Meeting at 8 P. M.

All Scoutmasters and their troops are invited to a special meeting in the Joseph Horne Co. auditorium, at which Miss Earhart, Mr. Putnam and Robert Dick Douglass, Jr., will speak.

One of a series of
publicity shots taken
on the roof of the
Copley Plaza in
Boston prior to the
1928 transatlantic
flight

The plaque at Burry
Port in South Wales
bearing the legend,
20 hours and 49
minutes – the correct
time according to
logbooks, but
probably not snappy
enough for Putnam's
book title

ERECTED
IN COMMEMORATION OF
MISS AMELIA EARHART, OF BOSTON, U.S.A.
THE FIRST WOMAN TO FLY ACROSS
THE ATLANTIC OCEAN,
WHO, WITH HER COMPANIONS,
WILMUR STULTZ & LOUIS GORDON,
FLEW FROM TREPASSEY, NEWFOUNDLAND,
TO BURRY PORT IN 20HRS 49 MINUTES
IN THE SEAPLANE NAMED "FRIENDSHIP"
ON JUNE 18TH 1928.

Amelia's Avro Avian after its ground loop in Pittsburgh, Pennsylvania, in 1928. The plane was quickly repaired to enable Amelia to make her return transcontinental flight

Amelia surrounded by crowds in Southampton, June 1928. Stultz and Gordon have been left on the periphery of the crowd. The woman wearing the feathered hat is Amy Phipps Guest

PHONE MYSTIC 1016
TELEPHONE NOANK

NOANK
CONNECTICUT

THE SQUARE HOUSE
CHURCH STREET

Dear Gyp

There are some things
which should be writ-
ten before we are married —
things we have talked
over before — most of
them

You must know
again my reluctance to
marry. my feeling that
I shatter thereby chances
in work which means
most to me. I feel
the move just now as
foolish as anything I
could do. I know: there

First page of the letter that Amelia presented to George Putnam on the day
of their wedding, February 7, 1931

lowered over the side wearing deep-sea diving equipment. She never reached the bottom because she noticed a leak in her suit and signalled by pulling on the line to be hauled in. On the following day, after repairs to the suit she dived successfully with instructor Frank Crilley (one of the world's most famous divers; he received the Congressional Medal of Honour in 1915 for his daring rescue of a diver trapped in wires), and walked along the sea bed at a depth of 35 feet, as far as their lead ropes would allow. There was little to see. They found only a clam shell and an empty milk bottle and after 15 minutes or so Amelia started to feel cold, so they came up. Later, dressed only in a swimsuit, she 'escaped' from the diving compartment. She wrote about it:

> On the bottom of the submarine is an unusual contrivance. It is an airtight chamber. By making the air pressure equal to that of the water one may step gayly [*sic*] forth into the Atlantic Ocean with never a drop coming into the chamber. The phenomenon is that of the inverted tumbler in a bowl of water where the water creeps up the tumbler only so far as the pressure of the imprisoned air will allow. Yes, I walked out the strange door into the green sea and swam through it into the sunlight. A swimsuit was the only equipment needed as the exit was only fifteen feet under . . .[35]

Her own version is a chatty, unexciting – though informative – magazine article, in which Amelia is at least as interested in the process of getting into the diving gear as the dive itself. The newspapers, however, could be relied upon to hype the incident into an adventure and some had her 'fired from the torpedo tube of a submarine at 100 ft', presenting a very different picture to the actual event.[36]

George was now so protective of Amelia's interests that others in the flying world were beginning to be directly affected by his aggressive strategy to make her the leading woman pilot. Lady Heath and Bill Lancaster, for example, had come to America that summer of 1929 to make the lecture tour that had been booked months earlier (as she had confided to George on a previous visit). On arrival they found that most of their engagements had been cancelled due to 'lack of interest', and that Amelia had been booked into every cancelled slot by the head of the lecture tour company. Lady Heath claimed later, in a conversation with Elinor Smith, that she had since discovered this had been engineered by George but felt she could not sue due to her husband's disapproval of litigation. Her friendship with Amelia quickly waned at this point.

Throughout late spring and into summer Amelia had been working in cooperation with other women on two projects: the first, to form an association for women pilots; the second, to organise a cross-country air race for women pilots. The race, called the Los Angeles to Cleveland Women's Air Derby, was to be the opening event of the National Air Races. It was a major achievement and well-organised, and thus Amelia was less than enchanted when humorist Will Rogers termed it 'The Powder-Puff Derby'. The name stuck and even Amelia eventually found herself referring to the entrants as 'powder-puffers'.[37]

There was no handicapping system (though there were two classes, one for the heavier planes and one for the smaller 'sport' types), so the bigger, more powerful aeroplanes would obviously stand the best chance of winning. Clearly the first woman home in the class for larger aeroplanes would be the one who got the acclaim and publicity. Aware of what the other competitors were using as their mounts for the race, Amelia had recognised that not only would she be outclassed in the Avian but she would have to fly in the small 'CW Class' if she raced it. She therefore set about looking for another aeroplane.

It was July before Amelia settled on the right one, a Lockheed Vega, registration number NC6911, previously flown by Charles Lindbergh as a demonstrator model and sometimes used as Mayor Jimmy Walker's hack. Lockheed had lent the Vega to TAT for trials during the summer of 1929 and Amelia had the use of it during this time. In July she sold the Avian and bought the big cabin monoplane, but within a few weeks had swapped it for a later model Vega (registration NC31E) that Lockheed Aircraft were using as a

demonstrator. It was this latter that she flew to California in early
August to compete in the race.

When Elinor Smith heard about this she was uneasy. The Vega
was undoubtedly the fastest aeroplane available but Elinor 'didn't
like it':

> The cockpit was high off the ground and your legs rested practi-
> cally under the engine mount, making the heat build-up pretty
> uncomfortable at times. I'd flown it just once, and everything the
> Bellanca was, the Vega wasn't. Fast, unstable, tricky near the
> ground with a monocoque, no-longer on fuselage that would
> collapse like a packet of cornflakes in a crash . . .[38]

Bearing in mind Amelia's performance at New Castle in March,
Elinor was concerned that Amelia would not be able to handle the
Vega, but shortly afterwards she received a phone call from George
Putnam. He hadn't forgotten her, he told her, he had her career very
much in his mind. At the meeting which followed he explained that
Amelia would be flying in the Women's Air Derby and following it
with a nationwide lecture tour. He then offered Elinor $75 a week
(an enormous sum in 1929) to pilot Amelia in the Derby and
around the country. Elinor was to do the difficult cross-country
flying, '. . . Amelia is not physically strong, you know. But of course
she must appear to be doing it. When pictures are being taken at the
various stops you must stand to her left, so her name will always
come up first in the captions . . .' When Elinor refused the offer
George resorted to bullying threats: 'You may *think* you have other
plans, but believe me, if you don't sign this you will never fly professionally again and certainly never in the New York area. You have
my word on that!'[39]

The youngster was upset, only too well aware that George had
the powerful contacts and the necessary influence to carry out his
threat, but she stuck to her decision. Rumours were circulating that
Amelia was taking secret refresher flying lessons from a private field
near Rye, but Elinor still wondered how Miss Earhart would cope
with the big aeroplane she regarded as unwieldy.[40]

The entrants in the Derby included two leading women pilots from overseas, the Australian Jesse 'Chubby' Miller, who had flown from London to Darwin as co-pilot to Bill Lancaster, and Thea Rasche from Germany. Lady Heath filed an entry but was unable to find a suitable aeroplane in time.[41]

Virtually every American woman pilot of note was lined up, as the starting flag went down at Clover Field, Santa Monica, that Sunday afternoon of 18 August 1929. Elinor Smith had hoped to enter but was offered a job putting on flying displays for the crowds who awaited the women racers at Chicago. Amelia said there were only thirty women eligible under the entrance requirements which insisted on a current licence and 100 hours of flying time, and of these thirty, twenty turned up on the starting line,[42] nineteen started and one, Mary von Mack, turned back before reaching the first control point. Although this put her out of the race, she followed the others and completed all the stages.

The race consisted of nine stages. The first day they were required to fly less than 100 miles to San Bernardino, but from then on the competitors rose before dawn each day and were in the air by sun-up to complete what can only be described as an endurance test of women and aeroplanes.

On the second leg the newspapers had a field day. Marvel Crosson's plane was seen to dive into the ground (her body was later found entangled in her parachute which had not had time to open as she baled out at too low an altitude). Thick mesquite undergrowth delayed the searchers and meanwhile reports of sabotage began to circulate for Claire Fahy's OX5-powered Travel Air was forced down when the wing braces snapped. Investigation led to the suspicion that drops of corrosive acid had been strategically placed at the sites of the damage. Thea Rasche was forced down with sand in her fuel tank and when reporters got to her she produced a cable received on the eve of the race warning her to 'be on the lookout' for sabotage. Bobbi Trout was also forced down with suspected sand or dirt in her fuel and there were immediate and predictable demands for the race to be called off to protect the lives of the flyers (notably *not* from these same flyers!) which were sensibly ignored by the organisers.

Amelia led on the second leg but on a refuelling stop at Yuma she overshot the field and upended the Vega in scrub when she hit a ridge. She blamed the crash on the fact that 'something had gone wrong with the stabilizers' but it was more likely that in the extreme heat and resultant 'thin' air resistance, the landing speed of the Vega was higher than she had previously experienced; sand had drifted over the runway making it difficult to identify and she overran it. The propeller was bent but a new one was flown in from Burbank within hours and she lost very little time.[43]

There were many forced landings during the race – not unusual in those days, when all pilots were used to landing, making mechanical adjustments and taking off again with the minimum of fuss; one, recorded by Amelia, was made by Ruth Elder who landed in a field of cattle. Having rolled to a stop the pilot sent up a silent prayer, 'Dear God, let them all be cows!'[44] Some contestants got lost or were blown off course and had to land to discover their whereabouts and/or refuel.

Margaret Perry felt unwell at the start of the race but took off anyway, despite her flu-like symptoms. Two days later she was hospitalised in Texas with typhoid fever. Blanche Noyes was flying at more than 3,000 feet over the western desert in Texas when she looked over her shoulder to see her plane on fire. She landed, put out the fire by throwing sand on it, and took off again despite having damaged her undercarriage.[45]

These incidents, widely reported owing to the amount of public interest generated in the 'race of flying beauties', caused more than one editor to react – 'Women have proven conclusively that they cannot fly' – and there was renewed backing of the earlier call for the race to be abandoned. In fact the race was a great success for sixteen finishers made it to Cleveland; one – Mae Haezlip – had joined them late as she had been unable to make the official start. Sportingly the other contestants agreed to allow her to compete.[46]

Amelia was to write later that despite the adverse criticism this was the highest percentage of finishers in any cross-country race to date, for men or women. In reality it was a highly commendable performance, given the unreliability of aircraft at that date, the fact that there were no navigational aids other than magnetic compasses and that aviation charts were still so basic that the competitors used those that were available in conjunction with Rand McNally road maps.[47] Feeling they had proved a point the competitors asked for and got, representation on the race committee in subsequent years.[48]

Waiting for Amelia at Cleveland became unbearable for George so, with Bill Lancaster to pilot him, he flew west to Cincinnati in a Great Lakes Trainer to meet her. 'Bill's entry in that race was "Chubby" Miller, mine A.E.' he recalled. After lunch with the women the two men took off ahead of the contestants but the engine stalled and they were lucky to climb out of the aeroplane in one piece, having 'ripped through the top branches of several trees' before effecting a pancake landing in a cornfield. As they rubbed their bruises they heard aircraft engines and the entire field of powder-puffers passed overhead. Although the men waved they were not spotted. Later, when George asked if Amelia would have come back for him if she had seen him, she grinned wickedly '. . . you wouldn't have wanted me to drop out of the race?'[49]

The race was won by Louise Thaden in a Travel Air with Gladys O'Donnell's clipped-wing Waco a close second. Both women had aeroplanes powered by the Wright Whirlwind J5 200-hp engine – as did Amelia and six other competitors. The Vega was generally considered to be 'the fastest ship' because of its streamlined design but Amelia was a poor third and when elapsed times were calculated she was a disappointing two hours behind Louise Thaden. Elinor Smith records Amelia's poor landing at Cleveland as the Vega bounced across the length of the vast airport with Amelia frantically braking and attempting to avoid a ground loop.[50]

'I was filled with admiration for her,' Elinor said, 'it was barely five months since the New Castle incident . . . and there was absolutely no way she could have built up enough air time to be at ease behind the controls of the fastest heavy monoplane in the air.' The landing speed of the Vega was at least one-third faster than any other plane in the race and Amelia must have been only too aware that if she allowed the speed to drop she could stall. '. . . One look at her drawn countenance when she flipped up the cockpit hood'

told Elinor and several other pilots who had watched the performance that 'this was gut courage that transcended the sanity of
reasoning.'[51] If Elinor's assessment of Amelia's piloting ability was
accurate then Amelia put up a first-class performance in achieving
third place in what was a very select gathering, especially in flying an
aircraft that was so difficult to handle.

A few days after the race Amelia called a meeting of women
pilots in her hotel suite. She outlined a plan formulated by herself,
Gladys O'Donnell, Ruth Nichols, Louise Thaden and Phoebe
Omlie to commemorate the Derby by forming an organisation
which would consolidate the gains made by the women in the race.
Elinor Smith was delighted to be invited and went along with the
proposal until Amelia insisted that they should press for equality in
racing with male pilots so that they could compete for big purses in
free-for-all competition.

At this stage Elinor and several others (Phoebe Omlie and Mary
Heath among them) objected. To date, few women had any experience of flying the big fast pure-racing machines in which the men
competed, which could only be described as huge engines with fuel
tanks to which were attached, almost as an afterthought, small
wings. 'Widow-makers' they were called, and they were certainly
lethal to many fine pilots. Those opposed to the idea argued that to
expose themselves to this type of competition could only betray the
women's lack of experience. Because of this disagreement over policy
Elinor Smith declined to become a charter member of the Ninety-
Nines, which would ultimately become arguably the most
prestigious organisation for women pilots.

The name supposedly arose because of a widely believed legend
that there were one hundred licensed women pilots in the USA
at that time and all except one joined the organisation (Neta Snook,
Amelia's first instructor, incorrectly claimed in a magazine article
that she was the one who declined) leaving ninety-nine assenting
women pilots. However this legend is not borne out by either the
Department of Commerce or Ninety-Nines' records. There were
more than 120 women with licenses of one type or another when
the invitations were sent out and in the following year, when the

charter deadline expired, ninety-nine applications had been received. Hence the name. Amelia was elected as first President of the organisation whose laudable aim was 'to provide closer relationship among pilots and to unite them in any movement that may be for their benefit or for that of aviation in general . . .'[52]

Putnam was rumoured to be annoyed with the Derby placings and later blamed Amelia's third place on the fact that the aeroplane had not been properly tuned before it left the Lockheed factory. These public statements by George became almost a joke in the flying industry for any adverse incident involving Amelia immediately called up a statement from George blaming the aeroplane or some mechanical defect. Whilst it naturally irritated the pilots, not to mention manufacturers of equipment, this unscrupulous behaviour was George's way of protecting his 'property'. His recipe for success had always been aggressive action. Amelia's willingness to allow these announcements to be made is less understandable.

Those adversely affected by George's methods smarted and disliked him intensely. He had the ability to create fear because of the power he wielded and it took a tough personality like Lindbergh or Smith to stand up to him. It is equally fair to say that there was a softer side to George Putnam for he was capable of great kindness and gentleness when he liked someone and would go to considerable lengths to help anyone with genuine talent and ability. The mistake some people have made about George is in assuming that the way he treated them was also the way he treated Amelia. They could hardly have been more wrong!

His relationship with Amelia had long since passed the point where she was a mere client and their obvious close rapport had not gone unnoticed. In the previous November in Chicago, for example, at her first meeting with George and Amelia, Elinor Smith had been in no doubt that their 'love affair was in full swing . . . for one thing there is an electricity between lovers that you can't miss, and the subtle pats and touchings between the two were unmistakable . . .' Nor did the sharp-eyed youngster miss the fact that the two were clearly sharing the double bed in the adjoining room of the suite.[53] Rumours of a romance were quashed but Amelia's claims that George meant nothing to her beyond a friend and business partner were negated when Dorothy left him, shortly after Amelia returned from the air races, and went to stay at Rye. Amelia's arrival at the Locust Avenue mansion was the final straw and the writer, Corey Ford, actually witnessed Dorothy's departure from George's 'handsome home at Rye, its duplex rooms decorated, appropriately enough with the pelts of dead lions'. It was during:

> a publication party he gave to launch one of his books, a celebrity-studded outdoors barbeque on the lawn behind his house with GP in chef's hat and apron presiding over the grill.
>
> At the height of the wing-ding, I left in search of the men's room, and wandered around to the front of the house. An express truck was parked outside, and as I opened the door I saw two movers carrying a trunk from the second floor. Dorothy Binney Putnam, GP's charming and vivacious wife, followed them downstairs, dressed in travelling clothes.
>
> 'Didn't you know? I'm divorcing George,' she said quite casually. 'He doesn't need me any more.'
>
> I strolled back to the party, where GP was gaily spearing frankfurters for Amelia Earhart . . .[54]

Dorothy went to Reno in September to establish residence in order to file for a divorce which became final in December.[55] Interviewed some years later, Amelia was to tell of her early feelings for George in what was possibly the only interview where she discussed her personal life with any frankness:

> I had no special feelings about Mr Putnam at first. I was too absorbed in the prospects of the trip and of my being the one to make it . . . of course before I had talked to him for very long I was conscious of the brilliant mind and keen insight of the man . . .

She then related how she had made the flight and gone to the Putnam's home to write the book:

Mr Putnam and I found that we had many things in common; I was interested in aviation, so was he. We both loved the outdoors, books and sport. And so we lunched together, and dined together, took long horseback rides together. Usually we were surrounded by many people, both he and I had many friends and were invited to the same parties. We came to depend on each other, yet it was only friendship between us, or so – at least – I thought at first. At least I didn't admit even to myself that I was in love . . . but at last the time came, I don't quite know when it happened, when I could deceive myself no longer. I couldn't continue telling myself that what I felt for GP was only friendship. I knew I had found the one person who could put up with me.[56]

Given George's record for always getting what he wanted, little imagination is needed to envision his pursuit of Amelia. That he loved her is beyond doubt, for he would never have parted from Dorothy over some light attachment, and contrary to popular belief that his interest in Amelia, and hers in him, was strictly business, their relationship became one of great depth according to George's elder son, David.[57] Many people interviewed testified that when George wanted to charm someone he became devastating, and so, for Amelia, the situation must have been a difficult one. Reared in a morally strict atmosphere she must have been torn between her feeling for him, and her avowed friendship for Dorothy, not least by the knowledge that the Putnams' separation was due, at least in part, to the amount of time she and George were spending together and George's discussion with Dorothy about the exact nature of his relationship with Amelia.

For George, too, the matter must have been painful. He had been married to Dorothy for nearly twenty years. She had been a loving partner, a good friend and an eminently suitable wife throughout those years and they had two sons whom they loved. His subsequent record as a husband (see chapter 22) reveals a man who needed a warm and loving relationship with his partner. Now he found himself in love with Amelia, possibly without any encouragement from her, although clearly she had been strongly drawn to him from the first. But George knew only one way; if you wanted something, you went all out and you got it, letting nothing stand in your way.

At about this time Amelia had a meal with Elinor Smith and said to her:

'GP has asked me to marry him. What do you think?' I said I didn't think a lot of it and the press wouldn't either. [At the time of this conversation Elinor had not heard of the Putnams' separation.]

She laughed and said, 'That's pretty much what I thought you'd say.' However she said she was already too involved and couldn't give him up. I don't know that she meant this emotionally, necessarily; I thought she saw what GP could do for her and she needed his power and push.[58]

CHAPTER 14

1929-1931

The grounds upon which Dorothy Binney successfully sued for divorce in December 1929 were George's 'failure to provide' for her and her two sons. Since leaving George she had met and fallen in love with Captain Frank Upton, formerly an officer on the liner *President Roosevelt*. A holder of the Congressional Medal of Honour, Captain Upton was also known for a heroic sea rescue of a shipful of passengers from a stricken vessel. Neither George nor Dorothy wanted unpleasant attention from the newspapers, particularly any speculation about possible future partners, so they made a private out-of-court agreement awarding George equal custody of the two sons to whose support he was to contribute.[1] Dorothy did not need his money and this was simply a method of obtaining a divorce with a minimum fuss.

George's success in promoting Amelia was not mirrored in his own career, however. The financial crash of 1929 spelled disaster for the publishing industry too, and G. P. Putnam's Sons was as affected as everyone else by falling sales. But Putnam's was also suffering from an internal situation. The president of the company was George's 85-year-old uncle, Major George Haven Putnam. 'The Major' had spent his entire life in publishing and though he had given George a free hand to build up 'the House' using his modern publishing methods, the old man clearly regretted those lost days of the nineteenth century when publishing was a slow and gentle process, without the need for hype and angles and contrived best-sellers. This wily old man saw the crash coming and pulled 'all of his

money' (presumably including that earned from the profitable previous ten years) out of Putnam's months before the crash and
'applied it to his estate', leaving only his original one-third shareholding.[2] This was a wise move on his part, but one which adversely
affected the company's cash flow at a vulnerable time.

Amelia spent the last months of 1929 in Los Angeles, working
for TAT and staying with the Madduxes[3] accompanied by her secretary, Nora Alsterlund. On 22 November she wrote to her mother
that she had been having a lovely time and flying a great deal.
'Today I think I broke the women's speed record in average time of
184.17 mph. I did one lap in 197 . . . in the new arrangement I am
half time with both eastern and western divisions of TAT.'[4]

Visiting her father, now married to his second wife, Helen, and
living at Eagerlock near Los Angeles, Amelia found him thin and ill
and worried about meeting his mortgage payments because he was
unable to work. Amelia subsequently repaid the outstanding mortgage of $2,000 and made over a freehold tenancy to her father, and
after his death (which she feared was not far off), to his widow. She
spent Christmas in California and was disappointed when the FAI
Contest Committee replied to her claim on the speed record:

> Please be advised that there is no category recognized by the
> F.A.I. for speed trials over a one mile straightaway course; there-
> fore this record can only be recognized as a 'Miscellaneous aircraft
> performance'. Maximum speed trials are only recognized by the
> F.A.I. when flown over a three kilometer course and timed by an
> electrical timing device which has been approved by the F.A.I . . .
> At the last meeting of the F.A.I. it was decided that when avi-
> atrices surpass an F.A.I. world record in their class, their
> performance shall be entered on the list of women's records and
> on the list of World's Records . . .[5]

George travelled to Paris and London where he adopted a desperate measure to obtain maximum publicity for a book which he
hoped would be a best-seller and thus help to retrieve the falling fortunes of Putnam's. The book had been written by Francesco Nitti,

nephew of the former Italian Premier, and the first man to escape from the Fascist penal colony on Lipari Island in the Mediterranean. The manuscript apparently exposed appalling prison conditions and spoke out against Mussolini. On 17 December, in Paris, George claimed that he had received an anonymous letter threatening retribution if he went ahead with the book's publication.

Adopting a manner of amused unconcern, he stated to the press on that occasion that such threats would not stop publication of the book. But on 30 December, in London, reportedly acting on the advice of Freddie Guest, he went to the police at Scotland Yard with two further letters, both decorated with fascist symbols, supposedly from the same group of fascists living in Paris, which threatened to kill George ('Pig . . . you will never reach New York alive') and blow up the Putnam offices in London and New York.

This time the police offered him round-the-clock protection until his planned departure on the SS *France* on 4 January. The matter was reported widely in both the British and American newspapers, thus providing the publicity he sought.[6] The publicity helped the book's sales a great deal and many years later George was to recall this successful publicity stunt (for that was what it was; he later confessed to his family and friends that he had written the letters himself) and attempt to use it again.[7]

When George arrived back in New York it was to the news that Dorothy was about to marry Frank Upton in the West Indies that week.[8] This must have assuaged any feelings of guilt he had over Amelia, who was in town to meet him, and to whom he immediately proposed.

Several writers have claimed that George proposed six times to Amelia, but George states in his biography of Amelia, *Soaring Wings*, that he 'proposed twice, at least'.[9] On this first occasion Amelia must have refused him, or asked for time to think about the matter. In any event, a marriage so soon after George's divorce would surely have confirmed the previous speculation about their relationship, which would not have helped Amelia's image.

George's attempts to make the Nitti book a best-seller became somewhat superfluous in February, when The Major died suddenly, leaving his Putnam's shareholding and his personal wealth to his son Palmer Cosslett Putnam. Palmer returned at once from Africa, where he had become a mining engineer, fired with enthusiasm to become a publisher and take his place at the head of the family business. He was in a powerful position thanks to his father's foresight, for he had that valuable commodity 'ready cash', of which there was little about after the financial crash in the previous year. On examining the books he expressed concern about the state of the firm, which at that stage was in need of a substantial capital injection, and suggested bringing 'new blood' into the house at senior executive level.[10]

In the ensuing family row ('to be avoided at almost any price', George was to write later), George offered to buy his cousin's stock and named a price which Palmer thought was considerably below its value. George, then vice president of the company, and only too well aware of the state of the publishing industry, considered the valuation he had put on the stock so fair that he quickly offered to sell his own holding to Palmer at the same valuation. This put George's holding at $100,000.

> My cousin bought, for which, at the time, I was glad . . . [but] a few years later he went into bankruptcy while he still owed me $75,000, which was very sad indeed. It was sad too for the House of Putnam. For after the engineer took over the controls, what with the depression and internal inflations of one sort and another, soon there were no more Putnams in the House our grandfather had founded.[11]

After George had left Putnam's, Palmer arranged a merger with Melvin Minton and Earle Balch (both of whom George had met in his army days and introduced into publishing). They had become Minton, Balch and Company and within a few years, just before its hundredth birthday, would own Putnam's. George was sorry to leave the family firm, but he recognised that nothing could be the same with his cousin in such a controlling position.

Reporting these events, *Time* magazine said

The departure from G.P. Putnam & Sons [*sic*] of G.P. Putnam was almost as newsworthy as the deal itself. In the past decade he has made himself conspicuous on the publishing scene. He is a man with a dangerous combination of literary ability, business acumen, energy . . . What Publicist Putnam intends to do in the future is not known. He may expand his cinematic activities, may publish on his own, may retire, may go off exploring. Perhaps he will do all these things. His cryptic statement of plans last week was 'If you played golf twelve years, you wouldn't stop all at once would you?'[12]

Throughout the spring of 1930 Edwin Earhart's health deteriorated. Amelia, who was commuting between Los Angeles and New York, saw him whenever she could but in a letter to Amy, Edwin stated, sadly, that 'even when she is in Los Angeles we do not see much of her so my information about her I get from the newspapers.'[13] During those months two senior executives, Gene Vidal and Paul Collins, had left TAT and Amelia was working with them to form a new airline which was to offer hourly round-trip services between New York, Philadelphia and Washington. The first shuttle!

In addition Amelia was writing articles for *Cosmopolitan* and various other journals such as *Aero-News and Mechanics* (and dealing with the massive correspondence that resulted from these); continuing her work with TAT; engaging the NAA in correspondence regarding setting up a committee to eliminate the headlining of aircraft accidents – 'you have no doubt noticed the exceptionally misleading and prominent reports which have appeared lately,' she wrote.[14]

She fitted in numerous speaking engagements while she travelled and was still plugging away at her old hobby-horse, the organisation for women pilots mooted in Cleveland the previous summer. In March 1930 the Ninety-Nines held its first meeting at which Amelia was elected president and Louise Thaden, secretary. Amelia made it her special responsibility to try to attract big prize money for women air race competitors.

She was, too, already toying with the idea of a solo transatlantic flight – a 'first' of her own – but then, every woman pilot of note had the same ambition. Although to reporters Amelia denied any such plans, to a friend she confided that she would like to do it, admitting frankly that she hadn't yet the necessary flying and navigation experience. 'Give me, say, eighteen months or two years . . .' she wrote.[15]

George, too, was busy. He was still managing Amelia and other clients while attempting to pick up his own publishing career. They spent time together whenever possible but there were 'long intervals of communication only by letter or telegram'. Later George remembered that he had bombarded her with instructions, and Amelia was so busy that 'the answers to my letters were usually my letters returned, with notations in pencil in the margin.'[16]

When they were together Amelia entertained George with amusing stories about her trips. After one lecture a woman had buttonholed her, saying, 'Do you know what my little boy said about your lecture today?'

'No,' Amelia had replied, asking dutifully, 'What did he say?'

'Well, he saw your picture beside the box-office and came running home crying Mommy, Mommy, Colonel Lindbergh's mother is going to speak at the theatre.'[17] Amelia's ready sense of humour never deserted her no matter how pressed she was, or how cornered by fame.

When in New York Amelia continued to stay in the AWA Club and, perhaps to allay her mother's concern, her secretary Nora Alsterlund moved in there, too. She never mentioned George to her mother during this period, though she wrote regularly, always sending 'a little something' to help financially. Amy was living with Muriel, who had given birth to a son, David, in April, but whose marriage was in difficulties. Finances were tight and Amy frequently had to ask Amelia for help. There were calls on her assistance too, from Edwin and Helen Earhart, though these were less frequent.

On one occasion Amelia wrote obviously in reply to a query from Amy:

Dear mother,
Enclosed is some cash. I just found your letter today and didn't
realize you'd be short of funds so soon. I shall not be in New
York very long I think, as I am going west again to pick up my
ship. There are several dates in the mid-west I must keep too.
Please let me know how Pidge fares.
    I am not marrying *anybody*.
        A.E.[18]

Amy's concern was no doubt prompted by misreported quotes.
To a close friend Amelia wrote at greater length, 'I am still unsold on
marriage. I don't want *anything* all of the time . . . I think I may
never be able to see marriage except as a cage until I am unfit for
work or fly or be active – and, of course, I wouldn't be desirable
then . . .'[19]
Early in the year she had written explaining that she was making
formal arrangements to provide for Amy, and her letter gives an
indication of her financial success:

I am enclosing a check for $100. Hereafter you will receive it
monthly from the Fifth Avenue Bank.
    I have put all my earnings into stocks and bonds and the
yearly income in your name. The list includes the $1000 dollar
bond of yours which you may have, of course, at any time . . .
Nora Alsterlund and I are living together in a large double
room at about half the rent of the suite. I am thus able to live
easily on what I make and you can have the other. I sent
clothing on because I thought it would please Pidge and was
probably needed and you wouldn't have purchased it . . . I have
just returned from Washington and Pittsburgh and am off
again to the west soon. I now have a job [it was a public
relations position organized by George] with the Pennsylvania
R.R. besides T.A.T. Maddux. I plan to work very hard this year
and little else but fly . . .[20]

When Amy voiced concern about the amount, Amelia responded

that her mother should 'not think you are taking my hard earned money', it was merely the interest earned on her investment 'that is extra to what I earn. I am living with Nora and very economical so there will be more and more accruing.'[21] These obviously satisfactory arrangements, no doubt engineered by George, must have put Amy's mind at rest for from this point on she did not hesitate to ask for help when it was needed.

June found Amelia at Grosse Isle Airport in Detroit. She had not taken lightly the refusal to acknowledge her speed record of the previous autumn and after much correspondence from her, and lobbying of the FAI by George, she was allowed to make an official attempt on the woman's speed record over 100 kilometres, which she set at 174.897 mph; the same day (25 June) she claimed the record over the same distance carrying a 500-kilogram payload at 171.438 mph, in a Vega owned by the Detroit Aircraft Corporation.[22] Ten days later she set a world speed record for women over the internationally recognised three-kilometre course, clocking up 181.18 mph. On her return home she found a letter from her father. He was obviously very ill and, with no time to write, she forwarded the letter to her mother by way of explanation, with a note scribbled on the back, 'Am heading west and will see him there.' She had only recently told Amy that Edwin was suffering from cancer and was probably too weak for surgery.

In August 1930 George joined the publishers Brewer and Warren as vice president.[23] After visiting her father, Amelia returned to New York and was hard at work on preparations for the new airline which had its inaugural flight on 1 September. Called the Ludington Line, it started with high hopes and with George's help they organised 'free flights for reporters' which gave them valuable free publicity, such as this interview Amelia gave to reporter Janet Mabie:

When we started the first of this month we hoped for a lot but we didn't expect anything. We expected the service would take hold gradually . . . that is the thing with transport in this country. We can't learn by European transport. We've our own conditions and we have nothing to go by.

We didn't expect to make money for a long time, we knew we'd make mistakes and have to find correctives. But what we build we intend to build solid and I think we have . . . The ten-passenger Stinson has justified itself as far as this service is concerned. Only once in 3900 hours of flying have we had a scrap of motor difficulties, a nut broke loose and fell into the crank case. The motor was replaced overnight without disrupting services . . .

We've got 20 landing fields on a 200-mile route. We sit down without any fuss if the weather turns . . .[24]

In September Helen Earhart cabled Amelia in New York advising her that her father was dying and wanted to see her. Amelia flew out immediately and spent a week there. He died peacefully a few hours after she left him on 23 September. She hurried back east where she had the usual round of engagements to fulfil and on the 25th was in Norfolk, Virginia where, according to newspaper reports, she 'made a spectacular visit to the city'. Her plane nosed over in landing at the Naval Air Station and she suffered scalp injuries which necessitated that she wear a turban to cover the bandages around her head.[25] Her passenger suffered a broken finger.[26] She had apparently been reaching for the brakes and leaning against the door when it opened and catapulted her backwards into the cabin. The plane ground-looped and ended up on its back. A few days later (2 October) 'full of tetanus' she wrote to her mother about Edwin's death and explained the crash:

I just returned from Dad to have a little crackup due to mechanical failure. The lock on the pilot's cockpit opened and let me out as I was leaning on it. I wasn't hurt much and neither was [the] Lockheed.

About Dad. The diagnosis was correct . . . he waged a hopeless fight against a thing which took all his nourishment . . . His big case was lost and we told him he had won. He couldn't have stood the disappointment so it was for the best . . . He asked about you and Pidge a lot, and I faked telegrams from you all.

He was an aristocrat as he went – all the weakness gone with
a little boy's brown puzzled eyes . . .
                   A.E.[27]

Her explanation of the crash to her mother was a considerable gloss-
ing-over of the facts for the Lockheed was so badly damaged that it
required a new fuselage and all its flying surfaces required repairs.[28]

Later that month Amelia accepted a proposal of marriage from
George, though two weeks later she again denied to reporters any
intention of marrying him.[29] On the following day, however, she
was with George when he admitted, smilingly, that he had obtained
a marriage licence, though they had no idea just then when they
might use it.[30] The sudden media interest may have been stimulated
by George's cryptic dedication to Amelia in his new book *Andre,
The Record of a Tragic Adventure* which read: 'To a favourite aeronaut
about to embark on a new adventure.'[31]

The licence had been obtained by George on 8 November 1930
and the couple planned to get married quietly almost immediately.
After the secret became public, however, there could be no hope of
the 'no fuss' occasion that Amelia particularly wished so the wedding
was postponed, requiring the judge to apply for a waiver because the
law in Connecticut set a defined period between the filing of intention and issue of a marriage licence.

A few weeks later, besieged every time they appeared in public, the
couple were still saying 'No' to reporters. George had a stock answer:
'In answer to the two questions I am constantly asked: "Am I getting
married?" the answer is "No." "When?" the answer is, "I don't know."'
Amelia assured her mother in a letter 'N.A. [her secretary] and I are
still going strong at the AWA.' According to Muriel, Amy opposed
the marriage because George was older and a divorced man (George,
who was then forty-two, was only ten years older than Amelia but her
age was being given as thirty), though since Amy herself was a divorcee
this seems an unreasonable prejudice. Amelia would never have let
such considerations colour her judgement, however, nor would her
mother's disapproval have influenced her decision. Any reservations
she had concerned her personal freedom and George had clearly

convinced her that he was prepared to accede to her wishes in this respect.

Her letters to her mother continued over Christmas and into the New Year. They were chatty letters full of family matters such as instruction about the suit she had sent for Christmas: 'Please go to a decent tailor and have the suit fitted . . . I want you to go into town with Nancy and buy a little brown hat to go with suit (a shade or two darker maybe) and a couple of pairs of gloves . . . then while you're at it get a dark blue hat . . . charge these and send me the bill . . . What is happening in the family? . . .' And there was business news such as 'I have taken another business with another woman; we've gone into partnership, I'll tell you the circumstances next time we meet.'[32] They were letters full of everything but the most important news, but then, she had never included her family in her important plans.

This dated back to the oceanic flight when Amelia had been distressed at Amy and Muriel's willingness to discuss with the press what Amelia considered to be very personal matters. She had now assumed a matriarchal position of provider and was in the throes of arranging a mortgage to enable Muriel to buy the house in West Medford which both Amy and Muriel felt sure would improve the latter's domestic situation.

On Wednesday 4 February in response to an invitation to visit her mother, who had the Challiss cousins staying with her, Amelia wrote a short note to say she wouldn't be home for the weekend but invited Amy and her guests to visit her the following weekend. 'I am due in Washington tonight and have a luncheon in Newark today. Cheerio. AE.'[33] She planned to spend the weekend with George. That Friday evening they decided, apparently on the spur of the moment, to use the marriage licence taken out on 8 November, three months earlier.

On Saturday 7 February 1931 Amelia and George were married in George's mother's home at Noank, Connecticut. 'For [Amelia],' George wrote, 'it was a heroic decision, touching something in her very much deeper than any mere problem of marriage which must be worked out with the . . . demands of a publicly important person. Her attitude towards responsibility was strict and methodical . . . she could toss off a scrambled word or phrase for fun's sake, but anything she thought enough of to undertake she could not play at.' George, too, had been warned of the dangers inherent in the proposed marriage, by his attorney, 'It may not be easy being married to a public character.'[34]

Nevertheless George telephoned his mother on Friday evening and told her they were driving up on the following day with the intention of getting married there; he also telephoned a friend of the family, Judge Anderson, to make the arrangements for the ceremony.

It was a clear cold day in the small New England fishing village that Saturday. There were no guests at the wedding, just the witnesses (one of George's uncles and the judge's son) and George's mother, who had not even had time to arrange flowers to decorate the house. But a large fire crackled brightly in the low-ceilinged sitting room that looked out over Long Island Sound and it had all Amelia asked – secrecy. She wore a simply cut brown suit and crepe blouse, with brown lizardskin shoes, 'no hat, of course'.[35]

Just before the judge was due to arrive Amelia handed George a letter and from the look on her face he realised that it was of vital importance to her. He wrote of the letter; 'It was pencilled longhand, with a terrible kind of care for each word, that it be fair and honest. A slip or two in spelling meticulously corrected; a few words crossed out, replaced by others monastically simple.'[36] It was undated, written on four sheets of grey writing paper headed The Square House, Noank, Connecticut (George's mother's home):

Dear Gyp
There are some things which should be writ before we are married – things we have talked over before – most of them.
　　You must know again my reluctance to marry, my feeling that I shatter thereby chances in work which mean most to me. I feel the move just now as foolish as anything I could do. I know there may be compensations, but have no heart to look ahead.

[In] our life together I want you to understand I shall not hold you to any medieval code of faithfulness to me, nor shall I consider myself bound to you similarly. If we can be honest I think the difficulties which arise may best be avoided should you or I become interested deeply (or in passing) with anyone else.

Please let us not interfere with the other's work or play, nor let the world see our private joys or disagreements. In this connection I may have to keep some place where I can go to be myself now and then, for I cannot guarantee to endure at all times the confinements of even an attractive cage.

I must extract a cruel promise, and that is you will let me go in a year if we find no happiness together.

I will do my best in every way and give you that part of me you know and seem to want.

AE[37]

An edited version of the letter was first published by George in his biography of Amelia, *Soaring Wings*, but it is believed that this is the first time it has appeared in a book in its unedited form. It is a most extraordinary testament. Few brides today, even given the relaxed conventions of the 1980s, would suggest to a bridegroom that sexual freedom for both parties was implicit in the marriage agreement.

That the points contained in the letter – or 'most of them' anyway – had been discussed by the couple indicates the level of their previous relationship and that Amelia was content to continue the liaison in its present form. It was George who wanted marriage, not – as his detractors have claimed – because he wanted to manipulate her, but because that was how George was. He did not possess Amelia's free-thinking approach and, being a romantic at heart, he wanted marriage with the woman he loved and to be a full partner in every sense of the word.[38]

Clearly when she wrote this letter Amelia was not madly in love with George, but his reaction to her written appeal perhaps reveals the reason why she was prepared to marry him. 'In her heart,' he said, 'she knew . . . that for good or ill, she must keep freedom in a measure which is not always possible in marriage. She had no selfish dream of the anatomy of freedom, but she did know it for an element without which she personally could not do, as some plants can do without water but cannot survive without air.'[39]

Amelia's fear of marriage may have been the result of her parents' experience, of having watched two intelligent, loving people turn sour and embittered in the confines of their union. Perhaps also, she still remembered the restrictions against which she had silently chafed when, even in her early twenties, she had been considered 'a daughter' and not an independent adult. Her success had provided her with an intoxicating independence both spiritual and financial and, much as she wanted the close companionship which she felt should be possible in marriage to George, she was not prepared to trade the former for the latter. She wanted both. George felt he could accommodate her wishes. Amelia has been described as emotionally undemonstrative, but Gore Vidal (Gene Vidal's son) explains: 'I can tell you that she was a very passionate person who felt things deeply. Of course it didn't always show with her – perhaps suppressed passion would be an accurate description.'[40]

After the wedding ceremony, for which they had to borrow his mother's platinum ring, having not had time to choose one, Amelia sat with the judge's son and talked about the development of a new autogyro in which she was interested. Then, after a glass of wine, she slipped a fur coat over her suit and the couple drove off to a secret destination; but not before George had telephoned his secretary Jo Berger to ask her to release the news. Within an hour the village post-mistress was bewildered. 'Wedding? I don't think there's been a wedding here today . . .' Mrs Putnam senior gave only the briefest interview. 'They didn't tell me where they were going so that I shouldn't be able to tell.' The statement released by Jo Berger gave merely the barest details of the marriage but did reveal that Amelia would retain her own name for business and writing purposes and that both would be back at work, as usual, on the following Monday morning.[41]

Amelia sent a cable to her sister asking her to break the news gently to Amy. Later, Amy made a short, dignified statement to the press: 'If Amelia is happy, and I am sure she is, then I am. I knew it was to take place, of course and I know Mr Putnam very well, but I didn't know the exact date . . .'[42]

Remembering her mother's disapproval, Amelia wrote to her:

Dear Mother

I want you to know I appreciate more than I can say the interview you gave . . . about my marriage. I was so proud of you. I am much happier than I expected I could ever be in that state. I believe the whole thing was for the best. Of course I go on in the same way as before as far as business is concerned. I haven't changed at all and will only be busier I suppose.

I have given up my A.W.A. [apartment] and moved to 42 W 58th Street just a few blocks away. I want you to come over as soon as you wish and see the apartment. I have two canaries and you know I've wanted one for ever so long. You can stay here at the hotel in another room or if you prefer at the A.W.A. Nora has moved uptown to the Columbia district . . .

I sent Muriel the $2,500 promised, I hope it will mean a lot to her, moving into a decent house . . . I am asking Pidge down here, maybe we could have a blowout together before she becomes too tied down [Muriel was pregnant again] – or is it obviously too late for her? Write me your plans.

AE[43]

Much has been made of the fact that Amelia retained her own name after her marriage, which was very unusual at that time, but in fact George as well as Amelia saw much merit in the move. After all, Amelia Earhart was an established property, the public would take time to react to the name Amelia Putnam. Undoubtedly Amelia did relish the individuality this gave her, but she was never bothered when she was addressed as Mrs Putnam and in private she often referred to herself in this manner,[44] while George frequently joked that he was often referred to as Mr Earhart.

CHAPTER 15

1931–1932

George wrote: 'When we were married our desk calendars were so full of pressing appointments that there was no time for a trip. I think that for AE there was a certain savour in the fact that the question of allowing even the gravest single step of her life up to that point to stand in the way of carrying on with her commitments, simply didn't arise.'[1]

The commitments George spoke of are borne out by newspaper archives. Both were deeply committed to their solo careers at that point and one or the other was constantly in the newspapers for attending functions, often as a guest speaker. George never failed to push out regular press releases. There were some newsworthy events in that year, however. After her marriage Amelia broke away from the Ludington Line following an undisclosed policy disagreement. Shortly afterwards George approached the Pitcairn company, manufacturers of an autogyro – an aircraft that was half-aeroplane, half-helicopter – about purchasing one.[2]

In the previous December Amelia had – 'just for fun' – made a test flight in an autogyro which was still new enough to make headlines. With virtually every prestigious flying record already broken by one of the dozen or so top women pilots, Amelia and George were looking for something which would keep Amelia's name a headliner, and the autogyro, they hoped, was just the vehicle.

On 8 April 1931 Amelia set an altitude record in the autogyro at Pitcairn Field, Pennsylvania, reaching an unofficial height of 19,000 feet on her first attempt and a recorded 18,500 feet on her second.

Amelia claimed this as an officially recognised height record. It is not recorded as such but the resultant crop of headlines confirmed that here was something worth cultivating. Amelia was the only woman flying an autogyro at the time. On 22 May she bought the Pitcairn PCA-2, registration NC 10780, stating that she wished to be the first person to fly a autogyro from coast to coast.[3] A few weeks later George arranged to sell the aircraft to Beechnut Packing Company, the chewing-gum manufacturers, who promptly loaned the aeroplane back to Amelia, paying her a retainer as a flying ambassador. Amelia actually enjoyed flying the weird-looking machine as well as finding it a challenge.[4]

After a few weeks recuperation from a tonsillectomy, Amelia set off from New York on 29 May, accompanied by her mechanic, Eddie de Vaught, on a tour that would take her via dozens of cities to Los Angeles. George's son, David Binney Putnam, still remembers being roped in to help with the publicity dreamed up by his father and Beechnut before Amelia took off, 'we had giant packets of Beechnut – about three feet long – which we were giving away';[5] and the autogyro had the words 'Beechnut Gum' emblazoned on its side.

At the end of her much-publicised transcontinental flight in what the newspapers insisted on calling 'the flying windmill' Amelia reached Los Angeles on 7 June, only to find that a previously unheard-of pilot – 25-year-old Johnny Miller from Poughkeepsie, New York – had made the trip a week before in an identical machine. Amelia was disappointed and George was furious. His explosive overreactions were well known but could be alarming to anyone witnessing them for the first time. In fact his tantrums lasted only minutes and subsided rapidly, they were more a release of tension, or an expression of frustration, than a reflection of a violent nature.

After some discussion it was decided that Amelia should return at once to New York, thus becoming the first person to make the return transcontinental flight in an autogyro. She certainly made headlines on this return flight, though they were not those she or George had hoped for. She stopped over in Abilene, Texas, on the return journey in order to attend an air fair. Naturally, the crowds were fascinated to see the autogyro and its woman pilot and Amelia made several demonstration flights during the day and gave some rides before deciding to leave. 'The crowd was desirous of seeing the autogyro closely,' she explained later, 'and I was taking off close to the crowd on that account . . .' As she took off a rotor clipped a landing light and fluttered 30 feet to land among parked cars, several of which were damaged, and showered the crowd with shards of damaged rotors and other debris. Both Amelia and the mechanic were uninjured but it was felt that the spectators had been put at grave risk and Amelia received an official reprimand from Clarence Young, then Assistant Secretary of Commerce for Aviation.[6]

Amelia answered the charges of carelessness by saying she had underestimated the distance required to get off safely and had been hit by a gust of wind, but that she retained control of the craft at all times and no one had been in danger. A replacement autogyro was hurriedly shipped out and Amelia continued her trip to Newark without further incident. A few hours after she handed the replacement aircraft back to its regular pilot he crashed it on landing.

Amelia continued to send hastily scribbled notes to Amy and in an invitation to her mother to visit Rye, she also explained the reprimand: 'The reprimand wasn't one really, mostly a chance for butting the Ludington Line and I [am] the goat. I am not a careless pilot and the letter doesn't say so.'[7] But the reprimand *was* galling particularly as she had been voted vice president of the NAA[8] shortly before setting out on her transcontinental trip.

Amelia found time after her return to write long letters of thanks to citizens of Abilene who had been kind to her after the crash, especially one family who had insisted on her staying with them and using their telephone. She arranged for George to call on them on his way to California a few weeks later. She spent the summer working from Rye – 'the city is so warm and it is hard to leave the sea even to fly . . .'[9] – and writing articles, in which she stressed the safety aspect of flying and exhorted more women to take it up.

In early September Amelia was demonstrating the autogyro at an

air show at the state fairgrounds in Detroit when it crashed on landing. George, who had driven there, was in deep conversation with
someone in the crowd and did not see the crash but heard the
sound and saw the look of horror on his companion's face:

> As I swung round I saw the giro, its rotors splintered, disappear
> in a cloud of smoke. I vaulted the rail and raced for the wreck.
> Never have I run so fast, until one of those guy wires caught my
> pumping legs exactly at the ankles. I did a complete outside loop,
> up into the air and over, landing full on my back . . . Coming to
> my senses – some of them at least – I saw AE emerge from the
> welter of dust (it wasn't smoke) and wave her hands in the air to
> show she was unhurt.[10]

George cracked three ribs but immediately put out a statement
that the crash was due to a structural fault, claiming that a landing
strut gave way as the wheels touched. The resultant heavy landing
crashed the fuselage to the ground, breaking the wires which supported the rotors which then dropped and sheared off the tail and
propeller. The aircraft was wrecked. 'My giro spill was a freak accident,' Amelia reported to her mother after the predictable headlines
had appeared:

> The landing gear gave way from a defect and I ground looped
> only. The rotors were smashed, as usual with giros, but there
> wasn't even a jar. GP fell over a rope running to pick me up and
> as he limped up I said 'It was all my fault,' meaning that he was
> hurt. The papers got it I said the crack was mine, which isn't
> accurate . . .'[11]

Despite her steady stream of letters, Amelia's relationship with
Amy and Muriel had begun to take a downturn. Under increasing
pressure she found the demands of her family irritating. Their concerns seemed to her to be petty and a critical note appears in her
letters to Amy, particularly of Muriel and Albert, who had not yet
formalised the loan agreement for the $2,500 Amelia had provided

for their house, and who were still finding it difficult to cope financially. Forgetting the days when money was not so readily available
to her she wrote curtly: 'Let me know how Pidge and Albert
progress, I don't know any way I can help them or you except by
trying to be banker for part of your funds for a while. If you want
to reach me you can do so through Nora at Rye.'

Later she allowed open exasperation to fill her letter:

December 1st 1931

Dear Mother

I am enclosing a check for $33. This plus the $17 I sent last
month makes $50. I am depositing the rest of the amount [of
$100 – the amount Amelia paid monthly to Amy] to your credit
here. I am very displeased at the use [to which] you have put
what I hoped you would save. I am not working to help Albert,
nor Pidge much as I care for her. If they had not had that money
perhaps they would have found means to economize before.

I do not mean to be harsh, but I know the family failing
about money. As for your paying board, such a thing is unthinkable as you have done all the house-keeping which more than
compensates. I would not, if I could, buy the bond. If there were
any assurance that things were run on a businesslike basis, there
might be some reason for helping.

It is true that I have a home and food but what I send you is
what I myself earn and it does not come from GP. I feel the
church gets some of what should go to living expenses and I
have no wish to continue that to Pidge's loss . . .[12]

Her position as a public figure had uncovered a natural assertive-
ness which was encouraged by George and so it seemed natural for
Amy and Muriel to turn to Amelia for help and guidance. But
Amelia's background had instilled a degree of financial prudence and
while, initially, she had enjoyed the novelty of being able to provide
treats for her family she now resented the fact that her generosity
was – to a certain extent – being taken for granted.

Muriel, in the throes of marital difficulties, was stung by her sister's strictures and it may be that both she and Amy blamed George for Amelia's new attitude, for neither woman really liked him.[13]

Under constant pressure, Amelia more and more treasured her time with George at the spacious house in Rye about 30 miles north-east of New York. Flanked by sandy beaches, the town had a number of large estates among old oaks and elm trees and the Putnam home was a pleasant place, vibrant with mementoes of George's many trips and adventures and with some startling interior decoration. One guest recalled sleeping in a room whose walls were decorated with jungle flora; another room was painted with water plants and tropical fish, so that one seemed to be sleeping in a fish tank.[14] From an informal 'English style' garden, guests entered the house through a reception hall tiled – somewhat startlingly – in sea-green ceramic tiles inset with Chinese medallions.

This led into a huge sitting room with windows along the length of one wall overlooking the terrace and gardens. A massive stone fireplace, kept well supplied with logs by George who 'loved to swing an axe',[15] was flanked by deep comfortable armchairs. Imported Chinese and Guatemalan rugs, Eastern embroideries, Chinese vases and Rockwell Kent paintings offered muted accents to the dark oak antique furniture. George's collections of exotica from his various travels around the world, from bearskins and walrus tusks to shrunken human heads and an old Spanish chest, filled rooms lined with books. In the 'Studio', where guests liked to gather after dinner, Amelia's trophies were displayed on the grand piano and in two alcoves. Portraits of George and Amelia hung over the carved staircase. With her peripatetic youth in mind, the old house must indeed have seemed truly a home at last.

It is doubtful that the time spent at Rye was always peaceful, for George was a lavish entertainer and the house was never empty of the writers and famous personalities that he constantly attracted, but Amelia felt no requirement to shine for visitors. Guests found her quiet, and a serene foil for George's brilliant magnetism.[16] When not working she loved to ride, or play golf, or swim in the Sound, and she found great relaxation in working in the gardens where pink and white dogwood bloomed each spring; she enjoyed the company of George's two sons who came to stay. She was especially close to David, who was now twenty-one years old, but the younger son, George, had contracted polio shortly after his parents' separation and constant physiotherapy meant he was unable to visit his father as often as did his elder brother.

As the year moved to a close the Putnams sent out a cheerful cartoon Christmas card depicting them both in an aeroplane flying between New York and Los Angeles. At some point after their marriage Amelia had realised, as she told a reporter, that what she had taken for so long as 'only friendship' had deepened into love. There was clearly no need for Amelia to exact payment for her 'cruel promise' of a year earlier. That she had found happiness with George was obvious from a poem she wrote for him:

> To touch your hand or see your face today
> Is joy. Your casual presence in a room
> Recalls the stars that watched us as we lay.
>
> I mark you in the moving crowd
> And see again those stars
> A warm night lent us long ago,
> We loved so then – we love so now.[17]

Probably there could have been no better match for Amelia Earhart than George Putnam. She was, he fully recognised, 'a loner' by nature[18] but her desire to live her own life fitted in well with his own lifestyle. Both were busy with their own careers and so there was no question of dependence but rather a pooling of resources. If George understood Amelia's needs then she understood his too, was tolerant of his aggressive, sometimes overbearing methods and found no difficulty in handling his brilliance, nor his often-bewildering mood changes.

Once he brought to her a marketing venture to sell children's hats bearing her name. George could see only the fact that at a cost of 50 cents and a selling price of three dollars it was a profitable project.

Amelia examined the hats and pronounced them cheap, firmly telling him she would not allow them to go on sale as she would have nothing to do with cheating children. One can only imagine George's frustrated reaction to Amelia's veto, but the contract was cancelled, none the less. There was a pronounced stubborn streak in Amelia and George must have realised immediately that on this occasion she was not going to change her mind.

During the winter months Amelia worked on a new book which she later called *The Fun of It*,[19] but in the back of her mind a plan was crystallising. One morning, according to George, she asked him over breakfast: 'Would you *mind* if I flew the Atlantic?'[20]

He knew that what she had in mind was a solo flight. 'I must have known for four years really that she wanted to. We talked of it from time to time, but always casually.' And he wrote of experiencing 'the fusion of a clutch at the heart, and something akin to elation, in the presence of so adventurous a spirit; but one could not *mind* her flying the Atlantic in the sense of putting out a proprietary hand to hold her back . . .'[21]

There were several good reasons for Amelia's wish to make that flight but first and foremost was a personal need to prove something to herself and to those critics who had jeered that she had merely been a passenger on the 1928 flight. Probably her own severest critic, she was well aware that her career had been built on a flight in which she played no active role and it hurt to have this pointed out. In the intervening time she had learned her craft, become an experienced and competent pilot and in a sense had 'earned' her place in aviation, yet she wanted, and needed, to prove that she *was* the best woman pilot. Thanks to George's skill in the field of publicity she was already firmly established as the best-*known* woman pilot.

There were other considerations. Several other women had preparations under way to make the flight and from the publicity angle George must have seen only too clearly that if another woman were to be first across the Atlantic it would not help Amelia's career. The most serious contestant was Elinor Smith who still made headlines despite George's efforts to subdue the girl whom newspapers had now nicknamed the 'Flying Flapper'. To George's chagrin Elinor had walked off with the annual award for 'Best Woman Pilot' in 1930.[22]

Elinor had acquired a Lockheed Vega similar to Amelia's with which to make the flight when the spring weather declared the transoceanic flight season open. Indeed she had intended to make the attempt in the previous summer but an accident in August at Garden City had wrecked the 'high speed [presumably retractable] landing gear' and by the time repairs had been made, including a conventional undercarriage, the weather slot had gone and the Atlantic 'season' was over for another year.

Amelia felt she had the necessary experience to make the solo attempt on the Atlantic and she badly wanted to take that record. She also had the ideal plane, the Vega, which – since its rebuild the previous fall – had been chartered to the Ludington Line, flying on a scheduled service between Philadelphia and Washington. There was one more factor; like George, Amelia relished the idea of adventure. There could be no question this time of her not realising how much water she had to cross, or of the fears of a transoceanic flier. She knew to a degree how accurate her navigation would have to be, and how much reliance she would be placing on her plane and instruments, not to mention her own ability and endurance.

Bernt Balchen was invited to Sunday lunch at Rye and over a game of croquet in the weak early April sunshine Amelia told him of her outline plan.

'Am I ready to do it?' she asked him when she had finished. 'Is the ship ready? Will you help me?' And after a brief moment of thought Balchen replied 'Yes, you can do it. The ship – when we are through with it – will be OK. And . . . I'll help.'[23] As before, only a very few were let in on the plan – her cousin Lucy (Toots) Challiss who was visiting at Rye, and Eddie Gorski, her mechanic. Amelia wanted to reserve the option to pull out at any time and therefore did not want the pressures of reporters, family or friends, nor even commercial interests. Nor did she wish to take the risk of precipitating a competitor into sudden flight.

As a cover story the press were informed that the Vega had been leased to Balchen. He was in the early stages of preparing for an already publicised polar flight and the plane was shipped to the old Fokker plant at Teterborough, New Jersey. There, under Balchen's instruction, Gorski went to work. It was first necessary to strengthen the fuselage to take the additional fuel tanks in the wings and cabin which would enable the Lockheed to carry 420 gallons of fuel and thus give her a range of over 3,200 miles. A new engine was also fitted. The old Wasp, which had done sterling work over the past three years, was removed and a new Supercharged Wasp engine which developed 500 hp was installed. The aeroplane in its smart red and gold livery was not given a name. Although it had become customary to name aeroplanes on record-breaking attempts, George was opposed to anything which might have detracted from the publicity and credit which would accrue to the name of Amelia Earhart. The aeroplane would not, therefore, be allowed to become a 'personality'; it was solely a vehicle for Amelia.[24]

The proposed flight date was set by George with his keen sense for a story and it was hoped that Amelia would leave exactly five years to the day that Lindbergh had made his flight on 20–21 May 1927. Amelia went along with this, recognising the news value of the coincidence, but ready at any time to abandon the project if Balchen reached the conclusion that she should not make the flight for any reason, or if she herself wished to pull out.[25]

By early 1932 no other person had successfully flown the Atlantic *alone* since Lindbergh, and though there had been some twenty flights by crewed aeroplanes (including the *Friendship* flight), what Amelia was planning was, in itself, a major venture.[26] Knowing that she would be castigated by certain elements of the media she made it clear in her earliest statements that she was not trying to prove anything and was well aware that the flight would not contribute anything to the science of aviation. 'It was clear in my mind that I was undertaking the flight merely for the fun of it. It was in a measure, a self-justification – proving to me, and to anyone else interested, that a woman with adequate experience could do it.'

That it was *necessary* to prove that a woman could succeed becomes evident from the attitude of Mary Heath, once a friend and now, because of George's behaviour, openly hostile towards Amelia. In an article in *Liberty Magazine* entitled 'Why I Believe Women Pilots Can't Fly the Atlantic – an outspoken warning by Lady Heath', this world-famous, experienced pilot confidently stated that it could not be done. 'It is plain suicide for any woman today', she claimed, and she had previously delivered her opinion in several lectures. Though almost certainly unaware of Amelia's imminent intention, she was a close friend and confidante of Elinor Smith who had made no secret of her proposed transatlantic attempt. Coincidentally the article hit the news-stands on the day Amelia took off, allowing a classic, though completely unintentional, piece of nose-thumbing from Amelia. In sending the article to *Liberty* Lady Heath's accompanying note had read '. . . do make an appeal if you can for women not to fly the Atlantic, even if you can't use my scribble. It is madness for them to attempt it and at least the first dozen will be drowned . . .'[27]

It was decided early on that Amelia would not set out to duplicate Lindbergh's course, for Balchen doubted her ability to endure such a long flight. It was agreed that she would aim for Paris as a provisional destination with the British Isles as the prime objective, but her departure point would be Harbour Grace, Newfoundland (Lindbergh had flown from New York), and to enable her to start in as 'fresh' a physical condition as possible, Balchen would pilot the plane to Newfoundland. If after her first landfall she felt able to continue to Paris, well and good, otherwise she was to set down anywhere.

That spring Amelia carried on with her usual round of speaking engagements. Most were fee-earners, but some were performed in a spirit of social concern, such as an address to the inmates of the Welfare Island workhouse, after which she was stopped for speeding and received a suspended sentence. From April she worked almost exclusively on the preparations for the flight, equipping the plane with additional instruments though in retrospect they seem basic enough: a drift indicator, and both aperiodic and gyroscopic compasses to supplement the magnetic one already fitted. With expert help she worked out the fuel system and how to best use it so that weight would be evenly distributed as each tank emptied. In this she was assisted by Major Edwin Aldrin.[28]

Instruction in blind flying techniques was vital and once the Lockheed was ready she took the opportunity to practise instrument flying whenever possible, 'until I felt really confident of my ability to handle the ship, without looking outside of the cockpit – that is, flying it solely with instruments.'[29] Through the middle weeks of May George and Amelia studied the Atlantic weather pattern charts with increasing interest. Once again George had recruited the personal assistance of 'Doc' Kimball[30] at the New York US Weather Bureau to provide detailed information of a 'slot' in which Amelia could safely get across. Doc Kimball, having seen seven women[31] perish in attempts to fly the Atlantic cooperated reluctantly, declaring 'When weather is at all possible we *may* tell a good man that he might make it. To all women we say NO. Unless conditions are extraordinarily good. And that is very seldom.'[32]

Amelia's letters to her mother were full of domestic trivia; her secretary was on vacation and she was finding it difficult coping with her heavy correspondence; the garden was just coming into spring flower; she advised her mother to make use of the 'scrub woming' hired to help out at Muriel's home; she sent a book for Sam Chapman – 'Will you forward it to him?'[33] There is no hint of the important event which was now occupying virtually her every waking thought.

On 18 May the outlook weather pattern made the projected departure date (20 May) look doubtful. A persistent trough of low pressure stationed over the eastern Atlantic threatened to dispense its rain and low cloud for a week or more. There was no improvement on the 19th, nor on the morning of the 20th. George went to New York to Doc Kimball's office while Amelia who had virtually abandoned the idea of a departure 'for some days', decided to drive over to the airfield. When she arrived at Teterborough Airport, Eddie Gorski told her that George was on the telephone. He and Kimball had just gone over the morning weather reports coming in from Atlantic shipping and key weather stations; not only was there clear weather over the Atlantic but there was good visibility all the way to Newfoundland – 'St John's, anyway', he told her, 'And by tomorrow the Atlantic looks as good as you're likely to get it for some time.' This 'slot' would not last, however.[34]

Amelia had a hurried conference with Balchen and decided immediately that she could be ready to leave at three o'clock. She drove home to change into flying clothes (riding jodhpurs, silk shirt and scarf, sweater and loose jacket), pack her leather flying suit, maps and a few odds and ends such as the elephant-toe bracelet which George had brought back from Liberia in 1929, and which it is said she regarded as a good-luck charm[35] (though she is on record as saying she didn't believe in luck: 'The best mascot is a good mechanic!').

> Five minutes was enough to pick up my things. Plus a lingering few more to drink in the beauty of a treasured sight. Beside and below our bedroom windows were dogwood trees, their blossoms in luxuriant full flower, unbelievable bouquets of white and pink flecked with the sunshine of spring.[36]

This was possibly the worst moment. The safe, calm old house with its peaceful garden full of sunshine and spring flowers. She must have wondered why she was risking her life when she could, without loss of face, remain safely at home. 'The actual doing of a dangerous thing, it seems to me, may require little courage. The preparation for it – the acceptance of the inevitable risks involved – may be a far greater test of morale', she once said.[37]

She allowed only moments for these fleeting thoughts before racing back to the airfield, reaching there at 2.55 p.m.; by 3.15 p.m. the Lockheed was in the air with Balchen at the controls and Amelia and Eddie Gorski resting in the cabin behind the auxiliary fuel tank.

They flew via St John's and when they arrived at Harbour Grace they found that weather reports were promising, though far from perfect. Knowing that George, by pre-arranged plan, would have now told Amy and Muriel about her flight, and remembering the contretemps of the previous flight, Amelia wired an instruction to George: TELEPHONE MY SISTER DIRECTIONS FOR PRESS INTERVIEWS and requested advice regarding her own media contact: IS RADIO BROADCASTING LOCAL STATIONS OK?,[38] to which George replied that she should avoid all broadcasting; he needed maximum impact to command the greatest fee from syndicating the 'scoop' news of the flight through the *New York Times*. Almost hourly reports on Atlantic weather conditions were cabled to Harbour Grace as well as encouraging forecasts from London.

Even the most detailed of these, however, seems little enough information with which to set off on such a hazardous journey in view of the number of times the words 'perhaps' and 'probable' occur in the text:

TO AMELIA EARHART, HARBOUR GRACE, NF MAY 20TH
NOON EST LOOKS SATISFACTORY. ONLY PROBABLE DIFFICULTY THOUGHT POSSIBLE EXTENDING FROM EASTERN ATLANTIC LOW SOUTH WESTWARD TO LATITUDE FORTY LONGITUDE FORTY SEVEN PROBABLY CONSIDERABLE CLOUDINESS. FORECAST HARBOUR GRACE LONGITUDE THIRTY FIVE WILL BE FORWARD SOON. EASTERN SITUATION APPARENTLY CLEARING UP SATISFACTORILY. FOLLOW-ING JUST RECEIVED FROM LONDON OUTLOOK TOMORROW EASTERN ATLANTIC FRESH NORTHWESTERN OR WESTERLY WINDS. SKY HALF TO HEAVY COVERED. CLOUDS FIFTEEN HUNDRED FEET SHOWERS VISIBILITY GOOD. BRITISH ISLES WIND SOUTH OR SOUTHWEST TWENTY TO THIRTY MILES AT TWO THOUSAND FEET BUT VARIABLE IN EASTERN DISTRICT. VARIABLE CLOUDS PERHAPS THUNDER AND RAIN. LOCAL FOG IRISH SEA ENGLISH CHANNEL. WESTERN EUROPE WIND SOUTHWEST OR WEST MODERATE TO FRESH VARIABLE CLOUDS PERHAPS THUNDER SHOWERS GP 2.50 PM[39]

In the early afternoon, while Balchen and Gorski completed the final mechanical check, Amelia went off to have a nap and it says a lot for her self-confidence that she was able to sleep. Just after 6.30 p.m. (local time) she was awakened and returned to the field. Balchen recalled her quiet and unobtrusive demeanour in his diary.

> She listens calmly, only biting her lip a little, as I go over with her the course to hold, and tell her what weather she can expect on the way across the ocean. She looks at me with a small lonely smile and says, 'Do you think I can make it?' and I grin back: 'You bet.' She crawls calmly into the cockpit of the big empty airplane, starts the engine, runs it up, checks the mags, and nods her head. We pull the chocks, and she is off . . .

Amelia remembered only Balchan's parting words: 'Okay. So-long. Good luck.'[40]

Despite the load the Lockheed rose easily and Amelia headed out over the open water in fair weather into a 'lingering sunset'.[41] As planned, it was exactly five years to the day that Lindbergh had set off on his historic flight across the Atlantic. A cable was sent to George AE TOOK OFF 712 NFLD PERFECT PERFORMANCE . . .[42] For George it was to be a long and anxious wait.

For a few hours the flight was uneventful but then, as she cruised along in the moonlight at 12,000 feet, her altimeter failed. In all her experience of flying she had never had this happen before and George later wrote that her reaction was one of awe rather than horror. From this point on she had no indication of her true height, a vital factor in instrument flying; however, she carried a barograph which would, at least, give her an indication of her climb and descent.[43]

Shortly afterwards a severe storm with lightning buffeted the Lockheed for about an hour and Amelia afterwards thought that she had probably wandered off course during this interlude. About four hours into the flight the exhaust manifold seam parted due to a bad weld. Noting the vibration, Amelia must have stood up and peered over the instrument panel through the gap under the rim of the cowling; there she could see the glow of flames and she immediately guessed what had happened.

She would have remembered a similar fiery glow from the

Friendship's exhaust on her previous ocean flight, and would have not been concerned by the flames *per se*, which she knew were caused by the burning of fuel and air under pressure and occurring in all vehicles (even in modern cars, but not seen because of the long exhaust), but particularly visible on aircraft with short or stubby exhausts and at night. She was then 'sorry she had looked at the break at all because the flames appeared so much worse than they did in the daytime'.[44] However she must have been concerned about the damage causing further problems, and indeed as the night wore on the manifold began to vibrate with increasing intensity. Later she admitted to being tempted, at this point, to return. However, since she was four hours out, thus requiring a four-hour return trip and a night landing in Newfoundland with a big fuel load, after some reflection she decided that the eight hours of total flying time would put her more than halfway across the ocean and she would fly on.[45]

After a while Amelia flew into clouds and decided to get over the top of them. She climbed for half an hour and then noticed that the plane was feeling sluggish; a film of slush on the windscreen had just alerted her to the fact that she had picked up ice when suddenly, without warning, the Lockheed went into a spin.

> How long we spun I do not know. I do know that I did my best to do exactly what one should do with a spinning plane and regained flying control as the warmth of the lower altitude melted the ice. As we righted and held level again, through the blackness below I could see the whitecaps, too close for comfort.[46]

She wrote that a glance at her barograph showed that she had lost 3,000 feet in the spin and now, still with no idea of her exact height she flew under the clouds until she ran into fog and decided that it was too dangerous to fly so low without visual checks. She climbed again, trying to find the happy medium between the fog and the ice and flew for some hours purely on instruments until dawn came. Flying eastward against the sun's passage the night was fortunately short, but even so that first glow of daylight must have been a welcome sight. The various incidents and problems had helped her to stay awake but she carried with her a small bottle of smelling salts to help maintain concentration. Later she confessed to almost 'losing her nerve over the ice', but remembering that Lindbergh had experienced a similar problem had given her courage.

As the sun rose she found it more comfortable to fly just inside the top of the clouds at about 10,000 feet, for the sun's brilliant reflection dazzled her if she flew on top; but as the morning wore on she decided to fly under the layers, even though 'they were very near the water'.[47] About two hours from her estimated first landfall (Valencia Island in southern Ireland) she turned on her reserve tank only to find that the cabin fuel gauge was leaking and that there was a steady drip of fuel into the cockpit and on her left shoulder.

Earlier, the metal of the exhaust manifold, burned for many hours by flames fuelled by hot gases, had split even further and the vibration had increased, which had caused Amelia extreme concern for the past hour or more. But now she became worried that the fumes of leaking fuel would reach the exhaust system and be ignited by the flames that she knew were there although they were not visible in the daylight. At this point she decided to put down at the first sight of land, wherever that might be.

Considering Bernt Balchen's expertise, that he was a very thorough and cautious man, and that he had given the plane a painstaking preflight check, it is surprising that so many things went wrong in such a short time.

Doc Kimball had warned that there was a belt of rain south of Amelia's course so when she ran into storm clouds in late morning she thought she was too far south and turned north-east hoping to reach the southern tip of Ireland. Later she claimed that she had probably been more or less on course for when land came into sight she found she had 'hit Ireland about the middle', but in fact her first landfall was Teelin Head, County Donegal in the north-west corner of Ireland and she was some 200 miles north of her stated track, which should have taken her across Dingle Bay in the south-west corner; indeed had she been another 50 miles north she would have missed Ireland altogether and flown on to Scotland.

Probably more exciting than actually sighting land was seeing a small fishing vessel about 100 miles off the coast. I was going by, as I wanted to reach land, but then decided to circle, that all might know I had got so far, anyway. I circled and received an answering signal. A whistle and some kind of bomb was set off. Of course I could not hear them, but I could see the smoke and the steam from the whistle. It was the first human contact since Newfoundland.[48]

Even when she sighted land Amelia had no way of accurately pin-pointing her position, and with no altimeter she was reluctant to fly on indefinitely without information about the height of any moun-tains she might encounter in the glowering thundery clouds that were all around her. When flying around the USA she had often used railroads to aid navigation, and now, fortunately, she spotted a railway track. A railway must, she reasoned, lead to a major town where there would be an airfield. She had yet to learn that Britain and Ireland were (and still are!) poorly served in the matter of land-ing fields and was surprised when the town she flew over had no airfield. Deciding that she would land anyway, she selected a large pasture and, after several low reconnaissance passes, landed in the long sloping meadow hoping to avoid the grazing cows. A lone, astonished, farm labourer saw her land.

Amelia cut the switches, climbed out of the plane and, as the man approached the plane, she called out. 'Where am I?'

Danny McCallion replied obligingly and with excruciating accu-racy.

'In Gallegher's pasture.'

CHAPTER 16

1932–1933

Although she had allowed for a flight of 3,200 miles Amelia actually flew 2,026 miles in 14 hours 54 minutes,[1] landing at Culmore near Londonderry in Northern Ireland at 1.45 p.m. (BST) on Saturday 21 May 1932. Having used only 350 gallons of the 420 carried by the Vega, she had enough left to fly for a further three hours or so. She considered the possibility of flying on to Croydon, near London, having established her position, but the condition of her aeroplane and her own physical tiredness convinced her to end the flight in Londonderry.

McCallion was not at all sure whether Amelia was man or woman when the boyish figure dressed in jodhpurs and shirt, short untidy hair uncombed, appeared.

'Have you come far?' he asked her. 'From America.' she replied. 'I was all stunned and didn't know what to say,' he recalled later.

Having only sipped at a small can of tomato juice during the entire flight Amelia asked where she could get a drink of water and McCallion led her to a nearby peat-roofed cottage where she drank several cups of tea while he ran for William Gallegher who owned the farm.[2] After investigating the truth of the unlikely tale carried by his normally sane cowman, Gallegher located a car which took Amelia to Londonderry, some five miles away. Meanwhile the local police were alerted and it seems that it was they who notified the *Londonderry Sentinel,* the first newspaper to receive the news. As teleprinters across the world chattered out details of her arrival, a reporter on the *New York Sunday Mail* reached immediately for the telephone and called George. He was lucky enough to break the news before anyone else. The scribbled notes made by George's secretary survive in the National Air and Space Museum library at the Smithsonian Institution in Washington, DC.

Landed in pasture
Londonderry Island [*sic*]
5 miles from London [*sic*]
Plane Ok
8.35 <u>Ireland</u>
London

These notes indicate that the reporter's geographical knowledge was poor; however, the telephone call ended a period of great anxiety for George who, interviewed during the flight, had remarked tensely, 'I guess I'm doing as well as can be expected!' 'He was wild like a bear,' his son David recalled, remembering the endless pacing of his father.[3] Now George was elated: '. . . tell her to telephone me wherever she is, all I want is to hear her voice and tell her she is the greatest woman in the world . . . I knew that if any woman could do this great feat she was the one; but I have been in deadly fear of the terrors of the Atlantic all night. For Heaven's sake tell her to telephone me at once. I shall not leave the phone . . .'[4]

George's nervousness had reached a crescendo when a telephone call from the Press Association advised that Amelia had crashed near Le Bourget. It was a mistake, a plane *had* crashed but it was 'twelve interminable minutes', George recalled, before he was told it was a false alarm and that, in fact, there was still no news of Amelia.[5]

For Amelia, though her physical weariness was obvious from telltale dark smudges under her eyes, it must have been a moment of great personal satisfaction. For now *she* had flown the Atlantic. On her own. And in doing so had broken several records:

She had become the first woman (and only the second person) to fly the Atlantic solo.
She had become the only *person* to fly it twice.

She had established a record for crossing it in the shortest time in
    any direction (previously held by Alcock and Brown in a time of
    16 hours 12 minutes)
She had established a record (2,026 miles) for the longest non-stop
    distance flown by a woman (previously held by Ruth Nichols
    with a distance of 1,977.6 miles)

On arrival in Londonderry Amelia went straight to a post office
where she sent cables before telephoning a London number where
'authorised' newsmen were standing by for her first-hand report of
the flight. Only when she had performed this pre-arranged duty did
she book a transatlantic call to George. Even as she waited, congratulatory cables and calls started to flood in, something she was
obviously prepared for.

When her call to George came through Amelia was able to tell
him a little about her flight: she had chosen for the last hours to fly
low over the ocean, she said, because 'I'd rather drown than
burn . . .' After giving George an outline of the flight for the *New
York Times* she was able to wash and eat before returning to Culmore
with two mechanics. She had earlier accepted an invitation to stay
the night at the home of a Mrs McClure, chatelaine of a large house
(Brook Hall) near Gallegher's farm, no doubt reflecting that she
stood a better chance of a peaceful night's rest there than in a
Londonderry hotel.

Next morning, having received the mechanics' report she decided
not to fly the plane to Croydon but to have it dismantled and
shipped over. She had received several offers to fly her to England
from such diverse quarters as the impressive Lady Bailey, and James
and Amy [Johnson] Mollison. On George's advice, however, she was
not prepared to share her limelight. Lady Bailey in fact flew to
Londonderry to greet Amelia but arrived shortly after Amelia had
left in a plane chartered from National Flying Services by
Paramount Newsmen (Movietone in England) who had bought
exclusive rights to filmed interviews.[6]

First, though, there was breakfast followed by photo calls and
interviews. Amelia was patient and chatty. She had taken off with

literally what she was wearing; she would have to borrow some money and clothes for all she had with her was $20; she had no intention of flying back to New York. Certainly more adept with reporters than after her previous flight, she talked about the flight in general terms, throwing in a few colourful terms such as 'Atlantic rollers'. She showed them some of the more impressive telegrams – from the President of the United States; the Prime Minister; Lord Londonderry; Andrew Mellon; Charles and Anne Lindbergh; Governor and Mrs Roosevelt; and from competitor Ruth Nichols (YOU BEAT ME TO IT FOR THE SECOND TIME). She kept to herself one which read WE KNEW YOU COULD DO IT AND NOW YOU HAVE, STOP CHEERS CONGRATULATIONS MUCH LOVE MOTHER AND MURIEL. And though she had accepted the invitation of the American Ambassador to stay at the Embassy in London, she was delighted to receive a cable from Lady Astor duplicating the invitation and offering to lend her a nightgown.

Amelia was persuaded to don her leather flying suit, start up the aeroplane and taxi it round the meadow for newsreel cameras, then, as she stopped the engine and emerged from the Lockheed, the small crowd that had gathered there cheered and threw their hats in the air. These pictures were circulated to cinemas within days, purporting to be live film of her landing after the flight – a harmless subterfuge aimed at an unsophisticated cinema-going audience.

In the early afternoon of 22 May Amelia took her leave of the Galleghers and departed for London in a Desoutter aeroplane which weighed less than the Vega's fuel load. She arrived in London to enthusiastic crowds and her short speech was heralded by a deafening clap of thunder and heavy rain which made her laugh. This unaffected behaviour did much to endear her to the crowd, especially as she showed no hurry to leave but stayed talking for a while, her short hairstyle unaffected by the weather. What Amelia did not see was fighting between Pathe and Paramount newsreelmen vying for the best filming position. Two of Pathe's men ended up with broken ribs in the scuffle! Amelia had already been distressed to learn that a plane carrying two reporters returning to London from Culmore had crashed killing both occupants.

Amelia's days in London were filled with dinners and public appearances, initially attended wearing borrowed clothes until she was able to buy some of her own. 'I lived mostly on credit', she said afterwards. George roared with laughter when told his wife was short of money. 'It won't be the first time she's landed in London broke!' he quipped. Amelia had spoken to him several times and in a conversation on 24 May, she asked him to join her for the remainder of her visit. In a letter to her mother Amelia said she hadn't been able to face the thought of coming home alone.[7] George made plans to sail on the 26th on the SS *Olympic* and meanwhile, though he was busy with plans for her New York reception, he took time to write to Amy:

Dear Mrs Earhart:
Thanks for the note. Of course I will take over the letters to Amelia. I am sure your cable addressed to her, London, has reached her.

. . . I am glad I am going over. We are coming back on a slow boat deliberately planned so A.E. can get a good rest, and naturally I will be able to shield her from much buffeting.

Will you let me know, please, if you and Mrs Morrissey, or either of you, care to come to New York to be here when Amelia arrives? Our friend Capt. Railey, is caring for all these things while I am away. Just write me here and my secretary will see that Capt. Railey gets your word. Accommodations will be arranged for you at the Hotel Biltmore, where we will stay, if you care to come. It will, I imagine, be a pretty hectic time. Likely we will be going to Washington that midnight.

Of course we would love to have you. On the other hand, possibly you would prefer to keep out of the circus and come to us a little later at Rye for a quiet visit.
                    Sincerely,
                    GPP[8]

In all her interviews Amelia made it clear that she had made the flight for purely personal reasons and she doubted that she would ever do it again. 'For one thing,' she said in a speech to the Institute of Journalists, 'it would take more than four years to convince my husband . . .' She claimed no advances for aviation as a result of her flight, though she did state firmly that she believed it would be only a short time before a commercial air service, probably in flying boats, would be crossing the Atlantic regularly.

Watching film of her arrivals in 1928 and 1932 one is immediately struck by the change in Amelia's attitude towards reporters. In 1928, though she answered questions readily enough, she was diffident and shy. In 1932 she 'hosts' the interviews, tossing in amusing remarks and playing with the reporters in a friendly manner. It is she who winds up the sessions with a confident 'Are there any other questions?' In a radio interview at the BBC she is not afraid to throw in words of her own invention. When the Lockheed picked up ice, she said, 'it felt bloggy'. And she broadcast a message to the American people after being told that she was to be awarded the Distinguished Flying Cross by Congress.

In what little time she could spare from the arduous round of public appearances Amelia wrote a final chapter for her book *The Fun of It* describing her flight in a brief, practical way. This was cabled to her publishers Harcourt and Brace in New York, 'a postscript,' she said, 'from overseas'. Predictably she was pictured daily with famous statesmen and socialites, celebrities from stage and aviation. Jim Mollison and Amy Johnson made regular contact – it would not be long before Mollison would make his own spectacular east to west flight across the ocean, the *hard* way, which experts said was virtually impossible due to constant adverse winds. And she not only met the Prince of Wales (later Edward VIII and subsequently Duke of Windsor) when he formally received her at Buckingham Palace on 25 May but she danced with him three times a few days later, at a charity ball. Amelia was a good dancer and made no secret of her enjoyment of the pastime. The two were reported as chatting happily together and later Amelia told reporters; 'Like all flyers he dances well', and, 'I hope the prince was amused.' She was distressed when she was reported as drawling 'Waal . . .' at him.

The Lockheed Vega, which had meanwhile arrived in London, was reassembled and put on display at Selfridges. The busy round of personal appearances continued until on 3 June she left England for Cherbourg on C. R. Fairey's yacht *Evadne* and there she met George for a private reunion before they entrained for Paris. It had been fifteen days, he recalled, since he'd taken leave of her:

Fairey met me at the landing ladder of his yacht.

'Hello,' he said. 'She's in there.'

AE was standing in the doorway.

'Hi!' she said casually.

It had a fine sound, that characteristic greeting. It took account of nothing – the strain and exactions of the flight, the chances that it would fail in mid-ocean – and it took account of everything. She was there, and there was nothing to be excited about . . .[9]

Later, over breakfast with the others on the *Evadne*, Amelia teased George with gentle humour. 'Generous allowance for a trip to Europe . . .' she said with a grin, referring to the $20 he had handed her at Teterborough, and later she reflected how shocking it was that she'd 'had to fly the Atlantic in order to get a new wardrobe'.[10]

In Paris, entranced by the city she had wanted to visit since earliest childhood, Amelia carried on the arduous tasks of a celebrity, but in the photographs of her there is a new luminosity in her face. There can be no question but that George's presence meant a great deal to her and he was a constant shadow. He was no stranger to Paris and his support gave Amelia a confident warmth in her handling of duties which might otherwise have warranted merely her practical, good-natured touch. Sometimes they appeared hand in hand, unusual, for both of them were intensely jealous of their personal lives and such public demonstrations of their relationship were rare.

Informally, the couple were lavishly entertained by the 'international' set based in Paris for the early summer – the outrageous Lady Mendl (Elsie de Wolfe) and Elsa Maxwell for example, and a couple who were later to prove valuable contacts, Jacques and Violette de Sibour.[11]

Formally, Amelia was made a Knight of the Legion of Honour, laid a wreath at the tomb of the Unknown Soldier, attended the Air Races and always, always, the couple were surrounded by happy crowds wanting to see and touch Amelia. Everywhere they went she was showered with bouquets of flowers and their rooms were banked with them. This caused a problem for George who suffered from hay fever and 'when introduced to an interested public was seen to be red-eyed and weeping'.[12] Amelia was modest and took a practical line about her achievements; when her courage was praised she replied, 'If it took courage I wouldn't have done it . . . I undertook the flight for my own pleasure and in a sense to justify myself.'

This line was clearly meant to deflect criticisms of the flight, which in some cases came from influential quarters, 'Amelia has given us a magnificent display of useless courage,' began M. E. Tracey in the *New York World Telegram*. Equally typical is this acerbic contribution from C. G. Grey, editor of *The Aeroplane*:

On Saturday, May 21st, Mrs G.P. Putnam, known professionally, or for purposes of publicity, as Miss Amelia Earhart, landed at Londonderry, in or near the Irish Free State, from Harbour Grace, Newfoundland. This proves that in 1932 with a modern aeroplane, a modern engine, and the latest navigational instruments, a woman is capable of doing what a mere man did in 1919, but in three hours less than the man's time.

We cannot think why she did it, except of course for her own gratification. It does nothing for the good of aviation. And . . . we all know that a good woman pilot is as good as an equally good man. And we all know that quite a number of men who are not by any means good pilots have got across the Atlantic whereas others who were remarkably good pilots have fallen in.

. . . Any further information on the subject of this flight may be gained from the daily press, and the cheaper the paper the more information the reader will get for his or her money.[13]

And in a letter to the president of the NAA (Amelia was vice president) one apparent misogynist wrote: 'Only an average flyer, she has pushed herself to the front by following the tactics of the feminists . . . Using a man-made perfect machine, tuned by men mechanics, trained by men flyers, [and a] course laid out by a man, by a lucky break she just managed to make the hop . . .'[14] It is difficult to know why Amelia attracted this sort of criticism (and there was more in the same vein even from other leading American newspapers) for though the flight, in itself, constituted no particular breakthrough, the mere fact that there were pilots prepared to risk all to gain records encouraged manufacturers to further technological effort. In a sense this was Amelia's – and all the other record-breaking flyers' – contribution to aviation.

In the public eye, too, the flight was a triumphant success at a time when newspapers carried daily reports of fatal air crashes. So her success encouraged confidence in aviation as a principle. Strange, this need to criticise the ability which is given to so few to reach out further than one's fellows; however, Grey's comments regarding 'cheap' newspaper reporting were accurate. Colourful accounts of Amelia landing with hardly a drop of fuel; within six feet of a hedge that would have wrecked her plane; killing cows as she landed; and various imaginary incidents which were supposed to have occurred during the flight are a trap for unwary researchers. Fortunately in the many speeches she was to make over the next months, Amelia took the opportunity to mock these spurious accounts . . . 'and no cow died, unless it was from fright!'

After Paris, Amelia and George travelled to Rome where they were granted an audience with the Pope and later met Mussolini who had sent a massive bouquet of red roses to her on her arrival in the Eternal City. But the main purpose of the trip was to attend the Congress of Trans-Oceanic Airmen organised by General Balboa, the Italian Minister for Air. George was particularly amused that, apart from Amelia, the only person to have flown the ocean twice, the convention members were exclusively male and 'well weighed down by medals'. There was no medal for Amelia – although she was to receive one later – 'It really was a troublesome situation. As far as Italy was concerned AE's sex was simply wrong . . .'[15]

Within days the Putnams were in Brussels for a private meal with the King and Queen of Belgium where Amelia was presented with the decoration of Chevalier of the Order of Leopold.[16] George, in morning suit, had had to borrow a top hat. Unfortunately it was several sizes too small and he carried it around uncomfortably hoping no occasion would arise when he might have to put it on his head. At a dinner party in Amelia's honour the couple met André Picard, the internationally renowned balloonist; George spent the evening unsuccessfully trying to persuade him to write a book.

It must have been a great relief to Amelia when on 15 June, nearly a month after she had taken off from Teterborough, New Jersey, she boarded the liner *Ile de France* to sail for New York. But she looked surprisingly relaxed as she acknowledged the cheers of those on the quayside, and was delighted when three light aeroplanes appeared over the ship to 'bomb' her with flowers.

A few days of rest on the ship were followed by the spectacle of New York at its most exuberant. Amelia was given a tickertape parade and mayoral address; welcoming crowds of thousands cheered the motorcade of dozens of cars containing civic dignitaries and aviation notables. Some of them were rivals in the field of aviation. When Elinor Smith, for example, warmly congratulated her, Amelia was quiet for a moment, recognising the magnitude of the young flyer's disappointment that she had not been the first woman to make the flight. Then she said, 'Thanks Elinor. It means a great deal to have you say that.'[17]

Amy and Muriel did not come to New York, perhaps because of George's eve-of-sailing letter, and on the following day George flew with Amelia to Washington where she was to receive from the President of the United States the Special Gold Medal struck by the National Geographic Society.

The society had, from time to time, honoured a select band of geographical pioneers but Amelia was the first woman to be so honoured. There were the usual rounds of lunches and dinners, including dinner at the White House, 'a solemn occasion', George recorded. On the day of her arrival the Senate approved the proposal to award Amelia the Distinguished Flying Cross.[18] Newsreel film shows that throughout, Amelia's slim and feminine presence seems calm, only slightly amused by it all. Almost always dressed in brown, according to newspaper reports, she is often the only woman without a hat, her fair curly hair lifted by summer breezes.

After Washington there were other cities, other parades, other welcomes. There were thousands of letters and cables each day. George was her constant support, not always able to be at her side but shadowing, occasionally taking her arm to steer her through a crowd, watchful, listening. This was his *business* after all. Sometimes a reporter looking for a different 'angle' interviewed George. His forthright views on feminine equality must have made good copy. Stating that it did his ego good to have his wife do something better than he, he finished:

> There is no question of my ever approaching Amelia's skill as a pilot . . . but I have licked her at plenty of things. If she were a gloating feminist, always harping on about her career and her success and never letting me get an oar into the conversation, I should probably have to sock her.

He then disposed of the idea that 'a woman's place is in the home' with the scornful rejoinder that it was a 'lot of bunk. AE does seem to me a particularly good sport who gets all the fun there is out of what goes on, whether it be flying or gardening or fan mail.'[19] This statement of George's seems to embody Amelia's entire approach to life: to put her entire concentration into whatever she was doing at the moment – work or play – and to *enjoy* it.

Amelia's book, *The Fun of It*,[20] with Amelia's postscript which told the story of the Atlantic flight, was published to coincide with her return. Each copy of the first edition contained a small 'phonograph record' of the speech she had made over the transatlantic radio link. This was George at his brilliant best, as a publicist *par excellence*.

When first contemplated, the book was to be written primarily to promote flying and in particular to encourage women to take up flying. As such, it might have sold in reasonable quantities to anyone interested in aviation, or to women college students and graduates, but that final chapter ensured its place on the best-seller lists.

Honours of all kinds continued to be heaped upon Amelia and the keys of various cities were bestowed at civic receptions; but perhaps the most valued award was Honorary Membership in the National Aeronautic Association. Fourteen men had previously received this distinction. 'I appreciate the honour very much,' Amelia wrote to Hiram Bingham, president of the NAA, 'indeed I do not think my exploit deserves it.'[21] Her diary for the remainder of 1932 was so full that when, in late June, Senator Bingham asked for a convenient date on which he might arrange a dinner honouring Orville Wright, she was hard pushed to come up with a free evening until December: 'I will endeavour to let you know six weeks in advance exactly what dates are open.'[22]

George's career also took a new turn at this point. In the months he had been with Brewer and Warren he had failed to make any significant impact, though his wealth of contacts had been invaluable. As he arrived back in the USA from Europe it was announced that he had been appointed Chairman of the Editorial Board of Paramount Studios where he was required to do for movies what he had done for publishing, i.e., identify viable projects from the hundreds of scripts that were submitted monthly, and to come up with original ideas. He would have to spend more than half his time in Los Angeles but as Amelia loved the California climate this obviously presented no great hardship. On 29 June there was a civic welcome at Boston, where Amelia briefly saw her family, but she stayed only one day. The Vega had been assembled and was available to fly and on 1 July she flew George and his son David Binney to California, primarily to attend the Olympic Games later in the month, but where Amelia and George both had business matters to pursue.

Barely ten days later, Amelia announced that she would make her trip back east a non-stop one to Newark, New Jersey.[23] No woman had so far flown non-stop from coast to coast. Ruth Nichols held the women's record for the fastest coast-to-coast crossing – though not non-stop – in a time of 29 hours 1.49 minutes.[24]

But Amelia told reporters she hoped to beat the time set by Frank Hawks[25] and the Met. Office predicted favourable tail winds; Amelia had merely to achieve the average speed she made on her transatlantic flight to beat Hawks's record of 18 hours 21.59 minutes, set five years earlier.

A forced landing (immediately, and somewhat predictably, blamed on component failure: a faulty fuel line, according to George's press release) at Columbus, Ohio, put the all-comers record out of reach. When she landed she was more than an hour behind Ruth Nichols's flying time and stated that she felt more tired than after her oceanic flight. She had been seated very uncomfortably on her parachute: '. . . I didn't carry one on the Atlantic flight because it wouldn't have done any good over the ocean . . .' She said she had no plans to attempt the record in the near future but hoped to 'one day, but would install special equipment for the purpose so she could fly at high altitude.' On this trip she said she did not exceed 13,000 feet as she crossed the Rockies.[26]

Although Amelia had not beaten Hawks's time, her elapsed time of 19 hours 14 minutes 40 seconds (flying time 17 hours 59 minutes 40 seconds) set a new women's record for the crossing, knocking nearly ten hours off Ruth Nichols's record. 'I wasn't trying for a record,' she told an Associated Press reporter. 'This flight was merely for practice in navigation.' This statement should be viewed in the context that her course had been plotted, and full navigation notes prepared for her, by former naval navigator Clarence S. Williams; but it was eminently sensible of her to have taken advantage of the best professional advice available. It must be remembered, however, that such assistance may not have been available to other women flyers. Amelia returned to California – and George – without further incident, though a few days later she was forced down again in northern California (it was a mechanical fault, again), when returning from a speaking engagement.

After a few days spent at the 1932 Olympic Games, accompanied by George and David Binney, Amelia returned to her packed

schedule, commuting several times each month between the east
and west coasts. On 25 August she made another attempt on the
coast-to-coast record and this time achieved her goal of a non-stop
flight (the first woman to do so). And while her time had still not,
as she had hoped, bettered Frank Hawks's, she broke the cross-
country distance record (2,478 miles) and her elapsed time of 19
hours 5 minutes broke her own record for the fastest flight by a
woman.

For some months Amelia had been trying to persuade her mother
to visit her at Rye that fall, but Amy had declined. It seems that
Amy disliked George from the start and though, for a while at least,
she later came to an acceptance of him, her dislike was never to dis-
appear entirely. This may have been rooted in jealousy. Amelia had
very little time to spare for Amy and their contact was reduced to
the regular letters which told her mother little about her real life,
concentrating in the main on mundane domestic matters. Each
month Amelia sent Amy's allowance and the accompanying letters
often had a disappointed tone when Amelia believed her money was
being spent frivolously by Muriel.

In October Amelia was voted Outstanding American Woman of
the year; she accepted on behalf of 'all women':

> When heavier-than-air craft were invented women followed just
> a few years behind men in their operation, and today women
> hold various records 34,000 feet altitude, 254 miles an hour
> speed, 3,600 miles non-stop, non-refuelling flight and recently
> two women remained in the air for eight days. I don't see how
> they did it!
>
> But just as important as these spectacular achievements is the
> everyday flying that 500 women are doing in this country. These
> women fly on all sorts of missions of business and pleasure, and
> I accept the medal for them too.

Recounting a laudatory article in the French press which compared her in glowing terms to Lindbergh, she continued with a grin:

All of it was too good to be true, and I knew there must be some catch in it. There was. The article ended with this query: '. . . but can she bake cakes?'

So I accept these awards (the title, a plaque and a chamois purse containing $1,000 in gold) [on] behalf of the cake bakers and all of those other women who can do some things quite as important, if not more important, than flying, as well as in the name of women flying today.[27]

Amelia's speeches always contained a firm but gentle reminder that women were the true equals of men. And she was not blind to the fact that the attitude of some women was responsible for sexism. 'Sex', she once said, 'has been used too long as a subterfuge by the inefficient woman who likes to make herself and others believe that it is not her incapability but her womanhood which is holding her back . . .'

Amelia *was* a feminist but she never resorted to the extremes of blatant feminism, nor did she need to do so. Indeed, apart from her membership in the Ninety-Nines and the National Women's Party, she maintained an opposition to any women-only organisation. Her thinking, her entire philosophy, was based on her certain knowledge that she was the equal of anyone, and in her marriage to George she was able to live in harmony with her concept of life. She actually denied being a feminist, disliking the connotation, saying that her opinions were merely 'modern thinking'. But her frequent speeches on the subject were made because she could see, even if she did not experience it herself, discrimination. In this too, George was her aide. He had smoothed her path in countless ways, and this should not be forgotten, nor discounted in assessing Amelia's career and achievements.

What did Amelia give George in return? The reflected kudos of her international celebrity, of course – partly created by himself, but she was no Trilby to his Svengali. George had provided the means for Amelia's own ability and courage to bubble to the surface. Had George wanted such celebrity for himself it is obvious that he could have achieved it some way or another. It was not fame *per se* that he hankered after, but the success of anything to which he put his brilliantly active mind. What is so surprising is how well Amelia filled the mould which George created for her as a publicity image. Or perhaps it was that George identified the greater qualities in Amelia long before they were apparent to anyone else.

Amelia, too, was practical in ways where George was impractical. She smoothed his exuberant excesses. And she had many shared loves with him: books; gardening; adventure; meeting and entertaining interesting people; music; the outdoor life; and a constant reaching upwards and outwards. What is more she obtained from everything she did, no matter how trivial, the utmost enjoyment, and this characteristic of hers was very dear to George. Everything about their relationship denies claims that their marriage was a mere business arrangement. On the evidence of Elinor Smith the two were already lovers shortly after Amelia returned from the *Friendship* trip; and Amelia's sister Muriel Morrissey was quite sure 'that it was a normal marriage in every sense of the word'.[28] To George's other wives (see chapters 21 and 22) and family members he was a warm, loving, sometimes extravagantly emotional man. He would not have settled for, and never could have been content with, a cold impersonal management/client arrangement.

In an interview in that fall of 1932, when asked about her husband, Amelia smiled and replied that she was:

> awfully proud of him. He is such a good sport about my flying. If he hadn't been I never could have made that ocean flight. Of course I wouldn't have expected him, and knew he wouldn't think of forbidding me to make the solo flight. But he could have tried to dissuade me, or he could have whined and made it unpleasant. If he had it would have taken too much out of me. Too much nervous energy to have opposed him . . . but he trusted my judgement. He doesn't know anything about flying, but he knows that I wouldn't have attempted anything that I didn't think I could do, that I wouldn't just dash into a thing without thought of preparation. He trusts my judgement about my ship, just as I trust his about books.[29]

There was no publicity, and no mention by Amelia in correspondence about a frightening incident on 22 October 1932. Amelia was landing in a crosswind when a Braniff Airlines aircraft somehow got over the top of her. Fortunately the incident was merely a near-miss, and was formally logged as such in the FAA files.

In December 1932 she was awarded an honorary degree (Doctor of Science) by Thiel College, the university which her father had attended. In her speech Amelia declared that her life was divided: '. . . fifty–fifty – aviation and marriage – and I guess one job is just about as big as the other.' Later, in a letter written to her mother on Christmas Eve, she unwittingly revealed the full tragedy of her father's life, and his early promise:

> I had an interesting time at Thiel. I met several people who were in Dad's class and others who knew him. I found his record for scholarship, ie, age of graduation, has never been equalled. He was fourteen when he entered college and only eighteen when he got his degree . . . Every one remembered Dad as so handsome and bright. His nickname was 'Kid'. I didn't know that slang was popular then. 'Kid Earhart' now sounds like a prize fighter . . .[30]

Throughout the winter and into spring 1933 Amelia's schedule of engagements was breathtaking. Her monthly letters to Amy are scattered with references to various cities, such as: 'I am just rushing to catch the [train] to Chicago'; two days after this she had an engagement in Portland, Oregon to which she flew in the Vega; then on to California.[31] This schedule, which worried Amy, seemed to have a bracing effect on Amelia. 'I am quite able to stand and weigh now as much as I ever have in my life. I have been drinking cream and gained ten pounds – so that's that.'[32]

Her letter in the month of April was extremely brief, but it had a certain novelty value if only for the headed writing paper:

> The White House,
> April 20th 1933

Dear Mother,
GP and I are staying here tonight. You may hear of our visit officially but this is a personal note . . .

Two paragraphs of unimportant trivia follow, the mouthwash she recommends Amy to use and a mention of some family photographs:

> That display of garter on sister's fat knee [Muriel's daughter, Amy Morrissey]. Do please have Pidge let the children wear sox so they don't look like bumpkins. And why the silly hair ribbon? I'll buy 'em 6 pairs of sox each if she will use them.[33]

An element of disapproval had crept into many of Amelia's letters and she often lectured her mother and sister on their clothes, sometimes sending money to buy a specific garment such as a dress, or suit, upon which she then gave minute instructions about accessories. Unintentional or not there is often an unpleasant air of patronage towards her family, whom she alternately loves and nags. She shows more genuine affection towards her Challiss cousins who often stayed at Rye, but then she never felt any responsibility towards her cousins, whereas she was Amy's support and resented the fact that she was also, sometimes, indirectly keeping the Morrissey family. Atavistically, she echoed her grandfather's deep-rooted conviction that a man should be able to provide for his family.

On a previous visit to the White House, when Hoover was President, George recorded the solemnity of the occasion and noted the gloom which seemed to pervade the entire building. He had felt chilled. Now his boyhood acquaintance, Franklin D. Roosevelt, had become President and the atmosphere had apparently lifted dramatically. 'The President's dwelling house,' George observed, 'miraculously became an American home – rather fabulous, to be sure, but homely in its simplicity, enormously informal a sort of combination clubhouse, workshop and drawing room, with rollicking overtones leaning at times to the slightly lunatic . . .' The relationship between the two men may have been of long standing, but George was 'GOP to the core',[34] and never deserted his Republican beliefs. It made for lively discussion, sometimes, in a Democratic administration. Amelia, though, supported FDR to the hilt, even trying to persuade her sister to vote for him.[35]

The Putnams were guests of the Roosevelts on a number of occasions (indeed this was not their first visit, they had dined there some months earlier; had been personal guests of the President at his Inauguration; and had attended a private reception party afterwards), and though it would be incorrect to say that they were close friends with the Roosevelts they undoubtedly enjoyed a relationship that was mutually rewarding.

Over dinner on this April 1933 visit, Eleanor Roosevelt confided that she had never flown at night and would like to see the lights of the capital city. Amelia immediately telephoned Eastern Airlines and organised a flight. Dressed in their evening clothes the two women drove to the airport and were taken on a flight over Washington and Baltimore. Some time later the first lady, who talked of getting a pilot's licence, actually went so far as to acquire a student permit but nothing ever came of this somewhat wistful ambition despite Amelia's promise to give the first lady personal tuition.

Meanwhile, Amelia's visit to Washington had a serious note. On the day after her dinner at the White House she was the guest speaker at a conference of 3,000 members of the influential Daughters of the American Revolution. Amelia's hardhitting speech criticised them sharply for agitating for strong rearmament without doing anything to obtain equality for women in the military organisations. Unless they were willing to bear arms for their country, she told them, they had no business adopting resolutions favouring a build-up of weapons. Her speech drew gasps of surprise, but many saw the sense of her arguments.

In fact Amelia was a self-confessed pacifist. As a young woman she had seen at first hand too much of the waste of war to see any glory in it. Within days there was another hint of the steely side of Amelia Earhart. The NAA of which it will be recalled she was not only an honorary member, but also vice president, announced that its house magazine was being farmed out to private enterprise for the agency's profit. For some months Amelia had become increasingly dissatisfied with the way the NAA was conducting its affairs and the bureaucratic approach that its president, Hiram Bingham, had adopted.

Amelia's public opposition to this move caused open conflict between herself and Hiram Bingham and resulted in a great deal of publicity which most people thought was inimical to the interests of aviation. Eventually she announced her resignation because of their policy differences – 'your viewpoint and mine are too dissimilar concerning fundamental policies to make any association desirable'[36] – amidst further publicity and in an exchange of extremely polite but bitter letters between her and Bingham.

Later Bingham wrote to Richard Byrd to ask him to stand as vice president in Amelia's place and commented briefly that the whole affair had started because George 'became excited about the magazine', and alleging that it was because George had planned to start a new magazine himself. In fact he had probably misinterpreted George's jokey announcement that he was thinking of starting a club, with a house magazine, for 'The Unknown Husbands of Famous Women'.

CHAPTER 17

1933–1935

With Amelia's career firmly established George now concentrated on his own work. His ability to evolve new ideas and devise special projects was given free rein in Hollywood and he was responsible for a number of innovative ideas. For one film he brought together ten top screen writers, each to write a single chapter of a mystery story. As each was handed the cumulative results of the work of the previous writers, the new twists and turns of a different mind were added. The finished story was used for the film *The Woman Accused*, and was modestly successful but it is now remembered chiefly for George's novel concept.

Amelia occasionally visited George at the studios and there was a crop of publicity shots of her pictured with stars such as Cary Grant, Mae West and Marlene Dietrich. In an interview about one of George's films, *Christopher Strong*, in which Katharine Hepburn played the part of a woman pilot, Amelia was asked for her thoughts on aviation movies and quickly warmed to a theme.

> I think it's too bad when aviation movies depend for their excitement on plane wrecks and lost flyers and all that sort of thing. Perhaps that's good drama but it certainly isn't modern aviation . . . There was a picture based on Air Mail, not long ago, in which planes crashed right and left. But that's no more representative of the air mail service than a train wreck every half hour or so would be truly representative of rail transportation.[1]

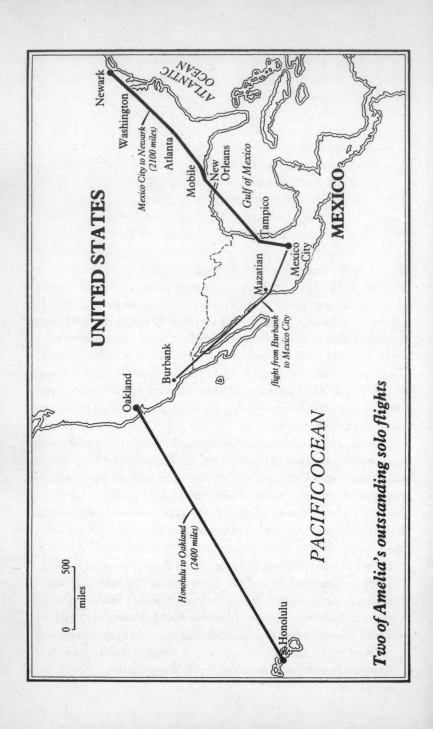

UNITED STATES

ATLANTIC OCEAN

Newark

Washington

Mexico City to Newark (2100 miles)

Atlanta

Mobile

New Orleans

Gulf of Mexico

Tampico

Mazatian

Mexico City

MEXICO

Burbank

flight from Burbank to Mexico City

Oakland

PACIFIC OCEAN

Honolulu to Oakland (2400 miles)

Honolulu

500

miles

0

Two of Amelia's outstanding solo flights

Asked in George's smiling presence whether war aviation movies
(an obvious reference to *Wings*, the first film in which George had
been involved before he met Amelia) did not throw the same melo-
dramatic spotlight on flying in general, Amelia spoke her mind:

> As an individual I'm opposed to war, anyway, and naturally I
> think it is extremely unfortunate that war should be emphasised,
> and to some extent glorified, in any kind of film . . . the destruc-
> tive possibilities of aviation are its least important attribute
> and . . . to put chief emphasis on the airplane as a weapon of war
> would be to distort its true place in the scheme of things.
> Aviation has grown up you know, it isn't a plaything any more. It
> has become a useful and serious industry . . .[2]

In radio broadcasts, personal appearances and lectures Amelia
constantly pushed her theme of Women in Aviation, and the safety
of aviation as a method of transport and by June 1933 she was busy
organising her own participation in the first of the National Air
Races to be open to men and women pilots. To her disappointment
she and Ruth Nichols were the only women contestants but this at
least ensured that the spotlight was firmly on Amelia. In the event
Ruth Nichols had to withdraw temporarily, because her plane was
not ready; but she and Amelia came to a private arrangement to fly
against each other's elapsed times for the $2,500 woman's prize. In
addition, together with the five men in the race, the two women
were competing for the Bendix Trophy and a $10,000 prize; given
the powerful machines the men were flying it was extremely unlikely
that either woman seriously thought she had a chance of winning.
Amelia's engine was 450 horsepower whereas the men's machines
were powered by 700 to 800 horsepower and more.

Prior to the race there was a minor family squabble by correspondence; partly because Amy had been 'helping' Muriel financially
again, and partly because Amy suggested taking her two young grandchildren on vacation. Amelia lectured:

> you are not to have both children . . . I will not permit it under

any circumstances. You are not the kind of woman who has not other interests but brats and I do not see the necessity of your being a drudge and nursemaid.[3]

Subsequent letters continued the theme:

Dear Mother,
I am sorry I cannot change about your taking two children at one time. I do not like to be arbitrary but I do not see any other way of doing things.[4]

Her next letter went further:

I want your solemn word that you will not try to [take] the two infants with you. I shall be compelled to withhold the monthly check if you do . . . it is bad for you and for them too, and as I have pointed out, for the Morrisseys. *It is absolutely out.*[5]

These letters, with their somewhat overbearing tones, not surprisingly created a painful period of relations between the two households, but Amelia (who continued to send the monthly allowances) held the upper hand. Eventually Amy spent her vacation at Rye later that summer.

Amelia turned her attention to the air races.

The time to beat was Roscoe Turner's record of 12 hours 33 minutes. Amelia did not finish with the other contestants. Although used to flying back and forth across the States she was delayed when her hatch cover broke loose in a rainstorm and she reported almost losing control of the plane. She landed for repairs, losing nearly an hour, but her arrival in Los Angeles was more than six hours behind that of her male competitors. Typically, within a day or so she publicly announced that her return journey to New York would be an attempt on the west–east record – her own, incidentally.

George was waiting at Newark, New Jersey, to greet Amelia after she clipped almost two hours off her previous record in an elapsed

time of 17 hours 7 minutes and 30 seconds. This was still disappointingly short of the men's time, but she reported being bothered
by fumes from a broken fuel line, and the hatch cover had again
blown open. She had been forced to fly for 75 miles holding the
hatch down and had sprained her hand in doing so.[6]

Amelia spent most of the summer of 1933 at Rye. Originally she
had planned to accompany George on a trip to Europe but when
Jim and Amy Mollison successfully piloted their de Havilland
Dragon *The Seafarer* across the Atlantic, 'the hard way' (east to west
against the prevailing winds) Amelia invited them to Rye as her
guests to recuperate. After circling Stratford Airport (Bridgeport,
Connecticut), Mollinson had been so exhausted that he underestimated his approach and the plane crash-landed in a swamp. They
were both injured but not seriously. During their visit a 'North
Atlantic Flight Club' was founded, its membership restricted to
those who had flown alone across the ocean. On that basis only five
pilots were eligible for membership: Charles Lindbergh, Wiley Post,
Jim Mollison, James Mattern and Amelia.

George's son David had also returned home after 'adventuring' in
South American jungles. Amelia was extremely fond of David, and
the feeling was mutual[7] so this was another reason for Amelia to stay
home. Finally, her mother consented to visit Rye, though whether
Amy's change of heart was connected with the fact that George was
away for eight weeks is not known.

It was a quiet summer but when George returned from Europe
the tempo increased, as it always did, and the usual crop of celebrities were to be found at Rye; Sir Hubert Wilkins, Bernt Balchen,
William Beebe, Roy Chapman Andrews, to name a few. Dinner parties inevitably finished up in 'the studio' where guests sprawled
comfortably to talk into the early morning of past adventures and
future plans. George, restless even as a host, often left the table to
telephone San Francisco or Los Angeles as a new idea occurred to
him.

Nothing escaped George and his concerns spilled over into so
many areas it is difficult to know how he found the time to hold
down a full-time job with Paramount. But despite his many

activities, and contrary to popular belief, he was not a wealthy man; most of his private income had been lost when his cousin had taken G. P. Putnam's Sons to the verge of bankruptcy and George never recovered the amount he had left invested in the publishing house. Nor was Amelia a wealthy woman. Between them, thanks to George's management and the fact that both were workaholics, they earned a considerable sum, it is true, but their constant entertaining, Amelia's aeroplanes, the upkeep of Rye, the salaries of their retinue, and a high-profile lifestyle used up their income almost as fast they earned it; while they were certainly not financially strapped there was, equally certainly, no huge fortune behind them. The 'millionaire' tag was all simply part of the Putnam image.

Amelia kept busy travelling and lecturing all over the USA. Her usual fee for a lecture was $250 but often she had to settle for less than this at 'fill-in' lectures, or for small organisations and colleges. The problem was that it was some time since Amelia had done anything *really* newsworthy and her lecture subjects, flying and opportunities for women, were a little worn, no matter how well she put them across . . .

George continued to commute between New York and Hollywood. Their Christmas card that year depicted a model of an old sailing ship and the printed message read: 'This is the Merchant Sailing Ship, George and Amelia . . . although no models ourselves at least we're still afloat, hopeful that in 1934 *your* ship may come in . . .'[8]

In the early part of 1934 Amelia launched a fashion house to manufacture and market clothes of her own design. They were sensible, classic-line clothes and would not be too out of place today. Shirt-waisted dresses, classic silk shirts, blouses with tails long enough not to ride up and reveal a midriff, slacks with permanent pleats, blazers and hip-length jackets. She specified washable fabrics and cool pastels, as well as classic navy and white combinations and the whole effect was quiet and tasteful. Amelia was confident that practical no-nonsense, well-made clothes selling for reasonable prices would be a sure-fire success. There were a few touches of genuine originality in the aviation theme which ran through the collection; tiny silver propellers served as buttons, silver screws fastened up a jersey dress, parachute silk was used as detail on blouses.

Amelia's first shop opened in Macy's, New York, a novel concept then – a shop within a store – and reported a brisk trade. Other outlets followed, but it was a brief success. By the end of the year it was wound up. There was the inevitable lecture tour in late spring 1934 but when in the fall George attempted to set up a new series of winter lectures for Amelia it rapidly became apparent that there were few takers at her usual $250 fee. Some new exploit would be needed, and further newspaper coverage, to bring her name into the forefront of the public mind.

Amelia had a new venture in mind already, though it would not reach fruition until the following year. Some months earlier Amelia had told a friend, Dot Leh, that her aeroplane needed an expensive overhaul, and that she would have to spend $10,000 on it to 'fix it up'. She was therefore thinking of selling it.[9] As the result of Dot Leh's connections and enquiries the Vega was sold in June for $7,500 to the Franklin Institute in Philadelphia as a permanent exhibition display.[10]

Before parting with the 'little red bus' (as she affectionately called it), Amelia removed the upgraded Wasp engine and substituted an obsolete model; she wanted her well-tried engine for the new aeroplane, also a Lockheed Vega. It was a later model in which Elinor Smith had been preparing an attempt to be the first woman to fly the Atlantic, a plan abandoned after Amelia successfully took that record. It was originally built to exacting specifications for Henry Mears of New York who had a 'round-the-world' flight in mind. Called the 'Vega Hi-speed Special', it carried the registration 965Y and was equipped with special fuel tanks, radio and streamlined landing gear and cowling. These latter appointments, together with a Hamilton Standard Controllable-pitch Propeller, gave the plane a speed of 200 mph and Amelia had her eye on further records as well as her constant journeys across the continent.

For the first time since their marriage George and Amelia found time in the summer of 1934 for a long vacation when they

'saddlepacked' into the wild mountainous country of the
Absaroka Mountains in Wyoming where an old friend of George's
(Carl Dunrud, a member of George's Greenland expedition) had
a ranch. With Dunrud as guide Amelia quickly came to understand her husband's lifelong love of mountains. They both rode
well – it was one of the ways they relaxed together during Rye
weekends – and now George tried to teach her to fish. Later she
was to observe engagingly:

> Whether I'm a good flyer is debatable. Whether or not I'm a fin-
> ished fisherman isn't.
>
> I'm not!
>
> 'Now,' I hear my husband admonish, 'drop your fly there –
> the dark eddy by that rock.'
>
> In that particular pool are several dark eddies and any number
> of rocks. Not that the exact locality makes any difference anyway
> because I'm not yet able to persuade my line to go where I wish
> it to.
>
> 'Not there. *There!*'
>
> 'Holy Cats!' The Lord and Master-Fisherman is becoming
> apoplectic. 'Let the line run out! Keep the tip up . . . gently . . .
> give the trout a chance. Now try another cast.'
>
> I do.
>
> 'Hells Bells! That's not a flail – that's a rod – only four ounces
> of delicate bamboo . . . just your wrist and forearm . . .'
>
> So it goes.
>
> 'After all,' . . . it's only human to talk back when he com-
> plains too bitterly because I've snapped the line and lost a
> promising trout . . . 'after all, what do *you* know about taking a
> plane off a small field?'
>
> 'Or a large one!' His grin is disarming.[11]

Amelia's record of the holiday conveys the warmth and depth of
their relationship and reveals a typical George, always expecting
perfection – he was at his best out of doors, even more so than in
business – his characteristic and unrestrained excitement in the

moment, the rising frustration which died in a laugh as suddenly as it had erupted. Amelia wrote:

In contrast . . . to the worries of a bewildered world was the crisp peacefulness of the Wyoming mountains with all the needs of living right at hand on the pack horses, a concentrated world of one's own, refreshing, restful, and remote . . .

It was an intensely happy period for them both and Amelia told George she'd like to spend more time there. Before the end of their vacation they filed a mining claim and commissioned the building of a small log cabin near the Dunrud ranch at Meeteetse.[12]

Shortly after their return to Rye, Amelia sprung another of her apparently artless remarks upon George. Just as she had mulled privately over her solo transatlantic trip, so she had quietly decided on her next venture; a trans-Pacific flight from the Hawaiian Islands to California, a flight of some 2,500 miles. George heard the news as he arrived home from the office:

One night in the autumn of 1934 she sat in golden *crepe* pyjamas on the 'liver-toaster' [club fender] round the fireplace at Rye reading the evening paper. As I came in from the train she looked up in the way of a person thinking out loud and said, 'I want to fly the Pacific soon.'

I had a brief-case and an armful of evening papers, but instead of going into the Hencoop (AE's disrespectful name for the office) to dump them I leaned against the arched doorway and said, 'You mean from San Francisco to Honolulu?'

She straightened a topaz link in one of her cuffs thoughtfully. 'No; the other way, it's easier to hit a continent than an island.'

'When do you want to do it?' I asked.

'Oh, fairly soon . . .'[13]

When Amelia made such plans George knew he would have to arrange the funding to prepare and equip the plane, and organise the logistics. For example the plane would need a thorough overhaul and would have to be shipped to Hawaii; special equipment for a transoceanic flight would need to be purchased and fitted. A record flight of this nature required not only planning and courage and practical organisation, but also cash. George knew just what to do, for a contact in the advertising world, Sydney Bowman, had for some weeks been running a $125,000 publicity campaign for the Hawaiian Sugar Planters Association in order to fight the Jones–Costigan Sugar Control Act adopted by Congress some months earlier. Bowman was quickly convinced of the value of climaxing this campaign with a successful record flight by Amelia and happily agreed to George's suggestion that the Association should sponsor Amelia for a $10,000 purse, with $5,000 payable on signing of contracts and the balance payable on the success of the attempted flight.[14]

In October the Putnams left Rye for California where the Vega was to be overhauled by Lockheed. As in the past, George had organised 'an expert' to oversee the technical aspects of the entire operation. On this occasion the expert was Paul Mantz.

George had met Mantz in 1928 during his involvement with the film *Wings*. Then the young pilot's dream had been to break into the movie business and he had provided a small team of stunt pilots to act out dogfights for the cameras. Mantz was a pilot of great brilliance with an instinctive feel for flight, and his experience of performing difficult stunts in the intervening years had taught him the value of precise planning to obtain successful results. He was an ideal man for the task of masterminding Amelia's flight, for he knew everyone worth knowing in the industry and was conversant with the latest developments in aviation technology.

Amelia and Paul Mantz got on well together and when a house near the Mantzes' home in North Hollywood became available to rent and George returned to New York, Amelia moved out of the Ambassador Hotel suite where she and George habitually stayed, and into the house at 10515 Valley Spring Lane, inviting Amy to join her there.[15]

In late November 1934 George telephoned Amelia with news of a fire that had destroyed a large part of their home at Rye. George had been staying with his mother in Noank, Connecticut, before joining Amelia in December for the trans-Pacific flight attempt. Since the house was to be empty all winter the caretaker had drained the water tanks and shut up the house, but without turning off the boiler. The resulting fire had taken a good hold when a neighbour spotted the flames and called for help.

One entire wing of the house was gutted, and irreplaceable Rockwell Kent paintings, books and papers were lost. Everything in the dining room was destroyed; the silver (much of it inherited from Earhart and Putnam ancestors) was a shapeless mass in a pile of ashes that was once an antique rosewood cabinet. A trunk containing all of Amelia's papers accumulated from childhood, including her poetry, letters and some stories she had been working on, had vanished.

Amelia's first thought, though, was for George's most treasured possessions. 'What about your father's books?' Fortunately they had been protected in a heavy glass-fronted bookcase that had been smoke-damaged and charred but had not burned and the books were largely undamaged. She was upset to learn that her papers (her 'peppers' as she called them) were gone. It was sad for them both, for they deeply loved their home. Practical as ever, George immediately commissioned the rebuilding programme.

During December preparations for the flight were finished and on the 22nd the Putnams and the Mantzes sailed for Hawaii aboard the *SS Lurline* with Amelia staunchily denying any suggestion of a trans-Pacific flight. Her declared intention was a short series of lectures and some flying around the islands.

Amelia wrote to her mother from the ship explaining how they were running the Vega's engine:

> . . . and it has barked a cheerful 'howdy' each time . . . the radio on the plane has been working wonderfully. At midnight I could pick up and talk to regular airway stations. Kingman Arizona heard perfectly . . . I'll have GP cable you when I start. My hope is to go on east so I shall not see you until later if that plan materializes . . .

Please try to have a good time. You have had so many squashed years . . . GP said you were an awfully good sport to stay alone in the little house. I said I had known that a long time. I have taken possession of the stuff in the zipper compartment of my brief case. Put it away until I turn up and if I don't – burn it. It consists of fragments that mean nothing to anyone but me . . .[16]

Although the transocean route had been flown before (by Sir Charles Kingsford-Smith) no person, male or female, had flown it solo. Amelia's plan was to land and refuel in California and fly on to Washington, DC. In January 1935 news of the sponsorship of Amelia's flight broke in the newspapers and the flight was vociferously denounced as a mere 'stunt' by editors. Nothing could be gained, they averred; Kingsford-Smith had already chartered the route; such flights should be attempted only in large planes equipped to stay afloat for several days. The papers calculated that under ideal conditions she might have 'only 50 gallons' of fuel left (i.e., more than two hours flying and almost 400 miles) if she were to make California. If she were to ditch, a costly search, risking lives of naval pilots, would have to be undertaken. There were some grounds for this attitude, for only a month earlier a fully crewed plane had disappeared on the same route entailing a fruitless 27-day full-scale search by army and navy planes and ships.[17] Ten pilots had already lost their lives attempting to make the crossing and if Amelia failed it could damage aviation in the eyes of the public.

As the papers thundered a concerted condemnation the navy refused to clear Amelia's departure, saying that her radio equipment had insufficient range for safety requirements. While they appreciated she could receive transmissions over the distance they questioned the ability of her radio to transmit over the 2,500-mile distance to Los Angeles station KFI. Paul Mantz, whose expertise ensured Amelia carried the latest radio equipment, immediately flew the Vega to 12,000 feet and was able to reach Kingman, Arizona and hold a conversation, effectively quashing the objection. In fact, Amelia's flight across the Pacific was the first in which a civilian aeroplane carried a two-way radio telephone. Because of the cost and weight, such equipment had previously been limited to larger transport aircraft.

The next snag was that the sponsors, who feared that bad publicity would damage their campaign, tried to back out of the venture. Amelia faced the Association's committee and scathingly told them that she could sense an aroma of cowardice in the room. However, she said, she fully intended to make the flight with or without their support. She got it.

All that remained was the weather. While Amelia waited for ideal conditions she and George stayed at the plush home of a wealthy friend of George's, waited upon by a large staff of Japanese servants, and Amelia wrote to Amy: 'We have lived like kings . . . GP and I wonder if we'll ever be satisfied with only one or two servants again . . .'[18]

It was 11 January before conditions were right and Paul Mantz would agree to Amelia's departure. He was confident that the plane was as ready as he and mechanic Ernie Tissot could make it, and the weather forecast was favourable. The Vega was loaded with 500 gallons of fuel and together with various extra equipment weighed more than 6,000 pounds.[19] However, Mantz reckoned that even with the excessive load the plane should lift off in 3,000 feet and Wheeler Field had a 6,000-foot grass strip. The army, whose airfield it was, had mowed a take-off strip and planted distance flags to aid Amelia in the take-off run. Heavy rain made the strip sticky but even so she lifted off, as Mantz had predicted, in just under 3,000 feet; but not before she noticed the ambulances and fire trucks standing by, servicemen with hand-held fire extinguishers and several women 'with handkerchiefs obviously ready for any emergency'. But it was the anxiety in the dead-white face of Ernie Tissot she saw as she pushed the throttle open and released the brakes.[20] Two hundred people and various newsreel cameras witnessed her departure.

For George, who had not slept the previous night and would not sleep while Amelia was airborne, the take-off was a period of supreme anxiety. He was no airman, and no mechanic, but he knew very well that this was the most dangerous moment of the flight.

Beside him Paul Mantz was willing the Vega into the sky. 'Get that tail up! *Get that tail up!*' he yelled at the top of his voice, adding various profane trimmings.[21]

As Amelia eased her aircraft into the air George sighed with relief and a reporter asked him how he felt. 'I'd rather have a baby,' he said smiling, meaning rather than fly himself (though perhaps it was also an ironical comment on the reversal of normal husband/wife roles). This was published nationwide as a frustrated wish to become a father, and stories that Miss Earhart's husband wished she'd give up flying and have a baby proliferated.

This time there were no frightening incidents and from her detailed description of the flight Amelia really enjoyed the experience. The Vega behaved perfectly and the only incidents which broke the apparent monotony were Amelia's regular radio contacts at quarter to and quarter past each hour when she reported in a somewhat unprofessional manner that 'Everything is okay.'[22] Once she saw a ship and was delighted to receive a Morse-code transmission from the radio operator, indicating that at 900 miles out she was dead on the course professionally laid out – as usual – for her by Clarence Williams.

A few hours out Amelia heard the radio announcer of the KGU commercial radio station in Honolulu suddenly announce: 'We are interrupting our musical program so that Mr Putnam may try to communicate with his wife.' Typically, George could not pass up such a wonderful opportunity for publicity:

And then some hundreds of miles out over the Pacific, I heard my husband's voice as though he were in the next room.

'A.E.' he said, 'the noise of your motor interferes with your messages. Please speak a little louder.'

A few minutes later I talked to him, through the little cup microphone – louder, as requested.[23]

The radio was a revelation. 'Miraculous!' Amelia said later. Using the call sign KHABQ Amelia could receive and transmit on frequencies 6,210 and 3,105 kilocycles. The confidence that this equipment gave Amelia was incalculable and though she disliked the effort involved in reeling in and out the long antenna through a hole in the cabin floor, she was delighted with the regular contact with radio stations. Once, after flying over a solid fog bank for hours she spoke out loud to herself: 'I'm getting tired of this fog.' This was picked up by radio stations as 'I'm getting tired' and was carried on the news broadcasts of west-coast news stations causing anxiety to her friends. But for George the regular sound of her voice was tremendous comfort, a tenuous link with Amelia. 'At least . . . this feature was a pleasant contrast to previous Atlantic flights with their long blank silences.'[24]

Amelia was some 20 miles south of her targeted landfall – the Golden Gate Bridge and Oakland – when she reached the Californian coast, but climbing up over the hills she could see San Francisco Bay under her port wingtip. By radio she announced, 'Am on course, will be in any moment now.' She landed at Oakland some 18 hours after leaving Honolulu.

Throughout the night her radio-telephone broadcasts had been heard on commercial radio stations and the public at large felt personally involved. At no point did she reveal her position, so that even Clarence Williams, who had prepared her charts, was unsure whether she would opt for a Los Angeles or San Francisco landfall, but after she announced at 7.55 a.m. that she was heading for Oakland, people began to surge to the airport.

The crowd of thousands – various estimates range from 5,000 to 10,000 – were at first not even sure that Amelia had arrived, for she landed at the far side of the field, almost out of sight, though her landing run and taxi towards the daunting reception was captured by newsreel cameras. After a short rest Amelia announced her intention to take off again for Washington, DC. She was tired after the flight, however, and despite the buoyancy created by success she recognised that it would be foolish to fly on without rest. She spent the night in an Oakland hotel after cabling George: SORRY I DID NOT DO BETTER.

George, relieved, cabled her a jokey telegram: SWELL JOB BUT HOPE IT DOESN'T BECOME A HABIT, before he boarded a ship to

return home the slow way; and President Roosevelt also sent congratulations and a long letter: 'You have scored again . . . [and]
shown even the "doubting Thomases" that aviation is a science
which cannot be limited to men only.'[25]

A few days later Amelia met George's ship and after a civic reception the two flew back to New York by scheduled airline.

Now there was no problem in finding organisations to book lectures at $250 each. And for the following months Amelia was 'on
the road' almost non-stop, too busy even to write to Amy. Every
night she telephoned George, sometimes asking him to contact
Amy and send her a check. Consequently:

Feb 11th 1935

Dear Mrs Earhart

In the first place, here is a check for the rent. Secondly here is a
check for $50 to help out immediate cash requirements. Third
I am sorry to report that it looks as though we are going to be
delayed in getting back to the coast. At least there is not much
chance of A.E. getting there until about 20th of March. Most
anything can happen to me. Affairs are even more than usually
hectic and uncertain! Anyway I will keep you informed.

Now here's one thing that seems to me important. I have
just learned that apparently we are paying $15 a month for the
board and lodging of a dog in an animal hospital. That is quite
absurd. That amount would support two starving people and
there are plenty of *them*!

Amelia is away in the middle west lecturing and so I am a bit
hazy in my knowledge. But as I understand it, we have some
obligation to take care of this dog. In paying the rent will you
please tell the agent that I will not accept further responsibility
for this dog. The owner or someone else, will have to take him
off our hands. And so please get him out of the hospital,
terminate the arrangement there, and give him to the agent. I
absolutely refuse to waste money in this minor and unjustified
way. I suspect you will sympathize with me. I would much rather
you bought a string of pearls or even a diamond bracelet!

AE is rolling around in the middlewest in her Franklin
lecturing every night, heaven help her, and is expected back on
the 26th. Incidentally you might mark on your calendar that
she is on the Beech-nut broadcast (Red Davis) on March 11,13
and 15th. Sincerely GPP[26]

Two days later a cable from Amelia in Wisconsin, despatched after
she had spoken to George by telephone, advised Amy: DISREGARD
WHAT GP WRITING ABOUT DOG WILL WRITE YOU MYSELF FIRST
MINUTE HERE IS VALENTINE CHEERIO. A.

The dog was part of the rental agreement and George's choler
would, she knew, probably have vanished even before the letter was
posted; he once admitted that his best letters were filed in the waste-
bin. Even so, it is not difficult to see how Amy's dislike of George
could have become so deep-rooted.

When the prestigious Harmon Awards were announced that
spring, for 1935, Amelia was awarded the title of America's outstanding airwoman. Both she and George had hoped for the title
'World's outstanding woman aviator' which she had held for the
past three years, but the committee was divided because of Jean
Batten's east-to-west solo flight across the South Atlantic. Eventually
the honours were shared between the two women. George counter-
acted Amelia's disappointment by referring to Amelia in subsequent
interviews as 'The First Lady of the air' – an obvious play on the title
accorded to President Roosevelt's wife.

At the same time, in a poll conducted by New York University's
journalist students it was found that, of world figures, the best-
known men were President Roosevelt and Hitler, while the
best-known women were Eleanor Roosevelt and Amelia Earhart.
Hardly surprising, when not a week passed without Amelia's name
in the papers for some reason or other. Much of this had been due
to George – now without a full-time business interest of his own –
but the natural cumulative effect of fame was also starting to take
effect. Some newspapers wondered if Amelia was planning a world
flight since she had, after her Pacific crossing, said on the radio that
it would be good practice and experience for future flights. Now,

asked to explain, she said enigmatically 'Everyone has his dreams. I like to be ready . . .' but denied plans for a world flight. When the reporter expressed a hope that she wouldn't attempt any more ocean flights Amelia reacted quickly and seriously. 'Why?' she asked. 'Do you think my luck might run out? Do you think luck only lasts so long and then lets a person down?'[27]

Having finished her tour of the midwest Amelia travelled to New York, where, at a reception, she met the consul-general of Mexico who suggested she should make a goodwill visit to Mexico City. 'It's the first time I've ever been asked anywhere,' she said later to George. 'I just *went* to Ireland.'[28]

Although Lindbergh had flown to Mexico City in 1927 from Washington,[29] the possibilities for Amelia inherent in this trip were not lost on George. A flight from Los Angeles to Mexico City with a return to the New York area would generate yet another burst of valuable publicity. With characteristic enthusiasm he catapulted into action, flying to Mexico City to organise the project.

The Mexican government agreed to issue a special postage stamp commemorating the flight and George recognised that he could finance the cost of the flight by organising a limited edition of what are now known as 'first day covers'. Seven hundred and eighty stamps[30] were produced. To satisfy international postal regulations 480 had to be placed on public sale but 300 were purchased by George to be carried by Amelia on her return to Newark, applied to autographed covers and sold to collectors.[31] To protect the rarity value of the issue and ensure that no further stamps could be produced, nor forgeries made, George provided the tube of special coloured ink and personally destroyed the lino cut.

George always maintained that 'Amelia never made profits from any flight . . . no single flight showed direct returns in black on the balance sheet.'[32] This statement is probably accurate (though very disingenuous), for the flights themselves created no direct revenue and were costly to finance. The profits came from the peripheral activities such as lecturing, books etc. George's idea of selling stamps was not only novel but also typical of his brilliance at innovative publicity and money-making schemes.

The flight to Mexico was planned for mid-April and meanwhile Amelia flew to Washington where she stayed at the White House for a few days while undertaking several engagements, among them a speech at the National Geographic Society, before going home to Rye. She wrote to Amy to say, a little wearily, 'I returned to New York and found myself signed for the most strenuous lecture engagement ever undertaken . . . I hope to start west the middle of this month. GP has left Paramount and is in a state trying to decide what alley he will run down. There are so many things to do.'[33]

In an interview in Washington Amelia was asked what she thought about the White House cuisine. Amelia replied that she had been so busy fulfilling engagements outside the White House that she'd hardly had any meals there. This became construed as a comment that she loved staying at the White House but never got enough to eat. She had already written a charming thank-you note, offering George's services for a matter under Mrs Roosevelt's consideration but now, exasperated and embarrassed, she quickly cabled a denial of the article and followed with a letter explaining the misunderstanding:

'Wa'll, I sure am glad to be here, and gosh, I sure do hope I'll meet the Prince of Wales,' was the quotation attributed to me in 1928 after the *Friendship* flight. It happened that *I said not one single word on the subject.* The whole was fabricated out of one reporter's imagination. I can laugh at it now. I only hope that one day I can laugh also at the preposterous 'starvation interview' the Press has had me give concerning my stay at the White House.

I believe you know me well enough to be sure I would never put out the kind of smart ungracious stuff it contained. Something I said (I can't think what yet) must have been misinterpreted and got passed round by word of mouth, since more than a week elapsed before it got into print.

I am humiliated that any incident should have occurred to mar what was to me so delightful an interlude . . . Perhaps you will let me raid the ice-box sometime, not because it's necessary but because it's fun.[34]

To which her hostess replied.

> You were such a perfect guest that I welcome you back at any
> time and you need not feel that you have to be out for every
> meal! We all feel we have not seen enough of you.
>   Affectionately
>   Eleanor Roosevelt

A handwritten PS reveals the First Lady's sense of humour and
perhaps the relationship between the two women: 'I shall give you
a key to the ice box next time!'[35]

On 19 April Amelia left to fly to Mexico where George awaited
her. Before take-off an act of sabotage was discovered. A drop of acid
had been placed on the rudder cables and they were almost eaten
through.[36] Eventually, after an otherwise uneventful flight Amelia
lost her way and landed some 50 miles short of her destination in a
dry lake bed. Redirected by peasants she flew on to Valbuena
Airport where George and Presidente Lazaro Cardenas were waiting
to welcome her. At an altitude of 8,000 feet Valbuena was too high
to enable Amelia to take off with a full fuel load, so the Mexican
Army prepared a three-mile long runway in a dried-out lake bed at
Texacoco. Amelia's return was delayed by poor weather and George
had to leave by commercial airline ahead of her.

It was 8 May before Amelia was able to leave and although this
leg of the venture, too, was uneventful she had fretted about the
long water crossing and promised herself that after this she would
make no further long flights over water with only a single engine.[37]

As usual George hyped the entire flight for all it was worth. The
result on this occasion was 'a frenzied mob of between 10,000 and
15,000 people' waiting at Newark, New Jersey, all determined to
touch Amelia or pat her as she alighted exhausted from her aeroplane. The police were unable to get close enough to protect her and
George, frustrated and angry, could only shout, 'This is the most
disgraceful scene I have ever witnessed . . .' Previously only
Lindbergh had provoked such scenes. The crowd was, however,
determinedly good-natured and carried Amelia, shoulder-high, to

the hangar where the official reception committee, and the frustrated George, waited with ill-concealed impatience.

Without a break Amelia returned to her packed lecture schedule though she managed to spend a few days toward the end of May in Los Angeles where she and Paul Mantz signed a partnership agreement. Amy had gone east to stay with the Morrisseys and George's mother had travelled out to visit the Putnams in Hollywood. The Putnams had planned to fly to Wyoming to repeat their vacation of the previous year but neither could find time.

One of the 'alleys' that George decided to run down, having left Paramount, was to join a consortium of businessmen to manufacture a training unit for parachute jumpers. Having being sold on the idea that pilots should be able to practise using parachutes in a safe environment, and realising the potential for sales of such a system to military outlets, George went into partnership to market 200-foot towers to which a safety line attached a standard parachute harness. Nowadays, these are familiar devices, but then it was a novel concept.

George launched his publicity campaign by having Amelia make the 'first jump in public' (others had tested it privately), and she was followed by a team of experienced parachute jumpers, Fay Gillis (a fellow member of the Ninety-Nines), an actress from a Broadway play and a reporter. George wondered if, in addition to the aviation industry and the army and navy (for whom it had primarily been designed), he might sell the idea to amusement parks and country fairs. The reporter doubted that the idea would catch on.

But there was a serious side to the circus atmosphere; army and navy chiefs were there to watch and place orders and Gene Vidal, Director of Air Commerce, had flown up for the demonstration and was persuaded by George to jump. George wrote to him next day:

Dear Gene,
In case you missed it here's what the New York Herald Tribune did this morning – front page and first page of second section. All the papers are correspondingly good. All four news reels, I think, will carry a yarn – they have some good stuff.

Publicitywise it was just about 100% success – far better than I
had dared expect.
                    Sincerely,
                    GPP[38]

The Putnams' peripatetic existence meant they had little time to
spend at the newly reconstructed house at Rye so they rented it to
a doctor for a year and based themselves in a New York hotel when
in the east and the Spring Valley Lane cottage when in California.
The heavy demands made on Amelia that spring took an inevitable
toll for in June she became ill with the old recurrent sinus problems.
An operation was followed by an attack of pleurisy and she was
bedridden for ten days. George, who had been in New York, flew
to her side; '[he] arrived yesterday, which helps . . .' she wrote Amy.
Her constant headache did not prevent Amelia's usual instructive
lecture when writing about the vacation Amy was to take with
Muriel:

> About clothes. Please remember you and Pidge attract attention
> as my relatives so spare me blowsies. I'd prefer you to get a few
> simple decent clothes, both of you. Not awful cheapies, so people
> who don't look below the surface won't have anything to converse
> about. Things you get now are cheaper and can be used next
> year . . .[39]

For some time Amelia hankered after a small house of their own
in North Hollywood. She loved the climate and the way of life
there, and her business partnership with Paul Mantz would require
her presence on a regular basis. George was opposed to the idea of
buying in California but, not unusually, Amelia got her way without
any fuss; George was, in any case, disposed to be amenable having
worried about Amelia's longer-than-usual convalescence. In late
June 1935 Amelia wrote to her mother from California:

> Today we bought a small house here. GP has been letting off
> steam since he arrived how he could not leave the east etc. But

Paul and I have kept him so busy with the funny businesses we
have stirred up that his bleat has grown less and less.

Imagine my surprise when day before yesterday he asked me
to drive him around Tolucca Lake district – where he had been
busy pointing out the impossibilities of renting even for a short
time. Well at the very end of Valley Spring Lane (I don't know
whether you ever walked there or not) was a little house with a
'For Sale' sign on it. It was on a square lot with two sides on the
golf course and a hundred foot lot on the other, now vacant.

We got home and he said 'I think I'll just call that real estate
man and see what he has to say.' The result was in four minutes
we were seeing the place and next day made an offer for it. GP
left at one today via United and actually two minutes before the
plane took off the real estate man rushed up and reported our
offer accepted. Whew.

. . . My ship is still undergoing repairs, that is repainting and
reupholstering and when it is finished I shall put it with Paul's
fleet for charter. We are going to start a flying school and plan all
kinds of things. GP is as keen as are we . . .[40]

Earlier in the year Amelia had announced that she had accepted
an appointment at Purdue University, Lafayette, Indiana, as a consultant in the department for the study of careers for women.
Although both she and the college's president (Dr Edward C.
Elliott) were aware that her involvement would be limited to a few
weeks each semester, Amelia was very keen on this appointment.

Amelia had met Elliott the previous year at a luncheon[41] and so
impressed him with her talk and positive attitude towards careers
for women, that he asked if she would visit the college and lecture
to the women students. As a result, a contract was negotiated with
Amelia as a 'visiting faculty member' at a salary of $2,000 a year.
In addition to the Women's Careers Department there was an
aeronautics department operating from the college's own airfield.
Here was an opportunity to encourage able young women not
only to forge worthwhile careers, but also to take up flying; two
subjects close to her heart. She continued to work determinedly at

her honorary position in the Ninety-Nines and wrote surprisingly long personal letters to female enquirers who were seriously interested in taking up aviation.

Throughout the summer of 1935 Amelia spent any spare time with Paul Mantz, planning the flying school and charter business. Sooner or later, she knew, she would have to give up record flying and when that day came this business would provide an income.

Amelia enjoyed Paul's company. He was fun and knew how to enjoy life. He 'played' in a way George never could but he was also a fine pilot respected by Amelia and others for his knowledge and expertise. And he had something that George had not; a *real* love of, and feel for, flying similar to her own. Furthermore he had the entrepreneurial spirit to use his ability to make money. In a sense he was a Putnam who could fly, and who could share all aspects of the flying experience with Amelia.

In late August, acting on a whim, the two decided to fly to the air races in Cleveland. Once there they made another spur-of-the-moment decision to enter the Bendix Trophy Race after Paul worked out that with their combined experience and the Vega's performance they could probably take fifth place. They duly 'cranked up' and, taking fifth place, won $500. For Amelia it was sheer fun. The freedom from absolute responsibility, Paul's overtly flirtatious manner, the feeling that in some way they were behaving deliciously childishly all contributed.

Amelia was kept so busy that fall that her notes to her mother were often no more than a line or two and it fell to George, sometimes after a telephonic nudge from Amelia, to write to Mrs Earhart keeping her in touch with her daughter's progress, sending her photos of the new house and pictures taken when they had flown with Paul over the Grand Canyon.

CHAPTER 18

1935-1937

Amelia's involvement with Purdue University was almost more a period of rest than another part of her schedule. She fitted in well with campus life, invariably staying at South Hall (now Duhme Hall) on her visits there. Of the 6,000 students on campus almost 1,000 were women[1] and women faculty members were as scarce as women students. Her lectures were over-subscribed but it was in off-duty hours that the students felt they got to know the woman they had previously read about in newspapers:

South Hall residents vied with each other to sit at Miss Earhart's table in the dining room . . . buttermilk became an overnight favourite beverage because it was her choice . . . These were the days when table manners were considered somewhat important . . . one thing you were supposed to do was keep your elbows off the table. Amelia's posture at table, when she was deep in conversation was apt to be sitting forward on the edge of her chair – both elbows on the table – and chin cupped in hands. Naturally the question was 'If Miss Earhart can do it why can't we?' The stock reply was 'As soon as you fly the Atlantic, you may!'

. . . after dinner . . . as many students who could would follow Miss Earhart into my room and sit around on the floor and talk and listen . . . she sat on the floor too – she was adaptable, easy and informal. It was during these times especially that we got to know some of the underlying beliefs and hopes and dreams that motivated our distinguished guest.

The conversations invariably centred around Miss Earhart's belief that women should have and really did have choices about what they could do with their lives. She believed and said that, of course women should be engineers or scientists; they could be physicians as well as nurses; they could manage businesses as well as be secretaries to managers. She believed in women's intelligence, their ability to learn, and their ability to do whatever they wanted to do . . . she saw no limitations on the aspirations [of women students].

There was no question that she, through her own achievements and persuasiveness, was an effective catalyst to heretofore unthinkable thoughts for all of us.[2]

Amelia took her role as visiting faculty member seriously and luckily some of her class lecture notes survive at Purdue, indicating her practical approach to encouraging the young women.[3]

A questionnaire she drafted for her students also survives inviting the answers to questions probably to be used in debate:

Why are you at College?
Do you really want a career?
Or are you doing it because your aunt says you ought to do it?
Or because you think it is the thing to do?
If you are married how does your husband fit into the picture?
What do you expect of him?
What part does he play in your life?

Ninety-two per cent of the women students who answered wanted a career.[4]

The demands on Amelia's time gave her few opportunities to write to her mother, and the few letters she did write at this time reveal an abruptness with Amy's affairs that was also visible in earlier letters when the pressures upon Amelia had been very great. Now, George was often Amy's correspondent, and as it is well documented that Amelia telephoned him every evening it is probable that he performed this small chore at her request, as on one occasion when Muriel arranged a dinner party with Amelia as guest of honour. Amelia wrote the briefest of notes cancelling it without explanation. Amy wrote and told her plainly what she thought of this arrogant behaviour and George read this to Amelia over the telephone. Although they agreed that George should write and explain, Amelia must have subsequently recognised that her curtness had caused hurt for she scribbled a note:

> Please tell Pidge when I wrote her about cancelling a dinner she was planning at Cambridge, I did not mean that GP and I would not be glad to eat at home with just *the family* if she wishes. That is if she will have a maid come in for whom I will gladly pay . . .

while George wrote simultaneously:

> I guess we will have to leave the decision in all this to Amelia. For self protection she simply has to be hard-boiled about getting away from people. Realize, please, this is a problem repeated two or three times a day every day for the last few months. I am meeting Amelia in Buffalo on Thursday and will take your letter with me.[5]

George fully recognised that the stresses of the past months were having an effect on his wife, but despite the strains of her busy life Amelia showed no desire to take even a temporary retirement. In a speech in December 1935 she hinted at what the future might hold for her. 'I'm looking for a tree on which new and better airplanes grow, and I'm looking for a shiny new one to shake down,' she said.[6] In fact she already had fixed in her mind the aeroplane she wanted.

In late November Paul Mantz had obtained a quotation on behalf of George and Amelia for a Lockheed Model 10E Electra. Prior to this other manufacturers had been canvassed and George wrote to Paul telling him that he had received a quotation from Sikorsky for one of their S-43 flying boats. At a price of $110,000[7] it was not under serious consideration but George suggested to Mantz that he let Lockheed know that Amelia would not automatically choose Lockheed, despite her past successes with their products. Amelia had recently scoffed at suggestions that she might be planning a round-the-world flight but it is obvious from the correspondence with aeroplane manufacturers that she had had such a venture very much in mind for some time. The price quoted by Lockheed was over $36,000 for a basic aeroplane; sophisticated equipment would cost as much again and would need to be fitted for the venture she had in mind.

News clippings of the period reveal that if Amelia was tired she never allowed it to show in her public life. To reporters she was always 'gracious', 'charming' and 'available for interview', and while she relied on George to contact Amy she had not forgotten Edwin's widow and clearly visited her stepmother from time to time on her frequent visits to Los Angeles. The little house in the California hills in which Edwin had died was no longer part of an isolated community. When Helen Earhart found that development taxes threatened to bankrupt her and that she might lose her home, Amelia stepped in and bought the house for $3,000, clearing all outstanding assessments at the same time. It is also obvious from her letters[8] that in addition to supporting Amy and often, to her chagrin, indirectly helping Muriel's husband, Amelia also 'contributed' every month to the upkeep of two Challiss cousins who were in financial difficulty.[9]

Amelia relied on George's support more and more. When she 'checked in' each night by telephone he masterminded the logistics of her tour, advising whether she had spoken at the same venue in the past so that her lectures, from specific descriptions of her record-breaking flights to 'Flying for Fun', could be altered to avoid giving the same speech. He provided information on whether the audience was likely to be a public one or consist of members of a private club.[10] George and Amelia's nightly chat was important to both of them but occasionally she finished too late to phone and sometimes when this happened she would send a cable next morning. A typical one reads: SORRY MISSED CALL LAST NIGHT APPRECIATE ROSES SEE YOU SOON. A.[11]

If there was a hint of difficulty in their marriage at this point (as future events were to suggest), and if the constant separations caused some coolness between them, there was no evidence of it at Christmas when George took Amelia for a walk one Sunday morning in bright cold sunshine along New York's Park Avenue, telling her he wanted to look at some bronzes of bears in a gallery there. Instead, showing her a magnificently carved chest he had commissioned many months earlier, he mumbled, 'There, how do you like that?' It was a few moments before Amelia realised that her initials were carved into a crest on the front and that the sides were encrusted with allegorical references to her various record flights – fishes for the oceans she had crossed, a shamrock for the landing at Culmore, etc. It was typical of George that having given so much thought to what was a precious item made by a brilliant master craftsman, he should present it in such an offhand manner. In fact it was his replacement for the rosewood cabinet that Amelia had treasured but which had been lost in the fire at Rye.[12]

The couple were to need confidence in their relationship, since shortly afterwards they received a verbal warning from Paul Mantz that his wife, Myrtle, was suing him for divorce alleging extreme mental and physical cruelty and, more importantly, alleging adultery with Amelia. Without question Paul was a ladies' man (a fact never denied by him), and Amelia had been drawn to him, but it is unlikely that their relationship ever went further than a mild attraction. She had spent a great deal of time with him. Often the two were alone on flying trips and certainly they spent long hours together planning their business ventures. She had been a guest at the Mantzes' home for a month on one occasion and for the odd weekends over a period of about a year. Myrtle was unable to offer any evidence to back up her charge against Amelia, and Paul took the witness stand himself precisely to clear Amelia from any damaging charges.

Unfortunately this well-intentioned act merely gave the newspapers an opportunity to run riot with sensational copy. Paul denied that he and Amelia had ever acted improperly. He also cross-charged mental cruelty, relating that Myrtle had once appeared in his bedroom and shot at him with a revolver and was insanely jealous without any foundation.

One witness for the plaintiff claimed she had attended a conference between Paul and Myrtle, held to attempt a reconciliation. Myrtle was said to have stated on that occasion, 'I know I am upset and jealous but I believe that if Miss Earhart would take her clothes and leave our house we would have a better chance of getting along.'[13]

The Mantzes' maid swore that Amelia and Paul had never been alone together in the house overnight. Indeed this had been the source of a violent quarrel for when the maid told Myrtle this, some months before the divorce case, Myrtle summarily dismissed her 'for lying'. When Paul took hold of Myrtle to stop her rounding on the unfortunate servant, a fierce struggle had started in front of embarrassed dinner guests.[14]

Amelia's name was cleared but she would have been naive not to have recognised that to some extent she had laid herself open to the accusations. George had been unhappy for some time about the amount of time Amelia spent with Paul but it was not in his nature (nor in the spirit of their marriage contract) to question her behaviour.

In one of George's letters to Amelia's mother he mentioned the affair briefly after giving her details of Amelia's itinerary.

If you have seen any of the clippings relative to Paul Mantz's divorce mess in Los Angeles, there is nothing to worry about. It was simply an effort by a cheap lawyer to get publicity for himself by perpetrating some innuendoes involving A.E.'s name. There was nothing we could do about it. Now it is all over.[15]

This time Amelia wrote at greater length:

Poor old Myrtle Mantz. She had to get nasty in the trial. The only two women she had not driven away from Paul paid for their loyalty by being dragged into a divorce suit. The silly accusations fell of their own weight and I cannot but feel she will eventually do something so disgraceful that the world will know what she is. Because, of course, after her self-inflicted publicity she will be watched. I really have been fortunate, for anyone who has a name in the paper is a target for all sorts of things . . .[16]

The question of whether Amelia did have an affair with Mantz has been raised many times. It is highly unlikely: Amelia was simply not Paul Mantz's type of woman. He was flamboyant by nature and his romances were with passionate, more obviously beautiful and extrovert women than Amelia. Even after his second marriage, which was a happy one, Mantz indulged in casual love affairs, but he was also capable of treating a woman on equal terms and in Amelia he probably recognised a kindred spirit. Any excitement the two shared emanated from a common love of flight, and plans for their proposed business ventures. Amelia enjoyed Mantz's company (few women would not), but if George was jealous of the time Amelia was able to spend with Paul (which is probable given his comments at a later date), it was most likely to have been because the respect and reliance she had previously only given to George, was now accorded also to Paul.

In particular she relied on Paul's advice in her plans for a round-the-world flight. Why did Amelia wish to fly around the world? She had surely already proven herself as a pilot of note and her news-worthiness was established beyond question. It was necessary for a variety of reasons. Initially she made record flights for publicity in order to build her reputation and to launch her career. Then, after she had received public acclaim, she felt unease that her career which meant so much to her, was based on what she considered a fabrication; she had *not earned* any credit by merely being a passenger of Stultz. Her Atlantic solo flight had put to rest any doubts about her ability for she had worked hard to acquire the necessary knowledge and experience, which together with her inherent courage, had enabled her to make that flight.

Since then her various exploits had established her as a competent pilot, the best-known woman flyer in the USA, thanks to George's superb management: and now she wanted and needed to make a final gesture. Neither she nor George could have been unaware that the public were tiring of record-breaking flights. Virtually every major record worth taking had been taken, and short of faster and faster flights from point A to point B there were few that would capture attention. One was flight in the stratosphere: an area of aviation that had been under exploration by Amelia's late friend Wiley Post before he was killed in an air accident in August 1935. (Wiley Post and Will Rogers were killed in a Lockheed Sirius equipped with floats. Undoubtedly the reduced performance of the aeroplane, due to the floats, had some bearing on the accident.) The other was a flight around the world by a woman.

The flight had already been achieved as early as 1924 by a US Army Service team, but probably more notably by Wiley Post. For good measure Post had flown it twice in his Lockheed Vega the *Winnie Mae*. On the first occasion, in June 1931, the one-eyed, partially deaf aviator had taken a navigator (Harold Gatty) and completed his transglobal circumnavigation in 8 days 15 hours 51 minutes.[17] This flight, Post readily admitted, did nothing for aviation, although it established his own reputation; at one point after a rough landing he had to beat the propeller back into shape with a hammer and a rock: colourful stuff, but it did not reflect the professional image of aviation that he wished to project.

Post subsequently set to work to learn about instruments such as the new automatic pilots and radio direction finders, primitive as they were in those early days of aviation, to prove that flying could be made safer and more accurate by modern technology. Two years later, in July 1933, using these instruments, he successfully accomplished a solo round-the-world flight in the *Winnie Mae* in 7 days 18 hours 49 minutes. His biggest problem, obviously, was lack of sleep but he ate only enough to keep himself alive; hunger, he said, helped to keep him awake! However, he had proven the value of instruments in aviation and on his return said that if man wanted to fly long distances safely and faster he would have to go higher; into the stratosphere where big winds – 'jet streams' – were known to exist which could add up to 200 mph to the speed of an aeroplane. He was working on this theory when he died and had achieved spectacular success when, wearing 'a pressure suit' of his own design he 'rode' the jet stream from Burbank, California to Cleveland, Ohio at an average speed of 227 mph in an aeroplane with a designed maximum speed of 168 mph.[18]

So Amelia's ambition to fly around the world would provide her with a major 'first' – she would be the first woman if successful – but also, as she was later to confide to the President, her course was 'unique'. Previous attempts had always been made to create time records and therefore the shortest possible route had been chosen. Amelia decided to travel the longest possible distance by traversing the world at its waist and thus eliminate the need to compete with existing records.

Amelia would never claim that this flight was being made purely for the fun of it, but she was quoted as saying that she was doing it to achieve a personal desire and 'I want it to be a thorough check of modern equipment. I expect to keep a log of what happened to personnel and machine under various conditions. Records such as these, be they of success or failure can do much to safeguard subsequent flights.'[19]

Funding for such a project was a critical factor. George and Amelia had no access to enough money to buy and equip the Lockheed Electra that Paul Mantz and Amelia had already decided was the most suitable plane for the proposed flight. (Even had they been able to contemplate the $110,000-plus needed to buy the Sikorsky, it was not an aeroplane that Amelia could have flown with confidence, though Paul later claimed he would have been happier if Amelia had selected a sea-plane.) In 1936 the amount required, even for the Electra, was a great deal of money and the Putnams certainly were not in a position to raise it on their own recognizance.

According to independent accounts by George, Amelia and President Elliott of Purdue University, it was George who first planted the idea of a 'Purdue flying laboratory' in Elliott's mind. There it bubbled around for a while until in the autumn of 1935, at a dinner party at the Elliots' home, Amelia outlined her 'dreams' for women and aviation, which coincidentally seemed remarkably similar to the aims and ideals of Elliott. Before the evening was over fellow guest David Ross offered to donate $50,000 towards the cost of providing a machine suitable for the flying laboratory. Further donations in cash and equipment were received from J. K. Lilly (of the Eli Lilly drug company), Vincent Bendix, and manufacturers Western Electric, Goodrich and Goodyear.[20]

This formed the basis of 'The Amelia Earhart Fund for Aeronautical Research'; its primary aim was to 'develop scientific and engineering data of vital importance to the aviation industry.[21] Many years later, when it was suggested that Amelia's flight was a spy mission, various writers would suggest that the money sum had been provided by the government and paid through Purdue merely in order to provide a 'cover' story. However, in a letter to me, and in various interviews, R. B. Stewart (then secretary-treasurer of Purdue University), who masterminded the fund, is adamant that there was no government involvement whatsoever.

> The PRF [Purdue Research Foundation] gave this money [from Ross and Lilly] to Miss Earhart so that she might buy her airplane . . . Contrary to popular belief, the money was not supplied by the United States government and Purdue University was not used as a smoke-screen to disguise any association with this mission. I sincerely hope you can set the record straight.[22]

A man of significant financial brilliance, Stewart had developed the Purdue Research Foundation five years earlier to fund a building programme and to provide fellowships. His skill in raising money in large amounts is demonstrated in the way he masterminded the college building fund:

> We were issuing Purdue University bonds to build dormitories and the Union building – all of them tax exempt. So I could receive a gift of a million dollars worth of stock on which the donor was getting interest and paying taxes on that interest. And I could say to that person, 'I'll get you out. I'll sell that stock to the research foundation. The foundation will pay cash of sufficient amount to buy you Purdue bonds and that income will be

tax-exempt so your net income will be the same. Now, when you die, then we cancel the Purdue bonds. The effect is – this is a deferred gift. There is no gift until you die. Actually, you're making money on it . . .'[23]

and it was this same brain that masterminded the fund to buy Amelia a 'flying laboratory'. Almost everyone at Purdue was impressed by Amelia and her record; there was general and genuine pleasure that she was part of their team and great enthusiasm at any opportunity to play some part in her career.

There were only a few critics; some of the older women – wives of professors, in the main – were shocked that she wore slacks not only around the dormitories but in Lafayette's soda fountain. Once she even came down to dinner wearing slacks which was not accepted dress in the conservative midwest.

Dean Potter huffily announced that Amelia was not scholastically qualified to be a member of the university faculty. A woman faculty member retorted that the dean was a scholar and didn't recognise the importance of motivating young people as well as educating them. Amelia merely mentioned that she had taught at Harvard University extension courses as long ago as the mid-twenties and felt she *was* qualified. Indeed, in terms of practical experience there was probably no one better qualified.

George had been put in charge of administrative arrangements for the aeroplane by Elliott and Stewart;[24] in March 1936 he advised Lockheed that the financial arrangements had been completed and he was in a position to make the initial payment but in view of the circumstances he looked for some price reduction. The equipment manufacturers, he felt, should be willing to supply at cost, because of potential publicity and especially since Amelia would make nothing out of the plane, 'all proceeds going directly to the Purdue Fund for aviation research'.

'Delivery is required June,' George wrote, 'so please step on it.' A month later he was writing again at great length advising Lockheed on technical matters such as engine size, fuel system, a special hatch cover; and to say that in Amelia's absence, Paul Mantz was the final authority on all technical matters. Stressing the need for confidentiality he instructed that the plane should be registered in his name and specified the Electra Model 10E which came with two Pratt and Whitney WASP S3H-I engines each capable of developing 550 horsepower. With the fuel loads she would be carrying in the extra tanks Amelia would need the power of the largest engines supplied by Lockheed for the Electra.[25]

Much thought was given to the radio equipment. Amelia (and George) had been extremely impressed with the radio telephone she had used in the Vega on her trans-Pacific flight and she was reluctant to revert to telegraphy which she said she had not practised for a number of years (probably not since the 1932 Atlantic solo, if then). Western Electric supplied a standard transport 50-watt radio transmitter (13 A) and a new, continuously adjustable, four-band receiver (20 A) with suitable power and remote control apparatus.[26] The equipment transmitted on 6,210 kcs (kilocycles, but now referred to as kiloherz), during the daytime and 3,105 kcs at night, standard aircraft frequencies, but was modified to incorporate an emergency frequency on 500 kcs which she could, if necessary, use in conjunction with a code transmitting key. To work effectively on 500 kcs a 250-foot trailing aerial was required. These aerials were technically effective but cumbersome to use as they were heavy and had to be let out and reeled in by means of a handle, a tiring job just before landing when there were many other jobs taking up a pilot's attention. They were also mechanically unreliable for in order to prevent the wire lashing about the aerial terminated in a heavy lead ball which was apt to break off under the strain imposed by the aircraft's speed through the air; the antenna then became useless. Both the radio and the code transmitter could be used by either the pilot or navigator from their respective positions in the cockpit and rear cabin.[27]

While George and Paul Mantz worked out the administrative details, Amelia continued her lecture tour, writing to her mother: 'The rumour about the world flight in June is applesauce. Confidentially I shall have a new airplane to play with then, I hope, but as I'm busy lecturing until May or thereabouts I shall not hop off in June. It would take months to prepare for such a trip – maybe a year.'[28] Amy's hopes may have risen about her daughter settling down by a line in this letter – 'I have a grand surprise for you. I can't tell you now but it's a swell one' – which was followed in several subsequent letters with a tantalising promise that she would 'probably come north to see you and unfold the great secret'.

Taken out of context these sentences have been used to suggest that Amelia may have been pregnant, but several letters in the archives at Radcliffe College's Schlessinger Library reveal merely that she and George had planned a surprise trip for Amy to visit Europe with a young cousin, Nancy Balis, as companion.

Everything had been planned by Amelia for Amy including lengthy lectures on *exactly* what to pack and how to pack it, even how to launder it. 'I have given you very decent stockings. Also everyday ones. Keep separate . . .'; detailed instructions followed on how to don silk (pre-nylon days) stockings, and how to remove them, to prevent them 'sagging'. More; 'if raining do not wear kid gloves. They'll spot . . . Keep manicured and have hair done every ten days . . .' Lists of minutiae contained what Amy might do, where she might go and what she might say:

> Please don't down the Roosevelt administration. It's all right to be reactionary inside but it is out of step with the times to sound off about the chosen people who have inherited or grabbed the earth. You must think of me when you converse and I believe the experiments carried on today point the way to a new social order when governments will be the voice of the proletariat far more than democracy ever can be. In all cases be careful of reporters . . .[29]

On 21 July 1936 Amelia was in Los Angeles to test-fly the Lockheed Electra 10E registration R16020 with Lockheed's test pilot, Elmer C. McLeod.[30] The inevitable news stories which accompanied the event described the plane as being capable of flying up to 4,500 miles non-stop and detailed the special state-of-the-art equipment on board. Amelia took formal delivery of the plane on 24 July, her thirty-ninth birthday.

Amelia was no doubt delighted with her new 'ship' but there were some drawbacks. It was no easy switch from the Vega to the Electra with its sophisticated controls and twin engines. It was a physically taxing aeroplane to fly and Amelia's reserves of physical energy did not run deep. But with Paul as her tutor she began learning how to master it. There were times when Paul grew angry at her seeming inability to grasp what to him were fundamentals of flying and he drove her hard. It was at Paul's insistence that she spent time in a Link trainer that he had installed in his hangar at Burbank; and there she learned about instrument flying in simulated conditions. But in fact Paul was never entirely satisfied with her ability to fly the Electra, no matter how much she practised, and despite his personal respect for her.[31]

A month earlier George had written to Eleanor Roosevelt on Amelia's behalf:

> to avail ourselves of the help which you kindly offered when we last saw you. Our wish is to be put in touch with the proper person in the State Department whose aid can be enlisted in connection with A.E.'s proposed world flight. We want appropriate guidance in securing the required permissions ... Do please emphasise that the project is for the present confidential. As you know A.E. likes to avoid advance discussion of flights – their realization depends upon so many factors.[32]

In referring this letter to Richard Southgate, Chief of Division of Protocol, the First Lady's secretary wrote:

> Mrs Roosevelt, upon her return to Washington, the other day, found George Palmer Putnam's letter to her and learned that you had kindly consented to take care of the things he wished done in the State Department.
> Mrs Roosevelt asked me to send you this special note to say that she had promised Mr Putnam to keep this matter confidential. She is sure you understand and that you will be *very* nice to him.[33]

The constant obsession with confidentiality regarding Amelia's flight in government papers appears to stem from this letter and Eleanor Roosevelt's; having received patronage on such a level George was never slow to hint at the relationship which Amelia and the First Lady enjoyed.[34]

Meanwhile George was liaising with Gene Vidal, once Amelia's colleague at TAT and now Director of Air Commerce:

I am told that hard surface runways are being installed in the Navy Field [Luke Field]. This is down at Pearl Harbor at sea level. On A.E.'s former flight she used Wheeler Field, which is Army and has some altitude and no hard surface runways. What I want to get is an exact description of the new runways, the total length of the pavement, the extra run and nature of the approaches. If they are not finished, I would like an estimate of what the condition will be as of, say, February. I do so hope you can get that information from the Navy Department.[35]

A week later, his follow-up letter has an intriguing paragraph implying that George is aware of something that Vidal wishes to keep secret:

By the way I golfed Saturday with George Leisure, the lawyer. *Remember?* . . . Well, George is kinda peeved at you. He says each time he meets you you have apparently forgotten him entirely – go through the motions of being introduced again. He felt you were just trying to high-hat him and pretending you never had that night meeting with him. I told him I knew that wasn't true but that you are sometimes dumb about names and faces! He asked me how many times you would finally have to meet him before you'd remember him. I am sure you do recall that he did render you a very great service one night. And naturally it is not unreasonable for him to be peeved. When are you coming up for more tennis?[36]

But only a month later Amelia was writing quixotically on Vidal's behalf, direct to Eleanor Roosevelt

> concerning a mean and unfortunate instance of political schem-
> ing . . . Aviation is my vocation and avocation. I should rather
> help the industry than progess myself. Thus I feel the pre-emp-
> tory dismissal of the Director of Air Commerce and two
> assistants substituting [a] legally trained individual for one of
> practical experience almost a calamity. There is little use of my
> trying to interest others in the President's cause when my heart is
> sick with the knowledge that an industry can be jeopardized and
> an individual's career blasted by what seems a personal feud . . .[37]

Her plea seems to have stimulated instantaneous action for although Vidal had already been dismissed and given one day's notice to clear his office, on 17 September Amelia cabled Mrs Roosevelt her thanks:

> for your helpfulness in the matter about which I wired you. Am
> informed outcome now promises to be satisfactory to Vidal
> whose loyalty merits the fair treatment which your interests
> securing. I am sure you understand that I was actuated by desire
> to serve the industry, the individual and the Administration.[38]

Eugene Vidal had been a close friend of the Putnams since the early days of Amelia's involvement with the TAT airline. Indeed it was through her influence with the Roosevelts that Vidal had been appointed to the post of Director of Air Commerce in 1935.[39] His son, Gore Vidal, was very much aware of the debt his father owed to Amelia. 'Eleanor was in love with Amelia and Amelia used this to get her way over lots of things; such as getting my father into the cabinet . . .'[40] From correspondence there is no doubt that George and Amelia had used this friendship, trading on his position and contacts, to short-circuit formalities when planning record flights. Permissions which usually took months to obtain were miraculously available to Amelia in days, for example. In particular Vidal's loss of office at the Bureau of Air Commerce at this moment would be a severe blow for he had access to official information that the Putnams could not get from any other source. Fortunately, her direct appeal to Eleanor Roosevelt paid off and Vidal was reinstated.

The summer passed quickly for Amelia. Apart from the usual round of lectures (her lecture file shows that in 1936 she gave 136 speeches and lectures. She usually drove because there was seldom a landing strip conveniently placed, driving through the night and sleeping during the day before delivering her speech and leaving immediately for the next venue) there was a residential visit to Purdue, and work for the Department of Commerce, in which for $1 a year she was commissioned to test a new direction finder.

Her correspondence took up a great deal of time; she wrote often to Gene Vidal on matters of aviation generally,[41] and a great number of responses to young women who wrote requesting advice on aviation as a career. In addition Amelia organised the women's handicap race at the 1936 National Air Races. Consequently it was George who met Amy in New York when she returned from her European trip; Amelia was simply too busy. In two months Amelia found time for only two hastily scribbled notes to Amy – the first to enclose pictures of the newly completed house in Hollywood, and the second to say that she and George would visit Boston to discuss her sister's rapidly escalating marital problem.[42]

Despite all the problems created by his divorce case the friendship between Amelia and Paul Mantz seems to have remained as strong as ever. Her reliance upon his technical advice was total. His knowledge of the latest developments was formidable and both Amelia and George must have recognised that the level of assistance that Paul could, perhaps uniquely, provide was essential for the round-the-world project.

Throughout these months George too was busy coordinating the logistics of Amelia's proposed flight. His own concerns seemed to have dwindled to ad hoc jobs such as steering a Paramount movie (*Go West Young Man* starring Mae West) through its New York premiere with all the resultant ballyhoo. George had formed a company, *Major Pictures*, to promote these activities, but it is clear that he spent most of his time during this period 'managing' Amelia Earhart. He wrote streams of letters to government and military departments requesting information on weather and charts of the Pacific. Some of the requested information was classified, he was advised, but the navy would assist where they could and two reports in particular, 'Climatic Features of the Pacific Island Region' and 'Detailed Information on Seaplane Anchorages and Landing Fields' which might be of help would be made available for George's examination if he could come to Washington.[43]

A proposal that Amelia should use in-flight refuelling on the longest section of her planned route occupied George for some weeks as did securing the services of professionals. Former naval navigator, Commander Clarence S. Williams, would prepare detailed charts of the entire route; and Amelia would take Harry Manning, a distinguished Master Mariner with the United States Lines, as navigator for the more difficult legs of the trip. Manning had commanded the SS *President Roosevelt*, on which Amelia had returned from England in 1928. They had been friends since and Manning, who was a radio ham and a pilot in his spare time, obtained three months' leave of absence from his employers in order to make the trip. A full-time mechanic, Bo McKneely, was employed, and Paul Mantz was contracted as 'Technical Adviser' at $100 a day.

The area of the Pacific Ocean over which Amelia would have to fly, with its myriad groups of islands, was not well charted (except by the British Admiralty, which was not consulted). During the previous two years various surveys had been carried out by the US Navy to correct charts which in some instances contained information provided by the navigators of clipper ships a century or more earlier. Clarence Williams would have known that the only way to get access to the latest information was through official channels – civilian records were pitifully inadequate for the trip Amelia planned. Recognising that in order to get the full cooperation that she would need from various government departments for the complicated Pacific section of her flight, Amelia wrote at length to the White House, this time to the final authority:

November 10th 1936

Dear Mr President,

Some time ago I told you and Mrs Roosevelt a little about my confidential plans for a world flight. As perhaps you know, through the co-operation of Purdue University I now have a magnificent twin-motor, all metal plane especially equipped for long distance flying.

For some months Mr Putnam and I have been preparing for a flight which I hope to attempt probably in March. The route, compared with previous flights, will be unique. It is east to west, and approximates the equator. Roughly it is from San Francisco to Honolulu: Honululu to Tokio[44] – or Honolulu to Brisbane; the regular Australia–England route as far west as Karachi; from Karachi to Aden; Aden via Khartoum across Central Africa to Dakar; Dakar to Natal, and thence to New York on the regular Pan American route.

Special survey work and map preparation is already under way on the less familiar portion of the route as, for instance, that in Africa.

The chief problem is the jump westward from Honolulu. The distance thence to Tokio is 3900 miles. I want to reduce as much as possible the hazard of the take-off at Honolulu with the excessive overload. With that in view, I am discussing with the Navy a possible <u>refuelling in the air over Midway Island</u>. If this can be arranged, I need to take much less gas from Honolulu, and with the Midway refuelling will have ample gasoline to reach Tokio. As mine is a land plane, the seaplane facilities at Wake, Guam, etc are useless.

This matter has been discussed in detail by Mr Putnam with Admiral Cook, who was most interested and friendly. Subsequently a detailed description of the project, and request for this assistance, was prepared. It is now on the desk of Admiral Standley, by whom it is being considered.

Some new seaplanes are being completed at San Diego for the Navy. They will be ferried in January or February to Honolulu. It is my desire to practise actual refuelling operations in the air over San Diego with one of these planes. That plane subsequently from Honolulu would be available for the Midway operation. I gather from Admiral Cook that technically there are no extraordinary difficulties. It is primarily a matter of policy and precedent.

In the past the Navy has been progressive in its pioneering and so broadminded in what we might call its 'public relations', that I think a project such as this (even involving a mere woman!) may appeal to Navy personnel. Its successful attainment might, I think, win for the Service, further popular friendship.

I should add the matter of international permissions etc., is being handled very helpfully by the State Department. The flight, by the way, has no commercial implications. The operation of my 'flying laboratory' is under the auspices of Purdue University. Like previous flights I am undertaking this one solely because I want to, and because I feel that women now and then have to do things to show what women can do.

Forgive the great length of this letter. I am just leaving for the west on a lecture tour and wanted to place my problems before you.

Knowing your own enthusiasm for voyaging, and your affectionate interest in Navy matters, I am asking you to help me secure Navy cooperation – that is if you think well of the project. If any information is wanted as to purpose plans, equipment etc., Mr Putnam can meet anyone you designate, any time, any where.

Very sincerely yours
Amelia Earhart

P.S. My plans are for the moment entirely confidential – no announcement has been made.[45]

The original of this letter in the Roosevelt files bears a handwritten scrawl across the top of the front page, 'Do what we can and contact Mr Putnam.' A formal memorandum was written to the Chief of Naval Operations in which 'the President hoped the Navy would do what they could to cooperate with Miss Amelia Earhart in her proposed flight and that in this connection, contact should be made with Mr Putnam'.[46]

Appropriate naval cooperation was thus secured (though George was advised that Amelia would have to take appropriate instruction on the in-flight refuelling procedures and bear the costs of the exercise – about $2,000) and because of Amelia's request all correspondence was stamped CONFIDENTIAL. It was probably through Gene Vidal that George learned of a possible alternative to the questionable flight refuelling proposals.

The Department of Commerce was about to establish an emergency field on tiny Howland Island, a convenient stage roughly half way between the Hawaiian Islands and New Guinea. Indeed, a construction party was due to leave Honolulu in early January to begin working on the project.[47]

The United States had begun a colonisation project on the uninhabited island of Howland on 2 April 1935; prior to this there was some doubt as to whether it was a British or American possession.[48] The declared intention of the US government at that stage was to assert United States sovereignty in order to use the island 'for weather observations and reporting and for the clearing of emergency landing strips'.[49] As Director of Air Commerce, Vidal became involved with the landing-strip project with the principal aim of providing emergency landing facilities for Pan American airlines who were just beginning surveys for proposed air services in that part of the Pacific. In May 1936 administration of the island became the responsibility of the Department of the Interior and there was a certain amount of internal political friction as each department fought for its rights. In June 1936 the Department of the Interior organised an expedition to Howland and the nearby islands of Baker and Jarvis, using the Coast Guard cutters SS *Itasca* and SS *Tiger*. The *Itasca*'s navigator took the opportunity to correct the coordinates of the island which appeared incorrectly on charts but it was some years before these corrections appeared on new hydrographic charts.

At some point in their many discussions regarding Amelia's flight,

Vidal undoubtedly mentioned Howland Island with its proposed landing strip. Such a landing seemed infinitely preferable to refuelling in flight for, apart from the degree of difficulty in the actual task of refuelling, there was Amelia's physical condition to take into account. How could she stay awake and alert over the period of 24 hours, flying the aeroplane with no one to 'spell' her occasionally? And how was she to fly the plane and manage the complicated manoeuvre of 'docking' the fuel lines? Paul Mantz had told them plainly that he thought it an inadvisable solution unless completely unavoidable.[50]

Amelia opted to land on Howland Island provided the strip was finished in time and she could obtain the necessary permissions. After much correspondence these were secured from departments as diverse as the Department of Air Commerce and the Coast Guard, but the construction of the landing strip had run foul of bureaucracy at the Treasury Department. Amelia once again asked President Roosevelt for help:

. . . am now informed apparently some question regarding WPA [Works Progress Administration] appropriation in amount three thousand dollars which covers all costs other than those borne by me for this mid Pacific pioneer landing field which permanently useful and valuable aeronautically and nationally. Requisition now on desk of A.V. Keene Bureau of Budget, Treasury Department. Understand its moving requires executive approval under circumstances could you expedite as immediate action vital . . . please forgive troublesome female flyer for whom the Howland Island project is key to world flight attempt.[51]

In reply she was advised that Federal funds had been allocated to enable the Bureau of Air Commerce to build the emergency landing field and that the working party was scheduled to leave Honolulu on 12 Jan.[52]

George and Amelia spent Christmas 1936 at Indio, California with financier Floyd Odlum and his wife, the noted aviatrix Jacqueline Cochran. Amelia and Jackie had been friends for some time and Odlum, a multi-millionaire, had made some contribution to the round-the-world flight fund. The relationship had initially got off to a rocky start when George took the same approach with Jackie as he had taken with Lady Heath and Elinor Smith and, just as with those two ladies, in Jackie he met a powerful character; but Jackie had the power of her husband's millions behind her. On their first meeting, Jackie said:

> He was very patronising, and said: 'Well, little girl, what's your ambition in flying?'
>
> 'To put your wife in the shade,' I replied.[53]

Such an unpromising start had not hindered the growth of a genuine friendship. Over Christmas Amelia and Jackie spent a great deal of time discussing aviation but, in particular, they shared an interest in telepathy and psychic phenomena. They evidently put their interest to some practical use for an aeroplane belonging to Western Air Express was reported missing on 15 December 1936. On 22 December Amelia telephoned the airline claiming to have had some sort of 'vision' in which a trapper had found the wreckage and looted it. A trapper subsequently turned up near Salt Lake City and reported finding the wreckage but disappeared without trace before giving the location. Amelia next predicted that she would make a startling discovery on 10 May concerning this wreckage, but there is no evidence that she ever did so.[54]

Quite what to make of these claims, so unlike the practical, even prosaic Amelia, is difficult to decide, and becomes more so in the light of subsequent events. On 27 December while Amelia was still a guest at Indio, a United Airlines scheduled flight was reported missing. Amelia reportedly telephoned the United Airlines office at Burbank and told them to search for the wreck at Saugas, a small town to the north of Burbank. The wreckage was duly found in the location she had given them.[55]

One further incident in this weird chain occurred two weeks later when a Western Express charter plane crashed. Amelia advised officials to search near Newhall, 15 miles north of Burbank, where again the wreckage was found as she predicted.[56] Later Jackie Cochran substantiated the newspaper reports of these events and claimed that they had a 'pact' to contact each other in case of emergency.[57]

Throughout January 1937 George continued to work on flight preparations while Amelia completed the last in her current series of lectures. A domestic crisis also intruded into her time when Muriel and Albert Morrissey decided to divorce. In a long letter dated 31 January Amelia berated her sister for 'giving in too much' to Albert. 'Given a little power over another, little natures swell to hideous proportions . . .' she scolded:

What's done is done. The problem is what to do now. In order to protect you – from yourself as much as anything – I want several things done. One, the stock which you bought with the thousand dollars Mother gave you is to be made over to GPP . . . Then Albert is to return the five hundred dollars to you which you gave him in a separate transaction . . . you will probably have to obtain a legal separation in order to get a monthly income. Please do not go to any old lawyer on this I am coming east this week and unless events move too fast, hold the legal part until I get to NY. If you have to see someone go to the man whose name I gave you before. And DON'T SIGN ANYTHING IN THE MEANTIME. Do not even write letters to Albert on she subject of the divorce or separation. Don't move out of the house away from Albert no matter how tough things may get . . . Perhaps Albert can be brought to his senses if GPP presses for the notes. I shall write to him to find out. Of course our money is gone [the money the Putnams had lent before Christmas]. That I can swallow, but it does make me sad to think that hard earned cash did no good . . .[58]

But there was little time to spare for family affairs as the date for the flight moved ever closer. A further factor was advised by Vidal; Pan American Airways intended to carry out a flight survey in March to pioneer a new air route to Auckland via Pago Pago. The US Navy and Coast Guard had been detailed to provide ships to assist on this survey; if Amelia could plan her trip to coincide with the flight, such assistance as they could render to Pan Am would also be available to her.[59]

In full possession of the arrangements made for the Pan Am escort, George travelled to Washington in early February to talk to chiefs at the US Navy. In their discussions they decided:

1. That two aviation mechanics from Pearl Harbor travel to Howland on the Coast Guard cutter *Duane* for the purpose of servicing the Lockheed; and further, that the USS *Ontario*, on station at Samoa stand by 'to act as plane guard' for the flight at some point about 1000 miles south-west of Howland Island and relay weather information to the *Duane* at Howland.

2. That the Governor of American Samoa, Pago Pago obtain weather conditions from Suva, Fiji, Australia and other locations and transmit data to *Duane*.

3. That USS *Swan* cruise to a position halfway between Honolulu and Howland Island to act as standby ship in case of an emergency and transmit weather information to Pearl Harbor and the *Duane*. (*Swan* to return to Pearl Harbor after Amelia's safe landing on Howland).

George then confirmed these 'requests' in writing to Admiral Leahy, Chief of Naval Operations, as part of a high-handed, name-dropping exercise that would be hard to beat for bare-faced cheek. And he got away with it, as he did with all his other requests; that Amelia might use Wheeler Field at Hawaii, for example.[60]

What does emerge clearly after examination of thousands of documents in American and British archives, is that any government involvement in the planning of Amelia's flight was solely at the behest of George and Amelia. Navy chiefs bridled, displaying reluctance and annoyance on occasions, but George bullied, cajoled and threatened until he got what he wanted. Every new privilege that was extended to this ace bargainer was quickly accepted and further privileges sought.

On 12 February Amelia, with Harry Manning in attendance,

held a press conference at the Barclay's Hotel, New York to announce the round-the-world flight. It was all that George could have hoped for with batteries of newsreel cameras and gangs of eager reporters. Amelia arrived late, indeed had even forgotten her own wedding anniversary celebration planned some weeks earlier, for which she was teased by George, but she quickly settled into her usual role of 'hosting' the interview.

One of George's main tasks was to ensure that Amelia reaped some financial reward from the flight. Remembering the success of the Mexican stamp issue when the stamps had quickly become great collectors' items, reaching a value of $100 within months, he had 10,000 special envelopes printed which Amelia would carry on the aeroplane. Immediately the flight had been formally announced in the press, Gimbels, the New York department store, started advertising the Amelia Earhart Special Cover in its philatelic advertisements. 'Most of the covers carried by Miss Earhart in previous flights are now worth between $25 and $200' the blurb ran, '. . . the covers will be postmarked at Oakland at the beginning and termination of the flight and also at a city in Australia or India. A Howland Island cachet, the first one in its history, will also be affixed to these covers . . . Price of this usual cover $2.50; same cover with Miss Earhart's autograph $5.00.'[61]

In addition to the special covers, George was already booking a post-flight lecture tour for Amelia at $500 per appearance. Despite the fact that the aeroplane and basic equipment had been provided for her by Purdue University, the Putnams had sunk a great deal of their personal money into the preparations and supplies for this flight. Indeed it would become obvious before too long that far from being wealthy the Putnams had very little in the way of financial reserves behind them and they were relying on the success of the project to rectify this position.

From New York Amelia flew to California, taking Harry Manning, Bo McKneely (the Lockheed mechanic) and George to make final preparations for her flight. Alighting in Blackwell, Oklahoma, when a minor fault occurred with the propeller syn-chronisation, the party were forced by bad weather to spend the night. George chose this moment to play one of his famous practical jokes.

While the party were dining he slipped away to the telephone and called the chief of police. Later when Amelia was driving out to the airport in a borrowed car she was stopped, booked for speeding and taken to the police station with Harry Manning belligerently complaining that they had seen no speed limit sign. In a hurry to get away Amelia elected to go to court immediately and pleaded 'Guilty'. The police judge, having given Amelia a lecture about speeding, turned to George, apparently not understanding the relationship, and asked, 'Are you responsible for this woman?' Relishing every moment of this George retorted: 'No your honour. I'm just a relative and I disown her.' The courtroom tittered and from George's expression Amelia began to suspect that she had been set up. The judge (whom George thought was in on the joke, but was not), fined Amelia the minimum amount of $1, since she was a visitor, and $3.50 costs. Later he asked George if the lady was really Amelia Earhart. 'I thought they were trying to kid me all the time . . .' he said.

Afterwards when the 'fine' had been returned to her, and they were all laughing about it, George more than anyone, Amelia wryly accepted George's little-boy victory. 'You've behaved pretty well up to now but I've half a mind to take off without you,' she said to him for the benefit of reporters, asking of one, 'how much is the bus fare to Burbank – for one?' Here she is reported to have called him a nickname not previously heard before: 'Muggy'.[62]

Amelia got her revenge in a neat fashion. Although George had long been a regular air traveller he continued to suffer from air sickness. Shortly after the couple's return to California he boarded a plane to return to New York and after about an hour he was handed a small package by the stewardess. It was from Amelia. He opened it to find a raw pork chop.[63]

The laughter always present between the two may have helped break the tension that had already started to build up in the team though for the next month there was precious little time for laughter. There were countless details to be worked out and checked, such as ensuring that supplies of aviation fuel and oil would be in place all along Amelia's route, often at places where Amelia hoped not to have to put down, but where extra fuel should be available 'just in case'. Jacques de Sibour of Standard Oil, whom she had met after her transatlantic flight in 1932, had experience of flying in the tropics; he also had many valuable contacts and was extraordinarily helpful to George in this respect. Not only fuel and oil, but also parcels of spares were shipped out to various destinations, to be available should they be needed.

There was, rightly, a great deal of discussion on the difficulties surrounding a landfall on Howland Island, a tiny barren dot in the Pacific ocean. Two miles wide and half a mile long, it is about 40 miles from the nearest land – Baker Island, some 25 miles north of the equator. It would take extraordinarily accurate navigation to locate this coral formation whose highest point was only 18 feet, but Manning seemed confident that he could do so.

Paul Mantz listened grimly to Manning's confident assertions. His own feeling was that using a sextant on the deck of a ship had nothing in common with celestial navigation from the roof hatch of an aeroplane and it may have been Paul who suggested that they engage Frederick Noonan, a former navigator on the Pan American Pacific Clipper routes across the Pacific. Noonan had made a dozen or so trips in the area, knew the problems that would be encountered and had experience in celestial navigation from a plane.

It was Paul Mantz who had designed the navigator's table and work area in the Electra after examining those on the Pan American Clippers. Noonan would have found all of the equipment familiar: there was a good-sized table on which to spread charts, and a glass inset in this worktop enabled the navigator to use the master aperiodic compass mounted underneath. A chronometer sat beside the table in rubber mounts, and other instruments fitted at this position were altimeter, air-speed and 'drift' indicators, a pelorus (sighting device for the compass) and a temperature gauge.

Noonan insisted that a bubble octant be installed in addition to the marine sextant[64] because his experience had taught him that the latter was inadequate for shooting from an aeroplane. The built-in 'bubble' level provided an artificial horizon in case the actual horizon was obscured by clouds or because the plane was too high. Further, he required at least one additional chronometer, he said.[65]

Born in Chicago in 1894, Noonan is reputed to have run away to sea in 1908. He rounded the Horn seven times, and served on the largest square-rigged ship (the *Crompton*: c. 1910) sailing under the Union Jack; during the First World War it is said that he served in the British merchant navy in the north Atlantic, and was torpedoed three times. He had learned his navigation at the Weems School of Navigation in Annapolis[66] and in 1925 he joined Pan American Airways as a navigation instructor.

After two years Pan Am transferred him to active work as a navigator on their Pacific Clipper flying boats and interspersed with this experience he had the task of mapping out the air routes to Hawaii, Midway, Wake Island, Guam, the Philippines and Hong Kong on which he is reputed to have made more than a dozen flights as navigator. For a while around 1930 he was also stationed at Port-au-Prince, Haiti as the station manager and it was rumoured among Pan Am employees that he was dismissed from Pan Am's service as a result of excessive drinking. Research has proved this to be inaccurate. He actually resigned because as a navigator and not a pilot, he could go no further in the company ranks. He had recently married and felt that his navigator's salary was insufficient for his new needs; he was then forty-four years old and wanted to make a new start.[67]

It was Noonan's intention to start a navigation school and he must have fully recognised that being part of Amelia's round-the-world trip would provide him with an incalculable amount of free publicity. But the stories of his heavy drinking seem too widely based to have no foundation: his contemporaries in the aircraft scene in California all 'knew' about this problem of Noonan's. It does not seem to have affected his work, however, and his professional reputation was that of a first-class navigator. Noonan was a heavy drinker not an alcoholic but it is ironic that Amelia should once again place her her trust, and the success of her flight, in the hands of a man with a reputation as a drinker.

Amelia said she fully appreciated the navigational difficulties involved in locating the island but she had four means of doing so. One: dead reckoning (an estimated position based on speed in a given direction maintained for a definite period); two: radio bearings from ships and shore stations; three: her radio direction finder; four: celestial navigation.

It was decided that Noonan would go along as far as Howland and return from there by ship. Manning would continue as far as Australia and Amelia would make the remainder of the journey alone. Shortly before the flight it was decided that Paul Mantz would join the crew as far as Honolulu. Mantz claims Amelia asked him to go along[68] but in an article written on the morning of the departure Amelia claimed Mantz had asked her specifically because his fiancée Terry was on her way to Hawaii and he thought it a good opportunity to join her there – 'We are leaving for Honolulu in a few minutes,' Amelia wrote for the *New York Herald Tribune*, 'and I have just made the most amusing discovery that I'm unwittingly playing the role of understudy to Cupid.' Elsewhere Amelia said that she thought she 'had just one more long flight in my system'.[69] And then? 'My lovely home in North Hollywood . . . California sunshine . . . books, friends, . . . many things.'

There were days of tedious delay due to bad weather, which grounded even commercial airlines; Oakland Airport had an unpaved runway which turned to a quagmire after heavy rain. But at last Amelia took off for Hawaii on 17 March 1937 with Manning, Noonan (appropriately, because it was St Patrick's day, wearing a bunch of shamrock in honour of his Irish ancestry) and Mantz on board, together with 947 gallons of fuel. There was no great departure scene – they had been at the airport and prepared to leave on several occasions in the past few days and the reporters were beginning to tire of the game. One, however, a photographer on the staff of the *San Francisco Chronicle*, rented an aeroplane and took a memorable picture of the Electra as it flew over the almost completed Golden Gate Bridge shortly after take-off. Sole rights to Amelia's story had been sold to the *Herald Tribune* newspaper group and as Amelia worked towards departure George had been bombarded with cables from the editor and proprietor (also his good friend), Helen Ogden Reid, stating that the exclusivity deal for Amelia's story meant that she should talk to *no one except* Tribune *representatives*. George replied that this would make Amelia look 'ridiculous'; she would give interviews explaining her position regarding personal statements to reporters, but must be free to answer general questions about her flight. If the *Tribune* were dissatisfied with this then he would prefer to 'wash out the arrangement and refund advances, rather than cause overmuch grief . . .'[70]

The 2,400 mile flight to Honolulu took only 15 hours 51 minutes, trimming over an hour off the record held by the Pan Am Clipper service, and this despite the fact that Amelia and Mantz claimed to have throttled back for most of the journey to 'save' the engines for the main flight yet to come. Amelia flew most of the time, with occasional periods of rest when Paul took over.

There were two very minor technical problems; icing caused an engine to run rough for a short time and a radio generator burned out when Harry Manning held down the Morse-code key to enable a shore-based direction finder to take a bearing on them. But Amelia's own commentary is interesting. Even though she was not carrying the full fuel load she anticipated taking on her longest hop, she did not feel able to manage the take-off alone.

> Paul Mantz and I had carefully worked out the piloting technique of that start. It was a team-play take-off – each with his own job, I at the controls, Paul handling throttles and retractable landing gear.[71]

An hour out from Oakland Amelia sighted a Pan American Clipper, 'silhouetted against a towering bank of cumulus, sunflecked clouds . . . this was the first time I had ever seen another plane at sea, and later I was to learn that in all their Pacific crossings up to then Pan American pilots had never sighted each other.' Coincidentally the pilot on that Clipper was Ed Musick, Noonan's former commander.

Both Amelia and Mantz were impressed with Noonan's navigation. Manning's role appears to have been one of checking the navigation and working the radio, but to Paul's annoyance he constantly came into the already cramped cockpit to shoot star sights through the cockpit hatch. It would have been better, Paul felt, if the hatch was in the main cabin. The flight gave Amelia her first opportunity to use the new RDF and Paul recorded that he was happy with her calm and professional approach.[72]

Noonan's navigation was accurate; when they brought the Electra down through the clouds their landfall was directly in front of them. Paul Mantz's biography *Hollywood Pilot* states that Amelia 'seemed to be tiring towards the end of the flight' and that as the Electra crossed over Honolulu's Wheeler Field 'Amelia had asked Paul to land the ship; she looked groggy from the long flight.'[73] She mentioned neither of these facts in her various accounts of the story but it does seem beyond doubt that it was at Amelia's request that Paul took over and landed the aeroplane, and Paul recalled that as he crossed Wheeler Field:

> I wrapped it around in a steep bank to check the wind sock. AE yelled 'Don't! Don't!' She was very fatigued and kind of exuberant. She calmed down when I made a normal approach and we landed . . .[74]

There was a delay in Hawaii before she attempted to take off on the most dangerous leg of her journey: the flight to Howland which lay more than 1,800 miles away. Noonan had flown similar routes on a dozen occasions previously and remained confident if naturally a little tense because of the media exposure. Mantz was to return to the mainland after Amelia's departure.

The 24-hour departure delay was said in an announcement to the press to be due to adverse weather conditions. In an internal report to the Chief of Naval Operations, however, US Naval Lieutenant Arnold E. True stated as part of his detailed report:

> The forecast issued by me and confirmed by Aerological personnel at Pearl Harbor was for favorable flying conditions over the entire route, except for cloudiness and showers near Pearl Harbor.

This forecast was verified by all subsequent weather reports over
the route. It is understood that her delay was occasioned by other
reasons.[75]

According to Paul Mantz, Amelia was simply too fatigued to
leave immediately and needed to rest before setting out on a very
physically taxing leg of the trip. Although the Honolulu–Howland
leg was some 600 miles shorter than the Oakland–Honolulu flight,
the navigational problems were clearly a source of anxiety. But after
a day's rest Amelia was ready to leave at daybreak on 20 March. In
the meantime Paul flew the Electra on a test flight after a few adjustments had been made to the propeller bearings, lubrication,[76] and
delivered it to Luke Field near Pearl Harbor. Luke Field's 3,000-foot
paved runway was more practical for a take-off with a 900-gallon
fuel load (this included 590 gallons of high-test military aviation
fuel – 100-octane, which Mantz had acquired 'by pulling a few
strings', to give extra boost at take-off).

Amelia and her crew sat for an hour in the pre-dawn light at the
end of the runway – floodlighting was switched on for her but she
waited for the sunrise – carrying out the routine pre-flight checks.
At last the Electra started to roll. There was a slight cross-wind and
Mantz's chief concern was Amelia's habit of correcting any swing of
the aircraft on the take-off run by increasing power in the opposite
engine to straighten up. Countless times he had told her that on
take-off she *must* use the rudder pedals to keep the plane straight,
that the throttles *must* be pushed smoothly forward together. Any
'jockeying' would create a dangerous yaw in direction and potentially lead to a ground loop. He said many times that Amelia had
never seemed to grasp the importance of this advice.[77]

The aircraft gathered speed and was about a thousand feet down
the runway – probably ten seconds from take-off – when the unthinkable happened. It appeared to drop its right wing. Amelia corrected by
reducing power on the opposite engine and the plane swung to the
left out of control in a classic ground loop. The undercarriage collapsed (the right wheel and the undercarriage were torn away) and the
machine careered along the runway on its belly spraying out showers

of sparks before coming to rest. Despite the fact that fuel was pouring out through the drain well in the damaged belly, there was – miraculously – no fire.[78]

Many years later it would be suggested that this crash was engineered by Amelia to buy time to plan a covert government mission but only a fool would hope to get away with such a dangerous ploy, and Amelia was certainly no fool. The official US Navy report on the accident, after consideration of the written and verbal evidence of several eyewitnesses found that:

> as the airplane gathered speed it swung slightly to the right. Miss Earhart corrected this tendency by throttling the left hand motor, the aircraft then began to swing to the left with increasing speed, characteristic of a ground loop. It tilted forward, right wing low and for 50 or 60 yards was supported by the right wheel only. The right hand landing-gear suddenly collapsed under the excessive load, followed by the left. The airplane spun sharply to the left sliding on its belly and amid a shower of sparks from the mat came to rest headed about 200 degrees from its initial course.[79]

Amelia had the presence of mind to cut the switches as soon as she knew she had lost control and the fire truck that had followed along the side of the runway reached the aeroplane within seconds. Witnesses said that Amelia stood up in the cockpit for a short time before crawling back through the cabin over the catwalk laid across the tops of the fuel tanks (usually she hoisted herself out through the hatch over the pilot's seat). Rescuers were already at the open cabin door and found Noonan calmly folding his charts saying that he'd be ready to go again next time Amelia wanted to try. As Amelia climbed out she appeared dazed and Mantz put an arm around her. 'Something must have gone wrong . . .' she told him.[80]

Manning was later to say of what he called 'the Honolulu fiasco' that the crash was purely due to Amelia's lack of ability as a pilot.[81] She had overcorrected and the heavily overweight aeroplane had been too much for the landing gear in the resultant ground loop, he said.[82] Predictably the Putnams blamed the accident on mechanical failure: 'Witnesses said a tire blew. However, studying the tracks carefully, I believe [that] possibly the landing gear's right shock absorber, as it lengthened, may have given way,' Amelia said.[83]

George, waiting in Oakland, had merely heard on the radio that Amelia was about to take off. Later he was to write that when the telephone rang he picked it up to hear:

'Putnam?'

'Yes.'

'Have you heard?' It was the Press Association. 'They crashed . . . the ship's in flames . . .'

The gang was looking at me.

'Here Bill [Bill Miller of the Depart of Commerce] . . . you take it.'

I could not listen further. I moved out into the cold morning, trying to walk steadily. In a few minutes they came racing after me. 'No fire . . . no fire at all. False report! No one hurt! . . .'

In 1932 in New York the telephone had told me falsely of a crack-up ending to the Atlantic solo – uncorrected for many minutes. And now, in 1937, the black wings brushed close again . . .[84]

Shortly afterwards George heard Amelia on the radio being asked if she'd try again. 'Of course,' she said, and hesitated. 'If it's possible . . . repairs . . . costs.' Immediately George 'shakily scribbled' a cable to his wife: SO LONG AS YOU AND THE BOYS ARE OK THE REST DOESN'T MATTER AFTER ALL ITS JUST ONE OF THOSE THINGS. WHETHER YOU WANT TO CALL IT A DAY OR KEEP GOING LATER IS EQUALLY JAKE WITH ME.[85] And an hour later Amelia telephoned him 'her voice weary with sadness'.[86] She told him she wanted to try again.

Practical as ever, George told her he'd make arrangements for the Electra to be shipped back. She and 'the boys' could take the SS *Malolo* back to California; it was sailing the following day at noon.[87] Meanwhile the 10,000 special covers had better be placed in the secure hands of the Honolulu postal authorities until they were needed again.[88]

In general the newspapers were kind to Amelia but a sour note was sounded by Major Al Williams, a highly respected flyer and a leader in aircraft development. In a swingeing personal attack on her he stated:

Like every other human enterprise, aviation suffers from a great number of ingeniously contrived rackets. Daring courageous individuals with nothing to lose and all to gain have used and are using aviation merely as a means toward quick fortune and fame. The worst racket of all is that of individually sponsored transoceanic flying . . . [where] the personal profit angle in dollars and cents, and the struggle for personal fame, have been carefully camouflaged and presented under the banner of 'scientific progress'.

. . . Amelia Earhart's 'Flying Laboratory' is the latest and most distressing racket that has been given to a trusting and enthusiastic public. There's nothing in that 'Flying Laboratory' beyond duplicates of the controls and apparatus to be found on board every major airline transport. And no one ever sat at the controls of her 'Flying Laboratory' who knew enough about the technical side of aviation to obtain a job on a first-class airline . . . Paul Mantz was the only pilot in the ship who knew how to take airplanes off and land them.

Nothing is said about the thousands of dollars which she and her manager-husband expected to get for thousands of stamp cachets carried in the 'Flying Laboratory'. Nothing at all was hinted of the fat lecture contracts, the magazine and book rights for stories of the flight . . . No, the whole affair was labelled 'purely scientific' for public consumption.

Williams then went on to destroy Amelia's reputation as a pilot:

She lost control of the plane during a take-off on the concrete runway on a standard Army airdrome and wrecked the 'Flying Laboratory'. And there again the public got a garbled story and a cleverly contrived explanation . . . plus a heroic story about cutting the switches and saving the lives of her crew. That ship got away from her on take-off – that's the low down.

Planes have to be held by clever pilots to straight courses on a getaway. And neither landing gear nor tires were designed to withstand being jammed into the ground. Her plane was a stock type which is carrying passengers and mail in this country day after day . . . It's time that the Bureau of Air Commerce took a hand in this business and it's my guess that the bureau will not grant Mrs Amelia Earhart permission to make another attempt – [and] it's high time that [they] put an end to aviation's biggest racket – 'Purely Scientific' ballyhoo . . .[89]

Al Williams was merely voicing what many in the aviation industry felt about Amelia's constant appearances in the media and probably she and George were very much aware of the groundswell of disapproval. George managed to have the article commented on and refuted by C. B. Allen, the redoubtable aviation correspondent of the *New York Herald Tribune*, but Amelia was white-faced and hurt when shown the Williams article. Her only comment to reporters, however, when questioned for her reaction was, 'I'm glad it wasn't a woman who wrote it.'[90]

CHAPTER 19

1937

George Putnam has sometimes been blamed for Amelia's final and fatal flight. It is said, and believed by many, that he insisted she have the aeroplane repaired and carry on with the original plan. But within minutes of the crash at Luke Field, even before speaking to George, Amelia had already told reporters that she wanted to try again. In her book, *Last Flight* (published posthumously), and in her numerous accounts of the crash she claimed that the thought had occurred to her even as the plane slewed to a halt among sparks at Luke Field. 'If we don't burn up I want to try again.'[1]

Undoubtedly George would not have argued with Amelia's decision and his cable to her, prior to their telephone conversation, was a genuine statement of his feelings on the matter. But her decision to carry on must have given George pause, for the plane was uninsured – no one would take the risk – so the damage to the Putnam exchequer was serious. Much of the cost of the trip had already been committed and was not recoverable; for example an engineer had been flown out to Karachi in order to overhaul the engines when she reached India. He arrived there only to find Amelia's flight abandoned so he had fly back again, all at Amelia's expense. There was a substantial bill from the US government for the work they had carried out on Amelia's behalf at Luke Field.[2] But the main expense was the repair and rebuild to the Electra by Lockheed.[3] The financial implications of a possible second failure were frightening.

'Friends helped generously,' Amelia recorded, but even so 'I more-or-less mortgaged my future. Without regret, however, for what are futures for?'[4] However, it was not only her own future that was mortgaged; it was also George's.

If Amelia had abandoned the entire idea, what then? Their losses were sustainable, but barely. Amelia (using her own money) had invested with Paul Mantz in several new businesses which were now coming to fruition.[5] There were plans for Amelia and George to start a new airline in partnership with Gene Vidal and Floyd Odlum. But Amelia knew that if she abandoned her plan she would henceforward be remembered as the woman who once tried to fly around the world and failed. Her previous achievements would be overshadowed by this failure. Worse, her ability as a pilot would always be called into question. It was unthinkable, given Amelia's character, her determination amounting to stubbornness, her pride in the reputation she had painfully acquired, that she would not have tried again.

George's role, as usual, was to provide the means for her to do it and to offer support. In the weeks following the accident it was George who arranged, through the navy, to make the necessary immediate repairs prior to crating and shipping the plane back to California.

After consultation with Clarence Williams, Amelia decided that since the second start was so much later in the year it would be safer to reverse the original flight plan and fly eastwards because of the weather conditions in the Caribbean and Africa. This required new diplomatic clearances as well as the extension of existing ones. George contacted their friend Jacques de Sibour who once again obtained permissions to overfly alien territories, relocated fuel, oil and supplies of spares and obtained new prevailing weather patterns.

And it was George who liaised with the navy and Coast Guard on the subject of guard ships and the provision of radio and direction-finding facilities for the flight; organised new overlays for the stamp covers (and the marketing of them); raised the money to pay for the Lockheed repairs and the additional costs of the rearranged flight; organised in advance the provision of customs formalities at each of her stops so that Amelia would run up against as little bureaucracy as possible; and booked Amelia into a series of seventy post-flight lectures at a fee of $500 per appearance.[6]

Amelia concentrated on the Electra and, perhaps chastened by her experience, flew with Paul Mantz to regain her confidence. Many hours were spent on 'homework'; simply absorbing the information obtained by George's administration machine about weather conditions, airport facilities and customs problems that she might meet at each stop along the way. Once again she planned the inventory, assessing each item in order to remove every ounce of unnecessary weight, now only too aware of the Electra's sensitivity when overladen.

Manning had told Amelia shortly after the Honolulu crash that he would not be able to accompany her as his leave of absence would expire before she could make a second attempt. Immediately after the crash he had publicly praised her coolness in cutting the switches and thus avoiding a certain fire. But many years later he was to say he made his decision because he had no faith in her ability, and it is obvious that their relationship had not been without its problems from the rest of his statement:

> Amelia Earhart was something of a prima donna. She gave the impression of being humble and shy; but she really had an ego, and could be as tough as nails when the occasion required it. I got very fed up with her bullheadedness several times. That's why she brought Noonan into the picture – in the event that I were to give up on the flight. AE herself was not a good navigator; and Noonan was a happy-go-lucky Irishman. He wasn't a 'constant' navigator; I always felt that he let things go far too long . . .[7]

In addition to arranging the practical details of the flight itself she spent time writing the first five chapters of her book *World Flight*.[8] Her intention was to make notes throughout the flight and mail them back to George at each stop. They would be transcribed and filed to await her return when she could use them to complete the book for early publication to take maximum advantage of the predictable publicity. Floyd Odlum made a $10,000 donation to the

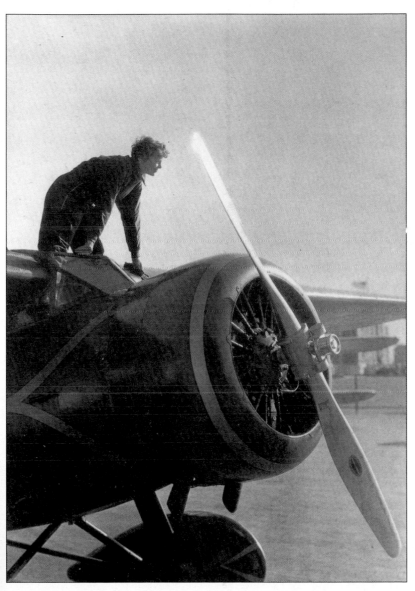

Amelia with her Lockheed Vega, which she called her 'little red bus'

George and Amelia at their home in Rye, New York, c. 1932

Amelia arranged an impromptu night flight over Baltimore, Maryland, and Washington, D.C., for Eleanor Roosevelt

Amelia takes a catnap. Photographed by George Putnam at their Hollywood home, c. 1935

The welcome accorded Amelia after she completed the first solo flight from Hawaii to the USA, 1935

Paul Mantz, Amelia, Harry Manning, and Fred Noonan, pictured prior to the takeoff from Oakland for Hawaii

Amelia in the cockpit of her Electra. It measured 4'6" wide by 4'8" high – cramped quarters for long flights with no co-pilot to relieve her at the controls

Amelia and George say their final goodbyes in Miami before takeoff on the fateful round-the-world flight

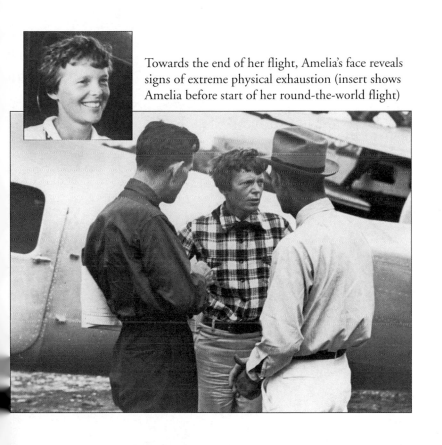

Towards the end of her flight, Amelia's face reveals signs of extreme physical exhaustion (insert shows Amelia before start of her round-the-world flight)

July 2, 1937: world headlines shrieked the news of Amelia's disappearance finances of the second attempt and because of this Amelia dedicated the book to him: 'To Floyd, with gratitude for all-weather friendship.'

There was always the never-ending flood of correspondence to be answered. On 14 May she received a request from her former employers, Denison House, to send a personal message to 'give a boost' to a fund-raising event. 'I am sorry my preoccupation with flight preparations prevents my doing anything active for Denison House,' Amelia replied. 'Further, aviation accidents are very expensive. However, here is $25 for use for *girls* in some way. I hope they have camp privileges these days . . .'[9]

Amy was still a guest at the house on Spring Valley Lane and at times the atmosphere there was less than harmonious. Amy was now sixty-eight years old, an intelligent woman who had been denied a career by virtue of the times in which she was born and brought up, and denied, by Edwin's behaviour, the comfortable family life which she felt should have been hers by birthright. She had sacrificed much for her daughters and was very possessive of them both; in a sense she never accepted that they were not still answerable to her. Amelia occasionally chafed at her mother's assumed dominion over her, but was in general able to cope because her own natural leadership asserted itself. Besides, she loved her mother, without being blind to her faults. She took Amy with her on several lecture tours, flying her across the continent on at least two occasions.

But the real problem was Amy's relationship with George whose disorganised lifestyle and often peremptory manners and flashes of temper ruffled Amy. She had not the sense to remain quiet and her way of dealing with the problem was to snipe at George whenever possible, which created tension between Amelia and Amy. Sometimes the constant criticism and acrimonious asides Amy made about George became embarrassing enough to cause Amelia to ban her mother from the dinner table and make her eat in her room until things improved.[10] George, however, was tolerant of Amy's scoldings (he otherwise found her to be a rather sweet, if improvident person) for Amelia's sake.

At the Putnam home, in addition to Amy, there was Jo Berger, the secretary whom Amelia and George had shared for some years and who often travelled with them between New York and Los Angeles, and a young woman general assistant, Margot De Carrie, who hero-worshipped Amelia, did secretarial work in Jo's absence and otherwise helped in many other ways such as meeting aeroplanes, ferrying guests around, and entertaining Amy. The house was run by Fred, the Filipino major-domo. There were also numerous casual callers and, just as at Rye, the house in the Hollywood hills could scarcely be called restful despite its tranquil setting.

One regular caller during May 1937 was Albert Bresnik, a young photographer whom George had designated 'Amelia Earhart's official photographer'; it was his way of attempting to control the release of photographs of Amelia, especially during the round-the-world trip. Originally Bresnik had been approached with the idea that he would join Amelia for one or two sections of the flight. 'The idea was that she would be meeting heads of state and VIPs along the way and if I went along as official photographer then we'd have total control of all photography concerned with the trip. I was 23 at the time and it would have been quite an achievement so I was very disappointed when told I wouldn't be going along.'[11]

One morning, a few days before Amelia left on her flight, Bresnik called on Amelia to show her proofs of some photographs he'd taken at a photo session:

> we were in the kitchen having coffee and I asked her what she was planning to do after the trip. I can't remember her exact words but she told me she thought there was a possibility she was pregnant and that when she came back she was going to be 'just a woman'.[12]

Lockheed worked hard to make the necessary repairs against the tight schedule. A considerable amount was done to 'strengthen' the Electra against the potential stresses of overloading, for the question of fuel loads was constantly on Amelia's mind after the Honolulu incident. The engines were thoroughly overhauled and on 18 May only a little over a month after it had returned to California, the newly rebuilt Electra was delivered to Amelia.

While the aeroplane had been undergoing repairs, Paul Mantz had been busy; although the Eclipse flowmeter and a Cambridge fuel analyser appeared to have worked well on the Oakland–Honolulu flight he returned both to the manufacturers for over-haul.[13] He also worked out a carefully planned table of throttle settings which he felt would enable Amelia to economise on fuel, but there was little else for him to do except occasionally accompany Amelia to Lockheed to oversee the repair work. He had noticed a new coldness in his relationship with George and a distance between himself and Amelia, but at the time he did not pay too much attention, thinking that it would blow over.

Two days after the delivery of the rebuilt Electra, Amelia and Paul flew to Oakland where they picked up 6,000 stamp covers that had been postmarked in Honolulu and returned for appropriate over-stamping with the words 'Second Take Off'. She was using the flight to Oakland as a test hop, Amelia told reporters, and she hoped she might get away around the beginning of June (at this point she had not publicly announced that her route would be a reversal of the original plan). After collecting the stamp covers the Electra returned to Burbank.

Paul Mantz was always bitter about what happened next. Even in the early sixties, nearly thirty years later, he reacted strongly when he spoke of it. Amelia left him in no doubt that she would be spending some days, perhaps even a week or more, in pre-flight preparations at Burbank and naturally Paul assumed he would be consulted. After their return to Burbank they discussed various aspects of the Electra's performance and handling. That evening Paul flew to St Louis to take part in an aerobatics competition; he intended to be gone for two days, leaving adequate time to assist Amelia before she left. But Paul had been deliberately left out of Amelia's real plans.

On the following day accompanied by George, Bo McKneely and Fred Noonan, Amelia took off on the first leg of her journey; from Los Angeles to Miami. She felt that rather than waste time in California she might as well make that first leg of the world flight a 'shake-down'; then if problems developed she could simply announce that it had been a proving flight and return the plane to Lockheed. There would be no adverse publicity because she had technically not yet started her trip.

When he heard on the radio of Amelia's departure from California for Florida on 21 May, Paul guessed immediately that Amelia had started her second attempt at the world flight and he was astounded and angry. He'd 'wanted to make a final check on her radio equipment, and of her fuel consumption, to run through the list of optimum power settings for each leg'. She'd been pushing too hard, trying to meet the tight schedules set up by George, he declared; too much time had been given to money-making schemes, advertising commitments and public appearances, and not enough time preparing for the flight.[14]

But above all he was hurt at the subterfuge involved, for he realised that in order to leave on 21 May Amelia must have made her decision some time earlier, yet she had not mentioned it during their flight to Oakland on the previous day. In fact the policy had been decided at least three weeks earlier, for then George wrote to Admiral Leahy outlining the details of the planned 'sneak take-off . . . which will occur probably between May 18th and 24th'.[15]

George was later to write that Amelia had once trusted Paul Mantz implicitly, but had lost faith in him prior to the flight and intended to dissolve her business partnerships with him after her return. Whether this is true or whether George was merely sniping at Mantz after their relationship deteriorated dramatically in 1939, is not known. If there was a reason why Amelia treated her former confidant in such a cavalier manner, the only people who could have known were Paul, Amelia and George and they never spoke of it to anyone.

But Paul was wrong in his assertion that it was at George's insistence that Amelia undertook the punishing work schedule. Amelia had become a workaholic and needed no urging. This flight was far more important to her than to George and she was especially aware of the financial cost of this second attempt, so she was prepared to work, and the work ethic was atavistically strong in her.

Paul's concern that Amelia had not paid enough attention to preparation was echoed by Amelia's radioman, Joseph Gurr, who was called in before the Oakland–Honolulu flight to repair a minor fault in the original radio installation. Gurr also felt that Amelia was too casual in her approach to safety features and preparation. He was concerned enough, before the first take-off, to check things out himself and had spent an entire day with Manning laying out all the safety equipment in front of the hangar, testing – as far as possible – everything. They inflated the life-raft, fired flares from the Very pistols, checked water and medical supplies. 'I do not know whether Amelia was checked out in the use of the equipment, but then Harry [Manning] was so no problem.'

But on another occasion Gurr was even more concerned by Amelia's attitude. He was particularly anxious that Amelia be instructed on the use of the radio and direction-finding equipment; he wanted to show her how to tune the receivers, how to operate the transmitter, learn correct radio procedures and the limitations of the system. Owing to her busy schedule Amelia was generally not available but at last she came along as Gurr requested and he began what he assumed would be a lengthy session of instruction. But after only an hour she said she had to leave for an appointment. 'We never covered actual operation such as taking a bearing with a direction finder, not even contacting another radio station,' he recalled.[16] Apart from the time she spent flying with Mantz it is believed that this was her only formal instruction in the use of the radio and communication system aboard the Electra.

After the Honolulu crash Gurr removed and checked the entire system. He was unhappy about the trailing antenna and on a test flight tried unsuccessfully to raise someone on the 500 kcs channel with the antenna unreeled. Afterwards he 'took the opportunity to re-design the top antenna installing a short stub mast behind the Direction Finding loop on top of the cockpit'. A wire antenna was fixed from this mast in a V leading back to the tops of the two rudders. 'It made a great deal of difference in radiated energy. Also, because of the added wire, this top antenna would now be more effective on 500 Kcs. The reel antenna was left on board.'[17]

From Burbank, Amelia and her three male passengers flew to Tucson, Arizona where they landed to refuel. As Amelia started up the engines the left one backfired and burst into flames, but this was soon under control with the plane's fire extinguisher system and Bo McKneely was on hand to cope with cleaning up the soot and replacing the burned rubber fittings. Next morning they flew on to New Orleans where they stopped overnight.

The Electra arrived at Miami on the following day, 23 May, and for the next week Amelia and McKneely worked with the mechanics at Pan American Airways to ready the Electra for the flight. According to the *Herald Tribune*'s aviation correspondent, C. B. Allen,[18] no one could fail to be impressed by the calm, unhurried manner in which Amelia went about the preparations for the flight. Allen was an old friend who had been a frequent guest at Rye, and his articles on Amelia tended to be of the *devotee* type.

She 'knew her stuff,' he reported, 'knew exactly what she wanted done . . . but also knew enough to let [the mechanics] alone while they did it . . . There was an almost audible clatter of chips falling off skeptical male shoulders.' He noted that she especially endeared them by her willingness to join in and help to push the plane in and out of the hangar, to sit on the floor under the plane and listen attentively when some technical matter was pointed out to her without worrying if her clothing had splatters of oil. She was happy to eat with the men at the airport diner, and although she once plaintively said she'd hoped to do a little sunbathing and swim, she was too occupied at the airport where in the cockpit of the all-metal plane in the searing heat beating down on the concrete apron she spent an hour running up the engines. When reminded she had said she wanted to sunbathe she laughed and said 'not the same thing at all . . . I wanted to soak up a little sunshine, not be fired by it'. Her smiling and cheerful presence won everyone's support at Miami. But she told Allen:

> I have a feeling that there is just about one more good flight left in my System and I hope this trip is it. Anyway when I have finished this job, I mean to give up long-distance 'stunt' flying.[19]

She told him that she was prompted by a number of reasons. Among them 'the repeated urgings' of George to give up hazardous flight attempts and her own feeling that she had done her fair share in this field. There was inevitable newsreel coverage and one clip records Amelia and George in their hotel, 'hamming' for the cameras.

'Now are you *sure* you don't want me to come along?' George asks with a smile.

'Well, of course you know I think a lot of you but 180 pounds of gasoline [pause] perhaps might be a little more valuable.'

'You mean you prefer 180 pounds of gasoline to 180 pounds of husband?' Mock incredulity.

Amelia giggles and hesitates before looking at him in smiling exasperation: 'I think you've guessed right . . .'

It is almost impossible not to be instinctively drawn to this Amelia with her natural intelligence, cheerful humour and quick smile. Watching these newsreel clips fifty years after their production, one might believe Amelia to be a product of the eighties, dressed in trousers and shirt with her short, undated hairstyle. She has the confidence of today's successful woman and great femininity.

Amelia hoped to get away on 30 May, but a test flight revealed a fault with the radio transmitter and also with the Sperry autopilot. The automatic pilot problem was resolved by changing the rudder control fitting but the radio fault was more persistent. The *Herald Tribune* reported on 30 May that, having tried unsuccessfully to raise a local radio station on both 3,105 and 6,210 kcs the Pan Am technicians inspected the system and decided that the problem lay 'with the new antenna recently installed on the flying laboratory'. They believed it to be of an improper length to give the transmitter its maximum efficiency and range and 'set to work this afternoon experimenting with various lengths and hope to have the problem solved in time for another test flight tomorrow'. Meanwhile Amelia got her wish to do a little sunbathing and fishing from a friend's yacht.[20]

Later George was to advise Paul Mantz that the radio had given endless trouble. 'As I understand it . . . the technicians decided . . . that the longer aerials were improper. One part of them just cancelled out the other, so they shortened the aerials and got the thing pretty well licked . . .' The 250-foot trailing aerial was discarded, possibly in the interests of saving weight, since Amelia clearly believed that it was not essential to the operation of the radio. One Morse-code key was returned to Western Electric and Joseph Gurr had kept the other; the Electra carried no keys but a carrier signal could be transmitted by holding down the microphone switch.

On 1 June a small crowd assembled at Miami before dawn to watch Amelia and Fred set off for California by the longest route that could be contrived. George's son David (accompanied by his wife, Nilla) was there and remembers George's transparent anxiety. Amelia showed no sign of nerves. Their public goodbye was recorded on newsreel film and shows Amelia sitting on the wing looking down on George and holding his hand. If the obvious affection between the two was enacted purely for the cameras both George and Amelia missed their true vocation. They should have gone into acting. On the previous evening she had told him:

> I know that if I fail or if I am lost you will be blamed for allowing me to leave on this trip; the backers of the flight will be blamed and everyone connected with it. But it's my responsibility and mine alone.[21]

For their private farewell George and Amelia retreated into the hangar building.

> There in the dim chill we perched briefly on cold concrete steps, her hands in mine. There is very little one says at such times.
> When Bo called that all was ready, Amelia's eyes were clear with the good light of the adventure that lay before her. But as she walked out to the [airplane] she seemed to me very small and slim and feminine . . .[22]

Amelia was a hundred miles away when she tuned into a Miami radio station to get a weather forecast only to hear the report of her take-off. 'In that manner that radio-folk sometimes have, the account of a very normal departure had become breathlessly exciting . . . it held me in cruel suspense as to whether I was going to get off safely . . .' she wrote.[23]

Amelia's first destination was San Juan, Puerto Rico, a 1,000-mile hop, but the territory over which they flew was well known to Noonan from his time with Pan Am, and the journey was uneventful. Amelia recorded that with Noonan's expert navigation (one landfall was one minute from the estimate he gave some hours earlier) and the Sperry autopilot, 'I was beginning to feel that long-range flying was becoming pretty sissy.'[24]

George called Amelia that night 'to talk over a few things, but especially, I suspect,' she recorded, '. . . just to say "Goodnight". That was pleasant.'[25] On the next legs, to Caripito (Venezuela) and Paramaribo (Surinam), Amelia estimated that despite 'bucking' headwinds they had averaged 148 mph.[26] They rested at the next stop, Fortaleza (Brazil), to refresh both themselves and the Electra before flying on to Natal, their take-off point for the South Atlantic leg to Dakar in Senegal, Africa.

For the 1,900-mile transoceanic flight Amelia loaded 850 gallons of fuel and 80 gallons of oil.[27] The crossing was uneventful, taking 13 hours 12 minutes and at about halfway they passed an Air France mail plane but could not make contact; Amelia explained, 'The mail plane's radio equipment, I believe, is telegraphic code, while mine, at the moment was exclusively voice telephone.'[28]

Once they descended over a ship to enable it to report their position; occasionally she allowed the Sperry autopilot to fly the Electra while she jotted notes in her log. One reads 'Gas fumes in plane from fuelling made me sick again this morning after starting. Stomach getting weak I guess.'[29] There are several such notes among her papers and this record of morning sickness adds credence to her admission in confidence to Al Bresnik that she thought she might be pregnant.

Although there was a catwalk over the fuel tanks that enabled

Noonan to join her in the cockpit when he was not working, there was a fishing line and pulley system rigged up between Amelia and the navigator's position to pass notes between the two. As they sighted the thin purple smudge of the African coast Fred passed Amelia the following note:

3.36 Change to 36 degrees.
Estimate 79 miles to
Dakar from 3.36 pm

Under this Amelia scrawled 'What put us north?'

Amelia's inclination was to turn north not south. She did not trust Noonan's assessment, perhaps because it was overcast and he had not been able to get a sextant shot to fix their position. For whatever reason she ignored his instruction and on reaching the coast turned left, following the shoreline north for about 50 miles when they found themselves at St Louis, Senegal. Had she done as Fred asked they would have arrived at Dakar, their intended destination, 163 miles to the south, within half an hour of 3.36 pm. Amelia was generous enough to admit her error in her cabled report to the *Herald Tribune*,[30] but this insistence on relying on her instinct rather than on Noonan's calculations did not augur well. Next morning they flew to Dakar where they stayed for a day to enable a small repair to be made to the fuel-meter and to have the engines checked before the flight across Africa.

The stop at Dakar was fairly typical. They did some sightseeing, had laundry done, and parcelled up for return to America anything not wanted on the remainder of the journey, such maps they had used so far, notes Amelia had jotted down for the book and various receipts and weather reports that would be helpful later in writing her book.

The subsequent flight over Africa: Gao (Mali), Fort Lamy (Ndjamena), El Fasher and Khartoum (Sudan) though hot, tediously long, and only occasionally exciting, was always interesting to Amelia, for she was seeing the places whose romance she had savoured as a child. She dwelt over the 'priceless names' in her log:

'Qala-en-Hahl, Umm Shinayshin, Abu Seid, Idd el Bashir, Fazi, Marabia Abu Fas . . .'

Noonan thought the navigation across the great continent more difficult than over water, for the few maps that were available were inaccurate and therefore totally misleading. Landmarks were few and information was limited to helpful comments such as: 'Swamp in rain; salt pan; rolling desert no trees; many remains of animals; two helig trees about four hundred metres apart ringbarked – they intersect the twenty-fourth meridian.' It was probably despite, rather than because of, such assistance that Noonan was able to write to his wife: '. . . we were lucky in always reaching our objectives. In all the distances I don't think we wandered off the course for half an hour, although there were times when I couldn't have bet a nickel on the accuracy of our assumed position.'[31]

Leaving Africa the pair flew down the Red Sea from Massawa (now Mits'iwa) to Assab (now Aseb). Originally Amelia had planned to fly from there to Aden en route to Karachi, but at Assab there was some doubt about whether it was desirable to make a stopover at Aden. The Electra therefore 'took on a full load of fuel' and set off on the long flight to India, hugging the 'Arabian shore'. For this stretch of her flight Jacques de Sibour had forwarded information and sketch maps of emergency landing grounds 'which I was able to obtain from the Air Ministry here [London] through the good offices of Sir Francis [Shelmerdine]. This data has never been released to an outside source before, so should be quite a help to Amelia when flying along this particular stretch.' While expressly forbidden to land on Arab territory Amelia was carrying credentials in Arabic. These had been prepared in the Cairo office of International Aviation Associates, the firm for whom de Sibour worked, and stated that Amelia was on an important mission on behalf of King George VI and that on no account must she be harmed. 'This might be useful should a forced landing have to be made . . .' de Sibour had informed George.[32]

The flight to Karachi was another first; no one had previously flown non-stop from the Red Sea to India before and Amelia was delighted to learn this from de Sibour on her arrival.

'There's a phone call for you' he said, after our greeting.

'Oh, yes.' My interest was mild. Probably a local newspaper.

Jacques persisted. 'From New York. GP on the wire.'

As casual as that! And we were almost exactly on the other side of the world.[33]

False reports that Amelia had taken off from Massawa (prior to the Assab stopover) for Karachi had placed the plane long overdue and created great anxiety for the welcoming committee and for George. In these days of instant communications it is easy to overlook the fact that Amelia was invariably out of contact when in flight. She told George she expected to be in Lae, New Guinea, about 23 or 24 June and home three or four days after that,[34] and confirmed this by cable next day after speaking to the mechanics who were to give her engines a major check and oil change.[35]

What George did not tell Amelia was that widespread rumours were circulating in America that at the conclusion of the trip she would divorce him in order to marry Paul Mantz. He could not discover the source of these rumours and knew there was no truth to them for Paul had recently married Terry and was from his own, and other witnesses' statements, 'crazy about her'. But George telephoned Paul after Walter Winchell told his national radio audience that rumours of Amelia divorcing George after her world trip to marry Mantz were untrue. 'Instead,' Winchell reported, 'she will marry an aviation inventor.'[36]

Paul and George had laughed about it but Gene Vidal's son, the American writer Gore Vidal, did not laugh and thinks there might have been a germ of truth in the rumours. He believes that Amelia was 'madly in love' with his father and states that had Gene given her any encouragement (which he had not) she would have divorced George and married Gene after the flight.[37] There is certainly no evidence to support any suggestion of a romance in the surviving letters between Amelia and Gene Vidal. They are extremely businesslike and convey mere friendship.

Indeed, despite the punishing schedule of the world flight, Amelia made time to write a personal note to George at each stop, usually a few scribbled lines on a page torn out of her stenographer's pad.[38] At Karachi, for example, she wrote:

I wish you were here. So many things you would enjoy . . . Perhaps some day we can fly together to some of the remote places of the world just for fun.[39]

From Karachi the Electra flew to Calcutta on 17 June; landing on an already sodden airfield, and with more rain forecast, they elected to refuel and take off immediately for Akyab (now Sitwe), Burma. 'That take-off was precarious, perhaps as risky as any we had,' Amelia wrote. 'The plane clung for what seemed like ages to the heavy sticky soil before the wheels finally lifted, and we cleared with nothing at all to spare the fringe of trees at the airdrome's edge.'[40]

By now Amelia and Noonan had been en route for 18 days (from Miami), 15 legs of the journey had been accomplished and they must both have felt reasonably confident with the mission so far. Any remaining doubts about Amelia's ability to fly the Electra competently must have been allayed by the number of flying hours and, more particularly, landings and take-offs she made under a wide variety of weather and airport conditions. The aeroplane had performed well and there had been no major problems.

After a short stop at Akyab they continued their eastward track but had to return to Akyab after running into a monsoon, a navigational feat accomplished by Fred Noonan's 'uncanny powers', Amelia observed, for they had zero visibility in the raging tempest.[41]

Flights to Rangoon, Bangkok, Singapore and Bandoeng (now Bandung), Java followed. At Bandoeng Amelia was told that George was on the telephone again. In this recorded conversation Amelia informed George that she would be back in California before 4 July and he immediately set to work to arrange a civic welcome there on Independence Day.

Take-off was again delayed by monsoon weather for some days but on 24 June they were able to get away and landed at Saurabaya, Indonesia. En route Amelia had experienced faults in some of her 'long distance instruments' so she returned to Bandoeng for repairs. The instruments concerned – the fuel analyser, flowmeter, and generator meter[42] – were not crucial to flight but would play an extremely important role over the Pacific where fuel would need to be monitored and conserved. These instruments had all given trouble previously, on several occasions; Amelia wanted to have them working properly.

The repairs, coupled with monsoon weather, forced Amelia to stay at Bandoeng for some days and she allowed herself to become a tourist.[43] At the nearby town of Batavia (now Jakarta), she toured the markets and purchased a small souvenir for a friend[44] and enjoyed the famous local dish, *rijstafel*, a meal of rice with twenty-one different courses of fish, chicken, meats, eggs, relishes, curries, nuts, fruits and vegetables.

Perhaps it was as a result of this meal that Amelia was smitten with a nasty and debilitating form of dysentery;[45] she was said to be extremely ill for a day or so. And perhaps this was also the origin of the undated scribbled jotting she made. 'Sick again this morning. Must be the petrol fumes.' Or perhaps not.

With health and weather conditions delaying them it was 27 June before Amelia and Noonan were able to leave Bandoeng for Port Darwin in Australia via Koepang (now Kupang), Indonesia. At Darwin they had the direction finder repaired. A fuse had blown; this was replaced and the instrument was checked out by Australian Royal Air Force Sergeant Stan Rose, who provided spare fuses and showed Amelia how to replace them. The parachutes were packed and shipped home; they would be of no value over the Pacific, Amelia explained.[46]

The couple reached Lae, Papua New Guinea on 29 June accomplishing the 1,200-mile flight in 7 hours and 43 minutes. At this point the Electra had flown some 22,000 miles and there were 7,000 more to go, all of them over the Pacific Ocean.

Amelia had hoped to get away from Lae before 30 June in order to ensure arrival in California on 4 July, as she had advised George in her phone conversations at Karachi and Bandoeng. Lae Airport was run by Guinea Airways, under their manager Eric Chaters, and it was he who organised mechanics to give the Electra a thorough 'going over'. Fortunately they were used to Lockheed aircraft as there was a sister ship to Amelia's Electra based on the field. Amelia wrote that:

> everyone has been as helpful and co-operative as possible – food, hot baths, mechanical service, radio and weather reports, advice from veteran pilots here – all combine to make us wish we could stay.[47]

Oil and oil filters were changed, spark plugs were cleaned and the engines were checked. The fluctuating fuel pump and the Sperry gyro had both been giving further trouble and these were repaired again.

Amelia and Fred Noonan spent the day of the 30th unpacking and repacking the plane. Every single item not absolutely essential to the flight was parcelled up and mailed home. Even Amelia's elephant-toe bracelet was returned[48] and there was not a spare ounce of weight left on the Electra after this exercise. Her obsession with weight may have been taken to extreme lengths for according to Harry Balfour, radio operator at Lae, survival equipment was also taken off. Balfour claimed that 'she unloaded all her surplus equipment on me including her [Very] pistol and ammunition, books, letters and facility books.'

Amelia cabled her last commissioned article for the *Herald Tribune*:

> 'Denmark's a prison' and Lae, attractive and unusual as it is appears to two flyers just as confining. Lockheed stands ready for longest hop weighted with gasoline and oil to capacity. However clouds and winds blowing wrong way conspired to keep her on the ground today. In addition FN has been unable account radio difficulties to set his chronometers lack knowledge their fastness or slowness. We shall try to get off tomorrow though we cannot be home by fourth of July as had hoped.[49]

Not much more than a month ago I was on the other shore of

the Pacific, looking westward. This evening, I look eastward over the Pacific. In those fast-moving days which have intervened, the whole width of the world had passed behind us – except this broad ocean. I shall be glad when we have the hazards of its navigation behind us.[50]

There were many pictures taken of Amelia and Fred at Lae. Amelia in particular looks extremely tired, ill even, with a puffiness about the eyes and sunken cheeks. The boyish smile is still evident but there is an emaciated look about her face and neck. She had been en route for a month by this time. In addition to spending twenty days actually flying the Electra, she had carried out the duties that might today be expected of visiting heads of state. Met by senior officials of government she was accorded VIP treatment which inevitably included a whirlwind sightseeing trip at every stage of her journey as well as a dinner of banquet proportions.

In her unofficial 'log' Amelia jokingly referred to 'the appalling habit of falling asleep after dinner and rising at 3 am to prepare for the next day's flight' that she and Fred had adopted.[51] By the time the two reached Lae they must have been close to the end of physical reserves, though Amelia looked to be coping less well with the rigours of the journey than Noonan.

At every stop there had been numerous details to cope with: customs clearance involving a thorough examination of the Lockheed; fumigation of the plane and equipment; scrutiny of their health and inoculation certificates; arranging hangarage or tie-down for the Electra; surpervising any repairs to equipment that had failed en route; planning for the next stage of the journey; ensuring that all the necessary permissions and flight maps and weather reports were available; that local radio frequencies were known. The long process of refuelling had to be watched carefully; all fuel had to be siphoned from the storage tanks 'spotted' along the length of her route by Standard Oil (and bearing the name AMELIA EARHART in bright colours), and strained through chamois leather filters to ensure no contamination. The details were endless.

Somehow, as well as handling all this, Amelia also coped with reporters *and* wrote a total of some 30,000 words about the journey as far as Lae, the bulk cabled home and published as a series of articles by the *Herald Tribune* and which were later used to compile a book called *Last Flight*. One wonders when she found time to sleep, and indeed, on her own evidence, she slept very little.

Not surprising then, that with her spell of sickness at Bandoeng, Amelia looked tired and ill during her time at Lae. But the key question is, did it affect her performance during the subsequent flight? Since it was physically taxing the answer is almost certainly that it did.

A further day's delay was encountered when Fred Noonan had not been able to set his chronometers because the time signals were not picked up on the Electra's radio, and Amelia cabled George:

> Radio misunderstanding and personnel unfitness probably will hold one day have asked Black for forecast for tomorrow you check meteorologist on job as FN must have star sights. Arrange credit if Tribune wishes more story.[52]

This cable has been much debated. In general, bearing in mind Fred Noonan's reputation for heavy drinking, it has been often misquoted as 'crew unfitness' to back up the theory that it was Noonan who was not fit to fly. But what if it referred to her own state of health? Perhaps it was Amelia who was unfit, not Fred Noonan. One has only to look at photographs to see the evident physical toll the flight had taken on her. And what about Amelia's preflight statement to Albert Bresnik that there was a possibility that she was pregnant? There are only her logged notes of being sick in the mornings to offer any substantiation to this, but could her message have been a warning to George? George never confided in anyone on this matter. Alternatively some years later there was a claim by her friend, Gene Vidal, that Amelia was undergoing an early menopause.[53] Clearly only one of these possibilities could be correct, but was either of them? Again, frustratingly, we may never learn the answers.

A great deal of emphasis has been placed on reports of Fred Noonan getting drunk on the night of their arrival at Lae after an argument with Amelia. These reports vary in description and reliable witnesses who were present that night do agree that he got 'very drunk' but only after Amelia and Noonan had already taken the decision not to fly on the following day:[54]

> The argument that caused Noonan to get drunk was over nothing very much. AE had been invited to a dinner party. Noonan was not personally invited though I think this was merely an oversight. Anyway he came down to the bar of the Cecil Hotel to find Eric Chaters and Jim Collopy all smartened up and ready to go for drinks. When asked if he was going Fred said 'No, but AE is . . .' leaving no doubt that he was disgruntled, and when asked what he'd have to drink he said 'whiskey'. The other guys were all drinking beer but he stayed on whiskey and got very drunk. Next day AE watched him like a hawk to make sure he didn't drink again.[55]

This drinking session of Noonan's is said to be behind Amelia's cabled message explaining the delay in departure but clearly it was not the only reason. More than likely the simple truth was merely that both Amelia and Fred were physically and mentally exhausted, and the extremely difficult leg from Lae to Howland which lay ahead imposed a new stress factor. It is known that she had delayed her flight from Hawaii on the first attempt due to tiredness, perhaps she now felt that a day's respite would enable her to fly more efficiently. Bad weather (it rained most of the next day) and Noonan's problem with setting the chronometers were also more likely factors in the delay than Noonan's rumoured hangover. That the two had reached a scratchy relationship is not impossible, of course; Manning has testified that Amelia could be difficult to work with. Her physical endurance was never great.

In speaking to George from Bandoeng Amelia obviously gave him no cause for concern for he continued to book engagements and, prior to her advice (by cable from Lae) that they could not now make it home by Sunday 4 July he had been sending messages to Amelia through the *Itasca*:

FOLLOWING FOR MISS EARHART UPON ARRIVAL HOWLAND ISLAND.
FLIGHT CONTINGENCIES PERMITTING IS SATURDAY ARRIVAL LIKELY.
SUNDAY LATEST. EITHER PERFECT. CONFIDENTIAL WANT YOU TO
KNOW VERY IMPORTANT RADIO COMMITMENT MONDAY NIGHT
NOTHING ELSE WHATEVER[56]

and later when her delayed start had become obvious:

PLEASE FORWARD EARHART LAE RUSH. IS THERE ANY LIKELIHOOD
OAKLAND ARRIVAL BY MONDAY MORNING REPLY VIA ITASCA[57]

The US Coast Guard cutter *Itasca* had been standing off
Howland Island for some days to act as a radio contact for Amelia.
The seaplane tender USS *Swan* was lying some 200 miles to the
northeast of Howland to act as plane guard on the Howland–
Hawaii leg. But for the difficult Lae–Howland flight the old, coal-
burning tug, the USS *Ontario* equipped with antiquated radio
system was to be Amelia's only help. During the original world
flight attempt, the *Itasca* and several other ships had been in the area
for the Pan American survey and Amelia had planned to take advantage of this arrangement. That the USS Naval and Coast Guard
chiefs were prepared to extend help to Amelia's second attempt was
down to George's persuasiveness which is well documented in
National Archive (Washington) files.

One of *Itasca's* problems was the amount of commercial radio
traffic that the flight created, from the press and from various officials
who had been involved by George (the cost of which was all borne
by George).[58] Added to this, communications in the area were very
poor. Cables for Amelia had to be routed through Samoa and took more
than twenty-four hours to reach her; *Itasca's* Commander Thompson
spent a considerable amount of time attempting to ascertain Amelia's
flight plan, radio schedule and communications data, as well as her
estimated time of arrival at Howland.

The charts laid out by Clarence Williams had been of immense
help on the journey so far, though Amelia had not adhered strictly
to the original flight plans. For the Lae–Howland flight, reciprocals

of the original Howland–Lae attempt had been prepared, together with the local data regarding Howland Island, that Williams had gleaned from the Hydrographers Office in Washington.

It is just possible that the following cable received by Amelia in Lae may have decided the flyers to depart from Clarence Williams's recommended direct course:

> The following from Narau. New Narau fixed light latitude 0.32 S; longitude 16.55 East. Five thousand candlepower 560 ft above sea level visible from ships to naked eye at 34 miles. Also there will be bright lighting all night on Island from phosphate workings . . .[59]

The island of Narau (now spelled Nauru) lay nearly 1,400 miles into the 2,556-mile flight and if stars were not visible for celestial navigation, the bright lights would give Noonan an excellent opportunity to check his position. Furthermore a detour to Narau would involve a deviation of only a few degrees north of the most logical course, a deviation easily corrected on the remaining part of the flight and involving little in the way of additional fuel.

Amelia estimated approximately 18½ hours for the 2,556-mile journey, based on the average speed she had achieved over the journey so far, approximately 145 mph. Part of the flight would have to be made at night, however, and since it was essential to reach Howland in daylight, a 'time slot' for the Lae departure had to be worked out.

Calculations were further complicated by the fact that they would be crossing two time zones and the International Dateline, and that Communications from the *Itasca* referred to US Navy time which divided hourly time zones into two half-hour ones. It was probably Noonan's suggestion that they leave at precisely 00.00 hours Greenwich Mean Time (GMT) in order to simplify matters. This would mean that GMT would also coincide with the elapsed time of flight (for example at 14.43 GMT they would have been in the air for 14 hours 43 minutes no matter what time zones or meridians they might have crossed) and ensure a daylight arrival over Howland.

During the past fifty years Noonan's professional skills have some-times been called into question; but research reveals that he was a careful, even pedantic worker.[60] Noonan had three chronometers in the Electra and at a reasonable guess one would be set at GMT, one at local time in Lae and one at local time Howland. As Amelia stressed, 'absolute accuracy in time was vital for the accuracy of celestial navigation . . . Howland is such a small spot in the Pacific that every aid to locating it must be available.'[61]

Both flyers were aware of the magnitude of the task ahead of them, of that there can be no doubt, but Noonan told various people at Lae that he was 'confident that he would have no trouble finding the island'.[62]

On the morning of 2 July 1937 the weather forecast was reason-ably favourable. There were headwinds of twelve to fifteen knots, partly cloudy conditions and rain squalls, but visibility was mostly unlimited.[63] All preparations were complete. Amelia made the deci-sion to leave.

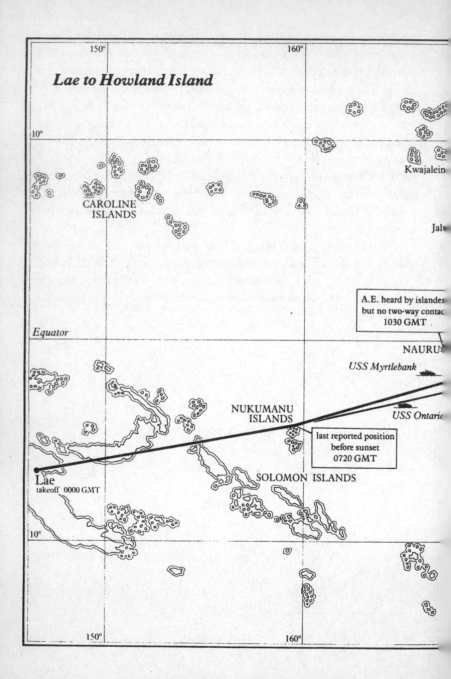

Lae to Howland Island

150° 160°

10°

Kwajalein

CAROLINE
ISLANDS

Jal

Equator

A.E. heard by islander
but no two-way conta
1030 GMT

NAURU

USS Myrtlebank

NUKUMANU
ISLANDS

USS Ontari

last reported position
before sunset
0720 GMT

Lae
takeoff 0000 GMT

SOLOMON ISLANDS

10°

150° 160°

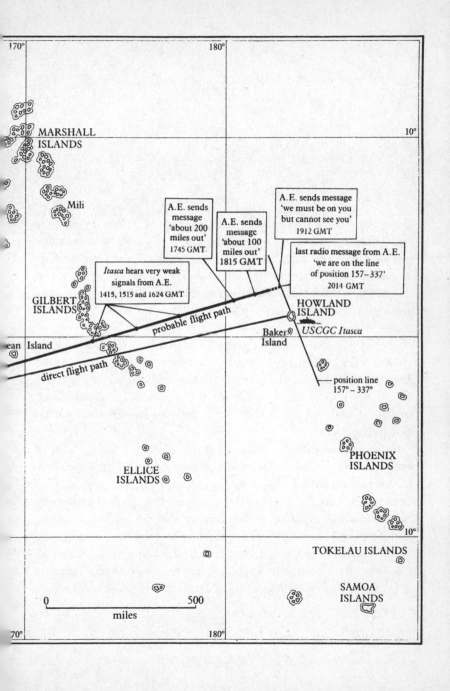

CHAPTER 20

1937

Since this book is a biography the author feels no obligation either to reach or to propound a theory, which could at best be speculation, about Amelia's fate. The facts, and the various theories have been carefully researched however, from thousands of original contemporary documents, and are presented in appendices for the reader, who may or may not choose to reach a conclusion.

At precisely 00.00 hours Greenwich Mean Time (10.00 a.m. local time at Lae) on Friday, 2 July 1937, Amelia Earhart lined up the Lockheed Electra on the runway at Lae and started her take-off run. It was 12.30 p.m. on 1 July at her destination, Howland Island, which lay two and a half time zones away and across the international dateline.[1]

It is believed that the Electra was loaded with 1,000 gallons of fuel;* less than its full capacity but probably the maximum possible for take-off on Lae's 1,000-yard unpaved runway. This would allow between 20 and 21 hours of flying, depending on how efficiently the aeroplane was flown. Before leaving the United States Amelia had predicted that the flight from Lae to Howland would take about eighteen and a half hours but according to *Itasca's* log, Commander Thompson expected her to arrive at Howland at approximately 19.30 hours (GMT). There is no evidence that

*See appendix for fuel information.

Amelia had ever taken off with such a heavy fuel load before this. For the Oakland–Honolulu flight the Electra carried 947 gallons but on that occasion Paul Mantz had been at her side, operating the throttles and retracting the landing gear.

The runway at Lae ended abruptly with a 25-foot drop to the waters of the Huon Gulf and witnesses stated that the take-off was 'hair-raising' for there was not a breath of wind to help the Electra into the air on that clear hot morning. Commercial pilot Mr Bert Heath, who was flying into Lae in his tri-motored Junkers aeroplane, watched the Electra's lumbering take-off run from high above the field. He recalled that close to the seaward end of the runway it was crossed by a dirt road. There was a high camber on this road and as the Electra hit the crest it bounced into the air and 'over the drop-off', flying so low over the sea that the propellers were 'throwing spray'. Mr Heath noted that the dust kicked up by the Electra over the dirt road hung about in the still air for some time and did not disperse quickly.[2]

A report by James Collopy (District Superintendent of Civil Aviation), stated:

> . . . after taking every yard of the 1000-yard runway from the north west end of the aerodrome towards the sea, the aircraft had not left the ground 50 yards from the end of the runway. When it did leave it sank away but was by this time over the sea. It continued to sink about five or six feet above the water and had not climbed to more than 100 feet before it disappeared from sight.
>
> In spite of this, however, it was obvious that the aircraft was well-handled and pilots of Guinea Airways who have flown Lockheed aircraft were loud in their praise of the take-off with such an overload.[3]

In the days that Amelia and Noonan had spent at New Guinea they made contact with Harry Balfour,[4] radio operator at Lae. Between them they arranged a radio schedule and after the Electra's take-off Balfour listened for Amelia's transmissions on her daytime frequency of 6,210 kilocycles; within the hour he received her first communication. From this point on the flight can only be pieced together by examination of the various radio transmissions that took place over the following twenty hours or so.*

The first radio communications between Amelia and Balfour were not logged, but Balfour is on record as stating that he was to contact with her every hour when position reports and height were received. Amelia's schedule was to transmit at 15 and 45 minutes past each hour, and listen on the hour and half hour to receive messages.

After about five hours Amelia reported that she was 'at 10,000 feet but reducing altitude because of banks of cumulus cloud', and two hours later she told Balfour that she was 'at 7,000 feet and making 150 miles per hour'. Amelia meant air speed; the Electra's ground speed would have been significantly less depending on the strength of the headwinds.

At 07.20 hours (GMT) Amelia provided a position 'latitude: 4 degrees 33.5' south; longitude: 159 degrees 07' east.' This placed the Electra more or less directly on the great-circle course for Howland Island, some 20 miles south-west of the Nukumanu Islands – which should have been visible as it was still daylight – and giving Noonan a perfect opportunity to check his navigation before nightfall. Although only a third of the way on the flight this was to be Amelia's only position report and thus it has great significance. (See map on pp 282–3)

An important factor is that having covered more than 846 miles (735 nautical miles; one nautical mile equals 1.151 statute miles), the Electra had achieved a ground speed of only 118 mph (103 knots),[5] considerably less than Amelia would have hoped for with an average airspeed of 150 mph. The shortfall is not unreasonable, however, if one takes into consideration a combination of the excess weight in the early stages of the flight when the Electra was slowly climbing to 10,000 feet, and stronger-than-forecast headwinds. The last weather report that Amelia is known to have received before

*See appendix for detailed radio log.

take-off forecast 12–15 mph east-south-east winds, but they were actually 25 mph.[6] Lae had transmitted the increased wind strength of '25 mph to the *Ontario* and 20 mph from there to Howland' but there is uncertainty that Amelia ever received this message owing to the 24-hour delay in transmission while cables were routed through Samoa.

Noonan could have determined the approximate wind strength and direction, though, by using the drift meter and smoke bombs, and if there had been any doubt at this time about whether they could complete the flight Amelia would have turned back (as she had at Karachi when conditions were marginal).

From the reported position near the Nukumanu Islands to Howland Island is 1,714 miles on the great-circle route laid out for Amelia by Clarence Williams. With a decreasing gross weight as the fuel was used up, and headwinds forecast to decrease to 20 mph the Electra was easily capable of averaging 130 mph or better, over the remaining distance, but this would give a revised estimated time of arrival (ETA) in the vicinity of Howland of 20.38 GMT leaving very little margin for error regarding fuel.

At 08.00 hours GMT, Amelia made her final radio contact with Balfour. At this stage her transmissions were becoming fainter but he was able to make out her message that she was 'on course for Howland Island at 12,000 feet'. When Amelia informed him that she was changing from her daytime frequency, 6,210 kilocycles, to her night-time one, 3,105 kilocycles, Balfour stated: 'We asked her to remain on her present frequency but she told me she wished to contact the American Coast Guard cutter *Itasca* so there was nothing to do about it but pass the terminal forecast to her and the upper air report from Ocean Island.'[7]

The USS *Ontario*, designated as Amelia's guard ship on that Lae–Howland flight, was lying 423 miles (368 nautical miles) from the Electra's last reported fix near the Nukumanu Islands. The *Ontario*'s position – latitude: 3 degrees 9′ south; longitude: 165 degrees 06′ east – put the ship less than ten miles north of Amelia's great-circle track. Amelia had previously requested by cable that the *Ontario* 'BROADCAST LETTER N FOR FIVE MINUTES AFTER HOUR

GMT FOUR HUNDRED KILOCYCLES WITH OWN CALL LETTERS REPEATED TWICE END EVERY MINUTE',[8] and this was done. *Ontario*'s captain, Lieutenant H. W. Blakeslee, recalls that it was 'rainy and overcast' that night. The ship had no light switched on but had one ready should they hear a plane.[9]

At 10.30 hours GMT, 3 hours and 10 minutes after Amelia had reported her position near the Nukumanu Islands to Balfour, residents on Nauru Island reported hearing Amelia say '. . . ship in sight ahead'.[10] Assuming that the ship Amelia reported was the *Ontario* the Electra was then maintaining an average ground speed of 125 mph, almost exactly what she should have been making with 25-mph reported headwinds and a fuel load approaching recommended operating levels. The reports from Nauru of what Amelia said are open to question, however, for some listeners claim Amelia actually said: '. . . lights in sight ahead.'[11]

It has been suggested that from the Nukumanu Islands, Noonan may have set a course for Nauru, some 607 miles to the north-east, in order to have one last opportunity to check his astro-navigation before setting out over open ocean; the sky was overcast and he may not have been able to take sextant bearings on celestial bodies. Such a detour would have added only 31 miles to the flight.[12] But it is much more likely that he continued on the direct great-circle course for Howland knowing that some 400 miles on that track the USS *Ontario* was waiting.

Lieutenant Blakeslee had no notification that Amelia had left Lae nor any acknowledgement from Amelia that she had heard *Ontario*'s morse signal. A watch was kept but the crew neither heard nor saw any sign of the Electra and two hours after the time Amelia was due to pass overhead, the ship, which had been on station for ten days, was ordered to return to port for essential supplies.[13]

Another possibility that has been suggested is that Amelia saw the SS *Myrtlebank*. The *Myrtlebank* was headed for Nauru and arrived there at dawn on the following day. At the time of Amelia's report this ship was lying at latitude 1 degree 40' south, longitude 166 degrees 45' east, some 44 miles north of Amelia's great-circle route.[14]

The suggestion that Amelia flew via Nauru seems unlikely, however, for in order for her to have been within visual distance (34 miles) of the lights on Nauru within 3 hours and 10 minutes after her last reported position, she would have been making a ground speed of 170 mph, a significant improvement over the previous calculated performance. On the other hand from 30 miles off Nauru she might have been able to see *both* the *Myrtlebank* and the lights on Nauru.

The flight via Nauru would have been possible, of course, if Amelia had transmitted her position to Balfour some time after it was plotted. Her casual attitude toward radio and reporting procedures makes this not unlikely (in the entire trip from Miami up to that point she had provided only seven position reports). The position report could have been provided by Noonan at any time following Amelia's previous radio contact, and it is not beyond credibility that having received it, Amelia waited until her 5.15 scheduled time to report. From the *Itasca* log alone, it is obvious that she was seldom pedantic about keeping to radio schedules.

The wife of the district administrator on Nauru, Mrs Garsia, noted in her diary for 2 July that Amelia had taken off from Lae and had been notified of the existence of the new Nauru light and local weather. She recorded picking up Amelia's radio transmissions on a shortwave receiver from 6 p.m. (Nauru time) but though they became increasingly loud Mrs Garsia could never make out what was being said. 'Amelia was due near or over Nauru at 9.40 pm but though we watched she did not come near.' It has been said that Nauru could never have picked up Amelia's radio signals if she had not been within 50 miles of the island, but Amelia had broadcast her position to Lae from almost 900 miles away; *Itasca*, subsequently, first heard Amelia's faint transmissions at something like the same distance; and on the following day a Nauru resident reported receiving Amelia's transmissions when she was in the vicinity of Howland Island.[15]

There is no real evidence as to the precise track of the aeroplane, after Nukumanu. No one saw or heard the plane fly over, and this fact alone has meant that no one can actually refute even the most outrageous theories regarding Amelia's course. Equally, no one can refute that she flew on a direct course for Howland in which case she must have flown over the Gilbert Islands at about 3 a.m. (local time) but no one there had been contacted in advance; no assistance was requested so no one was standing by.

From 10.30 hours GMT there was no radio contact from Amelia for several hours. At 12.42 hours GMT *Itasca* signalled Coast Guard Headquarters at San Francisco, where George was waiting for news, to advise that they had not heard from Amelia but saw 'no cause for concern as she is still 1,000 miles away'. It was 14.15 hours GMT before the first transmissions from Amelia were received by *Itasca* on 3,105 kilocycles.[16]

In the ship's radio room Chief Radioman Leo G. Bellarts was accompanied by Radiomen Thomas O'Hare and William Galten. A primary radio log, kept by Bellarts, was backed up by a secondary log maintained by one of his operators.[17] In addition to the two radio receivers there was a loudspeaker. Others waited in the room to hear Amelia: Commander Warner K. Thompson, *Itasca's* captain, and three of his officers, Lieutenant-Commanders Lee Baker and Frank Kenner, and Ensign William L. Sutter; Richard Black (later Admiral Black) from the Department of the Interior but representing George Putnam in respect of administrative details on this leg of the flight; and two press agency reporters H. N. Hanzlick of Associated Press and James Carey of United Press.

At first no one could make out what Amelia was saying above the static, but Bellarts caught her 'low monotone voice' saying: '. . . cloudy and overcast'. The two pressmen were familiar with Amelia's voice and agreed that it was she but could not decipher what she was saying. Bellarts sent weather forecasts to KHAQQ (Amelia's call sign) on *Itasca's* scheduled transmission times 14.30 and 15.00 hours GMT. Nothing was heard from Amelia during her 14.45 hours slot but this caused no particular concern. She was still a long way from Howland and no one was surprised that reception was poor over such a distance.

At 15.15 hours GMT Amelia came in on cue. '*Itasca* from Earhart. Overcast . . . will listen on hour and half hour on 3,105.'

Her voice was clearer this time and understood by others in the radio room. Fifteen minutes later Bellarts called KHAQQand gave details of the weather for the Howland Island area before asking: 'What is your position? When do you expect to reach Howland? *Itasca* has heard your phone so go ahead on key. Acknowledge this broadcast next schedule.' Each phrase was carefully repeated twice in accordance with the accepted code of practice.

No signal was picked up from Amelia during her next transmission time (15.45 hours GMT) so Bellarts repeated his previous message at 16.00 hours. When Amelia failed to report at 16.15 Bellarts waited eight minutes and transmitted weather by voice and Morse code on frequency 3,105 kilocycles.

As Bellarts finished calling, he switched to receive and picked up a faint transmission from KHAQQ which he logged as '. . . partly cloudy . . .', noting after it the code 'S1', indicating a very weak reception (signal strengths being measured on a table of 1–5. S1: very faint; S2: faint; S3: fair; S4: good; S5: very loud). A minute later Amelia transmitted again but so faintly that neither Bellarts or anyone else in the room could make any sense of it.

The *Itasca*'s log reveals that for the next hour and twenty minutes Bellarts sent weather data and his 'What is your position?' message at each scheduled transmission time, but nothing was heard from Amelia. At 17.44 hours she broke in at strength 3. '[want] bearing on 3,105, on hour, will whistle in mic.' Her transmission broke off but moments later she spoke again: 'about . . . 200 miles out. Approximately. Whistling now.' She whistled briefly but the transmission was too short for a direction finder to home in on the signal.

Dawn was now breaking, recorded in *Itasca*'s log at 17.45 hours GMT (6.15 a.m. ship's time). At 18.00 hours GMT Bellarts sent weather and requested Amelia's position, and at 18.15 Amelia's voice boomed in on schedule at strength 4: 'Please take bearing on us and report in half an hour I will make noise in microphone. About 100 miles out.' Bellarts recorded that, once again, she was on the air too briefly to take direction-finder bearings, but all on board the *Itasca* were heartened as the strength of her calls had increased indicating that she was getting closer.

Amelia's report that she was 'about 100 miles out' fitted in well with the time that *Itasca* expected her to arrive (19.30 hours GMT according to the ship's log), and they all confidently expected the Electra to appear overhead in an hour or so, but they heard nothing until 19.12 hours GMT when Amelia's voice filled the loudspeaker, signal strength 5 this time: maximum reception. Bellarts logged her call: 'KHAQQ calling *Itasca*. We must be on you but cannot see you but gas is running low. Been unable to reach you by radio. We are flying at altitude 1,000 feet.' But the secondary log reads: 'Earhart says running out of gas. Only half hour left/can't hear us at all/we hear her and are sending on 3,105 and 500 same time constantly and listening in for her frequently.'[18]

These two accounts have been taken by some researchers as sinister evidence. Why, they have asked, is Amelia sometimes quoted as saying: 'gas is running low . . .' and at other times: 'running out of gas, only half an hour left . . .'?

Reading the pages of these logs and pages of radio transmissions unrelated to the Earhart mission, the reason is obvious. This mission, while interesting, was really not very special. It was just another job for *Itasca*; the crew had performed a similar task some months earlier for the Pan Am survey. The men keeping those logs had no reason to believe that their scribbled 'radio shorthand' notes would be the subject of countless books. Busy with their duties they recorded the gist of what they heard, rather than the *precise* wording.

The message received at 19.12 hours GMT (7.42 a.m. ship's time) was actually written in the primary log by Bellarts as follows:

0742 KHAQQ CLING ITASCA WE MUST BE ON YOU BUT CANNOT SEE
U BUT GAS IS RUNNING LOW BEEN UNABLE TO REACH YOU BY
RADIO WE ARE FLYING AT 1,000 FEET

while the second log, in the same radio room, maintained by another radio operator, reads:

0740: EARHART ON NW SEZ RUNNING OUT OF GAS ½ HOUR LEFT
CAN'T HR US AT ALL/ WE HEAR HER AND ARE SENDING 3105 ES

500 SAME TIME CONSTANTLY AND LISTENING IN FER HER FRE-
QUENTLY

The reported version of what she actually said was made some
hours later, after the radio operators and others present in the
radio room had examined the written log and discussed *what*
had been said.[19] The sensational suggestions by several writers
that this was done on the instructions of the US government to
cover up or distort the facts may be discounted if only because of
the wealth of information that exists from so many different
sources, ranging from the military records, to the press (not
renowned for keeping secrets) and the inhabitants of various
islands. The explanation offered by *Itasca's* commanding officer is
more credible:

> The transcript of the radio logs from 0200 until 0930 is neces-
> sarily not complete due to the rapidity of events and also due to
> the Earhart exclusive use of voice, only partially received. At
> these times tuning was so essential that parts of the actual mes-
> sage may not be given. Officers of appropriate rank and
> experience were present . . . the radio log stands as it was written
> at the time and has not been changed or corrected. The transcript
> is an actual transcript [and] the portions [extracted above] form
> a true representation of the picture.[20]

Amelia's message that she was low on fuel caused some conster-
nation in the radio room, but there was little that Commander
Thompson and his crew could do other than set in motion provisional plans to go to the aid of the flyers in the event that they had
to ditch. On Howland Island a high frequency direction finder
had been installed, manned by Radioman Frank Cipriani, but when
Cipriani was contacted by the *Itasca* he reported that he was unable
to get any fixes on Amelia because her transmissions were too brief.
The equipment Cipriani was using was in any case very much
experimental and in the 'breadboard' stage. It had been brought to
Howland by Richard Black and was powered by a dry-cell battery

arrangement. In use for the whole night while Cipriani tried in vain to 'fix' on Amelia's transmissions, by daybreak – when it was most like to have been of use – the batteries had run down and were insufficient to power the unit.

Itasca was already making heavy black smoke which in the light breeze of under 10 mph drifted very little. Commander Thompson estimated that the smoke should have been visible for 20 miles or so. Over Howland the sky was clear and the sun already hot but to the north and north-west, 30 or 40 miles away, *Itasca's* crew could see formations of large cumulus clouds.

Thompson now decided to break with the radio schedule and transmit and receive on a continuous basis. At 19.13 hours GMT, within a minute of receiving Amelia's message that she was low on fuel, Bellarts transmitted by voice: '*Itasca* to KHAQQ. Received your message signal strength 5. Go ahead please.' He followed this with a long stream of letter As transmitted by Morse-code key on the 3,105 frequency. This was repeated at 19.17 hours with no response. Two minutes later, he tried again. '*Itasca* to KHAQQ: Your message okay please acknowledge with phone on 3,105.' Again he sent out a long series of AAAs by key.

Tension was beginning to build up in the radio room now. Amelia had not once acknowledged receiving any message from *Itasca* and her messages to them were brief and incomplete. But their apprehension must have been nothing to that experienced by Amelia and Fred Noonan who had now been in the air for over 19 hours. They were physically tired; there was no sight of Howland Island where Noonan clearly expected it to be; fuel supplies were running low and Amelia had not been able to make any radio contact. This meant not only was she unsure that her transmissions were being received but that she could not take direction-finder bearings on her DF unit. It is not difficult to imagine the concern that Amelia and Noonan were feeling.

At 19.28 hours GMT Amelia called *Itasca*: 'We are circling but cannot hear you, go ahead on 7,500 now or on the schedule time on half hour.' Again *Itasca* received her message at signal strength 5. Bellarts, confused by the sudden change of frequency, nevertheless immediately sent out a constant stream of AAAs on 7,500 as requested, and called by voice, 'Go ahead on 3,105.'

To the immense relief of everyone in the radio room, Amelia acknowledged receiving their message almost immediately: 'KHAQQ calling *Itasca*. We received your signals but unable to get a minimum. Please take a bearing on us and answer 3,105 with voice.' She then transmitted a series of long dashes for five seconds or so. The time was 19.30 hours GMT. It was the only time during the flight that Amelia was in two-way contact with *Itasca* and her reception of the transmission was too poor to enable her to tune her direction finder onto the signal.

Five minutes later having tried and failed to take a bearing on Amelia's transmission, *Itasca* radioed Frank Cipriani on Howland but he had been no more successful. Bellarts called on 3,105 again: '*Itasca* to KHAQQ. Your signals received okay. We are unable to hear you to take a bearing. It is impractical to take a bearing on 3,105 on your voice. How do you get that? Go ahead.' There was no response so he tried yet again, sending on 7,500 kilocycles since the only satisfactory contact had been received by Amelia on that frequency: '*Itasca* to KHAQQ. Go ahead on 3,105 or 500 kilo-cycles.'

For more than half an hour Bellarts sent voice and code signals, on all frequencies that he knew Amelia's radio was capable of receiving. The transmissions in the ship's log are interspersed with the laconic 'No answer' but the frustration and concern felt by all present were subsequently to be made obvious through the ship's log.

At 20.14 hours GMT the listeners in the radio room heard Amelia's voice for the last time. Volume was still strength 5 although it was not quite as clear as the previous transmission. She was sending on 3,105 kilocycles and spoke rapidly; some listeners described her transmission as sounding hurried and almost incoherent: 'KHAQQ to *Itasca*. We are on the line of position one five seven dash three three seven. Will repeat this message on 6,210 kilocycles. We are running north and south.'[21]

Bellarts immediately replied: '*Itasca* to KHAQQ. We heard you okay on 3,105 kilocycles. Please stay on 3,105 do not hear you on 6,210. Maintain QSO on 3,105.' He sent this by voice on 3,105 and by key on 7,500 kilocycles but nothing further was heard from Amelia on any frequency. *Itasca* continued to transmit on all frequencies until 21.30 hours GMT when Commander Thompson made the assumption that Amelia had ditched and set in motion the search procedure.

Commander Thompson had only the small amount of information Amelia had provided on which to base his search. There seemed no other reason for Amelia's report of flying 'at 1,000 feet' than that she was flying beneath a cloud base for it is easier to see over a greater distance at a higher altitude. Since the only cloud in the vicinity was to the north and north-west of Howland, Thompson concluded that the Electra's most likely position was in that sector. Furthermore, if Amelia had been in the clear skies surrounding and to the south and east of Howland she ought to have been able to see the pall of black smoke hanging over *Itasca*. Notifying San Francisco of his intention Thompson gave the command to proceed north at full steam.

Apart from the more sensational claims by writers who believe that Amelia and Noonan were not even in the vicinity of Howland when they disappeared, there has been much conjecture about what might have happened in the cockpit of the Electra during that flight. The main theories are that Amelia and Noonan had a disagreement causing Amelia to disregard his instructions (as she had done at Dakar); or that Noonan was suffering from a hangover and consequently was not up to the mental effort required, so that the Electra was lost due to his incompetence. The permutations and speculation are seemingly endless but unless the Electra is ever found we will never know the answer, and perhaps not even then.

What is certain is that Amelia and Noonan were exhausted. Even had they been fit and rested when they left Lae, which they were not, they had been awake for more than twenty-four hours, and flying for over twenty, when Amelia was last heard on the radio. The dimensions of the Electra's cockpit were, according to an article written by Amelia before her departure from the USA: 'four feet six inches by four feet six inches' and for the entire twenty hours Amelia would have been sitting in the same upright seat, unable to leave it at all. She was surrounded by equipment and would have found it difficult to stretch her limbs, though in smooth conditions she could allow the autopilot to fly the plane from time to time. The ceaseless engine noise in that confined space, and the vibration in the all-metal fuselage with its empty fuel tanks (also experienced by the crew of the 1967 commemorative flight to Howland in a Lockheed Electra), would have added greatly to the physical stress.[22]

Amelia's only contact with Noonan was on the occasions when he crawled over the fuel tanks and sat in the right-hand co-pilot's seat in the cockpit, when the two would have had to shout over the engine noise in order to communicate. Otherwise notes were passed between them on the end of a cleft bamboo pole or by using the pulley system.

Although Fred Noonan was able to stand up and stretch his legs in a limited manner, he would have been working all night in the cramped, poorly lit navigation area, also subject to the constant noise. In these circumstances it is not unlikely that he could have made a mathematical error at some point, which progressed through his final calculations.

The most likely scenario is that the plane was in the vicinity of Howland, may – at one point – have even been within visual distance, but missed it either due to clouds in the line of sight (a relatively small cloud could obscure such a small target)[23] or, if the flyers ever emerged into the clear air north of Howland, possibly missed the tiny island in the glare of the rising sun on the water. This, according to eyewitnesses, reduced visibility to a practical 15 miles or less, although the *Itasca* was making heavy black smoke at that time which at one point stretched for ten miles.[24]

What seems most likely is that Amelia ran out of fuel and was forced to land at sea shortly after her last verified message to *Itasca* at 20.14 hours GMT. Using extensive information gathered during eighteen years of research on the subject, Elgen and Marie Long claim to have pinpointed the most likely position[25] which is '35 miles west-north-west of the island . . . in an area perhaps 20 miles wide and 40 miles long.'[26]

Coincidentally, and perhaps curiously, using an entirely different line of investigation, a British researcher, Roy Nesbit (a former Royal Air Force navigator), has reached precisely the same conclusion.[27]

The author's conclusion is that Amelia probably went down within 100 miles of Howland Island, but for lack of proof in any direction it is not beyond the bounds of *possibility* that Amelia and Noonan were picked up by one of the Japanese fishing boats known to be several hundred miles to the north of Howland. Amelia reported running 'north and south on a line of position'.[28] This would be a line calculated by Noonan using a sun sight taken earlier in the day but the Electra might have been *anywhere* on that line because there was no second coordinate given and one assumes from Amelia's message that they were flying up and down the line within the area in which they expected to find the island.

There is substantial testimony to support the fact that a Caucasian couple was seen on the Japanese-mandated Marshall Islands (some 600 miles to the north of Howland) at some time around 1937 but that this couple was Amelia Earhart and Fred Noonan is open to serious doubt. The testimony of many islanders more than twenty years later may well have been given in the light of rewards offered for information, coupled with a genuine atavistic desire to please the questioner. There is no really convincing evidence that this was Amelia Earhart's ultimate fate, though the Japanese theory is discussed in an appendix to this book. All the documented facts point to the ditching off Howland Island which neither flyer survived.

It is known that Paul Mantz attempted to prepare Amelia, verbally, for a ditching in the Pacific in her Vega, prior to her solo trans-Pacific flight; and presumably may have gone through a similar routine for the Electra. Verbal instructions, however, would have been of minimal help in an actual sea landing.

Amelia would have known that she should keep the undercarriage retracted, but if she was completely out of fuel, as seems likely, she would have had to cope with a dead-stick forced landing on the water. Even over a smooth sea it is difficult to judge a plane's height above the water surface, and if she stalled too high, the impact alone would have been sufficient to have killed both occupants. In rough seas it would be even more difficult to judge height and such a stall, or even the effect of the waves in a rough patch of sea, would have caused severe damage to the Electra. When the *Itasca* steamed to the area under heavy cloud to the north of Howland Island, on 2 July, she reported a turbulent sea with waves four to six feet high.

Photographs of a new Bendix receiver installed in the Electra immediately before she left Miami were shown to the author by Elgen and Marie Long (see Appendix 2). They reveal that the unit was sited immediately in front of Amelia's head, mounted on the top of the instrument panel; its casing was a sharp-cornered metal box. If Amelia had hit her head on this in a ditching process (and it is difficult to see how she could have avoided it for she had no shoulder harness), it is probable that she would have been knocked unconscious. Noonan may have been in the cockpit, having been warned of an emergency landing, or he may have remained aft in the cabin.

Assuming Amelia remained conscious after a forced landing, that everything had gone according to the book – that she had lowered the flaps correctly, glided in perfectly, stalled out at the correct height above the water, and that the plane remained intact, there were other problems to take into account. The floating attitude of the Electra, due to the weight of the engines and empty fuel tanks, was nose down, tail up. With no way of escape through the cockpit hatch (which would be under water) Amelia would have had to scramble up the almost vertical slope of the fuel tanks, perhaps with the help of Noonan, or perhaps without his help if he was unconscious.

The life raft and emergency equipment were housed behind the rear cabin bulkhead, towards the tail of the plane, and even to have reached this would have required tremendous effort in an upended plane. It was then necessary to retrieve this not inconsiderable weight from stowage above head height (caused by the plane's nose-down attitude); partially inflate the raft using the CO_2 canister; open the cabin door; throw the life raft into the water and jump after it, continuing the inflation process once safely on board. No trace has ever been found of Amelia's life raft.

Lockheed Electras have made forced landings on water on at least ten occasions. One detailed report reads:

> The pilot experienced engine failure in the right engine and shortly afterwards lost some power in the left engine. He was able to land on a smooth sea, just off the Massachusetts coast, into a 10 mph wind with reduced power in one engine. The plane landed with tail down to allow the easiest deceleration and therefore lessen impact and as a consequence the pilot and all passengers got out safely and were picked up more or less immediately.
>
> The plane floated for eight minutes before sinking.[29]

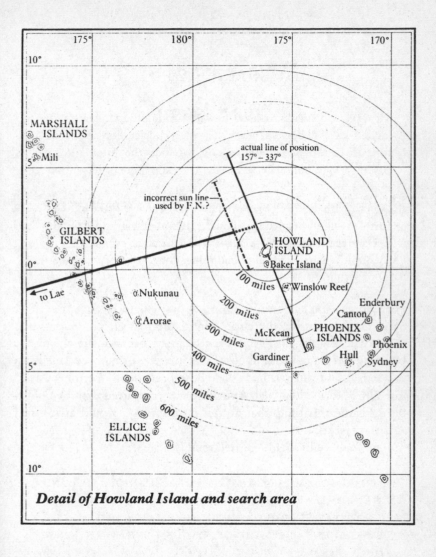

Detail of Howland Island and search area

Indicates probable track of the Electra using Noonan's navigational techniques. See also map of entire flight Lae to Howland on pages 282–283.

CHAPTER 21

1937–1939

Amelia Earhart to George Putnam: 'I know that if I fail or if I am lost you will be blamed for allowing me to leave on this trip; the backers of the flight will be blamed and everyone connected with it. But it's my responsibility and mine alone.'[1]

For George, who had been waiting at Coast Guard Headquarters in San Francisco during the entire flight, the news from *Itasca* was scarcely believable. There had been so many occasions in the past when he had waited with ill-concealed anxiety for news of Amelia's safe arrival, and when bad news had been passed to him erroneously, but all had turned out well. At first he was convinced that it would be the same this time, that at any minute news would arrive of Amelia's rescue.

The *Itasca's* cable had reported merely:

EARHART CONTACT 0742 REPORTED ONE HALF HOUR FUEL AND NO LANDFALL. POSITION DOUBTFUL. CONTACT 0646 REPORTED ONE HUNDRED MILES FROM ITASCA BUT NO RELATIVE BEARING. 0843 REPORTED LINE OF POSITION 157 DASH 337 BUT NO REFERENCE POINT PRESUME HOWLAND. ESTIMATE 1200 FOR MAXIMUM TIME ALOFT AND IF NON-ARRIVAL BY THAT TIME WILL COMMENCE SEARCH IN NORTHWEST QUADRANT FROM HOWLAND AS MOST PROBABLE AREA . . . UNDERSTAND SHE WILL FLOAT FOR LIMITED TIME.

George told *New York Herald Tribune* reporters, 'The plane should float, but I couldn't estimate for how long because a Lockheed plane has never been forced down at sea before. The plane's large wings and empty tanks should provide sufficient buoyancy, if it came to rest on the sea without being damaged. There was a two-man life raft aboard, together with lifebelts, flares, a Very pistol and a large yellow signal kite.'

Already steaming north *Itasca's* Commander Thompson began the search within three hours from Amelia's last contact. His next cable suggested that headquarters contact the navy to request a seaplane to assist him.

In the hours and days immediately following Amelia's last substantiated message, hope was kept alive by constant reports of radio signals purporting to have come from the Electra. The most significant was heard by Walter McMenamy who worked for Paul Mantz from time to time and who had maintained radio contact with Amelia during her solo trans-Pacific flight. McMenamy claimed that he intercepted weak Morse-code signals on the 6,210 kcs frequency about six hours after Amelia's final contact with *Itasca*: '. . . just the letters l-a-t' which he assumed was latitude, followed by indecipherable transmission. Although Amelia's Electra carried no code transmission key she could have transmitted a carrier signal by holding down the microphone switch. Later McMenamy claimed to have heard Amelia's voice, very faintly, calling 'SOS, SOS, SOS, KHAQQ, KHAQQ.'

Two hours later, Carl Pierson, also of Los Angeles, claimed to have picked up weak and indecipherable signals on 6,210 kcs.

It is interesting that despite the fact that these two amateur radio operators[2] were reporting radio contact throughout the next twelve hours, the San Francisco Coast Guard said they had heard nothing even though radio reception was unusually good and that they had three radio stations set constantly to monitor the appropriate wavelengths. Nothing was heard, either, by the Coast Guard's Pearl Harbor radio station, nor by *Itasca* and *Swan* who maintained their radio vigil. *Itasca's* Commander Thompson later concluded that what McMenamy and Pierson (and later, many other genuine radio operators) actually heard was probably the transmissions on 6,210 and 3,150 by *Itasca* herself, attempting to contact the lost flyers, for there were significant coincidences between the reported times of the messages and transmissions recorded in the ship's radio log.[3]

Because of George's publicity machine, every single known detail was published under banner headlines that Amelia was missing in the Pacific Ocean. It was a boon to hoaxers for they could invent messages (or send them on home radio sets) knowing which frequencies were applicable, the approximate location of Amelia's disappearance and enough personal information to enable faked messages to sound convincing.

From the start Paul Mantz doubted the authenticity of the reported signals, stating that the Electra's radio equipment was not capable of transmitting over any distance (even allowing for 'skip', the phenomenon that enables occasional freak radio reception hundreds/thousands of miles away) from sea level. Nor, except for the briefest period, could transmissions be made without the right engine being run to keep the batteries charged – a feat that could be accomplished only if the Electra were in the air or on land.

Donald R. Husted however, who had supervised the fitting of the Western Electric radio equipment, stated that he thought it was *possible*,[4] and Joseph Gurr, who spent many hours 'checking the systems out' at Burbank, told George that under favourable conditions and if '*everything*' was still working, it *could* transmit.[5]

It was not on the strength of the radio reports however, but in the belief that the empty fuel tanks would enable the plane to stay afloat for an indefinite time, and the knowledge that Amelia carried a life raft and emergency provisions, that a massive search was launched. Personally authorised by President Roosevelt, it involved nine naval ships and sixty-six aeroplanes at an estimated cost of over $4 million.

Only the *Itasca* and *Swan* were on station to start the search immediately;[6] the other ships had to be diverted from duties elsewhere. The aircraft carrier USS *Lexington*, for example, which was standing off Santa Barbara when the orders were dispatched, had been scheduled as the star attraction at the 'Marine Week' celebrations beginning on 4 July.[7] Ordered to Howland Island by Rear Admiral Manley on 3 July *Lexington* left immediately but took eleven days to reach the search area.

Within hours of Amelia being reported down a PBY flying boat with a crew of eight was dispatched from Hawaii to Howland to help in the search, as requested by Commander Thompson. Later, Thompson would pointedly mention in his report that throughout the PBY's flight *Itasca* had no difficulty in maintaining constant radio contact. The PBY was expected to arrive on the morning of 3 July, and *Itasca* therefore left the 'most likely' search area and returned to Howland Island to meet the plane. But some 700 miles north of Howland Island the seaplane sent the following radio message in Morse code:

> Last two hours in extremely bad weather between altitude 2,000 and 12,000 now, sleet, rain, electrical storms. In daylight conditions look equally bad cloud tops appear to be 18,000 feet or more. Am returning to Pearl harbor.[8]

Now understandably desperate for information, George pounced on every new rumour that was flashed to newspapers and wire services. His first request was that transmissions be sent every hour on the hour on 3,105 kcs '. . . just her initials, AE, followed by the questions: Land or water? North or south?'[9]

The twenty-four hours following Amelia's disappearance were spent as he had spent the previous twenty-four, at San Francisco's Coast Guard Headquarters waiting and hoping for a substantial report. Noonan's wife, Bea, joined him there to await news. Those present remembered how he paced back and forth for hours, in shirtsleeves, and with perspiration streaming down his face. 'AE will pull through,' he told the *Sunday Mirror*'s New York reporter. 'She has more courage than anyone I know. I am worried, of course, but I have confidence in her ability to handle any situation.' Once, irritated by Mrs Noonan's stifled sobs, he stopped to say: 'It's this way, Bea. One of two things has happened. Either they must have been killed outright – and that must come to all of us sooner or later – or

they are alive and will be picked up.' This statement was, understandably, no succour to the distraught bride of a few months who
promptly collapsed.[10]

George, though, was not able to use the luxury of retreat into
helplessness. He was a doer and psychologically unable to allow the
organisation of the search to be left to others. As the hours and days
wore on he could be seen twisting and struggling with the problem,
searching for new avenues of possibilities. After discussions with
Clarence Williams and Paul Mantz, for example, he decided that a
likely place for Amelia to have come down was several hundred
miles to the south of Howland, perhaps in the vicinity of the
Phoenix Islands, several of which, he said, were large enough for
Amelia to have 'made a pancake landing'. Using his normal bull-
dozing tactics to get his own way, George telephoned navy and
Coast Guard chiefs to request that ships be diverted from the organised search pattern to search the reefs in the Phoenix archipelago.

At George's request, Clarence Williams prepared a chart of the
great-circle 'base course' from Lae to Howland and on the assumption that Noonan would have obtained a drift angle soon after
take-off, estimated drift at 11 degrees (which would have been laid
off into the prevailing wind), or to the right of the original course.
The prolongation of this track, he said, passed 140 miles to the
south of Howland Island. He also warned George that it was just as
likely that the opposite might have happened, and drew another
track line 11 degrees to the left of the course, which passed 140
miles to the north of Howland. From these two lines he provided
George with what he called a 'cone of possibilities', which a staff
artist of the *Los Angeles Times* laid out and wired to many of the
daily papers around the world.

George immediately begged the navy to instruct the battleship
USS *Colorado* to search to the south-east as far as the Phoenix
Islands taking in the numerous reefs and coral atolls in that area.
Acceding to his request the *Colorado* made full steam to the area and
sent up its three 3U-3 spotter biplanes. The three young pilots
(Lieutenants John Lambrecht, William Short and Leonard Fox)
could not even locate the reefs which they had been instructed to

search. It was concluded that the charts were probably incorrect and, indeed, many years later the reefs were 'rediscovered' by cartographers.

The *Colorado* continued to search for the following five days, covering an area of more than 25,000 square miles. Every island of any size in the search area was visited: Endbury, Phoenix, Birnie, Sydney, McKean, Gardner, Canton and Hull, though only Hull Island was inhabited and the residents there had never heard of Amelia Earhart. The biggest problem the searchers felt Amelia might have, if she was down in the ocean, was sharks. The waters were so shark-infested that after a survey by the Royal Navy a year earlier they were considered unsafe for British commercial airliners to fly over and a proposed air route was abandoned.[11]

Gene Vidal claimed Amelia had told him that if she could not locate Howland she would turn back to the Gilbert Islands and consequently the Minesweeper USS *Swan* called on the Gilbert Islands and found the inhabitants highly excited by the unexpected contact from the outside world, but with no news of Amelia despite their having contacted all the larger islands in the group by radio. Some of the smaller islands in the archipelago lay up to 60 miles out but they were all eventually contacted without result.[12]

After the aircraft carrier *Lexington* arrived on station, sixty two of her aeroplanes covered an area of 151,556 square miles, and the *Lexington* was escorted by three new destroyers – the *Drayton*, *Lamson* and *Cushing* – who also participated in the meticulous search which eventually estimated to have covered more than a quarter of a million square miles of ocean.

Although the ships detailed from other duties took some days to arrive on the scene, the Coast Guard cutter *Itasca* spent seventeen days searching, from the first hours that Amelia was reported missing, and two British ships, the SS *Moorsby* and HMS *Achilles*, who were in the search area, also immediately joined in the search at the request of *Itasca*'s captain. The *New York Times* reported that the Japanese had detailed two vessels, the aircraft tender *Kamoie* and the survey ship *Koshu* to search the seas around the Marshall Islands some 600 miles to the north of Howland, and in all it was estimated that more than 4,000 men were involved.[13] Hopes were raised, briefly, by sight of what were taken to be green flares but these turned out to be meteorites or lightning;[14] a radio transmission was picked up by the British ship HMS *Achilles* on 3,105 which signed KHAQQ and said faintly, 'Give us a few dashes.' It was later decided that this probably emanated from *Itasca*. Another radio transmission was picked up by three radio operators on the naval station on Wailupe: '281 north Howland call KHAQQ beyond north don't hold with us much longer above water shut off.' Much later this was thought to be a hoax message that had originated in the Hawaiian Islands.[15] Even suspected hoax calls had to be investigated but, as Commander Thompson later pointed out, each time a hoax was investigated it pulled ships and planes away from the 'most likely quadrant', the area to the north-west of Howland. This area was searched thoroughly by *Itasca* during the day and night after Amelia's plane disappeared, however, and subsequently a much-extended area in that sector was searched during the following seventeen days, but it is doubtful whether the Electra would have still been afloat by that time.

As each new report was cabled to San Francisco by *Itasca* the transmissions were intercepted by wire services and Commander Thompson was inundated with lucrative offers for his 'unique story on Earhart rescue . . . and photographs' by newspaper editors anxious to scoop their competitors.

As the vast methodical search failed to turn up a single sighting, hope began to fade. At one point George was reported to have broken down in nervous collapse, but this brought forth a hasty denial:

I have not collapsed. I have indulged in no public sobbing. The nearest I have been to a hospital is the home of an old friend, Dr Ham Clay, who has lent me a helping hand. In the existing circumstances what is said about me is not of the least importance except that false reports heighten the anxiety of relations and friends. If I seem to have thrown in the sponge, it just makes it harder for them . . . if Amelia is dead it is the way she would have chosen.[16]

But despite his seeming rationality, George was now willing to try anything. His son David had flown to Oakland to join him while they awaited news, and remembers his father's desperation and the endless pacing of the floor at the Coast Guard radio station while George considered his next move.

Through Purdue's President Elliott came a cable from a correspondent suggesting that a position latitude 2 degrees, longitude 181 degrees should be searched. 'This position is 100 miles west of Howland,' the writer stated reasonably, and considering the much-publicised messages reported three days earlier by Wailupe naval station, it was too coincidental to be ignored. But when George requested that this position be searched he received a cable back from Admiral Leahy curtly advising him that it had already been thoroughly searched 'with negative results'.[17]

One apparently well-founded report emanated as the result of a radio listener who had tuned unknowingly into a popular radio programme called *March of Time* which 'dramatically simulated' the conversation between Amelia and the *Itasca*. The excited listener (an airport manager) immediately reported having heard Amelia and it was some time before it was realised what had happened.[18]

In her weekly newspaper column in the *New York Telegraph* on 7 July Eleanor Roosevelt noted her great anxiety over Amelia. 'I feel sure that if she comes through safely she will feel that what she has learned makes it all worth while. But her friends will wish science could be served without so much risk to a fine person whom many people love as a person and not as a pilot or adventurer.'[19]

President Roosevelt asked to be informed of the results of the search and on 20 July his secretary, Marvin H. McIntyre, sent the President an internal memo stating that Gene Vidal had been in close touch with the Amelia Earhart story, talking several times a day to George Putnam. 'He has some interesting sidelights and some speculations which are probably true as to what actually happened. You might find it interesting to spend 15 minutes with him,' he suggested. Roosevelt replied that he would be away until

26 July but would like to see Vidal for '5 or 10 minutes'.[20] In view of the suggestions that the President had an ulterior interest in the outcome of Amelia's flight, the archives reveal that he was prepared to devote a remarkably small amount of time to the matter.

A little later George wrote to McIntyre saying how much he appreciated the 'friendly personal co-operation which you have extended. Is there any way of ascertaining what the Japanese are actually doing – especially as regards a real search of the eastern fringe of the Marshall Islands? That is one of the most fruitful possible locations for wreckage.'[21]

Everyone was still working on the theory that the Electra would float and no attention was paid to Amelia's former radio mechanic Joe Gurr, who shyly voiced an opinion that the fuel tanks had vent openings in them 'through which the water could fill them in a certain length of time'.[22]

As the official search wound down George's own efforts grew more desperate. Though never allowing himself to become the victim of the more obvious crank messages that flooded in to him and to Amy, he did home in on some obscure possibilities. Shortly after Amelia's disappearance, for example, he recalled her 'telepathic' experience with Jackie Cochran a few months earlier.

According to Jackie's memoirs it was she and not Amelia who had located the missing airliners.[23] Further, she claimed, she had correctly 'seen Amelia and George having to land at Blackwell, Oklahoma in February (when George played the silly practical joke), and she had also been aware of the fire in Amelia's engine at Tucson on the first leg of her world flight, from Burbank to Miami. Shortly after Amelia went missing, Jackie related, George called on her at her Los Angeles apartment 'for the kind of help Amelia thought I might be able to give':

He was extremely excited . . . I told him where Amelia had gone down; that with the ditching of the plane Mr Noonan, the navigator, had fractured his skull against the bulkhead in the navigator's compartment and was unconscious; but that Amelia was alive and the plane was floating in a certain area. I named a boat called the *Itasca* which I had never heard of at the time, as a boat that was nearby, and I also named another Japanese fishing vessel in that area, the name of which I now forget. I begged Putnam to keep my name out of it but to get planes and ships out to the designated area. Navy planes and ships in abundance combed that area but found no trace. I followed the course of her drifting for days. It was always in the area being well combed.[24]

Three days later, Jackie claimed, she 'knew' Amelia had died.[25] This incident almost certainly lies behind George's intriguing cable to Daniel Roper, Secretary of Commerce:

Request your good offices in obtaining cooperation of British and Japanese in continuing search especially regarding Ellice, Gilbert and Marshall Islands, Ocean Island and area north-east of same. Also if possible request some of island northerly and north-westerly Pago Pago. Leave nothing undone looking toward securing information. Whatever it may be possible to do will be sincerely appreciated. For your confidential information extraordinary evidence seems to exist indicating castaway still living though of such strange nature cannot be official or publicly confirmed.[26]

Virtually the same message was despatched to the Secretary of the Navy and within days George offered a reward of $2,000 for information, and a guarantee to defray any costs involved in thorough searches of island groups such as the Gilberts.[27]

Estimates of the costs of the huge search were filtering into newspapers, which had been carrying the story on front pages, world-wide, for nearly a month. Indeed along with the Lindbergh baby kidnapping and the abdication of King Edward VIII to marry Wallis Simpson, the Earhart disappearance has long been regarded as one of the greatest news stories this century.

There was political criticism of the expenditure (estimated by newspapers at $4.5 million) involved in the search, but most people were able to accept that the ships and the men would have been engaged in some manoeuvre in any case. Besides, the search for

Amelia was not unique. Before Amelia's trans-Pacific solo in 1934 a similar search had been made in the Pacific for Captain Charles Ulm which occupied naval and Coast Guard ships and personnel for twenty-seven days. A spokesman for the navy told the *New York Times* that the opportunity to operate under service conditions over an important and little-known strategic area of the Pacific was an important by-product of the extensive search for Amelia.[28] Subsequently, Senator Davis, who formally raised the question of costs, was informed by letter that though the actual cost of fuel and oil involved in the search was $81,223.38[29] the expenditure was not merely philanthropic:

> The search made possible flights over islands and areas over which naval planes had never flown before, permitted a cursory survey of the area, which may help to correct charts and allowed a study of the weather and other operating conditions in a part of the Pacific which is becoming of increasing strategic importance.[30]

By now the administration felt they had done all they could regarding a purely civilian matter and George's continuous pressure for shifts of the scene of action were becoming an irritant. When, through the President's secretary, George asked if he was sure everything possible was still being done, the Secretary of State (Sumner Welles) wrote to McIntyre sending him the file of cables that they had sent to various missions.

> You will see from this file that we are doing everything we possibly can to be of help and I don't see that there is anything that you or I can say to him in reply to his letter, other than that you have seen the file of telegrams we have sent and are sure that we are doing everything we possibly can . . . The Japanese authorities have assured us that all fishing vessels have been told to keep on the lookout on the reefs and waters adjacent to the Marshall Islands. There isn't any way we can check up on what they are doing and we will have to take their word for it.[31]

On 18 July the search was officially abandoned by the ships in the Howland area and George, still desperately seeking any help he could muster, issued a press release from the National Geographic Society claiming that the search was incomplete. The Gilbert Islands, he said, had not been properly searched:

The Gilbert Islands are so far west that they mark where the east begins, they lie in the open Pacific just across the International date line, about 600 miles west of Howland Island and 1,600 miles south-west of Hawaii. Reason for searching so far from Miss Earhart's goal was the strong ocean current which swirls a titanic stream of the Pacific westward along the Equator in that area. The drift, aided by fairly constant trade winds, would carry a floating object westward from 10 to 40 miles a day. Natives have taken advantage of this current to make long oceanbound voyages in frail open canoes. There is a record of an 'involuntary' voyage of two natives whose boat was caught in the current and finally landed, three months later, 1,300 miles away.

The Gilbert Group consists of 16 coral islands festooned in a thin crescent across the equator . . . governed by Great Britain as part of the Crown Colony of Gilbert and Ellice Islands, of which the 200 square miles of dry land are scattered over a million square miles of high seas . . .[32]

'This release,' George was informed by the National Geographic Society, was 'circulated to 600 dailies and all press associations.'[33]

At the end of July, despite official opinion that Amelia had perished, George was still following up his own lines of enquiry. He flew to Washington, where he proceeded to badger anyone whom he could get to listen. To Amy, who was still staying in the Putnams' Hollywood home, he wrote, 'I am having conversations this afternoon with the White House and with many others. I find an extraordinary unanimous opinion that somehow, somewhere, Amelia is still alive. We are doing everything possible – at least we are trying to.'[34]

George's touching obsession with continuing the search is a

powerful argument about his emotional nature and his love for Amelia. No possibility was too obscure to warrant his interest. One of his requests was for the American Embassy in London to make a thorough search, at his expense:

> beginning at the following position: 174 degrees 10 minutes east longitude, 2 degrees 36 minutes north latitude. This is only 85 miles from Tarawa on Making Island bearing thence 106 degrees true. Mr Putnam believes he had authentic information that unchartered reef exists at that point and is regularly visited for turtles' eggs etc. by Gilbertese fishermen.[35]

But, one by one, George's leads came to nothing. 'I have the honour to inform you that the High Commissioner for the Western Pacific has reported that Captain Handley has returned after searching for Miss Amelia Earhart in the locality mentioned (174 deg. 10 mins east Long; 2 deg. 36 mins north Lat) . . . but that he found no trace of the reef referred to, or of Miss Earhart's plane.'[36] 'Foreign office advises that US vessels visited all Gilbert Islands.'[37] Finally all that was left for them to do was to forward to George the bills for expenses.[38]

The bills created their own problems for George because, to put it plainly, he had no money to meet them. 'For many years,' he was to explain later to Amy, he had been 'pouring my fullest energy and thoughtfulness and, largely, my income, into AE's activities and ambitions. And you know that the final tragedy and its aftermath involved me financially as much as, and even more than, the Estate. For which . . . I have no regrets. If we had to do it again. I'd spend everything I had again . . .'[39] He explained the position carefully on many occasions in an attempt to make Amy understand that the estate was not wealthy and that there was very little money after all debts had been settled.

> You must realize that she expected, properly, to make a great deal of money out of the results of the flight after her return. For instance she owned the ship entirely [Purdue had agreed to

present her with the Electra] which was worth $70,000 or more. Some of its purchase came from her and some from me, as well as the other larger contributors.[40]

George also told Amy later that during this period when he was coming to terms with Amelia's probable death he was '. . . knocked out and was no good to myself or anyone else,'[41] and this is borne out by friends. 'He was never the same man after Amelia disappeared, he changed a lot . . . became older, somehow . . .' was a typical comment.[42] But his pragmatism did not entirely desert him and he was able to recognise the opportunity to make some money for himself and Amelia's depleted estate immediately, by completing the book about the flight which had been commissioned before Amelia's departure by Harcourt, Brace & Co, the New York publishers.

One of the saddest experiences of these weeks had been the regular receipt of letters from Amelia, mailed from various stops along her route. Now he suggested to the publishers that he produce the book based on this 'informal log' of the flight which she had sent back to him. In fact it was mainly a compilation of her personal papers, articles she had written about her early years and her solo trans-Pacific and Mexican flights, added to the already published reports of the early stages of her flight which she had filed by cable with the *Herald Tribune* at her various stops. Her unpublished en-route world-flight jottings on less than fifty pages torn from a shorthand notepad were more aptly described as *aides-memoire* than pages of manuscript. However, George was fully aware that a book written (posthumously, as it were) by Amelia Earhart held more commercial interest than one written about her by someone else.

The book was retitled *Last Flight* and although George was insistent that it was entirely Amelia's own work, an examination of her notes and the finished product reveal that it owed a great deal to the hand of an editor. Amelia's 'log' in hard-to-read cramped scribble, made worse by the obvious vibration of the Electra, read, for example:

Caripito. Rain clouds hung around us this morning as we left. We flew low over the jungle most of the way to the coast then played hide and seek with rain storms until I decided I better give up watching the scenery and climb up on top of 8,000 feet topped all but highest. First big town Georgetown. Out at sea but could see neat fields along the coast . . . little clouds . . . white scrambled eggs.[43]

This became in *Last Flight*:

Rain clouds hung thick about Caripito as we left on the morning of June third. We flew over jungles to the coast and then played hide and seek with the showers until I decided I had better forgo the scenery, such as it was, and climb through the clouds into fair weather. An altitude of 8,000 feet topped all but the highest woolly pinnacles. In such a manoeuvre lies a recurrent delight of flying . . . now and then [the] sun illuminates mystic caves and roaring fortresses or shows giant cloud creatures mocking with lumpy paws the tiny man-made birds among them.[44]

To transcribe Amelia's notes and help with the physical production of the book, George recruited freelance journalist Janet Mabie. During the previous eight years Ms Mabie had written a number of articles about Amelia, and could be relied upon to give a favourable slant to any news story that George had wanted to 'break'. Later Ms Mabie was able to complain bitterly that she was never paid for the work she did on *Last Flight*, nor the syndicated articles that emanated from it,[45] but that George had merely advanced her the sum of $300, which she claimed was for 'expenses'. By October the manuscript was completed and though Ms Mabie claimed that she did most of the work it is equally clear from his correspondence that George, too, spent a great deal of time working on the project. Nor at the time did Janet Mabie dispute the title page:

LAST FLIGHT
by
Amelia Earhart
Arranged by George Palmer Putnam

But the matter was not to end there.

During the time that the book was being worked on, George was still seeking information, writing letters, and lobbying the administration for any proof of Amelia's fate. A life raft said to be similar to Amelia's was found off the Hawaiian coast and raised hopes again, briefly, until investigation proved it had originated elsewhere.[46] There was uncertainty about the type of life raft that the Electra actually carried but Margot De Carrie, George and Amelia's secretarial assistant, recalled that she had actually inflated it and tested it on Toluca Lake near the Putnams' Hollywood home. 'It wasn't very seaworthy,' she told reporters.

The US Coast Guard tracked down to hoaxers many of the calls purporting to come from Amelia.[47] A man who attempted to sell George 'information regarding Amelia's present whereabouts', using an old scarf of Amelia's as proof of his reliability, was traced and tried for attempted extortion. He was declared insane and committed to a mental hospital.[48]

By October George had concluded that Amelia was dead. He tried, tactfully, to convey this to Amy, who never really accepted that her daughter had perished, and only succeeded in upsetting the old lady. Muriel was more level-headed, recognising that if her sister had survived, they would have heard something in the intervening months. Under mounting pressure from creditors George filed a petition to be named trustee of Amelia's estate. This caused a flurry of letters between Amy and her mass of correspondents, many of whom were friends or casual contacts of Amelia's and with whom Amy kept in constant touch. To one, Benigua Green, who wrote protesting that George was 'giving up', he replied explaining patiently:

It became necessary for something definite to be done to simplify pending business matters. I did not choose to file her will or to take other similar steps that must come if and when we feel the chapter is definitely closed. Rather, on advice of counsel, I have sought to be appointed 'trustee for a missing person'. To date the law assumes AE is not dead but simply missing. In [her] absence a properly accredited representative is permitted by the court to conduct her business affairs. After an appropriate period if the missing person is not found then the will is probated, etc. So that is the situation I am sure you would like to know about it.[49]

In November 1937, *Last Flight* was published and though it never achieved the revenue George hoped for, it provided a regular income to the estate after the advance of $3,000 had been accounted for.[50] George included as an endpiece a note from Amelia to himself probably written prior to the first trans-Pacific flight:

Please know I am quite aware of the hazards . . .[51]

I want to do it because I want to do it. Women must try to do things as men have tried. When they fail their failure must be but a challenge to others.[52]

In December 1937 George joined an expedition to the Galapagos. He had a commission to produce an illustrated book and besides he had wanted to visit the islands ever since his first wife, Dorothy Binney, had gone there in 1922. He wrote affectionately to Amy, whom he had started to call 'Mother Earhart':

I could enjoy it all were the circumstances different. But naturally the thought keeps recurring how AE would have enjoyed it. And there are times the nightmare on the horizon blots out all else. At that I am glad I have broken away. It will do me much good. Already I am rested and sleeping well . . . But sometimes I feel that I am running away from something I should face at home. So . . . I am puzzled and far from happy, but there is nothing I can do about it. Mostly the days are filled with an effort to keep from thinking. The total emptiness is appalling.[53]

The expedition covered many weeks and it was spring before he returned. 'George', a friend was to tell me, 'was capable of the full gamut of emotions.'[54] His grief for Amelia was deep and real and not lessened by the fact that during those final weeks at sea he found solace in a relationship with Ione Reed, one of the women in the expedition. Given George's passionate nature it was hardly surprising that in the confined circumstances of the expedition he would succumb to a pretty and intelligent young woman who also found him extremely attractive. The two were discreet and the relationship continued for some months after their return but eventually it seems George found her company irritating and drove her off in a somewhat 'cruel' manner by deliberately provoking arguments and constantly finding fault.[55]

In George's absence many things had happened. A group of people headed by one Elmer Dimity (a parachute manufacturer who had known Amelia during the two years before her disappearance), with the approval of Amy, set up 'The Amelia Earhart Foundation'. It was a well-intentioned, though hopelessly inefficient organisation whose mission was to raise money to send a search/rescue expedition to the Pacific to discover whether Amelia was still alive, or if she was not, an explanation of the mystery.[56]

Dozens of organisations with whom Amelia had had connections (some extremely tenuous) erected memorials, others provided tributes in the form of scholarships and other honours, in Amelia's name. The ball that George had set rolling in 1928 had gathered speed by virtue of his publicity machine in the interim years, and now – as a result of the accident – it had acquired its own momentum which nothing and no one stop. It might be called the Amelia Earhart Legend.

George could not know the long-term effects on the public imagination of Amelia's disappearance, of course. All his energy was presently directed at trying to make a living. As he had told Amy, he had spent the previous two years working primarily on Amelia's behalf. Now, returned and rested after the South Atlantic trip, he took stock of his position. He was fifty-one years old, without a job and unable to use any of the assets in Amelia's estate, which –

though the net value did not amount to much – he had helped to create.

The fact that he was continuously referred to in the press as 'the "millionaire publisher" did not help much,' he told Amy, 'except to keep creditors happy.'[57]

Amy was one of George's major problems. The old lady was convinced – probably by the many sycophantic letters she received – that Amelia had left a substantial estate. Although the will at this stage had not been published, the nature of its contents was no secret: the bulk of Amelia's estate had been left to George (it had been assumed that Amy would predecease George), but the net income was to be used to support Amy during her lifetime. If George died before Amy, then everything would go to her and after her death to Muriel. At this time George was supporting Amy although he was recording the amounts he sent her and most of these were eventually properly offset against the estate.

During the summer of 1938 George began to make plans for his future. He set up a small publishing company of his own (George Palmer Putnam, Inc.) in leased offices at 6253 Hollywood Boulevard. Having secured an advance of $3,000 from Harcourt Brace he contacted Janet Mabie, announced that he was writing a biography of Amelia, and invited her to come to the house at Valley Spring Road and help him to write it. He would pay all expenses, he said, and though he could not give her a by-line he would formally acknowledge her help, and naturally would reach agreement on her remuneration. Ms Mabie was delighted and travelled from New York to California to begin work immediately, though in view of her subsequent claims that she had never been paid for the work she had done six months earlier on *Last Flight*, her alacrity in accepting this second commission seems peculiar.

There was a great deal of material: eighteen large scrapbooks crammed with news cuttings dating from Amelia's earlier days in aviation and hundreds of photographs, along with Amelia's own writings and George's recollections of events they had shared. Again, Ms Mabie would say that the entire work was hers, and indeed perhaps much of the compilation and typing was. But the many

surviving letters requesting information written by George to friends
and relatives of Amelia prove that he was not as detached from the
project as Janet Mabie was to attest.

'Dear Muriel,' (runs a typical letter from George)

> . . . forget the note I sent you the other day about the bronco. I
> found the verse.[58] Do you know the verse or rhyme or whatever
> it was that Amelia used to know concerned Simkin? [*sic*] I think
> Simkin was a cat. I have a hazy recollection that she was a pussy
> who wanted to drink her cream and have it too. Anyway at the
> beginning of our acquaintance AE called me Simkin and I find
> that in the code we set up for use in my messages to her at
> Trepassey I signed myself Simkin. If you can help me unravel that
> I will be grateful.[59]

From Muriel's reply came the following passage in the biography,
later published as *Soaring Wings*:

> When I'd known AE only a short time she began calling me
> 'Simpkin'.
> 'Why?' I asked her one day.
> It had, it seems, something to do with a book out of her child-
> hood reading. A tale of the Tailor of Gloucester who 'lived alone
> with his cat, which was called Simpkin'. Simpkin was a cat who
> believed that if holding one mouse in reserve against the danger
> of having time on one's hands – or paws – was wisdom, then
> holding a good number of mice in reserve . . . was even better. So
> Simpkin kept a flock – or whatever the grouping of mice is –
> always available by the simple expedient of housing them, one by
> one, under inverted teacups.[60]

George went on to explain how Amelia had seen the resemblance
in that although she was the centre of an important project just
then, in reality it was merely one of a group of enterprises in which
he was engaged. 'And so she privately called me Simpkin,' George
confided.

It was George who delved into Amelia's childhood and first discovered the often-told incidents such as her riding her sledge face-down as the boys did and, on one occasion, unable to stop, steering it straight between the fore and hind legs of a horse crossing her path as she careered downhill.

The end result was an interesting mosaic which has formed basic research for all subsequent biographies. 'Essentially informal and often unorderly', it further enhanced the heroic publicity-shy image of Amelia that George had striven to promote, with – it must be stressed – Amelia's full cooperation during her lifetime.

In September 1938 George told Amy in one of his regular letters that the book was almost completed and that he had 'been devoting almost all my time for the last couple of months to [it] . . . As I think you know Janet Mabie has been here for some time helping me . . .'[61] Following Amelia's disappearance the relationship between George and Amy had been much closer than previously, but over the next months it slowly disintegrated once George made it clear that he intended to try to establish proof of Amelia's death in order to have the will probated and to administer the estate in the manner in which Amelia had wished.

To establish the necessary proof for the court he wrote to Admiral Leahy,[62] who had commanded the search for Amelia, and through him obtained a sworn affidavit from Leigh Noyes, Captain of the USS *Lexington* on the scope and results of the search. It ended, 'No trace of either the Amelia Earhart plane or of its occupants was found.'[63]

One of the main contentions between George and Amy, however, was Amy's inability to accept that she must live on an income within the limits of Amelia's provisions for her, and that Amelia would not be there to bail her out whenever she got into financial difficulties as she had in the past. In addition she began to write tediously lengthy letters to George asking for this or that item belonging to Amelia to be sent to her; furs, coats, jewellery, small items of furniture or silver, etc.

Often these notes have an offensive tone and it is to George's credit that he remained courteous and helpful, never losing his patience at unwritten, but obvious innuendos that he was using the proceeds of the estate, and Amelia's property for his own enrichment. When Amelia's will was probated it was proven that George had acted properly and was simply stating the facts when he tried constantly to explain to Amy that there was no great fortune in Amelia's estate:

> It is also true, as I mentioned before, that the Estate owes some considerable bills. Unless some good luck comes over the hill for me during the next year, which would make it possible for me to absorb some of these charges, there will be precious little left of the Estate. Which is a situation we might as well all face . . . It has been my own suggestion from the first that, irrespective of the condition of the Estate, I elect to do what I can to care for your future and to help Muriel . . . Despite your unhappiness because things have not always been done just as you would like them, the facts I think demonstrate that I have done as much as I possibly can to be more than fair and considerate.[64]

Armed with the necessary statements from Richard B. Black and Captain Leigh Noyes (of the USS *Lexington*), and in the company of his employee, writer Charles 'Cap' Palmer, George went to Los Angeles city hall to file evidence – all, it seemed likely, that there ever would be – of Amelia's death. It was accepted by the court and the will was duly probated.

In essence, Amelia left all her household furniture, clothing and personal effects and jewellery to George. In addition, 'all the rest, residue and remainder of my estate, of whatever kind and nature . . . I give devise and bequeath to my [sole] trustee (George Palmer Putnam) in trust . . .' George was to administer the estate and, 'during the lifetime of Amy Otis Earhart, to pay over and distribute to her in quarterly or monthly instalments as she may elect, the net income therefrom . . . Upon her death, or if she shall predecease me, then upon my death to transfer or pay over the principal of the said trust to my husband George Palmer Putnam outright.' In the event of George predeceasing Amy then the estate would eventually be paid over to Muriel or her surviving issue.[65]

Eventually, receipts over the next few years would bring the actual gross value of the estate to $59,109[66] but authorised disbursements (every one meticulously receipted by George), for outstanding bills connected with the round-the-world flight, mortgage payments on the Valley Spring Lane property, Amy's upkeep and medical bills (over $7,000)[67] and sundry other items of expenditure such as taxes and property expenses, amounted to $45,329 leaving a net balance of only $13,780.

What is not generally known is that George had to sell his Rye home at this point, in order to remain solvent.[68] It is not generally known because George never talked of it. As he saw it, along with Amelia, he had gambled and lost. But the money was never important considering the greater loss of his wife and friend.

Almost unfailingly George wrote to Amy, often several times a month, telling her that she must keep her expenditure under control, that the estate could not help her if she overspent, that anything in excess of $125 a month (a frequent occurrence) came from his pocket which, though he didn't begrudge it, he couldn't afford it indefinitely.

George's reward for this has been a spate of accusations by Amelia's biographers implying that in some way he defrauded Amy and the estate. In fact his behaviour was exemplary in this respect, as can be seen by the estate records and his letters to Amy. Far from defrauding her, he had been considerably more generous to her than the estate's assets warranted.

Amy's distrust of George was continuously bolstered by her correspondents; she wrote up to fifty letters a week and was often uncomplimentary about him, claiming that he kept her short of money and that she was having to economise by going without food. Her monthly allowance was a reasonable sum in those Depression days and, as George told Amy, should be perfectly adequate if she would only plan her expenditure; 'a great many older people are living very pleasantly indeed on $125 a month . . . I cannot let you plunge blindly . . . just in the expectation that the Lord will provide. Because just now the Lord looks pretty poverty stricken!' Often these strictures ended with him sending some little item such as a trinket of Amelia's to soften his words, or a personal gift: 'Because I don't doubt that you are having extra financial difficulties just now I am enclosing herewith an additional check for $50.'[69]

George never managed to get through to Amy a realisation of the facts and it seems she went to her grave (long after George's own death) feeling that he had taken advantage of her. An examination of the letters she received from her friends shows a possible reason: 'Well as you once said, he is a poor lost creature. He was badly brought up and he has been spoilt all his life.' 'As for GP having to sell AE's things . . . words fail me. He should be willing to starve first.' 'I can't say it surprises me because nothing he does surprises me any more. But it does seem too bad. The thing that keeps recurring to me is how mortified AE would be that he could so poorly and ungraciously carry out what would be her normal wishes. I am afraid that she would be desperately ashamed . . . because she did have such good taste.'[70] Others told her George had 'no right to keep her short of the money which rightly belonged to her'. 'It is simply a matter of record . . .' one said, 'the estate is worth nearly $60,000.' Amy should tell him so!

In this particular matter, a protagonist was Janet Mabie, who had now fallen out with George over the biography *Soaring Wings*, and from whose pen dripped a ceaseless stream of vitriol aimed at him. It may be that she was justified to a greater or lesser extent, but the damage she did to the already tenuous relationship between George and Amy was enormous. She claimed that George had thrown her out of the house after a violent quarrel and had subsequently refused to pay her anything, stating that he had had to rewrite all her work.

This, she told Amy, was quite incorrect for she had read the book and 85 per cent of the finished work was exactly as she wrote it,

in exchange for my temerity to question his financial treatment of me he *removed* an acknowledgement of my work from the foreword. I never saw it but had been told it was 'beautiful'. But – he took it out before publication. I am not surprised but I am contemptuous.[71]

Each letter to Amy suggested that Ms Mabie should ghost-write a book about Amelia in collaboration with Amy, but to do this she needed Amelia's papers (those that had survived the fire at Rye), and the scrapbooks. Could Amy get them from George, she wondered, or could Amy persuade George to donate them to a foundation such as Purdue, where Ms Mabie could gain access without having to approach George?

It is more than probable that George treated Janet Mabie badly; a number of people such as Elinor Smith and Lady (Mary) Heath had similar tales to tell, and anyone unlucky enough to have George as an enemy was unfortunate indeed. But the reverse is equally true and there are many people who knew from George only generosity of spirit, although even his closest friends marvelled at his ability to explode in a most spectacular manner. But he remained impressive in the scope of his vision; 'George dared,' one friend said. 'He had power, knew, used it and enjoyed it. If George had been on the bridge of the *Titanic*, the iceberg wouldn't have had the gall to collide with him. Or if it had, George would have sunk the iceberg!'[72]

By now George had produced the first books under his own imprint 'G. P. Putnam'.[73] He continued to publish his own writing, however, through Harcourt Brace and this now included plans for his autobiography. The offices on Hollywood Boulevard were too big for George and Cap Palmer (whom George employed on an ad-hoc basis as ghost writer/editor/freelance writer). He therefore sublet part of his offices which 'were upstairs, over a tea room' which George promptly dubbed Menopause Manor. 'He had a great flair for attracting gifted people,' Cap Palmer recalled. 'And he got young talent who later made it big.' Pereira and Luckman, leading Californian architects, were just starting and they took space; further space was let to two young writers, Jerome Lawrence[74] and Robert E. Lee,[75] who were collectively referred to by George as 'the boys'.

Bob Lee recalls George during those days when he was trying to reestablish his life and career:

> It must have been a strange marriage; [although Lee never met Amelia] the world's most famous aviatrix and the iconoclastic publisher-explorer who loved the entire planet but had a short-fused impatience about most of the people who lived on it . . .
>
> Unquestionably, George was enormously attracted to women; a trim but husky hulk of a man, handsome, irascible, sly, opinionated, a total stranger to fear, gifted (or cursed) with a vinegar wit, the champion of raw charm. Though George and Amelia had exchanged some endearing letters I suspect it was something less than a marriage made in heaven, [but] . . . I know she was much in his mind.[76]

There was another reason, aside from the obvious need to regularise the administration of the estate, why George now needed to have Amelia declared legally dead. In the autumn of 1938 he had met Jean-Marie Cosigny James and from the start 'was strongly drawn to her'.

'GPP was never a loner,' Bob Lee stated, 'a wife was a lunar presence in his life. He could endure, temporarily, the dark of the moon, but he needed a feminine satellite to orbit his activity and tug at his emotional tides.'[77]

Jean-Marie was in the process of divorcing her husband William James, a Los Angeles attorney. She was extremely pretty, bright and amusing and good company. At that time, it was fashionable, among Beverly Hills housewives, to hold 'rather smart parties, *salons*, at which a guest speaker would attend. Often it would be a movie star or sometimes a writer, but always someone well known.'[78] Jean-Marie was on the salon circuit and always enjoyed them but particularly remembers one at which she arrived late. She had been working in her garden and had forgotten the time.

> When I arrived at my friend's house I was greeted with the words 'Hush! He's already started.'

I had no idea who the speaker was but as I walked in through the hall there was George Putnam speaking. He looked up at me, and looked, and looked. I was very conscious of his gaze but I found a seat and sat down and later, after he'd finished speaking he came over and said to me, without any preamble 'I'm going to marry you.'

He was so tall and so good looking that I was devastated. I loved him at first sight . . . he was alert and sharp and full of ideas, and though he was twenty-four years older than me he was always much *peppier*.

On the next occasion that we met, over dinner, he suggested that I should go over to see his house. I was very reluctant, and said I really couldn't think of going to a man's house alone. He roared with laughter. 'You must be kidding!' he said. 'You ought to see how many people live with me!'[79]

She soon found out what George was talking about. Usually he had his secretary, Jo Berger, and the Filipino house-boy, Fred, in residence. But the house was always filled with visitors, writers whom he was 'encouraging, who were invited to come and stay while they worked on a book; friends from back east . . .. he knew so many people.'

It did not take George long to obtain a consent to his proposal and Jeannie (as George quickly came to call her) broke the news to her disapproving family, while George told Amy and Muriel. Amy was incredulous; it was only a little over a year since Amelia had disappeared and she – at least – was convinced her daughter was still alive and would be found. Muriel was more sympathetic; she agreed with George that her sister had almost certainly perished within a very short time of her disappearance.[80]

At first Amy was wary in her meetings with Jeannie but this gradually became a tolerance of Jeannie and a condemnation of George. While never openly stating her feelings, Amy made it clear in many small ways that she held George indirectly responsible for Amelia's disappearance and, since his engagement, for his abandonment of Amelia. But Jeannie explained:

His feeling were never shallow – not for any of his wives – there was nothing superficial about him at all. But he couldn't stand not being married, not having a companion; he needed that background in his very busy life.

George and Jeannie had to wait for the various legal processes to formalise her divorce, and to free him by declaring Amelia dead. Under normal circumstances it took seven years before a missing person could be assumed legally dead. But George's attorneys argued that this was a special case. The entire world had witnessed the massive search for Amelia and detailed iron-clad testimony from senior naval officers was available to the court. Richard Black, Amelia's on-the-spot representative at Howland, ended his comprehensive statement on the entire flight and search with the sombre words: 'It is my belief and opinion that Amelia Earhart died on or about 2 July 1937.' The well-documented air/sea search, letters from inhabitants of island groups, and proof of George's own enquiries, subsequent to the official search, all led to an inevitable conclusion. On 5 January 1939 Amelia was declared legally dead.[81] Jeannie's divorce would not become final until 18 May.

Amy's letters to her former son-in-law now took on a bitter tone, and it is probable that she never forgave George for abandoning hope of Amelia's survival. In April she wrote from Berkeley, California, where she was living, as a temporary measure, in the Berkeley Women's City Club, telling him that she really *could not* live on the $125 a month that 'he allowed her'. She needed an increase, she said, and this ought to be possible as the entire income from the estate was legally hers. She gave details of a house she wished to rent, implying she felt it unfair that he should continue to live in Amelia's Spring Valley Lane property, and she enclosed a list of items left by Amelia that had special associations for her, and which she would like to have.

George wrote a long, patient reply saying that Amy's letter had troubled him greatly:

I do want to impress upon you that you have had, in the last year and a half, a great deal more than the 'income' from the Estate. Unfortunately I am not able to face more out of my own pocket . . .[82]

George explained how much was owed against the principal sum and that he paid the estate a fair rental for his occupancy of the property; he further went on to suggest how Amy should work out her monthly budget. Perhaps she should consider sharing a house with someone, he ventured. Amelia's papers, medals and certain books were being presented to Purdue University and some to the Women's Archives in New York. He would send most of the things she asked for, and though some of the hangings she had listed were 'always my own' he would let her have a couple; but he intended to sell the rest to realise some money on them if he could.

Perhaps you have some notion that I am embarking upon personal extravagances and extra expenditure in connection with my forthcoming marriage. While that is an intimate situation which concerns only myself, the fact is that the new set-up should involve some decrease in my own costs. I will continue to live as simply as I have in the past . . . Perhaps the comfort of companionship will not only make life more happily liveable, but also enlarge my earning abilities.[83]

He finished on a note of 'cheerful' news in a postscript that he had been approached regarding a 'possible sale of a motion picture based on the life of AE'.

Despite the seemingly lavish life-style at the Hollywood house with a full-time secretary, a house-boy, dinner parties for contacts whom George wished to influence, not to mention a constant stream of visitors and would-be writers, Cap Palmer remembers how financially tight things were for George at this time. To maintain credibility George was using the capital from the sale of his Rye house to bolster his image of success. But he needed to

earn enough money to live on, and when George suggested a
publicity stunt to promote a new book based on a success he'd
had many years earlier, Cap was frankly sceptical. 'No one will
ever fall for that!' he told George.[84]

George had published a novel called *The Man who Killed Hitler*.
European politics in the spring of 1939 gave the book a big potential
market and George felt that he could improve sales tremendously
with the assistance of a little media attention. Therefore in April he
informed the Los Angeles District Attorney's office that he had
received an anonymous letter threatening his life unless he halted
publication. A letter, written in German, appeared the following
night in many newspapers.

> If you have any regard for your future safety, stop publication of
> this book at once. The arm of Greater Germany reaches far and
> we have no desire to continue warning you. If you are wise you
> will do what we tell you because anything can happen to you and
> your future may be extinguished.[85]

George stated in interviews that the author of the novel, which
had gone on sale a week earlier, wished to remain anonymous. Also
that he (George) wasn't much worried about the threat.

Three weeks later (after several more letters, a threatening telephone call, and a bullet-riddled copy of the book had been received
by George's publishing firm, and after George had fired two shots
at a man climbing a tree outside his bedroom window), on Friday
13 May George got what he wanted – or almost. Headlines ran:
PUTNAM KIDNAPPED. 'Anti Hitler book seen as link.' George had
been discovered, bound and gagged, but otherwise unharmed, in a
partially built house near Bakersfield, California some hours after his
staff reported him missing.[86]

It was very similar to the 'Fascist plot' stunt George had pulled
off in 1929 but this time it misfired. Few people believed it and
some newspapers, scenting a ploy, openly voiced their suspicion.
Little action was taken by the authorities although George may
have been warned not to waste police time. No fool, George quickly

realised that he hadn't quite pulled it off but had no option than to bluff his way out. In a letter to Amy two days later he said sheepishly:

> As to myself, I look all right. It wasn't a pleasant experience and took a good deal out of me, but there was no physical harm done. I have had a pretty good rest over Sunday and am feeling nearly back to normal again . . . Next weekend . . . it might not be a bad idea for you to be unavailable . . . on the offchance that newspapers should seek some comment from you . . .[87]

Next weekend (on 21 May 1939) George married Jeannie in Boulder City, Nevada.

CHAPTER 22

1939–1950

Initially the marriage was a very happy one, and though George was concerned about his personal finances, especially the loss of income from some European investments due to the political situation, he felt he had made a new start. Encouraged by Amy, though, Jeannie 'was never really sure, in the early days, that Amelia was dead':

> I always thought there was a real possibility that she was still alive and might come walking in the door one morning. GP had no doubts, though he rarely talked about her – or Dorothy – but I knew he missed her very much.
>
> Fred, the houseboy, talked to me about AE a lot. I remember him telling me that just before she left on that final trip she took him to one side and said to him very carefully: 'Fred, I want you to take very good care of Mr Putnam.' Fred said he never forgot the manner in which she said this and he more or less regarded it as a sacred trust.
>
> We were very happy. George loved to give parties and Fred was marvellous, always knowing just what was needed. We always had lots of famous people there and it was very exciting. I remember Stokowski was a frequent visitor when he was dating Garbo – though she never came and of course we never mentioned her.
>
> Most of his income came from speaking tours and he was in great demand and away from home quite a lot. He used to have

the audience in the palm of his hand and was sometimes so funny that they would be in stitches.[1]

It was not always easy being married to George. He was still a great practical joker and Jeannie felt that some of his japes were 'rather cruel on the subject'. Jeannie, sweet-tempered and a little shy, was overawed by George's volatile disposition:

> I loved him very much but he had a terrible temper. It would just erupt and he would bellow at the top of his voice, not over big things, just some little incident that might irritate him. I remember we once had a new gardener and GP couldn't stand him from the moment we saw him, so whenever this man worked in the garden GP was unhappy. Once when he was working outside GP's study window the poor man did something, pruned a twig or some-thing . . . GP was up like a shot roaring at the top of his voice. 'Stop that you son of a bitch . . . !' Afterwards it was all forgotten – it was all bluster and noise really – but he was very impatient.
>
> If his secretary wasn't around to organize him he would just stuff all the papers he could find on his desk into a briefcase and rush off – of course he never had the correct papers when he got to where he was going. But he had an absolute knack of keeping people happy working for him. His staff loved him and were very loyal to him.[2]

George was still harassed by Amy's letters because the estate had still not, at that time, been probated. In addition 'The Amelia Earhart Foundation' was causing him concern with a flush of publicity releases aimed at fund-raising. Claiming that it had the support of President Roosevelt, Amelia's family, Paul Mantz and other connections of Amelia's, the Foundation announced a two-year search of the Pacific by the crew of an ocean-going yacht which would include Margot De Carrie, 'Amelia Earhart's per-sonal secretary'. Paul Mantz wrote immediately disassociating himself because although he 'wished to see the mystery solved it would be embarrassing to be misunderstood'.[3]

George, who had been questioned by reporters after the news releases, was more direct in his letter to the Foundation's principal, Elmer Dimity:

... As you realize, I know nothing. I have never been informed what money has been raised, nor what accounting, if any, has been made. I do not know who is associated with the project (except as it comes to me indirectly) nor what the plans are . . . I do find a great deal of publicity coming up hither and yon that Margot De Carrie was AE's secretary. You and AE's mother know that Margot, a very sweet and loyal girl, was never AE's secretary. She worked here at odd jobs and we graced her with that title to make things easier . . .[4]

After warning Dimity to keep all transactions 'within the bounds of careful business exactness', George wrote to Amy telling her, too, to be extremely careful. The name 'Amelia Earhart Foundation' was already in use by Purdue University, he reminded her; 'Naturally I must protect those who did so much for AE from any embarrassment. I do suggest you discuss this matter with Mr Dimity and see that I am equipped with a statement of facts . . .'[5]

Amy's reply was unpleasant despite George's carefully worded return letter explaining why the estate could not sanction the organization, 'especially in view of Paul Mantz's involvement'.[6] The estate had a claim against Mantz for the value of half the business in which he and Amelia had been partners, but there was a signed contract[7] which gave a surviving partner the entire business should one of them die, so the estate lost its claim. George thought this 'very unfair' and openly doubted that Amelia could have known what she was signing. George and Paul Mantz, never friends but tolerant of each other during Amelia's life-time, now became enemies.

To George's other sins was now added the charge by Amy that he really didn't want Amelia found, and surviving correspondence reveals Amy busily recruiting champions to her cause in the form of Paul Mantz and Dimity, by telling them how badly she was treated by George. Dimity wrote, 'I personally feel that the estate was left for your benefit and regardless of what anyone thinks proper you should have a sufficient amount monthly to live decently and without worry.'[8] Paul Mantz, on hearing that Amy was in dire straights immediately offered to make her a loan but after learning how much Amy was receiving from George, he rescinded his offer.[9] Dimity sent small amounts to Amy to bail her out of various small financial embarrassments; these were never repaid and it is clear that Amy was simply not able to manage money, which Amelia and George had always known.

But despite George's misgivings the foundation did organise a search of sorts. The skipper of the yacht *Yankee of Gloucester* diverted from a world cruise and at the Foundation's commission spent four weeks sailing around the Gilbert and Ellice Islands (which according to Navy Archives had already been thoroughly searched). A letter from the yacht's captain to Elmer Dimity stated that the results of the expedition were negligible, only one new point emerging: that Amelia's plane had been heard passing over the island of Tabiteuea during the night of 2 July. This statement places the Electra almost directly on its great-circle course from Lae to Howland. Captain Irving concluded, 'It is my opinion and that of all those with whom I have talked in this area that the search be considered finished and that everything humanly possible has been done to find any trace of Miss Earhart.'[10]

Unfortunately the money raised by the foundation had been spent on administration and publicity and Captain Irving's bill had to be paid by a member of the foundation who 'loaned' the sum of $1,800 for the expedition, an amount which was never repaid.[11] George's caution about the organisation was proven well-founded, although it must be stressed that its failure to perform was due to nothing more sinister than poor management; possibly George's open opposition may have also had a direct bearing on its failure to attract donations. But Dimity, who came to be known as 'Dilly-Dally Dimity' to his fellow members, was simply not capable of running the foundation that he had been instrumental in creating and it was wound up owing some $2,000.[12]

Since her disappearance there had been much correspondence

regarding the making of a film about Amelia. George worked on proposals from the film director Gabriel Pascal, and had set Cap Palmer to work drafting a screen treatment entitled: *For Woman, the World*. Amy meanwhile was approached by William C. Hollister, who proposed a film in which Amy and Muriel would play themselves. In a series of letters he offered Amy various sums for screen rights to Amelia's story, but 'not less than $15,000'. Katharine Hepburn, he said, would play Amelia.[13]

This must have seemed a tempting proposition to Amy; $15,000 *and* the opportunity to have Amelia portrayed as Amy felt she *ought* to be depicted:

Please do not think me mercenary [Amy wrote naively to Hollister]. To make the fitting memorial that you plan for my beloved daughter, I would do everything in my power gladly and willingly without money and without price, but there are other considerations – plans my daughter had for others dear to her . . . because of the deep love and understanding between us I wish to do these things. The way the Estate has been managed leaves me with very little and utterly impossible to carry out her wishes without something outside my small income.

. . . I have no specific information but believe we will find Mr Putnam has reserved rights to everything he might consider worth while, for my younger daughter and myself have thought only of our great loss, not what profit could be made from her dear name. For the sake of all of us I have kept as close as I could to Mr Putnam and have tried to be as near as possible to what he still calls me – Mother – though he is a difficult person to deal with . . .

. . . If our negotiations prove fruitful I shall have to have my attorney present . . . to protect me from Mr Putnam's plans of representing me which would mean his advantage would be first – he doesn't seem able to do differently . . . though he is kind in many ways.[14]

When George's discussion with Pascal came to nothing he contacted Hollister at Amy's request, only to find no substance to the proposals.

That spring George was distressed and unsettled when Jo Berger, the efficient and loyal secretary he had shared with Amelia for many years, died of cancer.[15] His financial situation had not greatly improved and his income from his lecture tours and publishing business was hardly keeping pace with his life-style, but he refused to reduce his standards.

Since Amelia's disappearance George had paid rent to the estate for the Spring Valley House. Now he decided it would be financially advantageous to rent the house to a tenant and buy a home of his own, somewhere out of town; preferably a cabin in the mountains where he would find the personal contentment he always felt in wild country but also where they could live more economically than in Hollywood. His business interests could be maintained by renting an apartment when he needed to be in Los Angeles. In due course the Spring Valley Lane house was let by the estate to the actor Eddie Albert, and George and Jeannie found their new home in Lone Pine, California, high in the Sierra Nevada mountains.

The couple had made vacation trips out of their searches through Tahoe, Oregon, San Jacinto, Carmel, Arizona and Yosemite. At every stop they enquired at gas stations, motels and coffee shops if anyone knew of a suitable cabin – or even an ideal place to build one. 'We . . . chased many rainbows, with disappointments at the end of them,' George recorded, but at last in the small town of Lone Pine in the Owens Valley they heard about a unique stone lodge at Whitney Portal. It had been built for a much-loved priest of the small community, but he had been killed in an automobile before he could take up residence.[16]

Thirty days after seeing the lodge, George owned it. The Putnam's new home nestled among huge boulders at an elevation of over 8,000 feet with a stunning view of Mt Whitney (highest peak in the continental United States) from its huge windows. Totally isolated, it was twelve miles and a 4,000 foot climb from Lone Pine, the nearest township. Hearing that Roosevelt had just named his house at Camp David Shangri-la, George decided to call the lodge Shangri-Putnam.[17]

The time they were able to spend in Shangri-Putnam was idyllic if short. George used it to write his autobiography, which he did 'in a very slapdash way at first . . .' Cap Palmer said. 'Having sold the idea and taken an advance from Duell Pierce and Sloane he simply pulled out a load of letters, files and articles and pasted them together. Then he gave them to me saying, "I want you to tell me honestly how great this is":

> Well, it was awful; and I told him it was a collection of junk, not a piece of writing at all. He'd had it typed into a manuscript and that was all. He screamed at me that I was Johnny-come-lately and what did I know about writing; then sent it off to Sam Sloane. When it was returned he screamed again. 'Damn it! What does Sam Sloane know about the book business.'
>
> Well, he had to do something because he'd spent the advance and he was a realist. Eventually he calmed down and I got him to take a look at it as if it were an unsolicited manuscript that had been sent to him for evaluation. After he'd read it he returned to me and said 'Damn it! It *is* junk!' and he got to work on it again.
>
> Occasionally I'd wander in and remind him of some incident or anecdote that he'd told me about and he'd say 'Didn't I have that in the book?' Each day George would write and I would edit and so the book was finally completed. Of course it was typical of him that it was mainly a collection of stories about other people – I've always said it ought to have been called *Autobiography about Other People..*
>
> He was a publicity hound but he never cared about publicity for *himself* – it was always for some project he was pushing, or some person he was promoting.[18]

George and Jeannie were staying in Los Angeles in the first week of December 1941. George had finished and delivered his manuscript that week and was concentrating on trying, yet again, to promote a film of Amelia. On Sunday the 7th they were to have lunch at Danny Kaye's house in Malibu. On the way there they stopped at some friends' for a drink; 'It was just a normal leisurely Sunday' said Jeannie:

> When we got there our friend came rushing out with shaving foam still over half his face. 'Have you heard?' he said.
>
> 'Heard what?' We hadn't had the car radio on, but apparently news had just broken about Pearl Harbor.
>
> Later we all walked on the beach and talked about what might happen and GP said to me: 'I'll call Roosevelt tonight.'[19]

As a result of his talk with Roosevelt George was offered a job in the Pentagon with the rank of colonel, but that didn't suit his plans at all. 'He didn't want a faceless job behind a desk', his son David told me. 'He wanted to *do* something.'[20] Cap Palmer agreed: 'He didn't want to leave Jeannie but he just was constitutionally *not able* to stand by and not get involved.' It took George about two weeks to organise matters the way he wanted them and then he went home to Jeannie and told her he'd enlisted. Within a short time he was wearing a captain's uniform.

George was still working at promoting a movie about Amelia. All his efforts, which revolved around Cap Palmer's screen treatment (based on a story by George called 'Lady with Wings: the life story of my wife, Amelia Earhart'), failed to come to fruition.[21] At one point Howard Hughes had been interested, in order to provide a vehicle for Katharine Hepburn, and there were various other syndicates interested but one by one the proposals disintegrated.

In the spring of 1942 RKO accepted a screenplay from scriptwriter Horace McCoy[22] entitled *Stand by to Die*. He had written it after speaking to one of the amateur radio operators who claimed to have heard Amelia's radio signals after she had officially disappeared. Although essentially a piece of fiction, the story contained elements which were directly based on some of Amelia's experiences (even the plane used for round-the-world flight scenes was a Lockheed Electra, though a smaller and later model than Amelia's), and very sensibly the studio made an offer to the Earhart estate for rights to certain parts of Amelia's story.

While George was unhappy that his own biographical treatment had been superseded by this highly fictionalised story, he was practical enough to realise that it was better for the estate to accept a reasonable sum ($7,500) than hold out indefinitely on the offchance that some day a film based on his work might be made. Besides, he reasoned, such a film might reawaken interest in Amelia, and enable a biographical motion picture to be made at a later date.

He signed on behalf of the estate, approving the original movie treatment but stipulating that any too-obvious resemblance to Amelia must be avoided. The movie was eventually released under the title *Flight for Freedom*, starring Rosalind Russell and Fred MacMurray and was the story of a 1930s aviatrix whose ambition was to fly around the world at the equator.

The film's heroine, Toni Carter, having completed the first leg of her flight, was about to take off on the second leg of the trip from Hawaii to Howland Island when she received a call from government officials in Washington, DC asking if she would take part in a secret mission under cover of her much-publicised world flight. Accordingly she deliberately crashed the plane on take-off, thus allowing time for the necessary preparations.

Subsequently, the plot called for her to fly by the same 'reverse' route as Amelia, land secretly on a small island in the Pacific and pretend to be 'lost', thereby enabling a huge air/sea search to take place which would allow Americans to overfly Japanese-mandated territory to ascertain what fortifications had been built.

The movie 'shocked' George for it showed the heroine madly in love with the man chosen by the navy to be her navigator. In view of the rumours that had circulated while Amelia had been on her last flight George felt the film hinted that Amelia had been in love with Fred Noonan. He sued RKO but settled out of court for a sum of $2,500. He made no public comment about the publicity for the movie, which included poster banners proclaiming 'The story they couldn't tell before Pearl Harbor' and 'Did Woman Flier Strike First Blow at Japs?'[23]

Pre-empting the movie's release, however, was an article written by George's friend and colleague, Charles 'Cap' Palmer, that appeared in the magazine *Skyways* under the title 'The War's First Casualty?' It referred to 'rumours that Amelia may have been on a government mission and had been captured by the Japanese'. The article reached no conclusion but it is now clear that this article was the first of the *genre* that might be called 'The Earhart Mystery', which is still very much alive and flourishing.[24]

Recently it has been suggested that this article was a publicity stunt organised by George to promote the film or a book, or alternatively – since 'Cap' was George's house writer – that it proves George knew something he could not tell the world more openly. But Cap Palmer denies this. Questioned for this book he stated that 'it was definitely not a promotion ploy':

> The suspicion that the Navy went to extraordinary effort and expense to 'search' for AE as a cover for getting cameras over the forbidden area was *ours* – *GP's* and mine – we had not the slightest hard information pointing to it.
>
> But the carrier *Lexington* left San Diego amazingly soon after the 'down' message, which led to the logical guess that the planes were loaded with cameras rather than rubber boats, and the motives were practical rather than humanitarian – especially since the *Lexington* couldn't possibly reach the site until days after AE and Noonan were certainly dead – with the Japanese knowing that world opinion would clobber them if they interfered with the 'rescue' attempt.
>
> The success of our Navy bombers later on indicated success of the mission/gamble. It may be that AE served her country wonderfully well . . . but there was never the faintest doubt in GP's mind that AE died within a few miles of Howland and the *Itasca*.[25]

The film was released at a time when almost everyone attended the cinema at least once a week, and many people came to believe that the film was based on fact, hence the growth of the Earhart Legend and the general willingness to accept sensational and outrageous theories. It is also possible that Amy came to believe this myth too, for in 1949 she implied as much at a press conference. Examination of her personal correspondence, however, makes it clear that she came to this conclusion only after the release of the film.[26]

It was some months before George was called to active duty for the service chiefs had a problem deciding what to do with this mid-fifty-year-old 'retread' (as he called himself), with his impressive connections. It was proposed that George, with his experience of arctic conditions, be posted to the north Atlantic, but eventually – after he reminded the army that he was still waiting for orders – he was instructed to report to the Army Air Force Officer Training School in Miami Beach, Florida.[27] After successfully completing the training courses where he was 'old enough to be the father of every man in his class'[28] he was transferred to the Air Intelligence School in Harrisburg, Pennsylvania. When he left there, with a commendation, his CO wrote:

> It is with much regret that I learn of your transfer from my command and it is desired to express officially and personally appreciation of your superior performance here at the Army Air Forces Air Intelligence School. Your work and accomplishments here . . . have been an inspiration to other officers working with you.[29]

The commendation earned George a promotion to major, a rank he treasured because of his boyhood affection for his uncle who had been known simply as 'The Major': George never sought further promotion.[30] In a letter to one of his many correspondents he explained his role in the war:

> 468th Bombardment Group
> Smoky Hill Army Airfield
> Salina, Kansas

> Dear Joe [Joseph Henry Jackson]
> . . . I have been with a combat unit here getting the big new secret bombers ready to take a hand in what goes on overseas.

The time is getting fairly close I imagine, when we will be shoving off.

I'm intelligence officer for a group of four squadrons and enjoy my rugged job immensely. Indeed I'm tickled no end to be with a gang like this, with plenty of geography and, likely, of adventure before us . . .[31]

At about the time of this letter George went home to California on leave. During the time he had been in the Army his marriage to Jeannie suffered irreversibly and to his dismay she told him she wanted a divorce. Jeannie, a dedicated Christian Scientist, was a gentle creature and felt she could no longer tolerate living in the eye of the hurricane with George, though she still professed to love him. 'I always loved him . . . I've never stopped loving him,' she said in June 1988. 'I should never have divorced him.'[32]

George returned to Salina confused and upset. Shortly afterwards Bob Lee telephoned him to ask if there was any news on a book he had written which George was attempting to have published. George was simply told it was a call from Hollywood, Lee recalled:

I don't think I merely imagined the sound of sinking disappointment when my voice came on the line. He thought it might be Jeannie calling him. I didn't realize that The Major and his wife were on the brink of marital bankruptcy. A few weeks later she began divorce proceedings. Grounds? Extreme cruelty. The inveterate fighter chose not to fight . . .[33]

Several things happened before George was 'shipped out'. The divorce went ahead smoothly, uncontested, and some months later at the home of mutual friends he met Margaret Haviland.

Like Amelia, Miss Haviland was a small-town girl. Born and raised in Michigan City, Indiana on the southernmost tip of Lake Michigan, she had a happy and secure childhood, attended good schools and eventually graduated from college with a Bachelor of Arts degree. In 1941 she was asked to return to her college to help in some fund-raising activities and this is what she was doing until 7 December 1941. Then,

> as American men were being mobilized and trained in many parts of the country a dire need sprang up for servicemen's clubs – places where they could write letters home, make phone calls, eat light lunches and enjoy entertainment. One of the largest such clubs was in Salina where it was not unusual to have 2000 to 3000 men in each evening . . . and it was from Salina that they all went overseas.[34]

Anxious to help in the war effort, Margaret was drafted to Salina, by the USO (which operated the clubs), as an executive. The relationship between Margaret and George, at that stage, was merely a friendship between two intelligent people who enjoyed each other's company and Margaret remembers that George was lonely and sad about the break-up of his marriage.

Quite by chance at this time George's son David was flying a B17 on a delivery mission and passed through Salina air base. He too remembers his father's depression over the break-up of the marriage but recalled that it didn't stop them having a marvellous evening together singing around a piano.[35] George's younger son, George Palmer Putnam Jr, was by this time an officer in the US Navy.

A week after David saw his father, George was on his way to India, and later flew over 'the Hump' (as he called the Himalayas) to China in the first B29 bomber squadron to make that trip. His role was Intelligence Officer for the squadron and once again he found himself the 'father of the unit'; his commanding officer was only twenty-three years old![36]

George's war service 'comprised in equal parts boredom, discomfort, disillusion and adventure', and indeed there must have been plenty of each, but overall he felt 'that curious satisfaction of being a part of such matters, a stimulation deep beyond that most of the ways of peace can offer.'[37] The squadron's task was to make the first bombing raids on Japan and it was George's responsibility to brief the young pilots before missions, to debrief them afterwards and generally update the intelligence data files for the men who came after them. He spent more than a year in the Far East and, as the unit moved around, often lived in the most basic conditions, 'off the land as the indigenous population did'. The army had managed to get weapons, ammunition and spares – the logistics of war – through to their lines, but rations were sparse.

Rice became a staple; 'If a peasant bought in a pig, they'd buy it and cook it. The pig may have been diseased but they had no choice; it was all there was. They used to have a thin gruel, porridge they called it, and even this had maggots in it.' George told friends that they 'often had to pick out the grubs before they could eat.'[38] Poor living conditions, polluted water and bad food inevitably took their toll of George who, despite appearances, had never been physically strong. He developed a parasitic infection in the kidneys and was eventually ordered home. He had plenty of time to think on the long Pacific voyage to America and decided that what he wanted more than anything, now, was to live full-time in his mountain home at Whitney Portal. There, he thought with affection, was 'cold clear water, an open fire, and a woodpile':

> Round about stood high country clothed with pines, scented with sage; a region of brawling streams, meadows bright with lupin, penstemon, and paintbrush; and, below, deserts with silver holly and gay carpets of tiny flowers, rimmed by purple hills, granite peaks.
>
> In every way so very different from Bengal, wet, dirty, stifling and crowded; or the raw, tragic hinterlands of China.[39]

At some time during this period of service George visited Saipan. By now stories that Amelia had been captured by the Japanese and taken to Saipan had started to circulate widely, fuelled by rumours that a white woman pilot had been seen there before the war and fanned by cinema-goers who had watched *Flight for Freedom*. George drove all over the island making extensive enquiries about the white woman flyer but he got no answers that gave him any hope that Amelia had ever been there.

In the spring of 1945, after his release from military hospital, he went directly to Cap Palmer's house in Hollywood and stayed there until the divorce became final.[40] Physically George bore the signs of his recent illness, but his great personality was not affected and his presence filled the Palmers' home for the weeks he stayed with them.

Soon after his return George 'very purposefully' started dating women, Cap Palmer said, 'but he wasn't looking for a woman, he was looking for a 'wife with whom to share his life':

women found him very attractive. One particular woman from Kansas, whom he had met when serving there wrote to him every day for years, her letters filled up a large box in the kitchen and then we started putting them in another box on the porch. All his ladies were very glamorous. Greer Garson was one. She *was* lovely, much more beautiful than in pictures and a lovely person.

One night he came home very shocked. The woman he had taken to dinner had, according to him, . . . 'made improper advances!'

'What happened?' we asked. 'She asked if I'd like to come in for the night!' he told us, appalled.

He was a bit like that, tough in business but innocent in many ways. For example he was always great friends with our daughter, Gay. The day after he met her we found them sitting talking together in Latin. Before the war she was a little girl and he would tell her bedtime stories. Well, the day he came home, after he'd greeted us he asked 'Where's Gay?' 'She's in the bath' I said, and before we could stop him he marched straight into the bathroom to give her a hug.

The problem was she'd grown up by then and was very embarrassed. He hadn't and didn't give it a thought.[41]

Margaret Haviland and George had kept in touch during the time he'd been overseas. The two met again and their friendship deepened into courtship. As usual George wasted no time, and though Peg (as Margaret preferred to be called) was reluctant to make such an important decision so quickly he swept her concerns aside. On 10 June they were married at a friend's home in Pasadena.

There were just a few friends present – and an army of pressmen. Bob Lee, the best man ('actually the worst' he recalled), and Jerry Lawrence, still collectively known as 'the boys', kept them waiting for two hours because of a flat tyre. 'Was George annoyed or irritated?' Bob wrote. 'Gross understatement. He was whopping MAD!' But the ceremony eventually got under way and when Peg went up to bed that night she was greeted by the spectacle of the marriage certificate stapled firmly to the bedroom door.[42]

After a short honeymoon George took Peg to the Whitney Portal lodge, high in the Sierras, where they spent that summer and winter. 'I dislike the cold and believe me it was cold at close to 9,000 feet,' Peg told me. 'But to keep me happy George organised expeditions into the hot sun of Death Valley some 80 miles away . . .' There, the couple used to stay at a small inn called Stove Pipe Wells. 'We used to go down on snowshoes to Lone Pine where the snowline ended and we had a car parked.'

During this time George wrote prolifically. Always an early riser he went straight to work at his typewriter. On the first morning of their residence at Whitney Portal Peg awoke to find a note on her bedside table:

Madam
Breakfast of canteloup, cream of wheat, toast and possum-with-hot-milk will be served either in the bedroom or on the terrace as desired. The time suggested is 10 am.

A simple luncheon is planned on the patio.

Dinner will be arranged at the Mt Whitney Grill. There will be Owens Valley steak, broiled and embellished with Swiss chard a la Shangri-Putnam, salad and chocolate pie. The Management wishes to know whether you desire Sauterne or Tokay as a beverage.

The Management also loves you very much and finds he

misses you greatly between the hours of six am and ten am (circa). Other times, too.

Ring, and service will appear . . .
The Management*

Peg was fascinated by George's fertile mind. his sense of fun, his raw energy, his need to 'never waste a minute'. An endless procession of house guests came up the steep winding narrow road to the stone lodge. 'The main house slept 14 people and higher up the mountain we had a guest house for eight more. In addition those who brought sleeping bags could use other little buildings. It was not unusual for us to sit down to breakfast with twenty-five at the table, or lunch for thirty-five or forty . . .' Peg remembered.

He wrote various books during this time, had a secretary living with us, sometimes two, and a houseman to do the chores. It was a mighty busy place. Streams of writers, mostly hopeful would-be writers, came for his advice and occasionally there came a good one.

My life consisted of seeing that we had plenty of food in the house, trucked up from Lone Pine, and that there was always enough clean bedlinen available. GP knew *everyone* of importance in America and they were all fascinated by what he was doing up there in the mountains and most came to see. No one ever wanted to leave . . .[43]

From time to time an echo of Amelia's legend would blow into their lives but mainly it was a time of work and relaxation and a time of great personal happiness for both George and Peg. George found many ways to express his love such as this note which Peg found in her Christmas stocking that first Christmas with 'a very large check':

*Temporary

Madam
I am instructed to turn over to you this slight check with the
understanding that it is to be spent exclusively on your
cherished person.
                    S. Claus.[44]

These intimate letters and notes convey a different George from
the one portrayed by his business associates, but according to his
family and closest friends he hadn't changed and had always been as
loving and playful in his personal relationships. So although most of
the letters between him and Amelia were destroyed in two house
fires[45] it is reasonably safe to assume that he was equally loving and
protective in his personal life with Amelia. Was this the real secret
of Amelia's ability to achieve – a secure home life coupled with the
sheer driving force of a partner who was able to make *anything*
happen?

Often Peg and George drove to Los Angeles where he would
conduct some piece of publishing business; sometimes he would
make a trip back east, or to his agent, Bye, in New York:

                    At [George] Bye's on Monday morning,
Wonderful
Your letters are a delight. I love you and miss you
ridiculously . . . Saw Ham Nelson [Bette Davis's first husband]
this morning; have red [*sic*] Helen's *Piney Bear* script, have
letter and script from Karl; as a huckster I am prancing from
one end of Manhattan to t'other.
   Dined last night at the Copacabana with the fabulous
parents of Mr Leeds. Now Sock is back from lunch and I must
vacate his typewriter, Love, love, love.

P.S.   A publishing fellow named Putnam
       Discovered he couldn't quite butnam
       What caused the hiatus
       Was meat and potatoes
       And eating whole pies without cutnam

and another:

> Miss you a lot. This is hard grind but I believe the results will
> please you. I love you a lot and miss you and wish I were with
> you. And nothing is so nice as being together on the hill in the
> coolth . . . including, of course, Basket [George's dog].
>   Kiss the boys [Bob and Jerry] for me . . . though I don't
> want to be misunderstood.[46]

Well aware of Peg's dread of winters on the mountain, George decided to do something about it. 'One day he came home with such a mischievous look on his face and eventually I got him to tell me what he'd been up to. "I've bought the Stove Pipe Wells inn for you, Peg. Now you'll never be cold in the winter," he said. It really tickled him to have a home in the highest possible position in America, and in the lowest too. He thought that was fantastic!'[47]

Since his return from active war service George had been troubled by periods of illness. The symptons were continuous and often distressing, '. . . but he would never say anything or complain; just every once in a while he'd say to me, "Peg. I think we've got to see a doctor in Trona . . ." and then I knew it was bad. But he was no invalid.' 'He loved to play tennis, hated to lose and rarely did,' Bob Lee recalled.[48]

George still derived a great deal of enjoyment from his practical jokes. One day when he and Peg were staying at Stove Pipe Wells he found there were some archaeological excavations not far away. Immediately he phoned his son David. 'Have you still got that old Eskimo skull?' he asked. 'Well, I'd like to borrow it!' Shortly afterwards those involved in the 'dig' were appalled to unearth a skull that was clearly that of an Eskimo from the floor of Death Valley.[49]

Owning the inn meant that someone had to be there constantly, so Peg had to spend time in Death Valley while George worked 'on the mountain' at his latest book *Up in Our Country*,[50] a conversational essay on the inhabitants, flora and fauna of the area.

'I still think this is a lovely place.' he wrote to Peg, mischievously, 'and am thinking of trying a want ad in the *Times* to see who'd like to share it with me . . .' The house was, as usual, full of guests and on this occasion there were several small children. 'As soon as I breakfast them they are off fishing. Domestic, that's what I am!'[51]

George had a way with children; he made them feel adult. They were never left out at his cocktail parties and were served special fruit juice drinks made to look identical to real cocktails; when the tray came round to a child it was presented so that the nearest drink was a 'special' and the child never knew he was being served anything different from anyone else.[52]

Many people who visited George and Peg at Whitney Portal recall their time there with affection. Typical is a letter from Helen Ogston – whom George encouraged to write the children's book *Piney Bear*.

> I personally appreciated George for his love of the English language. His conversation was a delight, his choice of words exquisite – just the right word to drop into a slot in a sentence. He also loved to tell stories but anything amusingly off-colour was told by suggestion.
>
> Once, standing in front of the large window framing Mount Whitney I asked him, 'Does it make the mountain any more beautiful because we know it is the highest?' George answered 'No, but it's like a beautiful woman. If you know she has a million dollars, she looks just a little bit better to you.'
>
> . . . Another time I rounded the corner of the guest house and banged my head on a low beam. It was a real bump that made me bite my lip. Because there were no tears George came over and gave me a gentle little kiss on the hurt spot.
>
> A wonderful mind, nary a mean streak . . . most of all I'm glad I knew him.[53]

In 1949 George was asked by Isaiah Bowman, an old friend and principal of Johns Hopkins University to serve on the Visiting Committee of the mathematics department. George had many such requests from various sources and he had served previously with the men on this committee. Now he suggested that the college 'try to find younger men, not with any thought of reducing the present incumbents, but by way of carrying the average age down a bit. Other than that I think the Committee is an excellent one and functions very well. I shall look forward to meeting with you again . . .'[54]

But George was never able to serve on the mathematics committee, for as the winter of 1949 set in he became too ill to travel. A few weeks later, just after Christmas, George was taken to Trona hospital with kidney failure and internal haemorrhages, and he died there on 4 January 1950 at the age of sixty-three.

Peg received hundreds of letters after George's death, many testifying to the inspiration they had received from him:

> What a complex character he was. He was a stormy petrel who incited all kind of reactions. I doubt very much whether he was ever more kind to any of his friends than he was to me. In many ways I think our relations were unique for he had a great deal to do with getting me started in exploration and on the first Byrd Expedition. He went out of his way to do many kind and thoughtful things for me. I look out on our snow covered campus this morning [Carleton College Minnesota] with a kind of depressed feeling . . . I wanted to tell you this because I have so many reasons to be grateful to George.
> Lawrence M. Gould[55]

Rockwell Kent, George's boyhood friend – and once his 'bridegroom' – wrote:

> I have never forgotten the ardent period when we lived together, nor been forgetful of the great friendship and belief in me that prompted him, over the disapproval of the older Putnams, to undertake the publishing of my first book, *Wilderness*, and, subsequently, *Voyaging* and *N by E*. I believe it would never have occurred to me to think of myself as a writer except for George's insistence that I was. And there was another aspect of George's friendship as a publisher . . . [he] never even suggested the alteration of a comma in anything I did.

Although for many years we had not only lived far apart but in many important respects had thought poles apart (I have always guessed that George was a conservative Republican, though I don't know) . . . I think we both felt that the friendship that had been established on Monhegan Island in 1906 was established for all our lives. I guess we never grew apart . . .[56]

George Agnew Chamberlain recalled:

an association that goes so far back into the past that I can't remember when George and I first met. What I do know is that we hit it off from the start and that our friendship never knew a set-back of any kind. This is no small thing to say for he was no easy man to know and the complexities of his character led him into collisions with people who hadn't the brain to unravel his personality. He was never well, even before the constraints of the war, but his terrific courage with which he rode along on nerve alone was something I constantly admired.[57]

These letters, and many others, define George's contribution to the lives of hundreds with whom he came into contact. His personal brand of dynamism, aggression, business acumen and belief that 'nothing was impossible', inspired many people to extend themselves into previously undreamed-of realms of achievement. Amelia Earhart was only one for whom this unusual and remarkable man made everything possible. That was his way. To inspire, and if necessary to provide, or help to provide, the practical means to turn dreams into reality.

Sometimes George's enthusiasm for a project overrode moral principles. He could not tolerate fools or dissemblers. And despite the glittering array of famous personalities who regularly beat a path to his door, he was just as impressed by a mountain dweller living in total contentment and alive to his whole world, as by the rich and famous who lived on their reputations.[58] He upset many people in his life and could not bear to be baulked. He could be an implacable and unpleasant enemy, crushing and vindictive if his projects were threatened; terrifying in a temper, menacingly cold when cornered and his active and fertile brain shot into overdrive at the merest hint of opposition.

But those who knew him well, who spent any time with him, loved the sheer vibrancy of life in his shadow. Life with George was turbulent, tumultuous, often disturbing, but always exciting. 'He was a very great man,' one friend said, simply.[59] It seems a fitting and apt epitaph, and one, I think, with which Amelia Earhart would have agreed.

George never knew of the fever that gripped the western world in the early 1960s when several writers produced books about Amelia which seemed to offer proof that she had been on a government spy mission when she made her last flight. Public interest in the subject was enormous, especially since it coincided with the Gary Powers U2 'spy-fly' affair.

The most famous of these books, Fred Goerner's *The Search for Amelia Earhart* proved to be a real blockbuster. Goerner was a CBS reporter who came across the story when a former Saipan islander gave a newspaper interview claiming she had seen Amelia Earhart and Fred Noonan being brought ashore there by Japanese soldiers before the war.

Amelia was back in the news again, and has really never left it since. From time to time a newspaper will run a story about her disappearance, hinting that another clue has been found (a flurry of correspondence usually results); a writer will produce a book or an article which debunks the theories of previous authors, putting forward yet another new theory and insisting that this is what *really* happened to Amelia.

Even Fred Goerner now states that Amelia was not on a spying mission, though he does believe she fell into Japanese hands and died in captivity. The spy theory, at least, is almost put to rest and the mass of declassified official documents reveal that confidentiality was maintained because of the early requests from Amelia and George for secrecy about her flight plans. But the mystery of what happened to Amelia and Fred Noonan after that last radio message remains very much alive and there are several organisations, as well as individuals, planning further searches for the remains of the Electra.

Opinions vary as to where the plane might have ended up before running out of fuel, but based on what is known (i.e from Amelia's radio contacts) it was probably in the ocean somewhere in the vicinity of Howland Island. After much research into dozens of theories I have concluded that Elgen and Marie Long (and Roy Nesbit, who recently wrote a series of magazine articles) are most likely to be correct in their hypothesis that the Electra ran out of fuel and was forced down about 40 miles north-north-west of the Island. The Longs recently established a fund to finance a properly organised search, but have in the meantime personally financed a survey of the ocean bed in the area in which they will start their search. They needed to know whether the area consisted of a flat sea bottom, or whether it consists of chasms and deep gulleys. The reason is obvious; on a flat surface any wreckage would stand out, 'like a basketball on a gym floor,' Elgen says.

Elgen Long is a careful man by nature. A senior pilot with the 'Flying Tigers' airline until his retirement a few years ago, he also made a record-breaking solo world flight of his own. He understands the stresses on a pilot involved in this type of venture and the technicalities of navigation and radio/radio direction finding. He is also well aware that in the fifty-odd years since the Electra disappeared, deterioration on a massive scale is likely to have taken place and that what he is searching for may be mere scraps of metal, but he is determined to resolve the mystery.

But what is left of Amelia herself; of the free spirit of which those who knew her well were fortunate enough to catch glimpses? Amelia's legacy is the legend of an ordinary girl growing into an extraordinary woman who dared to attempt seemingly unattainable goals in a man's world. It is impossible to evaluate the inspiration that Amelia handed down to the generations of women who came after her. Impossible too, to evaluate the motivation that Amelia and her contemporaries, the pioneers of civil aviation, provided for designers and manufacturers; for always these record-breaking pilots demanded better, faster and safer equipment, and they flew constantly at the outer limits of technology. Often, like Amelia, they paid the ultimate price, but the aeroplanes of today are a direct result.

I set out to research this book with only the faintest impressions of my subjects. I thought of Amelia hazily, as a female Lindbergh, and had a deeply unfavourable impression of George Palmer Putnam from my conversation with Paul Mantz so many years earlier. My work has involved interviewing family, friends and business contacts of both, as well as reviewing their letters and writing. Research not only changed those initial impressions and created annoyance that George has been so misinterpreted, but left me with a genuine regret that I never met him. He must have been an exceptional man to have been the springboard for Amelia's abilities. A friend told me:

> AE had to conquer George almost as Lindbergh had to conquer the Atlantic, yet it was GPP's hell-fire determination that provided *design* for these adventures of hers, and pulled them off. I wonder if the slim, frail girl-in-slacks would have startled the world without the explosive, pragmatic apostle of the impossible to goad her on.
>
> When glory shone, it was *her* limelight – the evenings at the White House, weekends at Hyde Park, the invitations from Royalty, the confrontation with Il Duce, whom GPP had denounced in print. One night George told the details of that meeting; the coldness with which [Mussolini] had received him, while dancing fond attendance on his illustrious wife. 'Mr Earhart' undoubtedly chafed at this 'stage-door Johnny' role, but both husband and wife knew they had a good thing going and I suspect Amelia needed George more than George needed her.[60]

What George and Amelia each brought to their relationship was exactly what was required to stimulate the unique talents of the other person. And the combination of their individual ability enhanced the regard they had for each other and deepened into love. It was an unusual love, at times, but a deep and genuine one, which deserves its place in Amelia's story.

APPENDIX 1

Radio communications
Amelia's radio communications with Lae, and subsequently with *Itasca* comprise the only documented evidence of the events leading up to her disappearance.

GMT & time elapsed	Local[1] time at Lae	
00.00	10.00 a.m.	Take-off from Lae
05.00	3.00 p.m.	EARHART TO LAE: 'AT 10,000 FT BUT REDUCING ALTITUDE BECAUSE OF BANKS OF CUMULUS CLOUD
07.00	5.00 p.m.	EARHART TO LAE: 'AT 7,000 FT AND MAKING 150 MPH'
07.20	5.20 p.m.	EARHART TO LAE: '. . . POSITION LATITUDE: 4 DEGREES 33.5' SOUTH, LONGITUDE: 159 DEGREES 07' EAST'
08.00	6.00 p.m.	EARHART TO LAE: 'ON COURSE FOR HOWLAND ISLAND AT 12,000 FT.

Note: All the above were received from Amelia by Harry Balfour. Balfour is on record as stating that he was in contact with Amelia every hour when position reports and height were received from her. Since her transmission times were at 15 and 45 minutes past each hour it is probable that the times given are approximate, with the exception of the one contact at 5.20 (07.20 GMT) which was reported in full detail to *Itasca* on 3 July. These snatched versions of her initial radio transmissions are all that have ever been recorded.

At the last contact she informed Balfour that she was changing from her daytime radio frequency (6,210 kcs) to her night-time one (3,105 kcs).[2] 'We requested her to remain on her present frequency but she told me she wished to contact the American Coast Guard Cutter *Itasca* so there was nothing to do about it but pass the terminal forecast to her and the upper air report from Ocean Island . . .'

10.30   8.00 p.m.   EARHART OVERHEARD BY NAURU RADIO '. . . A SHIP IN SIGHT AHEAD . . .' This message appeared in the log of the USS *Lexington*.[3]

However in 1969, former Nauru resident T. H. Cude claimed he had heard her say 'Lights in sight ahead' which led him to believe she had seen either the beam of the Nauru light, which was visible for 34 miles, or the lights of the phosphate workings, which had been left switched on purposely.

No two-way transmission was established but Amelia's voice was heard by several people on Nauru on short wave radio.[4]

The following extracts are taken from the official report of Commander Warner Thompson, *Itasca*'s captain, and the ship's two radio logs.

GMT & time elapsed	Local time at Howland	
12.42	1.12 a.m.	*Itasca* to San Francisco: Have not heard Earhart signals up to this time but see no cause for concern as plane is still 1000 miles away . . .
13.45	2.15 a.m.	*Itasca* log: 'Nothing on 3105'
14.00	2.30 a.m.	*Itasca* log: 'Itasca to Earhart on phone 3105'
14.15	2.45 a.m.	*Itasca* log: 'Heard Earhart plane on 3105 but unreadable through static.' Radio operator Leo Bellarts however caught Amelia's low monotone voice and reported that she said . . . CLOUDY AND OVERCAST . . . Various people were present, including two reporters familiar with Amelia's voice, they agreed it was she but could not decipher the message.
14.30	3.00 a.m.	*Itasca* log: 'Sent weather to KHAQQ'
14.45	3.15 a.m.	*Itasca* log: 'Nothing heard from Earhart.'
15.00	3.30 a.m.	*Itasca log:* 'Sent weather. KHAQQ from Itasca: What is your position? When do you expect to reach Howland? Itasca has heard your phone go ahead on key. Acknowledge this broadcast next schedule.' [Weather referred to is weather at Howland].

15.15	3.45 a.m.	EARHART: 'ITASCA FROM EARHART. OVERCAST . . . WILL LISTEN ON HOUR AND HALF HOUR ON 3,105.'
15.30	4.00 a.m.	*Itasca* log: 'Broadcast weather on phone 3,105 . . . and key 3,105.' Also transmitted: 'What is your position? When do you expect to arrive Howland? We are receiving your signals please acknowledge this message on your next schedule.'
15.45	4.15 a.m.	*Itasca* log: 'Earhart unheard on 3,105 this time.'
16.00	4.30 a.m.	*Itasca* log: 'Repeated previous transmission.'
16.23	4.53 a.m.	*Itasca* log: 'Sent weather/code/phone/3,105 kcs.'
16.24	4.54 a.m.	EARHART: '. . . PARTLY CLOUDY . . . (Volume S-1 *very faint*)
16.25	4.55 a.m.	*Itasca* log: 'Earhart broke in on phone – unreadable.'
16.30	5.00 a.m.	*Itasca* log: 'Sent weather, "What is your position etc."'
16.43	5.13 a.m.	*Itasca* log: 'Earhart signals unheard on 3,150.'
17.00	5.30 a.m.	*Itasca* log: 'Sent weather, "What is your position etc."'
17.15	5.45 a.m.	*Itasca* log: 'No hear during [scheduled time].'
17.30	6.00 a.m.	*Itasca* log: 'Sent weather data.'
17.44	6.14 a.m.	EARHART: '[WANT] BEARING ON 3105/ON HOUR/WILL WHISTLE IN MIC.'
17.45	6.15 a.m.	EARHART: ABOUT 200 MILES OUT. APPROXIMATELY. WHISTLING NOW.' (Volume S3 *fair*) *Note:* Sunrise was recorded in log at 6.15 a.m.
18.00	6.30 a.m.	*Itasca* log: 'Sent weather and asked position.'
18.12	6.42 a.m.	*Itasca* log: 'KHAQQ came on air with fairly clear signals calling *Itasca*.'
18.15	6.45 a.m.	EARHART: 'PLEASE TAKE BEARING ON US AND REPORT IN HALF HOUR I WILL MAKE NOISE IN MICROPHONE – ABOUT 100 MILES out. *Itasca* log: 'Earhart signal strength 4 but on air so briefly bearings impossible.'
18.30	7.00 a.m.	*Itasca* log: 'Sent weather, maintained contact on 500 kcs for "homing".'
18.48	7.18 a.m.	*Itasca*: 'Cannot take bearing on 3,105 very good/please send on 500 or do you wish to take bearings on us/go ahead please.' Log: 'no answer.'
19.00	7.30 a.m.	*Itasca:* 'Please acknowledge our signals on key please.' Log: 'unanswered.'
19.12	7.42 a.m.	EARHART: 'KHAQQ CALLING ITASCA WE MUST BE ON YOU BUT CANNOT SEE YOU BUT GAS IS RUNNING LOW BEEN UNABLE TO REACH YOU BY RADIO WE ARE FLYING AT ALTITUDE 1,000 FEET.' *Itasca* log: 'Other log reads – Earhart says running out

of gas only half hour left [verified as heard by other witnesses]/can't hear us at all/we hear her and are sending on 3,105 and 500 same time constantly and listening in for her frequently.'

Note: Itasca had two logs in radio room.

| 19.13 | 7.43 a.m. | *Itasca*: 'Received your message signal strength 5 (sent AAAs etc on 500 and 3,105) Go ahead. |

Note: considering the power of Amelia's transmitter – 50 watts – the strength of these signals (S5 is the maximum possible) indicates that she must have been very close to *Itasca* at this point. According to the Commanding Officer, 'It was also the time we expected her to arrive.'

19.17	7.47 a.m.	*Itasca*: 'Received your message signal strength 5 (sent AAAs on 3,105).'
19.19	7.49 a.m.	*Itasca*: 'Your message okay please acknowledge with phone on 3,105 (keyed AAAs)'
19.29	7.58 a.m.	EARHART: 'WE ARE CIRCLING BUT CANNOT HEAR YOU GO AHEAD ON 7,500 EITHER NOW OR ON THE SCHEDULE TIME ON HALF HOUR.'

(Volume S5 very loud, maximum strength on meter).

| 19.29 | 7.59 a.m. | *Itasca*: 'AAAAAAAAAAAA (on 7,500). Go ahead on 3,105.' |
| 19.30 | 8.00 a.m. | EARHART: 'KHAQQ CALLING ITASCA WE RECEIVED YOUR SIGNALS BUT UNABLE TO GET A MINIMUM PLEASE TAKE BEARING ON US AND ANSWER 3105 WITH VOICE ('sent long dashes on 3105 for 5 seconds or so') |

(This was the only direct reply that *Itasca* received from KHAQQ. It was later believed that she turned away at this point).

| 19.35 | 8.05 a.m. | *Itasca*: 'Your signals received okay we are unable to hear you to take a bearing it is impractical to take a bearing on 3,105 on your voice/how do you get that?/go ahead.' |
| 19.36 | 8.06 a.m. | *Itasca*: 'Go ahead on 3,105 or 500 kilo-cycles.' |

Log: 'Itasca sending on 7,500 as her only acknowledgement was for signals on 7500.'

19.37	8.07 a.m.	*Itasca*: 'Go ahead.'
19.42	8.11 a.m.	*Itasca*: 'Itasca to Earhart. Did you get transmission on 7,500 kcs/go ahead on 500 kcs so that we may take a bearing on you/it is impossible to take a bearing on 3,105 kilo-cycles/please acknowledge.'
19.43	8.12 a.m.	*Itasca* log: 'repeated above message on 7500.'
19.45	8.15 a.m.	*Itasca*: 'Do you hear my signals on 7,500 kcs or 3,105

		please acknowledge receipt on 3,105/go ahead.' Log entry: 'sent on 3,105 and repeated on 7,500.'
19.48	8.18 a.m.	*Itasca:* 'Will you please acknowledge our signals on 7,500 or 3,105/go ahead with 3105.' Log entry: 'no answer.'
20.03	8.33 a.m.	*Itasca:* 'Will you please come in and answer on 3,105/we are transmitting constantly on 7,500 kcs and we do not hear you on 3,105/please answer on 3,105/go ahead.' Log note: 'this unanswered.'
20.04	8.34 a.m.	*Itasca:* 'Answer on 3,105 kcs with phone/how are signals coming in/go ahead.'
20.14	8.44 a.m.	EARHART: 'WE ARE ON THE LINE OF POSITION 157–337, WILL REPEAT THIS MESSAGE ON 6,210 KCS. WAIT, LISTENING ON 6,210 KCS. WE ARE RUNNING NORTH AND SOUTH' (on 3105 – volume S5).
20.17	8.47 a.m.	*Itasca:* 'We heard you okay on 3,105 kcs. Please stay on 3,105 do not hear you on 6,210 maintain QSO on 3,105.' Log note: 'This broadcast by voice on 3,105 and by key on 7,500. Nothing was heard on 3,105 or 6,210.'

In addition to the above transmissions *Itasca* transmitted other numerous voice and code messages to which there was no response. Those above are merely the more important ones which show that the radio schedule requested by Amelia was maintained. In most cases although a precise time was given, the transmission lasted several minutes or more while the message was repeated in line with conventional radio procedure.

APPENDIX 2

Technical aspects of the Lae–Howland flight: Fuel; Navigation, Radio and RDF

Fuel

The amount of fuel carried by the Electra determined its flying time and range, so it has been an important factor in plotting the most likely area of Amelia's forced landing; but it has kept countless researchers guessing. Amelia's decision about the amount of fuel she carried would have been made in the knowledge of the distance involved (Lae to Howland is 2,561 miles),[1] and the conditions affecting take-off at Lae.

In her final telegram to the *Herald Tribune*, Amelia stated that the plane was 'weighted to capacity'. Did she mean by this that the plane was full to the capacity of the fuel tanks (1,150 gallons according to Lockheed's archives)? Or did she mean – mindful of her experience at Luke Field, Honolulu, in the previous March – to the maximum capacity she thought she could safely manage on the take-off at Lae? There is conflicting evidence.

James Collopy, district superintendent of civil aviation in Papua New Guinea, reported after Amelia's disappearance that 'according to Captain Noonan' the Electra was carrying 1,100 gallons of fuel, which included 50 gallons of 100-octane fuel. The high-octane fuel was intended to be used during the take-off to give extra power; the balance was 87-octane aviation gas, and there were 64 gallons of oil.[2] Earhart researchers Elgen and Marie Long recently interviewed Robert Ivedale, the mechanic who worked on the Electra at Lae who also claimed that the Electra had 1,100 gallons on board when Amelia took off from Lae.[3]

The airport at Lae used Imperial measures. If 1,100 imperial gallons had been pumped aboard the Electra this would have been the equivalent of 1,321 US gallons – clearly impossible as there was not that capacity. So perhaps there is room for doubt in the statements made by Collopy and Ivedale simply because of the conversion factor.

Noonan told reporters on the eve of take-off that they would be carrying '950 gallons of petrol – sufficient to give a still-air cruising range of 2,750 miles',[4] and although one hesitates to believe newspaper reports over the first-hand evidence of Collopy and Ivedale, they are worth examining. One report by the Aviation Correspondent of the Sydney *Telegraph*, quoted Noonan saying that with 950 gallons 'the plane was overloaded by two tons'. This is almost exactly what was said before the flight from Oakland to Honolulu, three months earlier on the first attempt at the round-the-world flight. Was it an accurate report? Would Noonan, a responsible and experienced navigator, consider a theoretical margin of less than 10 per cent adequate on a flight where there was no alternative landing site and the destination was potentially difficult to locate?

It seems improbable; and yet when Amelia flew from Oakland to Honolulu in company with Paul Mantz, Harry Manning and Fred Noonan, the Electra carried only 947 gallons for the 2,400 mile flight (which took 15 hours 51.5 minutes). And afterwards Amelia stated that of the 947 gallons 'more than four hours' fuel remained'[5], but during that flight Paul Mantz had monitored fuel consumption and throttle controls for he was always unhappy at Amelia's tendency to fly with the throttles wide open. Fuel conservation was an important issue, hence the two instruments that Mantz had insisted on fitting aboard the Electra as an aid to the economic use of fuel.

Amelia's disastrous attempted take-off from Luke Field (which had a 1,000 yard concrete runway), was made with 900 US gallons of fuel on board. In a press interview on 24 April at Burbank Amelia said she felt that the 'Electra had ground looped because it was overloaded'. If Amelia considered the Electra to be overloaded with 900 gallons for take-off on a concrete runway, how could she possibly consider that she could take off with 1,100 gallons on Lae's *unpaved* runway of 1,000 yards?

The Luke Field crash undoubtedly made a big impression on Amelia and there is no evidence that she had ever taken off in the Electra with a fuel load of more than 1,000 gallons. A cable from George to Jacques de Sibour indicated that tests would be made with 850 and 1,000 gallons, but it is not known if this was ever carried out.[6] Furthermore, manufacturer's specifications indicate that the Electra was *not capable* of taking off with a fuel load of 1,100 gallons in 1,000 yards in still air conditions.[7]

Even taking into account the fact that Amelia's plane had been stripped of all superfluous equipment/effects, and that magnesium alloys had been used for various parts of the plane in order to reduce weight, the minimum possible net weight of the aeroplane would have been 9,200 pounds.[8]

A US gallon of aviation fuel (0.8327 of an imperial gallon) weighs 6 pounds (an imperial gallon of aviation fuel weighs 7.2 pounds); and 1,100 US gallons of fuel weighs 6,600 pounds. If Collopy and Ivedale were correct the gross weight of the aeroplane with 1,100 US gallons of fuel would have been a minimum of 15,800 pounds. Lockheed figures show that with this gross weight, take-off of the *standard* Model 10 under the prevailing conditions at Lae (hot, humid, still air) would have required more than 2,500 yards (7,500 feet) of runway.[9]

Allowing for the additional power available because Amelia's 10E model was fitted with twin 550hp Wasps, the maximum gross weight limit for a take-off on Lae's 1,000 yards (3,000 feet) runway would be 15,300 pounds. With a net weight of 9,200 pounds the aeroplane could have carried only 1,000 (US) gallons at the outside.

First-hand information also exists that Amelia never intended to carry more than 1,000 gallons (even before her Honolulu disaster). In order to obtain the necessary permission to overfly British territories during the round-the-world flight, Jacques de Sibour had approached Sir Francis Shelmerdine (Director of Civil Aviation) on her behalf. Following his meeting de Sibour suggested to Amelia that she should write a personal letter to allay Shelmerdine's concerns. In this letter Amelia states:

> . . . Your interest is no doubt in its fuel tankage; i.e. 1,150 gallons. Such amount provides a maximum cruising range of 4,000 miles. My longest hops over the Pacific are about 2,500 miles – at which time I shall carry probably 1,000 gallons of gasoline.[10]

Various researchers have highlighted pieces of circumstantial evidence in order to advance theories regarding the amount of fuel in the Electra's tanks when Amelia took off from Lae, but in fact no hard evidence has ever been discovered. A scrap of paper on which Amelia had scrawled some figures relates to fuel taken on board and totals 684 gallons. It was mailed to George from Lae but as it was included with Amelia's notes of the journey from Bandoeng there is no way of knowing whether it related to the fuel taken on board at Lae or Darwin or some other place.[11]

In the light of Lockheed's figures on the plane's performance, fuel consumption, the prevailing conditions and the amount of time that Amelia was *known* to be in the air, it is unlikely that Amelia was carrying more than a thousand gallons, which would have given her between 20 and 21 hours range depending on how efficiently she flew the aeroplane. She expected the flight to take about eighteen and a half hours but headwinds of 10 mph greater than forecast, if encountered over the entire trip, would add an extra two hours to the flight.

Amelia's last message to *Itasca* was transmitted after 20 hours and 14 minutes of flight.

Fuel consumption

At Paul Mantz's suggestion the Electra had been equipped with a 'fuel analyser' to measure the effect of the fuel and air mixture on the power output and enable the pilot to select the most efficient and economic combination. In flight trials, Mantz worked out the most effective settings for various stages of flight and these had worked remarkably well on the Oakland–Honolulu flight in March. Records exist at Lockheed showing that

Amelia was reasonably proficient at operating this instrument using settings provided by Mantz.

From these and manufacturer's figures,[12] it can reasonably be assumed that during the take-off and fight to gain airspeed and height the fuel consumption may have been as high as 100 gallons an hour; and the long slow climb of the heavily burdened plane to 10,000 feet would burn fuel at a rate of approximately 70 gallons an hour.[13] Once the fuel load reduced to within recommended levels the fuel consumption could drop to 38 gallons an hour while still maintaining an airspeed of 150 mph. Thus, a speculative (and very approximate), attempt can be made to calculate the amount of fuel used during the time Amelia was known to be in the air.

Take-off and gain airspeed	.33 hours at 100 gph	33 gallons
Climb to 10,000 feet	5 hours at 70 gph	350 gallons
Descend to 7,000 and cruise (say)	5 hours at 50 gph	250 gallons
Remaining time at maximum efficiency	10 hours at 38 gph	380 gallon
Total fuel consumption		1,013 gallons

It should be remembered however that fuel consumption would take a gradual curve between these reference points and the application of a reasonable 5 per cent contingency to cover this fact could put consumption as low as 956 US gallons or as high as 1070 US gallons.

Navigation

Amelia and Noonan had two navigational choices. They could either fly a great circle course (as set out by Clarence Williams) relying totally on frequent star sightings, or Noonan could have plotted a constant compass bearing (rhumb line)[14] course for Howland. In northern latitudes the great circle route (while appearing to be longer on a map) is more direct since it follows the earth's curvature. But the difference between the two alternatives at the equatorial latitudes between Lae and Howland would be only 50 miles or so.

Whichever system was chosen, Noonan would frequently check his position by shooting what he called 'the heavenly bodies' (sun. moon, planets and stars). He is on record stating that fixes based on stellar observations at night were more reliable than those taken during the day because of the ability to cross-check.

During the day cross checks could be made 'by crossing a line of position [derived by sun shots] with a radio direction finding (RDF) bearing'; but, he said, this was not totally reliable 'due to the amount of error which would be introduced by even a small angular error in long range DF bearings'. Noonan understood, and had considerable experience working with direction finders, and had used them successfully in his work in the Pacific with Pan American.

Knowing Noonan's navigational methods, which are a matter of record,[15] it is possible to ascertain his tactics on this occasion. At some point before the aeroplane reached Howland Island, having ascertained a position by celestial navigation, Noonan would plot a course that would take them either well to the north or well to the south of the island. It did not matter which, it was only necessary to be *sure* that the island was somewhere to the north, or somewhere to the south, when they arrived at a parallel position. This system of navigation was pioneered by Francis Chichester in 1931 (when he flew in his Gipsy Moth to the remote Howe and Norfolk Islands en route from New Zealand to Australia):

> I had worked out a fine system of navigation. I had found that I could follow an invisible curved path to the island by taking sextant shots of the sun every hour; this was based on the fact that measuring the height of the sun above the horizon with a sextant enabled one to calculate the distance of the [air]plane from the spot vertically below the sun on the surface of the earth. . . . I had to aim well to one side of the island in case error in the dead reckoning caused by a faulty compass reading, or undetected wind effect, should put me on the wrong side of the island. And the island being out of sight, I must be certain when I turned to the right I was turning towards it, and not away from it. This system was afterwards dubbed by one of my friends as 'my theory of deliberate error'.[16]

In Chichester's case he introduced a deliberate error of 200 miles; in other words he flew to a position which he assumed was 200 miles to the north of the island which was his destination. It is known from several contributions to Weems Navigation Manual, by Noonan, between 1931 and 1935, that he was an adherent of this 'find the island' system and had used it successfully to navigate the Pan Am clippers to Pacific islands.

From what is known it is most probable that Noonan chose to aim to the north of Howland. Radio transmissions from Amelia to *Itasca* during the early hours reported 'cloudy and overcast' conditions. A little over an hour before her final radio contact Amelia said they were flying at 1,000 feet. The most probable reason for this was cloud since they would have been able to see further at a higher altitude and had they been in clear weather they would have obviously taken advantage of greater visibility.

Howland itself, and the area south and east of it, was in clear sunlight with occasional scattered small clouds. The crew of *Itasca*, however, reported thick cloud in an area estimated to be forty miles to the north and west of Howland. This cloud, said Air Corps observer, Lt Cooper, would have prevented the flyers seeing the island from a distance greater than ten miles unless the clouds were very high above them. But the *Itasca*, which was lying north-eastward of the Island, was emitting thick black smoke which hung around for several hours and which Commander Thompson felt should have been visible up to 30 miles away.[17]

Had Noonan elected to aim south of Howland Island the Electra would have been flying in clear and cloudless skies; but in that case had the line of position 157–337 been accurate Amelia and Noonan could hardly have missed seeing Baker Island (a little under forty miles to the south).

Assuming, then, that when the Electra reached the point on the plotted course where Noonan could have been reasonably certain that Howland Island lay approximately due south of them (a position which could be confirmed by a sun shot) he would have advised Amelia to turn right and fly in a southerly direction until the island was reached. This sounds simple but Sir Francis Chichester noted his own doubts when he first put his theory to the test:

> I had a feeling of despair. After flying in one direction for hour after hour over markless, signless sea, my instinct revolted at suddenly changing direction in mid-ocean . . . I had been so long on the same heading that the island must lay ahead not to the right. I was attacked by panic . . . [18]

It is tempting to wonder if Amelia experienced these same feelings of doubt, for everything indicates that it was a reliance on her own similar instinct that led her to ignore Noonan's navigational instruction on the flight to Dakar when she turned north instead of south and put them 163 miles north of their destination.

In order to obtain an accurate line of position Noonan would have used tables from the *Nautical Almanac for 1937* which provided details of the sun's azimuth[19] which for 17.55 GMT – sunrise – on July 2nd 1937 was 067 degrees.

The fact that Amelia gave a line of position has led many researchers to suppose that Noonan achieved an actual sun shot because according to the relevant almanac it was an accurate one for that morning. However, using the information in the almanac it was possible for him to have *precomputed* lines of position in advance using sun-pointing angles, azimuths and attitudes at (say) 6.15 a.m. (sunrise), 7.30 a.m. and 8.30 a.m. so that in the event of his not being able to see the sun due to cloud he would at least have a theoretical north/south line at dawn.[20]

The problem in this case is, in simplistic terms, that although the Electra was flying south on the line of position that Amelia gave, the line would not necessarily intersect with Howland Island unless Noonan's dead reckoning position (which assumed they were due north of the island), was accurate. They may, for example, have been 'running north and south' on a line which was thirty or forty miles short of the island (i.e. parallel to Noonan's supposed position). Furthermore, even with a sextant shot at the sun it was impossible for Noonan to know how far north of the island they were without a bearing on, for example a radio signal.

Amelia reported that they were running north and south ('N ES S' in the radio operator's shorthand code is north and south, and those present in the radio room agreed this is what she said, and repeated in correct radio transmission procedure), and not north *to* south; which provides reason to believe that she may have turned – at least once on this line and was hunting for Howland along a length which allowed for a reasonable error factor; perhaps 50 or 60 miles.

Noonan clearly believed that they should have located the island at approximately 7.42 ship's time (19.12 GMT) and was so sure that he instructed Amelia to 'circle', which she reported sixteen minutes later at 7.58 (19.28 GMT). Two minutes later, she reported that she had received *Itasca's* signals but was 'unable to get a minimum' on which to tune her direction finder. It was the only reply which indicated that she ever received any signals from *Itasca* during that flight and hence it is assumed that at that point she was closest to Howland Island.

One wonders why, if Amelia and Noonan were so certain that they must be in the vicinity of Howland Island ('must be on you but cannot see you') they did not engage in a 'square search'; that is to fly in a square pattern which increases in size progressively by the distance visible to the naked eye. Theoretically, provided one has sufficient fuel, the target must be located sooner or later. Had Amelia been carrying 1,100 gallons when she took off she would have almost certainly had sufficient fuel to have performed this manoeuvre. But she had already reported that she was low on fuel. An hour and two minutes before her last radio contact she had reported either that she was low on fuel or that she had only approximately half an hour's supply left. It would not be possible for her to be more precise – there was always a quantity of fuel which could not be used due to attitude of the plane/gravity et cetera, and it is unlikely that she would know what that amount might be.

There is one further navigational factor to take into consideration which in itself is insufficient explanation for Amelia's disappearance, but it might have been part of the reason why Amelia and Noonan never located Howland Island.

The area of the Pacific around Howland was largely unknown and poorly charted. The reported positions (latitude and longitude) of the many uninhabited islands dated from the logs of sailing ships a century or more earlier. Clarence Williams, Amelia's navigational consultant, had used the co-ordinates of Howland given in *Lippinott's Geographical Dictionary of the World*, and used by the US Navy Department's Hydrographers Office. On Amelia's charts Williams clearly marked the island's position as Latitude 0 degrees 49'00 North; Longitude 176 degrees 43'09 West – correct according to *Lippincott* in the spring of 1937.

Ironically, in the survey conducted a year earlier, the *Itasca* had corrected this position to Latitude 0 degrees 48'06 North; Longitude 176 degrees 38'12 West, but the change had not found its way into print when Williams consulted the Hydrographers Office.[21]

The difference amounts to just under six miles. Howland Island was not where Amelia and Noonan expected it to be.

Radio and DF

It is generally agreed that the overriding factor leading to Amelia's disappearance was her lack of expertise in radio communications. Commander Thompson stated: 'Viewed from the fact that Miss Earhart's flight was largely dependent on radio communication, her attitude towards arrangements were casual to say the least.'[22]

It seems certain that had Amelia ever been able to establish reasonable two-way communication with *Itasca* the end result would have been very different and tragedy averted.

The radio aboard Electra was always assumed to have been the Western Electric equipment fitted by Joe Gurr. Elgen Long's research, however, indicates that this may be incorrect. He interviewed a former Bendix employee who stated that before Amelia left Miami she was persuaded by Bendix to discard the Western Electric equipment for the new Bendix RA-1 series. The Longs have also located photographs of the Electra's interior, taken at Miami, showing an RA-1 receiver fitted on top of the instrument panel directly in front of Amelia. 'Bendix offered Amelia $5,000 to ditch the Western Electric gear . . .' Elgen Long told me. The reason was obvious: the publicity surrounding a successful navigation of the world using *entirely* Bendix equipment would be very valuable. Furthermore Bendix was one of the major original backers of the Purdue 'Flying Laboratory' project and had given $20,000 to the second world flight coffers.

Elgen Long also states that he has further proof of this via Stan Rose, the mechanic who checked Amelia's radio and DF equipment at Danvin and who replaced the blown fuse. Rose apparently stated that *all* the radio equipment was Bendix.

There is one further piece of evidence for this claim: a letter from Lockheed on the subject of 'Radio Equipment of Earhart Electra' dated 30 July 1937 which states: '. . . we have good reason to believe that additional equipment was installed by Miss Earhart in Miami.'[23] Perhaps this was one of the reasons for the confusion that has arisen over the years regarding what frequencies were available to Amelia.

The *Itasca's* instructions were that Amelia's plane was 'equipped with a 50 watt transmitter for operation on 500, 3,105, and 6,210 kilocycles, and with a receiver covering all frequencies. The direction finder covers 200 to 1500 kilocycles.' A subsequent message corrected this cable, advising that the direction finder covered 200–1400 kcs. *Itasca* was also informed that 'on the previous trip [Oakland to Honolulu] communications were handled by Pan American Airways with the Electra working on 3,105 and Pan American on 2,986 kilocycles.[24] But George advised *Itasca* 'when Amelia Earhart took off from Miami she stated she would not try to communicate with any radio station but would broadcast her position every 15 and 45 minutes past each hour . . . her receiver will be used most of the time taking radio bearings.'[25] (Records show that Amelia did not transmit her position on a regular basis at any stage of the trip.)

Itasca acknowledged this communication, requested information on the frequency best suited to Amelia's 'homing device' and asked her to designate, 'time and type of our signal. We will give smoke by day and searchlight by night'.[26] But Commander Black commented, 'It will be noted in the event that the *Itasca* was to be used as a homing-in agency, and was to transmit on 3,105, that it would be impossible for the plane to receive the above frequencies on its direction finder the range of which was 200-1400.'

Subsequently, *Itasca* received the following messages from Amelia regarding communications:

HOMING DEVICE COVERS FROM 200–1500 AND 2400–800 KILO-CYCLES ANY FREQUENCIES NOT REPEAT NOT NEAR ENDS BANDS SUITABLE.[27] Another read: SUGGEST ONTARIO STAND BY ON 400 KCS TO TRANSMIT LETTER N FIVE MINUTES ON REQUEST WITH STATION CALL LETTERS REPEATED TWICE AND EVERY MINUTE. SWAN TRANSMIT VOICE 9 MEGACYCLES OR IF I UNABLE RECEIVE BE READY ON 900 KCS. ITASCA TRANSMIT LETTER A, POSITION, OWN CALL LETTERS AS ABOVE ON HALF HOUR 7.5 MEGACYCLES. POSITION SHIPS AND OUR LEAVING WILL DETERMINE BROADCAST TIMES SPECIFICALLY. IF FREQUENCIES MENTIONED UNSUITABLE NIGHT WORK INFORM ME LAE. I WILL GIVE LONG CALL BY VOICE 3105 KCS QUARTER AFTER HOUR POSSIBLY QUARTER TO.[28] While a further cable instructed: REPORT IN ENGLISH NOT [Morse] CODE ESPECIALLY WHILE FLYING WILL BROADCAST HOURLY QUARTER PAST HOUR GCT [Greenwich Civil Time][29]

To which *Itasca* replied:

FOLLOWING FOR AMELIA EARHART PUTNAM LAE QUOTE ITASCA TRANSMITTERS CALIBRATED 7500 6210 500 425 KCS CW AND EITHER CW OR MCW. ITASCA DIRECTION FINDER FREQUENCY RANGE 550 TO 270 KCS.[30]

It has been stated that Amelia was never informed that in addition to the direction finder on *Itasca*, another direction finder, an experimental high-frequency piece of equipment, had been installed on Howland Island. So experimental that it was still in the 'breadboard' stage of development. Paul Mantz's biographer states that Paul had arranged to borrow this DF from the navy and, working for George as Amelia's formal representative at Howland, Richard Black had arranged the installation and operation of the unit. But the equipment was mentioned in a cable from George to Admiral Leahy dated 29 April 1937,[31] before Amelia left on the round-the-world flight, so it appears highly unlikely that Amelia would not have been aware of its existence. There was no evidence, however, that it was of any assistance in the project, though *Itasca* maintained contact with the operator, Frank Cipriani, constantly and a log was kept of the operation. At the time when Amelia was closest and the Howland Island short-wave DF might have been most useful, it was running low on power, the dry-cell battery arrangement rigged up by *Itasca*'s engineers almost exhausted from the night's work and in need of recharging. According to an official report by Lt Daniel Cooper of the Air Corp, who was on Howland Island as an official observer, the equipment on Howland Island was capable of working on 3,105 kcs but Amelia never transmitted for a long enough period to enable Cipriani to obtain a bearing on her.[32]

In summing up the mission Commander Thompson stated:

. . . Ship's direction finder manned at 0725 [ship's time]
Itasca transmitters were accurately calibrated
Itasca signals clearly received by other [radio] units
Itasca fully covered all Earhart schedules 7,500, 3,105 etc
Earhart never answered *Itasca* questions and never gave a position. Communications were never really established.
Earhart acknowledged receiving *Itasca* signals at 0800 [ship's time]. This formed the only case and was apparently for signals sent by *Itasca* on 7,500.
Earhart could not secure null on *Itasca* signals.
Earhart's last message was hurried, frantic, and apparently not complete. Earhart did not return to air on 6,210.
Earhart was on air very briefly and apparently over modulated. The attempts of the radioman on Howland to secure cut failed.
Judging from signal strength Earhart was closest between 0730 and 084446, when her signal strength was 5 with a 50 watt transmitter.
Earhart probably had receiver trouble.
Earhart apparently did not know position.
Earhart asked *Itasca* to take bearings on her. This was never planned. Earhart knew that *Itasca* could give her accurate bearings on 500 [kcs] and yet never transmitted on 500 in order for *Itasca* to assist her. Earhart knew that she could use 500 when close in if necessary.
The signals which Earhart acknowledged were transmitted on 7,500. Her direction finder loop could not handle this frequency. It is possible she was referring to other signals.[33]

Commander Thompson did not know that Amelia could almost certainly not communicate on 500 kcs because the 250-foot trailing antenna, necessary for operating on that frequency, had been left in the USA, along with the code keys. It was said that neither Amelia nor Noonan could use code at operational speeds, though both must surely have been capable of tapping out a call sign letter. For some reason Amelia had convinced herself that she did not need code and that voice communications were adequate. In respect of the direction finder, Elgen and Marie Long have conducted research using an antenna system identical to that used on Amelia's Electra. 'The directional qualities were practically nil. It didn't have high points of nulls and voids on it. So the waves radiating from it would be very little, regardless of what direction the antenna or airplane was pointed at the time.'[34]

Amelia's Lockheed Electra 10E – sundry specifications for the round-the-world flight:
Normally a ten-passenger plane, the Electra had been cleared of all seats and about half of the cabin was filled with additional fuel tanks with a capacity of 753 gallons. The wing tanks were capable of taking 398 gallons – total capacity 1,151 gallons.[35]

About 18 inches off the floor is a wide chart table. Beneath it, visible through a glass inset in the table top is a master aperodic compass. Special windows of flat glass have been installed on both sides of the aircraft, free from the distortion of standard cabin windows. Through them the navigator makes his celestial observations using a bubble sextant. A pelorus also is mounted for use at both windows.

An arrangement has been devised to open the cabin door about four inches, where it is held rigidly in place. A Pioneer Drift Indicator is mounted for looking down through this aperture to check wind drift on the earth or sea below. For this work flares are used at night over water, smoke bombs in daylight. Beside the chart table are mounted three chronometers, altimeter, air speed indicator and temperature gauge. A Bendix Direction Finder was fitted, its loop mounted on the top of the cockpit is adjustable by Amelia from inside the cockpit.

Amelia's entire wardrobe all in matching shades of brown fits into one small suitcase. In the fuselage there will be a two man rubber lifeboat, instantly inflatable from capsules of carbon dioxide. Likewise a Very pistol for firing distress signals, flares that ignite the surface of the water and as Amelia says, 'A very orange kite'.[36]

APPENDIX 3

The 'Earhart Mystery' theories

Probably it was the film *Flight for Freedom*, screened in 1943, which first planted the idea in many people's minds that Amelia's disappearance may not have been a straightforward 'ditch' in the Pacific Ocean. Rumours eddied and swirled throughout the war that Amelia had, either deliberately or accidentally, flown over Japanese mandated territory, been forced to land and taken prisoner. Some people believed that after the war she would be found and liberated.

In March 1944 in the Marshall Islands a native called Elieu Jibambam talked to US Navy Lieutenant Eugene Bogan. Elieu said he had been told by a late friend, a Japanese trader called Ajima, that an American woman flyer had come down on a reef near Jaluit Island and was picked up by a Japanese ship. Ajima told him the woman was a spy and had been taken away by soldiers to another island. Bogan reported this to his senior officer but no official report was filed on the grounds that it might raise false hopes that Amelia Earhart was still alive.[1]

The *American Weekly* ran a story about Amelia on 10 September 1944 after the island of Saipan was taken by the US Marines. The article told how marines had found a photograph album filled with pictures of Amelia in her sports togs in a captured barracks. Although Amelia had not carried such an album with her on her last flight, the finding of this item somehow bolstered belief that there was a connection between the album and Amelia's disappearance.[2]

It was probably because of this story together with talk that a Caucasian woman pilot had been seen there before the war that George Putnam made a point of visiting Saipan. With *carte blanche* to go anywhere, and talk to anyone, George travelled all over the island and questioned numerous people. Later he told his family and close friends that he never discovered a single piece of information that led him to believe Amelia had ever been there. George Putnam, the great publicist, would *never* have passed up an opportunity to write a sensational book and make a war heroine of Amelia had there been the slightest hint of a story. Accusations that he did not want Amelia found because he had remarried are patently without foundation; by then he was divorced from Jeannie and had not yet begun courting Peg.

George was always convinced that Amelia had run out of fuel somewhere near Howland Island and had died either during the emergency landing at sea, or very shortly afterwards. He did, however, strongly believe that the massive sea and air search for Amelia had probably also been used to gather information about a sensitive area in the Pacific.[3]

In 1944–45 Thomas E. Devine, a sergeant in the US Army Postal Corps, was based at Saipan. Two incidents caused him to become involved in the Amelia Earhart mystery. In early July 1944 he heard rumours that Amelia Earhart's plane was locked in a hangar at Aslito Airfield. Devine went to the airfield and saw a twin engine metal airplane in a hangar which he stated bore the registration NR16020. Shortly afterwards, he claimed, the aeroplane was destroyed by the US Army. About a year later, at the Japanese cemetery of Garapan, he and a friend were shown a grass-covered spot by a native woman who, through an interpreter, told them it marked the grave of two white flyers, one of whom was a woman.[4]

Jacqueline 'Jackie' Cochran, who also had a personal interest in Amelia's fate, had headed up the WASPS organization of women ferry pilots during the war. When hostilities ceased she was directed by General 'Hap' Arnold to make an official investigation into the role of women in the Imperial Japanese Air Force. In Jackie's autobiography *Stars at Noon*, written in 1954, she related how, while engaged on this mission, she discovered 'numerous clippings and photographs about Amelia Earhart, Jimmie Doolittle and other American pilots including myself. There were several files on Amelia Earhart at the Dai-Ichi building in Tokyo.'[5]

Jackie did not describe the contents of those files and some writers have implied that there is a sinister reason for this. But had the files revealed anything contrary to Jackie's belief that Amelia had ditched and drowned, surely she would have commented on the fact, or else not repeated in the same book her *certainty*, because of her telepathic abilities, that her friend had died after drifting on the ocean for several days. It is likely that the files contained nothing more than a collection of cuttings and photographs (there were so many newspaper articles and stories on Amelia), and Jackie never mentioned them because she felt they were unimportant.[6]

After the war ended, the rumours remained so widespread that the US Navy Department was compelled to take the unusual step of formally denying that Amelia had been involved in any military operation during her round-the-world flight. They also stated that no evidence had been found in captured documents, nor from interrogation of Japanese prisoners, that Amelia had fallen into Japanese hands. But in the meantime thousands of American servicemen had liberated islands all over the Pacific. Undoubtedly, in view of the rapidly growing Amelia Earhart legend many would have asked questions or talked about the subject to islanders.

In 1945, a dentist serving with the US Navy on the island of Saipan in the Marianas was told by his young assistant Josephine Blanco that she recalled seeing a twin-engine plane land on the water in Saipan Harbour. She was able to fix the date as summer 1937 because she was eleven years old that year and about to start attending a new school. Her brother-in-law was Japanese and she was taking lunch to him in a restricted area which she had a pass to enter. When the girl met her brother-in-law he took her to see 'the American woman' who had been taken off the plane. To the child's surprise the woman was wearing what appeared to be men's clothing (slacks and shirt) and also wore her hair short like a man. The woman was accompanied by a tall man. The two captives were led away to a clearing in nearby woods by soldiers; Josephine heard shots and the soldiers returned alone.

Ms Blanco later married, became Josephine Akiyama and settled in California. Both she and her former employer told this story to Captain Paul L. Briand Jr, an assistant professor of English at the USAF Academy in Colorado, who had been interested in Amelia's story. As a result Captain Briand wrote his book *Daughter of the Sky*, published in 1960, in which he outlined Mrs Akiyama's testimony and suggested that Amelia might have wandered off course during the night while Noonan slept.[7]

For Captain Briand's theory to be correct, Amelia's error would have had to have been more than 100 degrees from the point of her last reported position; instead of flying east she would have had to fly north-west. But a simple glance at her compasses (she had more than one) would have told Amelia she was flying almost in the opposite direction.

And what about the evidence of *Itasca*'s radio log and those who heard Amelia's transmissions at strength five towards the end of her flight? For *Itasca* to have received strength five signals from Amelia's 50-watt transmitter from the Mariana Islands was most improbable, especially during daylight hours (the condition known as 'skip' which can cause freak radio reception is more common at night). What is more the Marianas are a very large group of islands covering a huge area of the North Pacific Ocean. Amelia could hardly have been out of sight of land for the length of time reported, had she been in the Marianas and flying the course she would have to have steered to get there from the Nukumanu Islands. Captain Briand maintained his belief, however, that Amelia had finished her flight in Saipan and in 1967 wrote to Ann Pellegreno that he was convinced Amelia and Noonan had been captured and executed.

In 1960, just before the publication of Paul Briand's book, a San Francisco-based CBS journalist, Fred Goerner, came across Mrs Akiyama's story in a local paper. Goerner spent more than five years investigating the matter which included four trips to Saipan, during which he interviewed more than two hundred people, as well as investigation of the role played by US military organizations in Amelia's flight.

Goerner concluded that Amelia had been on a covert mission for the US government; that she had detoured to Truk for the purpose of taking photographs of Japanese fortifications; and that she had subsequently become lost in a tropical storm during the night. Goerner's contention was that she landed in the lagoon at Mili Atoll in the south-eastern Marshall Islands some seven hundred miles north-west of Howland Island. She waded ashore to get help for Noonan who had hurt his head in the landing. Later, some eleven days after the Electra had landed, a Japanese fishing boat arrived at the island and took Amelia and Noonan aboard, transferring them either to the seaplane tender *Kamoi* or the survey ship *Koshu*. They were taken to Jaluit, then Kwajalein, and finally to Japanese military headquarters in Saipan for questioning.

'Death may have been a release they both desired,' Goerner said on the final page of his best-selling *The Search for Amelia Earhart*. The frontispiece was a photograph of Amelia sitting on the running board of a car with a Japanese driver. The caption said pointedly that the photograph had been among the effects of a captured Japanese officer during the 1944 invasion. But the photograph was later identified as having been taken before Amelia's round-the-world flight; the driver was employed by Standard Oil and the bracelet Amelia is wearing in the photograph (the elephant hoof bangle with silver insets) is part of the Ninety-Nines collection, so could not have been with her on her final flight.[8]

After the Goerner book came a whole crop of theories. Marines Everett Hansen and Billy Burks who were on Saipan in 1944 claim that under the command of a Captain Griswold they excavated a grave. The remains of two bodies were taken away by Captain Griswold. When Burks and Hansen asked what it was all about, Griswold is said to have winked and said mysteriously: 'Did you ever hear about Amelia Earhart?'[9]

Donald Kothera had seen a civilian plane without its engines in a canyon on Saipan in 1946. With a friend, Joe Davidson, he returned to the island in 1967 and interviewed islanders who claim that they remember seeing Amelia and Noonan there in 1937. The result was a book entitled *Amelia Earhart Returns from Saipan*.[10]

Many people who set out to prove that Amelia was captured and died in Japanese hands, contacted Amy. For the old lady the possibility that her daughter had died in the service of her country was a more palatable explanation for Amelia's disappearance than that Amelia had simply got lost and run out of fuel. Amy told newsmen in 1949 that she believed Amelia to have been on a mission for the US government: 'Amelia said there were things she couldn't tell me . . .' But there were always things Amy could not be told prior to one of Amelia's record-breaking flights, and the reason was that Amelia could not rely on her mother not to reveal her plans.

Perhaps one of the most bizarre episodes of all was based on (initially, at least) genuinely detailed and well-assembled initial research by Joe Gervais from which he produced a manuscript called 'Operation Earhart'. Like Goerner, Gervais maintained that Amelia was a spy whose mission had been to fly over

Truk and the Marshalls to photograph them, and was then to 'get lost' on Canton Island. He had first tried to visit Saipan in 1969 but unlike Goerner (who was an accredited pressman) could not get permission. Instead he went to Guam and questioned natives who had formerly lived on Saipan. He continued his research for six years but when Goerner's book was published it was scornful of Gervais's work (a surprising act towards a fellow author and contemporary researcher), which temporarily hampered Gervais for he lost a great deal of credence. This did not deter him, however.

In 1965 while lunching on Long Island Gervais met a woman who was wearing an oakleaf decoration that may only be worn by holders of the American Distinguished Flying Cross. Gervais thought that she looked exactly as Amelia Earhart would have looked had she survived. He spoke to the woman, Irene Bolam, and she told him in conversation that she belonged to the Ninety-Nines and Zonta. After a complicated calculation, Gervais concluded that the woman *was* Amelia Earhart, who had survived the flight, having successfully accomplished her spy mission. But, Gervais claimed, she had wished to opt out of her high-powered former life so the government had secretly brought her back to the United States and given her a new identity.

She (Amelia, according to Gervais) later married and a key factor in Gervais's new theory was that the letters in her husband's name (Guy Bolam) could be made to represent each of the eight islands of the Phoenix Group. Furthermore, this produced a code which equated to the correct co-ordinates of Hull Island (Gull Island being the Pacific Island where Toni Carter, heroine of *Flight for Freedom* was supposed to 'get lost'. The coincidence was too much for Mr Gervais to accept). Despite evidence from Mrs Bolam's friends, such as aviatrix Viola Gentry who had known both Mrs Bolam *and* Amelia Earhart in 1928, Gervais insisted that no records (pilot's licence etc) of Mrs Bolam existed prior to 1937.

Gervais was even more convinced when he found photographs of an Electra 10E which had crashed in the mountains in California bearing the registration number NR16020. He maintained that Amelia had never taken the Electra 10E on her round-the-world flight, that she had actually flown a larger military version called the Lockheed XC-35 which had supercharged engines, a cruising range of forty hours and a speed in excess of 200 mph and was test-flown in May 1937. This, Gervais maintained, was the real reason for Amelia's crash in Hawaii on the first attempt, so that the XC-35 could be substituted when the original Electra was being rebuilt at Lockheed.

After a book called *Amelia Earhart Lives* written by Joe Klaas (who had worked with Gervais for some years on the story) was published in 1970, Mrs Bolam had to sue Gervais. One of the pictures in his book showed Amelia in Japanese dress being served with tea and it was hinted that this was evidence of her temporary capture; but the picture concerned was taken in Hawaii prior to her solo trans-Pacific flight when she was staying in a house full of Japanese servants. The aeroplane with the same number as Amelia's Electra was a sister ship bought by Paul Mantz after the war; he had obtained permission to use Amelia's old registration. Only one Lockheed XC-35 was ever built and it was in a museum in the USA when Gervais wrote his book, so it could not have been shot down over a Pacific Island as he claimed.[11]

And so it went on, the Earhart legend. Subsequent books on the subject tended to use what was known and build on it and so were less subject to the traps and pitfalls suffered by earlier writers. Among the more credible is one by Vincent Loomis, *Amelia Earhart – The Final Story;* his theory about where the Electra landed is shared by Oliver Knaggs in *Amelia Earhart – Her Last Flight.* Both writers believe that after failing to locate Howland, Amelia turned and headed for the Gilbert Islands, but a navigational error put her over the Marshalls where the Electra landed in a lagoon at Mili Atoll. From here the flyers were taken by the Japanese to Saipan where Fred was executed after throwing a bowl of food into the face of his guard, and Amelia died of dysentery.

Paul Mantz and Muriel Morrissey were each concerned enough by the crop of stories to write to Eleanor Roosevelt. Both received her personal assurance that Amelia was not involved in a government mission.[12] Senior Japanese officers who were stationed in the Marianas and the Marshalls and who would have known if two American flyers were captured have been interviewed. Having served prison terms for their part in war crimes they have nothing to fear from confession at this point and yet they still profess to know nothing.

But there is such a wealth of evidence from islanders who claim to have seen two white flyers (many say one was a woman, but not all), both in the Marshall Islands and Saipan before the war, that it would be irresponsible to dismiss it out of hand. Serious discrepancies exist, however, between the verbal evidence of eye witnesses presented in the various books, and sometimes even within the same narrative. The Electra has been 'seen' crashing in the sea off several different islands, but turning up intact in another. It has also been witnessed in a series of different locations, sometimes as a wreck, sometimes only slightly damaged; and it has also been seen as it was destroyed by the US Army. Amelia has been summarily executed on landing in some stories, and has been incarcerated in a jail according to other witnesses. Sometimes witnesses claim that she was not jailed but lived in semi-captivity in a hotel, free to come and go within a limited area. Most witnesses, though, say that the woman flyer died of dysentery. Many were shown photographs of Amelia with the question 'Was this the woman?' The answer was invariably 'Yes.'

There were even claims that Amelia may have been 'Tokyo Rose', the wartime woman 'disc-jockey' who beguiled Pacific-based American troops. Tokyo Rose had a marked American (New York) accent and it is not impossible to imagine some seabee remarking idly that it must be Amelia Earhart. Laughable as this may seem George once made a special trip to the front lines to listen to a Tokyo Rose broadcast in order to confirm that the voice was positively not Amelia's.

With so many eye-witnesses (the number seems to grow each year despite the passing of time) it must be assumed that there probably were two white flyers on Saipan and/or the Marshalls before the war. Whether these two flyers were Amelia Earhart and Fred Noonan is open to serious doubt.

No *hard* evidence has ever been found or presented, in spite of countless thousands of research hours in American and Japanese military archives, and after millions of words have been written on the subject by scores of authors, to prove that Amelia and Noonan survived an emergency landing in the ocean in the vicinity of Howland Island.

As stated in a previous chapter, the theory that Amelia was a spy is now almost dead. The welter of documents released by the US government, and those available in the Roosevelt Library at Hyde Park, must convince all but the most cynical researcher that there was no covert operation involved in Amelia's disappearance. Apart from anything else Amelia's flight over the area concerned in these theories would have been at night, yet Amelia had no equipment available for night-time photography. Much of the credit for exploding the spy theory must go to Dick Strippel for a highly readable and technically laudable book, *Amelia Earhart – The Myth and the Reality*, published in 1972. Even Fred Goerner now agrees that Amelia was not a spy, but like many others he is convinced that Amelia ended up in the hands of the Japanese and died in captivity[13].

Notes on other principals in this book:

Amy Otis Earhart died on 29 October 1962 at the age of ninety-five.

Muriel Earhart Morrissey gave lectures on the subject of her sister for many years, and donated the family papers to the Schlesinger Library at Radcliffe College. This is now one of the primary sources of information on Amelia Earhart's life. Muriel died in 1998 aged ninety-eight.

Jean-Marie, George's third wife, remarried Mr George T. Asp.

Peg, George's fourth, and last, wife continued to run the Stove Pipe Wells hotel after his death. His estate was not – contrary to speculation – enormous. As tourism increased, by dint of hard work she built up the business, increasing the original tiny accommodation to take 265 persons and achieved a first-class reputation for comfort and standards. In 1962 she met Willard Lewis and they were married.

Paul Mantz became one of the most famous of Hollywood's aviation movie stuntmen. If this conveys the impression of a 'daredevil flyer' it is correct, he was meticulous and precise, devising and planning his every move. Almost inevitably, though, he was killed as a result of his profession, while making the movie *The Flight of the Phoenix* in 1965.

APPENDIX 4

CHRONOLOGY OF IMPORTANT EVENTS IN AMELIA EARHART'S LIFE

Age on 24 July	Year	
	1897	Amelia Mary Earhart, first child of Edwin and Amy Otis Earhart, is born (July 24) in Atchison, Kansas.
11	1908	Amelia sees her first aeroplane, at the Iowa State Fair.
21	1918	Amelia becomes a nurse at Spadina Military Convalescent Hospital in Toronto, Canada.
22	1919	Returns to the United States to live with her sister and mother in Massachusetts. Enrols in fall as medical student at Columbia University.
23	1920	Leaves Columbia University after one semester. Joins parents who are living in Los Angeles. Meets Sam Chapman. Takes first flight with Frank Hawks.
24	1921	Takes flying lessons from Neta Snook and buys first aeroplane (Kinner Airster).
25	1922	Sets unofficial women's altitude record of 14,000 feet.
26	1923	Becomes engaged to Sam Chapman.
27	1924	Amy and Edwin Earhart separate and begin divorce proceedings. Amelia sells Kinner Airster and buys automobile in which she drives her mother from California to Massachusetts, where they settle with Muriel.
29	1926	Becomes social worker at Denison House.
30	1927	Receives call from Captain H. H. Railey, who later asked if she would like to be the first woman to fly across the Atlantic. Writes Ruth Nichols regarding forming an organisation for women who fly.
31	1928	Becomes first woman to cross Atlantic by air, as a passenger (17–18 June). Buys Avro Avian airplane. Writes *20 Hrs. 40 Min.* Announces that her engagement to Sam Chapman is ended. Makes first solo-return transcontinental flight by a woman (September–October).

32	1929	Acquires Lockheed Vega and competes in first Women's Air Derby (Santa Monica, California, to Cleveland, Ohio), taking third place. George Palmer Putnam and his wife, Dorothy, separate.
33	1930	Becomes first president of the Ninety-Nines, the first women pilots' organisation. Joins Ludington Lines airline as vice president. Edwin Earhart dies of cancer. George Putnam's divorce becomes final. Amelia sets women's speed record of 181.18 mph over a three-kilometre course (July). Acquires transport license (October).
34	1931	Amelia marries George Putnam (7 February). Acquires an autogiro and achieves altitude record for autogiro of 18,451 feet (April), then becomes first person to make solo-return trans-continental flight in an autogiro (May–June).
35	1932	Writes *The Fun of It*. Becomes first woman (and only the second person) to fly the Atlantic solo, and the first person to cross the Atlantic twice by air (20–21 May, the fifth anniversary of Charles Lindbergh's transatlantic flight). Sets women's record for fastest non-stop transcontinental flight (Los Angeles to Newark, New Jersey) in 19 hours and 5 minutes (August). Receives the following awards: Distinguished Flying Cross, given by the US Congress The Cross of Knight of the Legion of Honor, given by the French government Gold Medal of the National Geographic Society, presented to Amelia by President Herbert Hoover Honorary membership in the National Aeronautic Association. Wins the Harmon Trophy as America's Outstanding Airwoman.
36	1933	Visits the White House as guest of the Roosevelts. Participates in National Air Races in Cleveland, Ohio. Breaks own transcontinental record in time of 17 hours, 7 minutes, and 30 seconds. Wins the Harmon Trophy.
37	1934	Wins the Harmon Trophy for the third year in a row.
38	1935	Becomes first person to fly solo across the Pacific Ocean from Honolulu, Hawaii, to Oakland, California (2,408 miles), in 17 hours and 7 minutes (11–12 January). Becomes first person to fly solo from Los Angeles to Mexico (April), by official invitation of the Mexican government. After record-breaking return flight from Mexico City to Newark, New Jersey, Amelia is mobbed

by welcoming crowds. Named America's Outstanding Airwoman by Harmon Trophy committee. Competes in National Air Race with Paul Mantz.

39	1936	Takes delivery of Lockheed twin-engined airplane termed the 'Flying Laboratory', which was financed by Purdue University (July). Starts planning round-the-world flight.
39	1937	First leg of round-the-world flight (Oakland, California, to Honolulu, Hawaii) sets record for east–west crossing in 15 hours and 47 minutes (17 March); Amelia ground loops while taking off for Howland Island (20 March), and aeroplane is badly damaged. Aeroplane is repaired and a second attempt at world flight begins from Miami, Florida, on 1 June, 1937. On 2 July, after completing 22,000 miles of the flight, Amelia and her navigator, Fred Noonan, take off from Lae, New Guinea, for Howland Island. Several radio contacts are subsequently made but neither the aeroplane nor the flyers are ever seen again.

NOTES AND SOURCES

Abbreviations used in notes:
AE Amelia Earhart
AOE Amelia Otis Earhart
GPP George Palmer Putnam
MEM Muriel Earhart Morrissey

INTRODUCTION

1 *Southampton Daily Echo*, 19 June 1928.
2 *Ibid.*
3 *Ibid.*
4 Amelia Earhart, 'Lucky Turning Point', *New York Herald Tribune*, n/d.
5 George Palmer Putnam, 'Amelia's Career Described', *Providence Sunday Journal*, 19 September 1937.

CHAPTER 1

1 Schlesinger Library, Radcliffe College, Cambridge Massachusetts. Ref.: A129 Folder 2(d) 'History of Altman family'.
2 *Ibid.*
3 *Ibid.* Ref.: A129, Folder 2(a) 'A Brief History of Earhart Ancestors'.
4 *Ibid.* Ref.: A129, Folder 2(a) and 2(d).
5 *Ibid.* Ref.: A129, Folder 2(a).
6 *Ibid.*
7 *Ibid.* Ref.: A129, Folder 1 'Genealogy of Isaac Otis, his family and descendants' (29 sheets).
8 Butler Library, Columbia University, New York. Oral History Collection. Ref.: Amy Otis Earhart.
9 A. T. Andreas, *History of State of Kansas*, privately published, Chicago, 1883, p. 396.
10 Paragraph refers specifically to settler George Million. Information from

article entitled 'Early Atchison' provided by Atchison County Library Local history collection.

11 *Ibid.*

12 *Ibid.* Ref.: *Happenings in 1858.*

13 *Ibid.* Local History – general file.

14 Butler Library, Oral History Collection. Ref.: Amy Otis Earhart.

15 Andreas, *History of State of Kansas,* p. 396.

16 *Atchison Globe,* 27 April 1905.

17 Butler Library, Oral History Collection. Ref.: Amy Otis Earhart.

18 *Ibid.* Family legend has it that each time another child arrived the judge built on another room.

19 Andreas, *History of State of Kansas,* p 396.

20 Butler Library, Oral History Collection. Ref.: Amy Otis Earhart.

21 *Ibid.* In her second recorded interview Amy states that she satisfied the entrance requirements for Wellesley College.

22 *Ibid.*

23 Muriel Earhart Morrissey, *Courage is the Price,* McCormick-Armstrong, 1963.

24 Butler Library, Oral History Collection. Ref.: Amy Otis Earhart.

25 *Ibid.*

26 Baptismal Register, Trinity Episcopalian Church, Atchison, Kansas. Also, the *Atchison Globe,* 27 July 1897.

27 Butler Library, Oral History Collection. Ref.: Amy Otis Earhart.

CHAPTER 2

1 Jean L. Backus, *Letters from Amelia,* Beacon Press, Boston, 1982, p. 18. Morrissey, *Courage is the Price,* pp 80–81.

2 *Ibid.*

3 Morrissey, *Courage is the Price,* p. 27. Letter dated 12 May 1903.

4 Author's interview with Mrs Muriel Morrissey, Medford, Mass., June 1987.

5 Amelia Earhart, *The Fun of It,* Harcourt Brace Jovanovich, New York, 1932, p. 11.

6 *Ibid.,* p. 12; also Butler Library, Oral History Collection. Ref.: Amy Otis Earhart.

7 *Atchison Globe,* special edition, 21 June 1963.

8 Butler Library, Oral History Collection. Ref.: Amy Otis Earhart.

9 Backus, *Letters from Amelia,* p. 15.

10 Butler Library, Oral History Collection. Ref.: Amy Otis Earhart.

11 Mrs M. O. O'Keefe: *Atchison Globe,* 21 July 1963.

12 Morrissey, *Courage is the Price,* p. 52.

13 Mrs M. O. O'Keefe: *Atchison Globe,* 21 July 1963.

14 Atchison Museum, Earhart Collection.

15   Backus, *Letters from Amelia*, p. 18.
16   Schlesinger Library. Ref.: 83–M69.
17   Helen Rogers to AE, 30 June 1932; Schlesinger Library Collection.
18   Butler Library, Oral History Collection. Ref.: Amy Otis Earhart.
19   Morrissey, *Courage is the Price*, p. 78.
20   *Ibid.*
21   Backus, *Letters from Amelia*, p. 20.
22   Letter from Mather, Rock Island Line, dated 5 December 1912. Schlesinger Library. Ref.: 83–M69.
23   Butler Library, Oral History Collection. Ref.: Amy Otis Earhart.
24   *Ibid.*
25   Backus, *Letters from Amelia*, p. 18.
26   Schlesinger Library. Ref.: 83–M69.
27   Morrissey, *Courage is the Price*, p. 88.

CHAPTER 3

1   *Los Angeles Times*, 19 June 1928, 'Dad Proud . . .', p. 2.
2   Morrissey, *Courage is the Price*, p. 96.
3   *Ibid.*
4   Backus, *Letters from Amelia*, p. 22.
5   Morrissey, *Courage is the Price*, p. 99.
6   ΛE to ΛOE, Schlesinger Library. Ref.: 83–M69 dated Saturday (March 1917).
7   *Ibid.*, Tuesday (31 July 1917).
8   *Ibid.*, 8 August 1917.
9   *Ibid.*, 14 August 1917.
10 Butler Library, Oral History Collection. Ref.: Amy Otis Earhart.
11 Schlesinger Library. Ref.: 83–M69, undated (November 1917).
12 *Ibid.* Two letters dated 31 October and November (undated) 1917.
13 *Ibid.* November 1917.
14 Bill for School Fees from Ogontz School for Girls dated 11 June 1917. Schlesinger Library, Ref.: 83–M69.
15 Earhart, *The Fun of It*, p. 19.
16 *Ibid.*
17 *Ibid.*, p. 20.
18 *Ibid.*
19 Schlesinger Library. Ref.: 84–M21, written from Northampton, Mass. on 26 December 1918.
20 Earhart, *The Fun of It*, p. 21.
21 Schlesinger Library, 13 March 1919. Ref.: 84–M21.
22 Earhart, *The Fun of It*, p. 21.
23 *Ibid.*
24 Pilots' licences, registration cards at Columbia and Harvard, etc.

25 AE to AOE., no date, probably September 1919. Schlesinger Library. Ref.: 83–M69.

26 Earhart, *The Fun of It*, p. 23.

27 Muriel Earhart Morrissey and Carol L. Osborne, *Amelia My Courageous Sister*, Osborne Publishers, Inc., California, 1987, p. 57.

28 Neta Snook Southern, *I Taught Amelia to Fly*, Vantage Press, New York, 1974, p. 104.

CHAPTER 4

1 But enacted under his successor, Franklin D. Roosevelt.

2 Morrissey, *Courage is the Price*, p. 119.

3 Earhart, *The Fun of It*, p. 24.

4 *Ibid.*

5 Amelia Earhart, *20 Hrs. 40 Min.*, G. P. Putnam's Sons, New York 1928, p. 46.

6 Operated by Emery Rogers, this was the first commercial field in Los Angeles. It was located west of Wilshire Boulevard.

7 Earhart, *The Fun of It*, p. 25.

8 *Ibid.*

9 *Ibid.*

10 Southern, *I Taught Amelia to Fly*, pp 92–5.

12 *Ibid.*, p. 92.

12 *Ibid.*, p. 95.

13 George Palmer Putnam, *Soaring Wings*, Harrop & Co., London, 1939, p. 44.

14 Southern, *I Taught Amelia to Fly*, p. 1.

15 Morrissey, *Courage is the Price*, p. 102.

16 Southern, *I Taught Amelia to Fly*, pp 105–6.

17 Earhart, *The Fun of It*, pp 25–6.

18 Southern, *I Taught Amelia to Fly*, p. 106.

19 *Ibid.*, p. 110.

20 *Ibid.*

21 *Ibid.*

22 *Ibid.*, p. 122.

23 *Ibid.*

24 *Ibid.*, p. 124.

25 Earhart, *20 Hrs. 40 Min.*, p. 66.

26 *Ibid.*, p. 67.

27 Earhart, *The Fun of It*, p. 27.

28 According to Neta Snook Southern's log book, she gave Amelia five hours' instruction in the Canuck and fifteen hours in the Kinner 'Canary'. Further hours were required with John Mòntijo before Amelia went solo. A good average for students is reckoned to be (and was then) twelve hours.

29 This aeroplane was the first of the DC aircraft, had a 56-foot wingspan,

a twelve-cylinder Liberty engine and was the first aeroplane to carry its own weight as a payload.

30 Southern, *I Taught Amelia to Fly*, p. 126.

31 *Ibid.*

32 *News Press*, St Joseph, Mo. 20 Febuary 1977, interview with Neta Snook Southern.

33 *American Magazine*, August 1932, p. 72.

34 Earhart, *20 Hrs. 40 Min.*, p. 56.

35 Any reasonably intelligent person can become a good and proficient pilot but it has been recognised for some time by the Air Forces of the world that some people have instinctive ability in the air. Today, prospective jet fighter pilots can be recognised long before they set foot in an aeroplane because this skill is apparent even in flight simulators. For natural pilots the air is simply their element, and the ability which makes such pilots outstanding appears to be inbuilt; it cannot be learned.

CHAPTER 5

1 *American Magazine* (no date but probably late 1928), p. 72; AE's Scrapbooks at Purdue.

2 Elgen and Marie Long's taped interview with Lloyd Royer.

3 *American Magazine*, p. 72.

4 *American Magazine*, August 1932, p. 15.

5 Long's Royer interview.

6 Letter from AE to Lloyd Royer, 5 October 1921; Long's Royer interview, courtesy of Marie and Elgen Long.

7 *Los Angeles Examiner*, 8 August 1922.

8 This record does not appear in official archives. Ruth Law had already reached 14,000 feet some years earlier but as there were no separate classifications for women's records and they had not exceeded the altitude achieved by men, such attempts and achievements were regarded as 'unofficial'.

   Many such unofficial 'women's records' (recognised by the aviation fraternity) were set until the first officially recorded woman's altitude was set by Louise Thaden in December 1928 when she reached 20,260 feet.

9 Earhart, *20 Hrs. 40 Min.*, pp 80–1.

10 Amelia was later to claim, uncorrectly, that this was the first licence issued to an American woman.

11 Letters to the author from AE's cousins Ann Cain Tibbetts and Doryce McKelvy.

12 Long's Royer interview.

13 John Underwood, *Madcaps, Millionaires and 'Mose'*, Heritage Press, 1984. (See reproduction of official programme on back cover of this book.)

14 Earhart, *20 Hrs. 40 Min.*, pp 85–6.

15 Long's Royer interview.

16 Long's Royer interview.
17 Amelia's student registration card at Columbia University.
18 Earhart, *The Fun of It*, p. 48.
19 Putnam, *Soaring Wings*, p. 47.
20 Earhart, *20 Hrs. 40 Min.*, p. 86.
21 Letter from Waldo Waterman, first vice president of The Early Birds 19 April 1962. File: Amelia Earhart General, NA&SM Library Smithsonian Institution, Washington, DC. Mr Waterman was the subsequent owner, but had little use from the plane as it suffered a broken crankshaft shortly after his purchase.
22 Earhart, *20 Hrs. 40 Min.*, p. 88.
23 Long's Royer interview.
24 AE to Lloyd Royer: letter in possession of Elgen and Marie Long by whose kind permission it is reproduced here.
25 Earhart, *The Fun of It*, p. 52.
26 *Ibid.*
27 76 Brook Street, West Medford.
28 Job application form: Denison House records: Schlesinger Library.
29 Their company 'Montijo and Royer' was formed to build a five-passenger cabin biplane called 'The California Coupe', information courtesy John Underwood.
30 AE to Lloyd Royer. Letter in Amelia Earhart General file NA&SM Library, Smithsonian Institution, Washington, DC.
31 Women's Union files, Radcliffe College, Cambridge, Mass.
32 Backus, *Letters from Amelia*, p. 62.
33 Putnam, *Soaring Wings*, p. 54.
34 *Christian Science Monitor* clipping, undated but in 1928 scrapbook, front page.
35 Unidentified news clipping in AE's scrapbook, *c.* 1928.
36 AE to Bernard Wiesman, 6 May 1928: Purdue.
37 Earhart, *The Fun of It*, pp 59–60.

CHAPTER 6

1 G. P. Putnam, *Wide Margins*, Harcourt Brace and Company, New York, 1942,
2 *Ibid.*, p. 3.
3 *Ibid.*, p. 25.
4 *Ibid.*, pp 23–4.
5 *Ibid.*, p. 7.
6 *Ibid.*, p. 30.
7 *Ibid.*, pp 34–5.
8 *Ibid.*, pp 41–2.
9 *Ibid.*, pp 38–9.

10   *Ibid.*, p. 38.
11   *Dictionary of American Art*, John Murray, London, 1979.
12   Putnam, *Wide Margins*, pp 43–7.
13   *Ibid.*, p. 45.
14   *Ibid.*, p. 47.
15   Harvard College Archives (Students' records), Cambridge, Mass. Letter dated 17 March 1908.
16   Putnam, *Wide Margins*, p. 49.
17   *Ibid.*, p. 49.
18   Wellesley College Archives. Class of 1910 biographical records and reunion books.
19   Theodore John Winthrop, *The Canoe and the Saddle* (publisher unknown), British Library shelfmark 12704.K.34, 1863.
20   Putnam, *Wide Margins*, pp 48–9.
21   *Ibid*, p. 49.

CHAPTER 7

Apart from the various newspapers cited for chapters 7 to 9 there are two main sources of information. One is GPP's own autobiography *Wide Margins*; the other is a thesis written in June 1966 by James LeRoy Crowell of Bend, Oregon, entitled 'Frontier Publisher – A Romantic View of George Palmer Putnam's Career at The Bend *Bulletin* 1910–1914'. Mr Crowell has most generously allowed me to use the results of his college research, his excellent thesis and his scholarship.

1   James LeRoy Crowell, *Frontier Publisher*, June 1966, Bend, Oregon, USA, pp 21–2.
2   Putnam, *Wide Margins*, p. 51.
3   *Ibid.*, pp 51–2.
4   *Ibid.*, p. 53.
5   *Ibid.*
6   GP stated in *Wide Margins*, apparently incorrectly, that there were 1,200 people in Bend, but Crowell points out that the Federal census of 1910 lists 536 living in Bend. 'The discrepancy lies in the statistics of the precinct of Deschutes, which had 616 residents [which] had been annexed to Bend.' Crowell, *Frontier Publisher*, p. 53.
7   Crowell, *Frontier Publisher*, p. 50. The author makes the point that $300, in the days when a wholesome meal could be purchased at the hotel for 35 cents, gave Putnam a great advantage over the average newcomer to Bend in 1909.
8   *Ibid.*, p. 52.
9   *Ibid.*, p. 3.
10   *Ibid.*, p. 75.
11   *Bulletin*, 18 August 1909.

12   Crowell, *Frontier Publisher*, p. 82.
13   'Palmer Bend' (George Palmer Putnam), *The Smiting of the Rock*, G. P. Putnam's Sons, New York, 1919.
14   Crowell, *Frontier Publisher*, p. 88.
15   *Bulletin*, 16 February 1910.
16   Crowell, *Frontier Publisher*, p. 90.
17   Bulletin, 16 March 1910. However, Mr Crowell states on p. 2 of *Frontier Publisher* that GP merely obtained a half interest.
18   Putnam, *Wide Margins*, p. 62.
19   *Ibid.*
20   Crowell, *Frontier Publisher*, pp 95–6.
21   Wellesley College Archives. Class of 1910 biographical records and reunion books.
22   Pinelyn, 606 Congress Street, Bend.
23   George Palmer Putnam, *In the Southland of North America*, G. P. Putnam's Sons, New York, 1913.
24   *Bulletin*, 15 November 1911.
25   Crowell, *Frontier Publisher*, p. 141.
26   Putnam, *Wide Margins*, p. 65.
27   *Ibid.*
28   *Ibid.*, p. 67.
29   Crowell, *Frontier Publisher*, pp 145–6.
30   Putnam, *Wide Margins*, pp 54–5.
31   *Ibid.*
32   *Ibid.*
33   Crowell, *Frontier Publisher*, p. 151.
34   Putnam, *Wide Margins*, p. 64.
35   Wellesley College Archives. Class of 1910 biographical records and reunion books.
36   Crowell, *Frontier Publisher*, p. 61.
37   *Ibid.*, p. 135.
38   Putnam, *Wide Margins*, p. 68.
39   *Ibid.*, pp 55–6.
40   Wellesley College Archives. Class of 1910 biographical records and reunion books.
41   Crowell, *Frontier Publisher*, p. 194.
42   *Portland Oregonian*, 28 November 1914.
43   Crowell, *Frontier Publisher*, p. 139–140.
44   *Ibid.*

CHAPTER 8

1   Putnam, *Wide Margins*, p. 79.
2   *Ibid.*

3   *Ibid.*
4   Crowell, *Frontier Publisher*, p. 213.
5   *Ibid.*, p. 214.
6   Honourable Discharge Papers G. P. Putnam: Oregon National Guard, 30 December 1916.
7   *Bend Bulletin*, 6 September 1916.
8   Crowell, *Frontier Publisher*, p. 217.
9   Putnam, *Wide Margins*, p. 79.
10 *Ibid.*
11 Putnam, *Wide Margins*, pp 4 and 10.
12 *Ibid.*
13 Honourable Discharge from Army, document dated 20 December 1918.
14 *Who was Who 1951–1960*; see also Putnam, *Wide Margins*, p. 14.
15 Crowell, *Frontier Publisher*, p. 223.
16 Putnam, *Wide Margins*, p. 80.
17 *Ladies' Home Journal*, 1 May 1920, p. 41; *Collier's Magazine*, 5 June 1920, p.54.
18 Putnam, *Wide Margins*, p. 94.
19 *Ibid.*, p. 91.
20 A neighbour at Rye, Mrs Caroline O'Day.
21 Putnam, *Wide Margins*, p. 94.
22 *Ibid.*, p. 164.
23 *Publisher's Weekly*, 1921.
24 William J. Robinson, *Married Love and Happiness*, Critic and Guide, New York, 1922.
25 Corey Ford, *The Time for Laughter*, pp 203–5.
26 *Ibid.*
27 Crowell, *Frontier Publisher*, p. 235.
28 Putnam, *Wide Margins*, pp 109–10.
29 *Ibid.*, p. 153 and Putnam family tradition.

CHAPTER 9

1   Author's interview with 'Cap' Palmer, Los Angeles, June 1988.
2   Putnam, *Wide Margins*, p. 252.
3   *Ibid.*, p. 217.
4   *New York Times*, 21 February 1916, Section IX, p. 7.
5   Formerly named the *Effie Morrissey*.
6   *New York Times*, 21 June 1926, p. 1.
7   *Geographical Review*, vol. XVIII no. 1, January 1928, p. 4; *New York Times*, 21 February 1926.
8   Dan Streeter, *An Arctic Rodeo*, G. P. Putnam's Sons, New York, 1919.
9   David Binney Putnam, *David Goes Voyaging*, G. P. Putnam's Sons, New York, 1925.

10   *Idem.; David Goes to Greenland,* 1927; *David Goes to Baffin Land,* 1928.
11   Putnam, *Wide Margins,* pp 252–3.
12   *New York Times,* 21 June 1926, p. 1.
13   *New York Times,* 11 May 1926, p. 3.
14   Streeter, *Arctic Rodeo,* p. 226.
15   *New York Times,* 19 August 1926, p. 1.
16   *Ibid.,* 25 September 1926, pp 1–3.
17   Putnam, *Wide Margins,* p. 373.
18   *New York Times,* 3 October 1926, p. 20.
19   Expedition sponsors were James B. Ford and Frederick C. Waltcott of the American Geographical Society Council, W. F. Kenny of New York, Gustavus D. Pope of Detroit, and George Grey Barnard of New York; the Museum of the American Indian, Heye Foundation, and the Buffalo Society of Natural Sciences. George Palmer Putnam (director of the expedition), underwrote the balance.
20   *New York Times,* 11 September 1927, p. 1.
21   Edward Jablonski, *Atlantic Fever,* Macmillan, New York, 1972, p 294.
22   Walter S. Ross, *The Last Hero,* Harper and Row, Inc., New York, 1964, p. 139.
23   Charles A. Lindbergh, *The Spirit of St Louis,* Charles Scribner's Sons, New York, 1953, p. 504.
24   Putnam, *Wide Margins,* pp 231–42.
25   Lindbergh, *The Spirit of St Louis,* p. 547.
26   Putnam, *Wide Margins,* p. 232.
27   *Geographical Review,* vol. XVIII, no. 1, p. 4.
28   Putnam, *Wide Margins,* p. 234.
29   *Ibid.*
30   *Geographical Review,* vol. XVIII, no. 1, p. 4.
31   Lindbergh, *The Spirit of St Louis,* p. 547.
32   Putnam, *Wide Margins,* p. 235.
33   Lindbergh, *The Spirit of St Louis,* p. 547.
34   Putnam, *Wide Margins,* p. 235.
35   *Ibid.,* p. 236.
36   *Ibid.,* p. 233. Lindbergh eventually received about $200,000 in royalties on sales of *We.*
37   *Ibid.,* p. 237.
38   *Geographical Review,* vol. XVIII, no. 1, p. 4.
39   Richard Evelyn Byrd, *Skyward,* G. P. Putnam's Sons, New York, 1928. In recognition of his flight over the South Pole on 29 November 1929 Byrd was promoted to the rank of Rear-Admiral USN (Rtd) by an Act of Congress.
40   Putnam, *Wide Margins,* pp 301–3; see also Paul O'Neil, *Barnstormers and Speed Kings,* Time Life Books, New York, 1981, pp 59–63.
41   *Time* magazine, 25 August 1930.
42   Putnam, *Wide Margins,* p. 236.
43   *Ibid.*

CHAPTER 10

1   Putnam, *Wide Margins*, p. 293.
2   Hilton H. Railey, *Touch'd with Madness*, Carrick and Evans, New York, 1938, p. 100.
3   *Ibid.*
4   Putnam, *Wide Margins*, p. 293.
5   *Ibid.*
6   Railey, *Touch'd with Madness*, p. 101.
7   Putnam, *Wide Margins*, p. 171.
8   *Ibid.*, p. 294.
9   Railey, *Touch'd with Madness*, p. 103.
10 *Ibid.*
11 *Ibid.*, p. 104.
12 Earhart, *20 Hrs. 40 Min.*, p. 100.
13 *Ibid.*, 101.
14 Jablonski, *Atlantic Fever*, p. 190; *New York Times*, 2 July 1929, Obituary of Wilmer Stultz.
15 Letter to author from Richard K. Smith (air historian) 22 November 1987; and article by Richard S. Allen, *Air Britain Digest.*
16 *Ibid.*
17 Peggy Phipps Boegner and Richard Gashot, *Halcyon Days*, Old Westbury Gardens and Harry N. Abrams Inc., New York, 1986.
18 *Ibid.*
19 Frederick Guest: highly decorated for war service, Freddie – as he was universally known – served as assistant private secretary to his cousin, Winston Churchill (as Parliamentary Under-Secretary of State for Colonies; President of the Board of Trade and latterly as Home Secretary); he then served in various key positions in the Treasury before becoming Secretary of State for Air and President of the Air Council.
20 See various references in Bror Blixen, *The African Letters*, St Martin's Press, New York, 1988.
21 *Halcyon Days*, Boegner, pp 192–3.
22 Letter to the author from Mrs Helen Ogston regarding her conversation with McCracken.
23 Amelia Earhart, 'Lucky Turning Point', *New York Herald Tribune*, n/d .
24 *Miami Herald*, 22 May 1937.
25 'Amelia's Career' described by George Putnam, *Providence Sunday Journal*, 19 September 1957.
26 *Illustrated Love Magazine*, January 1932, pp 25–7, Interview with Amelia Earhart; courtesy of Purdue University collection: Ref.: AE's scrapbooks.
27 *Ibid.*
28 Morrissey and Osborne, *Amelia, My Courageous Sister*, p. 78.

CHAPTER 11

1   Corey Ford, *The Time for Laughter*, pp 101–3; Earhart, *20 Hrs. 40 Min.*, pp 96–101.
2   Earhart, *20 Hrs. 40 Min.*, p. 101.
3   Railey, *Touch'd with Madness*, p. 103.
4   Special Collections Library, Purdue University, Lafayette, Indiana. Ref.: I (A:2).
5   Letters to the author from Richard S. Allen and Richard K. Smith.
6   Earhart, *20 Hrs. 40 Min.*, p. 100.
7   *Ibid.*
8   *Ibid.*, p. 109.
9   *Ibid.*
10 AE's will. Seaver Centre, Los Angeles Museum, Ref.: L2100 PI 58.
11 *Ibid.*
12 George Palmer Putnam found these two letters some months after Amelia's disappearance, held together with a perished rubber hand. Paperclipped to them was the note 'Popping off letters'.
13 Earhart, *20 Hrs. 40 Min.*, p. 121.
14 *Spur* magazine, 15 July 1928, p. 39.
15 Anne Morrow Lindbergh, *Hour of Gold, Hour of Lead*, Harcourt Brace Jovanovich, New York, 1973, p. 121.
16 Article by Julia Railey in *Boston Evening Post*, exact date unknown, 1928.
17 Putnam, *Soaring Wings*, p. 58.
18 Author's interview with Cap Palmer, Los Angeles, June 1988.
19 Letter to the author from Richard K. Smith.
20 Earhart, *20 Hrs. 40 Min.*, p. 131.
21 *Lantern*, July–August 1928.
22 *Cosmopolitan* magazine, 'The Man who Tells the flyers: Go!', May 1929.
23 *Spur* magazine, 15 July 1928, p. 39.
24 *Ibid.*
25 *20 Hrs. 40 Min.*, p. 165.
26 Letter to the author from Richard K. Smith.
27 Jablonski, *Atlantic Fever*, p. 206.
28 *Time* magazine, 18 June 1928.
29 Earhart, *20 Hrs. 40 Min.*, pp 165–6.
30 Special Collections Library, Purdue University. File I:B (1928), cable dated 12 June 1928.
31 *Ibid.*, Cable dated 13 June 1928, 1 p.m.
32 *Ibid.*
33 Earhart, *20 Hrs. 40 Min.*, p. 166.
34 Special Collections Library, Purdue University. File I:B (1928), cable dated 13 June 1928, 5 p.m.
35 *Ibid.*, 10.30 p.m. I:A3 (1928).
36 *Ibid.*, File I:B13 (1928).

37 Letter to the author from Richard K. Smith.
38 Cable, Putnam/Earhart in Purdu University Archives, I/B 91928).
    Atlantic Flight file.
39 Putnam, *Soaring Wings*, pp 64–5.
40 *Ibid.*, p. 65.
41 Earhart, *20 Hrs. 40 Min.*, p. 170.
42 Putnam, *Soaring Wings*, p. 65.
43 Letter to the author from Richard K. Smith.
44 Earhart, *20 Hrs. 40 Min.*, p. 170.

CHAPTER 12

1 *Los Angeles Times*, 18 June 1928, p. 2.
2 *New York Times*, 18 June 1928, p. 1.
3 Earhart, *20 Hrs. 40 Min.*, pp 171–6.
4 *Ibid.*, p. 182.
5 *Ibid.*, p. 187, also unidentified newspaper cutting in NA&SM Library:
   Amelia Earhart General File: F0171300.
6 English daily papers, 19–20 June 1928.
7 *20 Hrs. 40 Min.*, p. 199.
8 Cyril Jeffries, *I Was There*, commemorative booklet by Burry Port
   Chamber of Commerce, May 1978.
9 Amelia interview in *Los Angeles Times*, 19 June 1928, p. 2.
10 Amelia had taken up fencing in Boston the previous winter.
11 *New York Sun*, 20 June 1928.
12 Mr Williams, resident of Burry Port in unidentified newspaper cutting
    dated 1987: Purdue University's collection of AE's scrapbooks.
13 Part of AE's log was reproduced in the programme of a Reception given
    by the City of Medford.
14 *New York Times*, 19 June 1928, p. 1.
15 *Los Angeles Times*, 18 June 1928, p. 2.
16 Copy of original cable at Purdue: File I:El.
17 Putnam, *Soaring Wings*, p. 66.
18 *Southern Daily Echo*, 19 June 1928, p. 1.
19 *New York Sun*, 20 June 1928, p. 1.
20 Not traced; probably among the papers destroyed by fire at Whitney
    Portal in 1953 (see chapter 22). Amelia's reply is at Purdue: File I:EI.
21 *Flight*, editorial, 21 June 1928.
22 Lady Heath to AE, 20 June 1928. Purdue File I:D17.
23 *Daily Express*, 25 June 1928.
24 *Ibid.*
25 Unidentified cutting in AE's scrapbooks at Purdue. This speech was
    repeated several times after she returned to the USA, see specifically
    New York Times, 29 July 1928.

26 Earhart, *20 Hrs. 40 Min.*, p. 209.
    Author's note: Beryl Markham, who flew the Atlantic from east to west in 1936, said much the same after sailing back to England. She later told a friend that if she had any comprehension of the amount of water she would never have made the flight.
27 Earhart, *The Fun of It*, p. 87.
28 Unidentified cine-clipping in the author's collection.
29 19 June 1928, p. 2.
30 George Putnam told this story several times in newspaper articles, many years afterwards. See also Morrissey, *Courage is the Price*, p. 167.
31 Cable to Porter Adams, 9 July 1928; NA&SM Library; Amelia Earhart General File, F0171300 Smithsonian Inst., Washington, DC.
32 Letter from Clarence Young, Assistant Secretary for Aeronautics, to Porter Adams dated 3 August 1928, *ibid.*
33 Letter to Clarence Young from Porter Adams, *ibid.*
34 AE to RB July 1928; also Byrd's reply dated 30 July 1928, *ibid.*
35 *New York Times*, 31 July 1928, p. 8.

CHAPTER 13

1   Earhart, *20 Hrs. 40 Min.*, p. 280.
2   AE to AOE, 12 August 1928. Schlesinger Library File: 83–M69.
3   *Ibid.*, 26 August 1928.
4   Elinor Smith, *Aviatrix*, Harcourt Brace, Jovanovich, New York, 1981, p. 135.
5   *20 Hrs. 40 Min.*, p. 280.
6   Transcript of author's interview with Mrs Jean-Marie Asp, San Diego California, June 1988.
7   *New York Times*, 1 September 1928, p. 1.
8   Earhart, *The Fun of It*, p. 91.
9   Putnam, *Soaring Wings*, p. 79.
10 *New York Times*, 1 October 1928, p. 14.
11 *Ibid.*, 5 October 1928, p. 27.
12 Putnam, *Soaring Wings*, p. 81.
13 *New York Times*, 23 November 1928, p. 22.
14 Smith, *Aviatrix*, p. 70.
15 *Ibid.*, p. 71.
16 Transcript of author's interviews with Elinor Smith Sullivan, Santa Clara, California, June 1987 and July 1988.
17 Putnam, *Wide Margins*, pp 286–7.
18 Donna Veca and Skip Mazzio, *Just Plane Crazy*, biography of Bobbi Trout, Osborne Publishers Inc., California, 1987, p. 106.
19 GPP to Stephen Mather. Berkeley College library, special collections. Mather File.
20 *New York Times*, 26 December 1928.

21 Smith, *Aviatrix*, p. 102.

22 *Ibid.*, p. 103.

23 Smith, *Aviatrix*, pp 93–4 and author's cited interviews with Elinor Smith Sullivan (see p. 391).

24 *Ibid.*

25 *Ibid.*

26 *New York Times*, 29 March 1929, p. 16.

27 Extract from Amelia's second log book which began on 20 July 1929 and ended 2 March 1932; information courtesy of Richard Sanders Allen. The log book is in the possession of a collector in Culver City, California.

28 *New York Times*, 29 March 1929, 'Amelia Earhart is fourth woman to whom transport licence is granted. Others are 1: Ruth Nichols; 2: Phoebe Omlie; 3: Lady Mary Heath . . . although other women hold "limited commercial" licences.'

29 Harry Bruno, *Wings Over America*, Halcyon House, New York, 1942, p. 222.

30 *New York Times*, 1 July 1929, p. 1.

31 *New York Times*, 16 July 1929.

32 Amelia Earhart, 'Afraid to Fly?', *Cosmopolitan* magazine, July 1929.

33 *Ibid.*

34 'Fly America First', *Cosmopolitan* magazine, October 1929.

35 'Adventures Beneath the Sea', *Cosmopolitan* magazine, August 1929.

36 Many letters and phone calls between the author and freelance aviation researcher, Mr Peter Stevenson, were needed before the hyperbole was recognized as such. At one point Mr Stevenson dared the author to duplicate AE's exit from a submarine. The author declined.

37 Earhart, *The Fun of It*, p. 153.

38 Smith, *Aviatrix*, p. 108.

39 *Ibid.* Note: This interview between Elinor Smith and GP obviously occurred before the rule change. Originally applicants had to be accompanied by a mechanic. A flood of entries from Hollywood actresses in partnership with qualified male-pilot 'mechanics' resulted in a transparent attempt to obtain free publicity. Accordingly the rules were changed and entrants had to fly the course solo.

40 Author's interview with Elinor Smith Sullivan.

41 *Ibid.*

42 Earhart, *The Fun of It*, pp 152–3.

43 *Yuma Morning Sun*, 20 August 1929, p. 1; see also *New York Times* and *New York Sun*, 20 and 21 August 1929.

44 Earhart, *The Fun of It*, pp 153–4; see also *AAHS Magazine*, Fall 1963 issue, pp 223–4.

45 Judy Lomax, *Women of the Air*, John Murray, London, 1986, pp 55–7; Veca and Mazzio, *Just Plane Crazy*, pp 114–27.

46 *Ibid.*

47 Lomax, *Women of the Air*, p. 56.

48   *AAHS Magazine*, Fall 1963.
49   Putnam, *Wide Margins*, p. 287.
50   Smith, *Aviatrix*, p. 133.
51   *Ibid.*, p. 134.
52   Ninety-Nines' Newsletter from AE to members dated 19 January 1932; Ninety-Nines; Archives, Oklahoma; also Library of Congress reading room: TL 501.N5.
53   Letter to the author from Mrs Elinor Smith Sullivan, 29 November 1988.
54   Ford, *The Time for Laughter*, p. 205.
55   *New York Times*, 27 September 1929, p. 11.
56   Cutting in AE's scrapbook for 1932: believed to be from *The Illustrated Love Magazine*, January 1932, pp 25–7.
57   From transcript of author's interview with Mr David Binney Putnam Fort Pierce, Florida, June 1988.
58   Elinor Smith Sullivan interview, Santa Clara, California, June 1988.

CHAPTER 14

1   *New York Times*, 19 December 1929.
2   *Ibid.*, 21 March 1930.
3   Maddux was a close friend of Lindbergh's and President of Maddux Airlines.
4   AE to AOE; Schlesinger Library. Ref. 83–M69.
5   Luke Christopher, Secretary FAI to J. Mikrent, Directing Official of Speed Trial held in Los Angeles on 22 November 1929.
6   *New York Times* and *The Times* (London) covered this event in most issues between 30 December 1930 and 4 January 1930.
7   Transcript of author's interview with Charles 'Cap' Palmer, Los Angeles, June 1988.
8   *New York Times*, 30 January 1930. The marriage took place in the West Indies on 12 January.
9   Both Amelia's sister; Muriel Morrissey, and the writer Jean Backus stated that George proposed six times to Amelia. See: Backus, *Letters from Amelia*, p. 87, and Morrissey, *Amelia, My Courageous Sister*, but George is on record saying she refused him 'twice, at least', see *Soaring Wings*, p. 76. I was unable to find any original source for this information which is now often quoted. It is possible that George told Muriel, but unfortunately she has been too ill recently to be interviewed again.
10 Putnam, *Wide Margins*, p. 300.
11 *Ibid.*
12 *Time*, 25 August 1930, p. 39.
13 AE to AOE; 19 April 1930: Schlesinger Library. Ref.: 83–M69.
14 Letter from AE's secretary to F. Neely at the NAA, 2 December; NA&SM Library, Smithsonian Institution, Washington DC. File.

Amelia Earhart General, FO171300.

15 Backus, *Letters From Amelia*, p. 93.

16 Putnam, *Soaring Wings*, p. 79.

17 *Ibid.*, p. 93.

18 AE to AOE; undated: addressed from AWA Clubhouse, 353 West 57th, New York. Schlesinger Library. Ref.: 83–M69.

19 Putnam, *Wide Margins*, p. 76.

20 AE to AOE, February 1930. Schlesinger Library. Ref.: 83–M69.

21 AE to AOE, 25 February 1930. Schlesinger Library. Ref.: 83–M69.

22 Information courtesy Mr Richard Sanders Allen. Note that courses were measured, for reasons of international competition, in metres. Amelia's speed record was subsequently converted in miles per hour.

23 *Publisher's Weekly*, 30 August 1930, p. 757.

24 Syndicated article in unidentified newspaper: from Amelia's scrapbook at Purdue University. In the first thirty days the line carried 5,000 passengers according to a letter she wrote to her mother in October, see Schlesinger Library. Ref.: 83–M69.

25 *Virginia Pilot*, 25 September 1930, p. 1.

26 Mr Carl Harper.

27 AE to AOE, 2 October 1930. Schlesinger Library. Ref: 83–M69.

28 Letter to the author from Mr Richard Sanders Allen.

29 *New York Times*, 10 November 1930, p. 11.

30 *Ibid.*, 11 November 1930, p. 27.

31 George Palmer Putnam, *Andre, The Record of a Tragic Adventure*, G. P. Putnam's Sons, 1930.

32 Letters dated 31 December and 19 January 1931 to AOE from AE. Schlesinger Library. Ref.: 83–M69.

33 AE to AOE, 4 February 1931; Schlesinger Library. Ref.: 83–M69.

34 Putnam, *Wide Margins*, p. 282.

35 Putnam, *Soaring Wings*, p. 77.

36 *Ibid.*, p. 78.

37 AE to GPP. Seaver Center, Los Angeles Museum, Ref. 2100 Pl 58–137. The original letter is part of the museum's Betty Bowers collection. For many years it was thought that this letter had been destroyed in the fire at Lone Pine after George's death.

38 Transcript notes of author's interview with Mr and Mrs Charles 'Cap' Palmer, Los Angeles, California, June 1988. Mr Palmer was a close friend and colleague of GP's and his relationship is mentioned in later chapters of this book.

39 Putnam, *Soaring Wings*, p. 77.

40 Author's telephone interview with Gore Vidal, 21 January 1988.

41 *New York Times*, 9 February 1931, p. 1; and many other newspapers.

42 Unidentified Boston newspaper, 7 February 1931. Newsclipping in AE's 1931 scrapbook. Purdue University.

43   AE to AOE, 22 February 1931. Schlesinger Library. Ref.: 83–M69.
44   AE to AOE '. . . Mrs Putman is here (can't spell my own name!)'; see letter 16 September 1933. Schlesinger Library. Ref.: 83–M69.

CHAPTER 15

1   Putnam, *Soaring Wings*, p. 81.
2   Frank Kingston-Smith, *Legacy of Wings*, p. 176.
3   *Ibid.*, p. 183.
4   *Ibid.*, p. 188.
5   Transcript of author's interview with David Binney Putnam, Fort Pierce, Florida, June 1988.
6   *New York Times*, 20 June 1931; also letter AE to AOE, July 1931 Schlesinger Library.
7   AE to AOE, 27 April 1931; 27 June 1931 and July 1931: Schlesinger Library.
8   Cable to AE from Hiram Bingham dated 24 April 1931: Amelia Earhart General File: FO171300; NA&SM Library, Smithsonian Institution, Washington, DC.
9   AE to Mr and Mrs Oldham of Abilene, 17 July 1931. *Ibid.*
10   Putnam, *Soaring Wings*, p. 194.
11   AE to AOE, 17 September 1931. Schlesinger Library.
12   *Ibid.*, 1 December 1931. Schlesinger Library.
13   Transcripts of author's interviews with Mr David Binney Putnam and Mrs Margaret Lewis, June 1988.
14   Letter to the author from Elspeth Huxley, January 1988.
15   Transcript of author's interview with Mr George Palmer Putnam Jr, Boynton Beach, Florida, June 1988.
16   Letter to the author from Elspeth Huxley, January 1988.
17   Putnam, *Soaring Wings*, p. 160.
18   *Ibid.*, p. 105.
19   Earhart, *The Fun of It.*
20   Putnam, *Soaring Wings*, pp 97–8.
21   *Ibid.*
22   Organised by the American Society for the Promotion of Aviation.
23   Putnam, *Soaring Wings*, pp 98–9.
24   Letter to the author from Mr Richard K. Smith, 22 November 1987.
25   Putnam, *Soaring Wings*, p. 102.
26   Bert Hinkler had flown the South Atlantic solo, in November 1931.
27   Lady Mary Heath, 'Why I Believe Women Pilots Can't Fly the Atlantic', *Liberty Magazine*, 21 May 1932, pp 46–51.
28   Father of Major Edwin E. Aldrin, astronaut in crew of Apollo XI; second man to walk on the moon in July 1969.
29   Earhart, *The Fun of It*, p. 212.

30   Dr James H. Kimball.
31   Heath, 'Why I Believe . . .'
32   *Ibid.*
33   AE to AOE, 4 May 1932. Schlesinger Library.
34   Putnam, *Soaring Wings*, pp 102–3.
35   Loretta Gragg, Resource Center of the Ninety-Nines, Inc., Will Rogers Airport, Oklahoma City, Oklahoma, June 1987.
36   Amelia Earhart, *Last Flight*, Harcourt Brace, Harrop, 1938, p. 17.
37   Amelia Earhart, 'Women and Courage', *Cosmopolitan* magazine, September 1932.
38   Cable AE to GP, 19 May 1932. Purdue File III:A1.
39   *Ibid.* File III:A2.
40   Earhart, *Last Flight*, p. 18.
41   Earhart, *The Fun of It*, pp 212–14.
42   To GPP from 'Parkes', 20 May 1932. Purdue File III:A3.
43   Barographs were instruments commonly used to record the variations in height during flight. They were often sealed to prevent tampering, and used on altitude record attempts and on flying tests to give an indication of the pilot's ability to maintain straight and level flight.
44   *The Times* (London), 23 May 1932.
45   *Yorkshire Post*, 23 May 1932.
46   Putnam, *Soaring Wings*, p. 106.
47   Earhart, *The Fun of It*, p. 217.
48   *National Geographic Magazine*, 'The Society's Special Medal Award to Amelia Earhart', July 1932, pp 358–67.

CHAPTER 16

1   There is a great deal of confusion about the actual time of this flight. The National Geographic Society, in its award to her, stated that the time was 16 hours 12 minutes. On examination this confusion appears to have been caused because of the time zones; a misunderstanding of how British Summer Time (BST) works; and a correction for the time Amelia claimed to have spent (some 15 minutes) circling the pasture.
      She left Newfoundland at 7.12 p.m. local time which equates to 11.12 p.m. BST and landed at Culmore shortly before 2 p.m. BST on the following day.
2   In various reports Mr Gallegher is named as James and Robert, while his surname is sometimes spelled Galagher or Gallagher. I have used Amelia's version.
3   Article by Janet Mabie titled: 'Conversations', from unidentified magazine, date *circa* 1932. In Amelia's scrapbooks housed at Purdue University.
4   *Sunday Mail*, 22 May 1932, p. 1.

5   Putnam, *Soaring Wings*, p. 112.
6   The pilot of the charter plane, I.W.C. MacKenzie, expressed his admiration of Amelia's flying when he saw the field in which she had landed. 'With the Vega's high landing speed it was no mean feat to bring the big airplane into such a limited space,' he said.
7   AE to AOE; written from 4 St James Square – Lady Astor's London house – 2 June 1932. Schlesinger Library.
8   GPP to AOE, 26 May 1932. Schlesinger Library.
9   Putnam, *Soaring Wings*, p. 112.
10 *Ibid.*
11 Violette de Sibour was the daughter of Gordon Selfridge (owner of the famous London department store). The de Sibours became firm friends of the Putnams.
12 *American Weekly News* article by George, no date *c.* 1933.
13 *The Aeroplane*, 25 May 1932, p. 924.
14 8 May 1932: Smithsonian.
15 Putnam, *Soaring Wings*, p. 117.
16 To AE from the Ambassade de Belgique, Washington, 11 July 1932. Purdue File III.G2
17 *Boston Evening Transcript*, 20 June 1932.
18 *Congressional Record*, Monday 20 June 1932.
19 *Saturday Review*, December 1932.
20 Earhart, *The Fun of It.*
21 AE to Hiram Bingham: Smithsonian.
22 *Ibid.*, 19 July 1932.
23 Amelia had to return east for the official 'launch' of a new automobile, the Essex 'Terraplane'.
24 Ruth Nichols's flying time had been 13 hours 21 minutes but due to a delay in Witchita her elapsed time was 29 hours 1 minute 49 seconds.
25 Air racing champion and the man who had piloted Amelia on her first flight.
26 *New York Times* cutting, probably 13 July 1932.
27 *Philadelphia Enquirer*, 6 October 1932.
28 Transcript of author's interview with Muriel Morrissey, Medford Mass., June 1987.
29 *Morning Journal*, Marquette, Michigan, 25 October 1932.
30 AE to AOE, 24 December 1932: Schlesinger Library.
31 AE to AOE, letters dated 27 January and 14 February 1932. Schlesinger Library.
32 *Ibid.*
33 *Ibid.*, 20 April 1933.
34 Letter to the author from Mr Robert E. Lee.
35 Transcript of the *Amelia Earhart Symposium* held at NASM, Smithsonian Institution, Washington, DC, 1983.

36 AE to Hiram Bingham: NASM Library files: Smithsonian Institution, Washington, DC.

CHAPTER 17

1 *Screenland*, June 1933, pp 29–30.
2 *Ibid.*
3 AE to AOE, 8 June 1933. Schlesinger Library.
4 *Ibid.*, 14 June 1933.
5 *Ibid.*, probably 4 July 1933.
6 *New York Sunday Mirror*, 9 July 1933, p. 1.
7 Transcript notes of author's interview with David Binney Putnam, Fort Pierce, Florida, June 1988.
8 Atchison Library, Amelia Earhart collection, Atchison, Kansas.
9 Letter from John H. Leh to F. Goerner dated 6 March 1967. Amelia Earhart General File: NA&SM.
10 It was later transferred to the National Air and Space Museum at the Smithsonian Institution where it may be seen on permanent display.
11 Amelia Earhart 'Flying and Fly-Fishing', *Outdoors*, December 1934, pp 16 *et seq.*
12 Carl Dunrud, 'Amelia Earhart in Wyoming', *In Wyoming*, date unknown – c. 1970, p. 31.
13 Putnam, *Soaring Wings*, p. 235.
14 *Oakland Tribune*, 3 January 1935.
15 Backus, *Letters From Amelia*, p. 158.
16 AE to AOE, 26 December 1934. Schlesinger Library.
17 Nothing was ever found of C.P.T. Ulm, his crew or aeroplane. John Williams, 'Earhart Plan for Solo Hop opposed', *Los Angeles Times*, undated newsclipping. Purdue.
18 AE to AOE, 6 January 1935. Schlesinger Library.
19 Amelia Earhart, 'My Flight from Hawaii,' *National Geographic Magazine*, May 1935, pp 593, 609.
20 *Ibid.*
21 George Palmer Putnam, 'A Flyer's Husband', *Forum and Century*, June 1935, pp 330–2.
22 Various newspaper reports: specifically *Oakland Tribune*, 12 January 1935.
23 Earhart, 'My Flight from Hawaii', p. 596.
24 Putnam, 'A Flyer's Husband', p. 330.
25 President Roosevelt to AE, 18 January 1935. Purdue.
26 GP to AOE, February 1935. Schlesinger Library.
27 . . . *World Herald* [full title unreadable], 19 February 1935.
28 Putnam, 'A Flyer's Husband'.

29 It was during Lindbergh's flight to Mexico that he met his future wife, Anne Morrow Lindbergh, daughter of his hosts.

30 Stamp value: twenty centavos.

31 George Palmer Putnam, 'A Husband's Farewell to his Wife', *North American Newspaper Alliance*, September 1937.

32 *Ibid.*

33 AE to AOE, written on White House paper, 4 March 1935, Schlesinger Library.

34 AE to Mrs Eleanor Roosevelt, 14 March 1935. Purdue.

35 Eleanor Roosevelt to AE, 19(?) March 1935. Purdue.

36 Putnam, *Soaring Wings*, p. 220.

37 Earhart, *Last Flight*, p. 4.

38 GPP to Gene Vidal, 3 June 1935. University of Wyoming, Laramie, Wy. Vidal collection, by kind permission of Mr Vidal's widow.

39 AE to AOE, 5 July 1935. Schlesinger Library.

40 *Ibid.*, 28 July 1935. Schlesinger Library.

41 Ruth Freehafer, *R. B. Stewart and Purdue University*, Purdue University Press, Lafayette, Indiana, 1983.

CHAPTER 18

1 Earhart, *Last Flight*, p. 46. By 1975 there were over 12,000 women students at Purdue University.

2 A personal recollection of Amelia Earhart written by Helen Schleman, 13 April 1975. Also letter from Ms Schleman to the author, October 1988.

3 Amelia Earhart files. Special Collections Library, Purdue University. Specifically XII:A3.

4 Earhart, *Soaring Wings*, p. 228.

5 GPP to AOE, 26 November 1935, Schlesinger Library.

6 *Brockton Daily Enterprize*, 11 December 1935.

7 Don Dwiggins, *Hollywood Pilot*, Doubleday, 1967 p. 95.

8 AE to AOE, 17 December 1935.

9 *Ibid.*

10 AE to GP, 18 April 1936. Purdue.

11 *Ibid.*, 25 November (probably) 1936.

12 *Christian Science Monitor* (Boston), 25 January 1936.

13 *Los Angeles Times*, 3 March 1936, p. 1.

14 *Ibid.*

15 GPP to AOE, 4 March 1936, Schlesinger Library.

16 AE to AOE, 23 March 1936, Schlesinger Library.

17 Terry Gwynn-Jones, *Magnificent Gamblers*, Orbis Publishing Company, London, 1981, pp 79–86.

18 *Ibid.*

19 *Boston Globe*, 18 March 1937.

20　Freehafer, *R. B. Stewart.*

21　*Ibid.*

22　Letter to the author from R. B. Stewart dated 22 November 1987.

23　Freehafer, *R. B. Stewart.*

24　Draft of Associated Press Release by Foster Hailey, 19 April 1936.

25　The engines supplied to Amelia were the *civilian equivalent* of the engines specified for the military version of the Electra model 10E. There was nothing 'special or secret' about them according to Lockheed files.

26　Morrissey and Osborne, *Amelia, My Courageous Sister,* p. 178.

27　*Oakland Tribune,* 7 March 1937, 'Miss Earhart makes detailed preparations for World Flight.'

28　AE to AOE, 1 April 1936. Schlesinger Library.

29　Long letter from AE to AOE, written in pencil and undated but probably late May or early June 1936, headed 'Suggestions and Comments'. Schlesinger Library.

30　The letter 'R' designates Restricted use. Amelia had applied for a licence covering 'Long distance flights and research'. At a later date the US licence registration letter 'N' would be added, viz: NR 16020.

31　Dwiggins, *Hollywood Pilot,* pp 101–2. Also author's conversations with the late Paul Mantz *c.* 1962.

32　GP to Eleanor Roosevelt, June 1936. Purdue.

33　Letter from Eleanor Roosevelt's secretary to Richard Southgate, 29 June 1936, US Navy Archives.

34　*Ibid.*

35　GPP to Gene Vidal, 3 August 1936. Vidal papers, Wyoming University.

36　*Ibid.,* 11 August 1936.

37　AE to Eleanor Roosevelt, cable dated 15 September 1936. NA&SM file: Amelia Earhart General.

38　*Ibid.,* 17 September 1936.

39　AE to F. D. Roosevelt, 5 November 1935. Ref. 83–M69, Schlesinger Library.

40　Author's telephone interview with Gore Vidal, 21 January 1988.

41　Sundry letters in following collections: Wyoming University; Purdue; Schlesinger Library; NA&SM library.

42　AE and GP provided a loan to try to alleviate the financial problems and save the marriage.

43　Letters 1–14 October 1936 between GP and Captain A. G. Reid, USN: US Navy archives.

44　Generally accepted spelling for Tokyo in 1937. The new version was not generally adopted in the west until after the Second World War.

45　AE to the President, 10 November 1936: Purdue File VII: A1.

46　Internal Memorandum: Paul Bastedo to Chief of Navy Operations, 16 October. US Navy Archives.

47　Memorandum regarding discussion between Mr Miller of Air Commerce and Commander Hill. Dated 3 February 1937. US Navy archives.

48 Letter and article (unpublished) from Lt J. G. Johnson (who served aboard the *Itasca* on the 1936 exploratory mission to Howland); to *New York Times* editor, 18 March 1937. File F0171300, NA&SM, Smithsonian Institution, Washington, DC.

49 Dick Strippel, *Amelia Earhart: The Myth and the Reality*, Exposition Press, New York 1972, p. 40.

50 Dwiggins, *Hollywood Pilot*, pp 97–8.

51 AE to President Roosevelt, 8 January 1937. Purdue File VII: A1.

52 Letter from Assistant Secretary to the President dated 12 January, 1936. Purdue File VII:A1.

53 Sound Archives collection: Columbia University, New York. Aviation tapes.

54 Sundry cuttings in Amelia Earhart's scrapbooks at Purdue. Specifically *Cleveland Press* and *New York Daily Mirror*, 16 February 1937.

55 *Ibid.*

56 *Ibid.*

57 Jacqueline Cochran, *The Stars at Noon*, Robert Hale, 1955, pp 87–91.

58 AE to MEM, 31 January 1937. Schlesinger Library.

59 Strippel, *Amelia Earhart*.

60 Sundry letters and internal memorandum in National Archives, Washington, DC, January to May 1937: File number FO 171300.

61 *Airpost Journal*, vol 8, 8 February 1937.

62 *Blackwell Sunday Tribune* (Oklahoma), 21 February 1937, p. 1.

63 Putnam, *Soaring Wings*, p. 212 (this incident also repeated in another context in article by GPP, unidentified news cutting in scrapbooks at Purdue).

64 *Time*, 19 July 1937, pp 45–6.

65 *Oakland Tribune*, 7 March 1937.

66 Letter from Lt-Cmdr P. V. H. Weems, *Popular Aviation Magazine* (USA), May 1938.

67 Transcript of author's interview with Elgen and Marie Long, San Mateo, California, 2 July 1988.

68 Dwiggins, *Hollywood Pilot*, p. 99.

69 Cable from C. B. Allen (in Oakland) to *New York Herald Tribune*, 3 July 1937, 3 p.m.: Purdue File VIII:D4.

70 Cable from GP to *Herald Tribune:* Purdue File VII.C3.

71 Earhart, *Last Flight*, pp 57–8.

72 Dwiggins, *Hollywood Pilot*, p. 100.

73 *Ibid.*, pp 100–101.

74 *Ibid.*, p. 102.

75 Memorandum from Lt Arnold E. True to Chief of Naval Operations Ref. SECNAV 1315–1544. US Naval Archives, date obscured, *c.* April 1937.

76 *Time* magazine, 29 March 1937, p. 36.

77 Dwiggins, *Hollywood Pilot*, pp 99 and 103.

78 Eyewitness report of George Miller (civilian employee at Luke Field) and others, Exhibits C–F to the official board of enquiry, 23 March 1937 US Naval Archives.

79 Official report from Cmdr of Hawaiian Air Depot, Luke Field, to the official board of enquiry, *ibid.*

80 *Time* magazine, 29 March 1937, p. 36.

81 Fred Goerner's speech at Amelia Earhart Symposium at Smithsonian Institution.

82 Another eyewitness, Pan Am's 'Captain Lodi' said it looked to him as though the accident had been caused because she had neglected to lock the tailwheel.

83 Earhart, *Last Flight*, p. 71.

84 Putnam, *Soaring Wings*, p. 261.

85 *Ibid.*, p. 260.

86 *Ibid.*

87 The *Advertiser* (Hawaii), 20 March 1937.

88 *New York Herald Tribune*, 20 March 1937; Backus, *Letters from Amelia*, p. 213.

89 *Cleveland Press*, 31 March 1937; also syndicated to other newspapers.

90 *New York Herald Tribune*, 7 April 1937.

CHAPTER 19

1 Earhart, *Last Flight*, p. 73.

2 Letter and invoice in the amount of $1,086.10 dated 13 May 1937, National Archives, Ref. Y197.

3 Lockheed's bill was $14,000.

4 Earhart, *Last Flight*, p. 78. Among the donations from 'generous friends' was a check from Richard Byrd for $1500, exactly the amount Amelia had given him for the Antarctic Expedition in 1929.

5 Called *United Air Services Ltd*, the business included aeroplane charter and a flying school.

6 Author's interview with Elgen and Marie Long, San Mateo, California, 2 July 1988.

7 Frederick Goerner's speech to Amelia Earhart Symposium in 1983 to Smithsonian Institution, Washington, DC. A full transcript of the symposium appeared in *Aviation Journal* (California) in various issues from April 1983 to May 1984. Mr Goerner's speech appears in the February 1984 issue, p. 5.

8 *World Flight* was the proposed title for Amelia's book. But it was published posthumously under the title *Last Flight*.

9 Schlesinger Library, Radcliffe College: Denison House Records.

10 Author's interview with Mrs Margaret Putnam Lewis (GP's fourth and last wife), Los Angeles, California, 29 June 1988.

11 Author's interview with Albert Bresnik, Los Angeles, California, 28 June 1988.

12 *Ibid.*

13 Dwiggins, *Hollywood Pilot*, p. 104.

14 *Ibid.*

15 GPP to Admiral Leahy, 8 May 1937. US Naval Archives.

16 Joseph Gurr to Fred Goerner. Letter on file at NA&SM Library Smithsonian Institution, Washington, DC. Earhart General File FO 171300.

17 *Ibid.*

18 C. B. Allen, Aviation Correspondent of the *Herald Tribune* from 1923 to 1953. A long-time friend of George's, he had written many articles about Amelia from the time of her 1928 flight and had answered the damaging Williams article following the crash in Hawaii.

19 *New York Herald Tribune*, 8 July 1937.

20 Letter to the author from Mrs William Lee Reed, 22 January, 1989. Amelia spent a few days aboard the yacht 'Brownie' deep-sea fishing and relaxing with Mrs Reed's parents the Bruce McIntoshes.

21 Unidentified newspaper article by GPP (probably September 1937). Scrapbook no 18; Purdue University's Special Collections Library.

22 Putnam, *Wide Margins*, pp 297–8.

23 Earhart, *Last Flight*, pp 97–8.

24 *Ibid.*, p. 100.

25 *Ibid.*, p. 102.

26 *Ibid.*, p. 110. Author's note: In giving the names of cities where Amelia stopped on her last flight I have used the names and spellings as they appeared in her log. Many have since changed and where necessary for clarity I have also given the present name in brackets.

27 *New York Herald Tribune*, 8 June 1937.

28 Earhart, *Last Flight*, p. 129.

29 *Ibid.*, p. 130.

30 *New York Herald Tribune*, 8 June 1937.

31 Earhart, *Last Flight*, p. 152.

32 De Sibour to GPP, 29 April, 1937. Purdue File VIII: A1.

33 Earhart, *Last Flight*, p. 180.

34 GPP to AOE, 16 June 1937: Schlesinger Library.

35 AE to GPP 17 June 1937. Purdue File VIII: B3.

36 Dwiggins, *Hollywood Pilot*, p. 108.

37 Transcript of author's conversation with Mr Gore Vidal, 21 January 1988. See also Gore Vidal, *Armageddon*, André Deutsch, London, pp 25–9.

38 The original pages of Amelia's informal log are held in Purdue File VIII: B.

39 Putnam, *Wide Margins*, p. 292.

40   Earhart, *Last Flight*, p. 195.
41   *Ibid.*, p. 197.
42   *Ibid.*, pp 211–12: see also Morrissey and Osborne, *Amelia, My Courageous Sister*, pp 220–4.
43   Earhart, *Last Flight*, pp 212–13.
44   Elgen and Marie Long interview.
45   *Ibid.*
46   Earhart, *Last Flight*, p. 217.
47   *Ibid.*, p. 222.
48   Amelia's bracelet was subsequently donated to the Ninety-Nines, and is held at their headquarters in Oklahoma City as part of their extensive Amelia Earhart collection.
49   Cable dated 31 June 1937, Purdue Fae VIII: B2.
50   Earhart, *Last Flight*, pp 225–6.
51   *Ibid.*, p. 102.
52   AE to GPP, cable dated 30 June 1937. Purdue File VIII: B4.
53   Transcript of author's conversation with Mr Gore Vidal, 21 January 1988. See also *Armageddon* pp 25–9.
     Because of the source I have given this suggestion of an early menopause considerable attention in my researches. I have now discounted it for two reasons:
     1. Since Amelia was only thirty-nine years old, this is not only 'disagreeably early' but most unlikely and George would surely have known about it, yet he told no one, not even his family, subsequent wives or closest friends.
     2. It is doubtful that Amelia, liberated as she was, given the mores of 1937, would have found it easy to discuss such a matter with a male friend.
54   Ann Holtgren Pellegreno, *World Flight*, Iowa State University Press, 1971, p. 144.
55   Elgen and Marie Long interview.
56   *Itasca* log, US Navy Archives, p. 27.
57   *Ibid.*, p. 29
58   *Ibid.*, p. 9.
59   Cable, Purdue File VIII: II6.
60   It was Noonan who specified the navigational equipment for the first Pan American Clipper services in 1935; a choice not made because he necessarily considered one instrument 'superior' to another but by the fact that the equipment he recommended he 'had used extensively . . . and [it] had been proven satisfactory'. The following is an extract from a letter from Fred Noonan to Lieutenant-Commander P.V.H. Weems (founder of the Weems School of Navigation in Maryland), 11 May 1935, and published in *Popular Aviation Magazine* (USA) May 1938. I have quoted it at length because it reveals Noonan's working methods:

'. . . for instance parallel rulers versus protractors – and I suspect that plain prejudice which actuates so many of us, carried some weight . . . parallel rulers, where room permits their use, are more satisfactory for rapid plotting of long range Direction Finding bearings . . . those carried were of the Captain Fields Improved type – graduated in degrees – and consequently the greatest objection to their use in aircraft, namely creeping when referring to compass roses, was removed.

. . . Time pieces carried were a Longines Civil Time Chronometer and Longines second-setting watch. The latter was set to correct GCT [Greenwich Civil Time, a synonym for Greenwich Mean Time (GMT) the base time at Greenwich, London, from which all other world times are taken], at all times by checking with the chronometer. Two sextants were carried, a pioneer bubble octant and a mariner's sextant. The former was used for all sights; the latter as a preventer. I also carried a Dalton Mark VII Navigational Computer, which I find a great convenience.

. . . fixes were determined entirely by stellar observations at night. These fixes were more reliable than would be possible by crossing a line of position with a Direction Finding bearing, due to the amount of error which would be introduced by even a small angular error in the long range Direction Finding bearings. By day, having only the single heavenly body for determining the lines of position, we did not cross the bearings, however during daylight hours we were nearer the radio stations and consequently the error introduced was considerably reduced.

The accuracy of fixes was very gratifying. By that an accuracy of approximately ten miles is implied. My experience is that such a degree of accuracy is about the average one might expect in aerial navigation . . . The greatest difficulty is, of course, the determination of drift angle. We carried smoke bombs and water flares for this purpose [these were not entirely satisfactory due to cloud] and consequently the difference between 'no wind' positions and fixes established by observation were utilized, entirely for determination of drift angle, and, of course, wind direction, and velocity for laying new courses. However [where sudden wind shifts could be expected] reliance would necessarily have to be placed on Direction Finding bearings despite their lack of extreme accuracy.

In addition to the actual navigation I maintained a very detailed log . . . in addition to recording courses, variation, deviation, track made good, indicated and true air speeds etc, a complete meteorological record was kept. As you may imagine, each hour represented 60 very busy minutes.

I consider the development of the Greenwich Hour Angle the greatest contribution to the science of navigation . . . and have used it exclusively since first published in the Air Almanac. The second-setting watch runs it a close second as a time saver and an aid tending to mini-

mize errors . . . I suppose you wonder which method I use for compu-
tation of observations. I use Dreisonstok exclusively. Probably another
prejudice but I have used it since it first became available in 1927 or
1928 and still prefer it.'

61 *New York Herald Tribune*, 3 July 1937, p. 1.
62 Report by J. A. Collopy (District Superintendent of Civil Aviation at
    Lae) 28 August 1937, File WF2 'Search' No: 9. Schlesinger Library.
63 Cable, File WF2 'Weather'. Schlesinger Library.

CHAPTER 20

1 The international dateline referred to is the 180th meridian.
      The US Navy and Coast Guards subdivide hourly time zones into
   half hours and it is this 'ship's time' which is referred to as local time at
   Howland in all logs and reports used in this chapter: *Itasca* log: reel C,
   US Navy Archives microfilm on Amelia Earhart.
2 Pellegreno, *World Flight*, p. 144; see also Vincent Loomis, *Amelia
   Earhart*, Random House, 1985, p. 11.
3 Report by J. A. Collopy dated 28 August 1937; copies in Purdue,
   Schlesinger, and Smithsonian archives.
4 Balfour was later to claim to the writer Vincent Loomis that Amelia had
   asked him to go along with her as radio operator. This seems extraordinary when she had stripped the plane of every item of personal luggage,
   every slip of paper and even discarded safety equipment in order to carry
   a greater fuel load.
5 All distances quoted for this flight have been checked using the computer
   at the Royal Geographical Society, London using verified coordinates;
   they do not necessarily agree with contemporary assessments of distances
   between points, some of which have proved to be incorrect.
6 British Earhart-researcher, Roy Nesbit, examined the meteorological
   records for Nauru and the British Gilbert and Ellice Islands for 2 July
   1937 which are held at the National Meteorological Archives, Bracknell,
   Berkshire. He discovered that winds at a 'medium height' were 25 mph
   from due east. This also equates to reports in the *Itasca* log that winds in
   the first sector of the flight were 'stronger than forecast'.
7 Letter from Harry Balfour to Dr Robert Townley, 31 December 1969.
   However, a report by Paul Rafford states that Balfour told him he had
   been unable to pass the met report to AE which gave 25-mph headwinds.
   Both documents in NA&SM Library, Smithsonian Institution,
   Washington, DC.
8 *Itasca* radio transcripts report. Ref. 8018–2200 30 June 1937, p. 32;
   National Archives, Washington, DC.
9 Note from Captain Blakeslee to Mr Pete Stevenson 24 May 1988, given
   to the author by Mr Stevenson.

10 Official report by the commands of *Itasca*, p. 2, 'Known Facts (no 17)'. US Navy Archives. Also, similar report by captain of the USS *Lexington*, p. 2; National Archives, Washington, DC.

11 Letter from T. H. Cude (Director of Police at Nauru in 1937) to Francis X. Holbrook. NA&SM Library, Smithsonian Institution, Washington, DC.

12 Figures provided by computer at The Royal Geographical Society, London.

13 Note from Captain Blakeslee, 24 May 1988, to Mr Peter Stephenson.

14 *Itasca's* log.

15 *Ibid.*, see also appendix No. 1.

16 All radio communications between Amelia Earhart and *Itasca* are taken directly from the *Itasca's* radio log, and from the official report of the incident made by *Itasca's* captain, Commander Warner Thompson. Detailed extracts from this log will be found in Appendix No. 1. The original documents are freely available for researchers at the National Archives Building; and on microfilm reels A–F of the US Navy file on Amelia Earhart; and at the office of US Coast Guard; all in Washington DC.

17 *Itasca* report on Earhart search, p. 36.

18 *Itasca* radio log, p. 42.

19 *Itasca* report, p. 35.

20 That final message, interpreted above in the *Itasca* report, appears in the log *exactly* as follows:

KHAQQ TO ITASCA WE ARE ON LINE 157 337 WL REPT MSG WE WILL REPT N ESS S THIS ON 6,210 KCS WAIT 3,105/A3 AS(?)ʹ KHAQQ TSMISION 'WE ARE RUNNING ON LINE LSNIN 6,210 KCS'.

21 Pellegreno, *World Flight.*

22 In June/July 1967 on the thirtieth anniversary of Amelia's last flight a commemorative round-the-world flight was made in a standard Lockheed Electra, model 10. Piloted by Anne Pellegreno, co-piloted by Bill Payne and navigated by Bill Polhemus they found difficulty in locating Howland even with the vastly superior communication technology available to them. Ms Pellegreno recorded the story of this flight in her book *World Flight*, q.v.

23 *Itasca* report, pp 43 and 49.

24 *Ibid.*

25 Elgen and Marie Long have already conducted several impressive underwater studies in conjunction with Hawaiian-based oceanographic laboratories. It is their intention to launch a massive underwater search/survey for the Electra, using submarines of the type used to locate the *Titanic*.

26 Based on the Longs' theory, the Electra lies at a depth of 16,800 feet.
27 Roy Nesbit, 'What DID Happen to Amelia Earhart?' *Aeroplane Monthly*, January and February 1989.
28 *Itasca* log, p. 45.
29 August 1967; Air accident reports FAA Archives. None of the ten Lockheed Electra aircraft involved in the reported sea landings broke up as a result of the landing. This incident also reported in Pellegreno, *World Flight*, no p/n; see section 'The Earhart Controversy'.

CHAPTER 21

1 *New York Herald Tribune*, 4 July 1937, p. 1.
2 Although both men were using radios from home as 'amateurs' both were in fact skilled professional radio operators.
3 *Itasca* report, p. 104. Other messages, Thompson maintained, were 'criminally false transmissions'.
4 *San Francisco Chronicle*, 6 July 1937, p. 1.
5 Letter from Joseph H. Gurr dated 3 May 1982 to author Fred Goerner, NA&SM Library, Earhart file. Note that Mantz was not aware of all the work Gurr had carried out. Mantz assumed that the only aerial available for transmissions on 500 kcs was the trailing one that Amelia had 'left behind because she felt it a nuisance'. In fact it seems possible that because Gurr 'had fitted a loading coil and resonated the top antenna system' with wire antennae to the two tail surfaces that Amelia, at least, believed this new arrangement worked equally well and therefore left the trailing antenna because it seemed surplus to requirements.
6 The USS *Swan* was 200 miles from Howland waiting to act as plane guard on the Howland–Honolulu leg. See the *Washington Post*, 3 July, p. 1.
7 *San Francisco Chronicle*, 5 July, p. 1.
8 *Itasca* report, p. 57.
9 *New York Herald Tribune*, p. 1.
10 *Time magazine*, 12 July 1937.
11 *New York Times*, 8 July 1937.
12 Letter to Secretary of Navy Department from W. A. Levett, Acting Officer-in-charge, Beru, Gilbert Islands. US Navy Archives 361030.
13 *New York Herald Tribune*, 7 July 1937, p. 1.
14 *Itasca* report. p. 76.
15 *Ibid.*
16 *San Francisco Chronicle*, 9 July, p. 1.
17 Cable from Admiral Leahy to GP, Purdue Special Collections File X:B3.
18 *Itasca* report, p. 88.
19 Eleanor Roosevelt, 'My Day', *New York Telegraph*, 7 July 1937.
20 Franklin D. Roosevelt Library, Hyde Park, New York.

21 *Ibid.*, 31 July 1937 and Purdue Special Collections file X:B7.

22 Letter from Joseph H. Gurr dated 3 May 1982, NA&SM Library, Earhart file. Belief in the theory of the buoyancy of metal aeroplanes was dispelled during World War II when a great number of all-metal aeroplanes ditched and sank almost immediately.

23 Cochrane, *The Stars at Noon*, pp 90–91.

24 *Ibid.*

25 This episode reported in *Stars at Noon* differs from Miss Cochran's statements to an interviewer in tapes held in Columbia University's Sound Archive library. There she states that she was 'on a ship on the way to Europe when Amelia went missing'.

Her claims that she had never heard the name *Itasca* are also surprising since it had been publicised that the *Itasca* would stand by for radio contact during the first planned attempt on the world flight and for three weeks the newspapers had been carrying reports that *Itasca* was standing by at Howland to meet Amelia. It seems highly unlikely that Jackie Cochran could have missed all these reports of her friend's flight in which she must, surely, have been interested.

26 US Navy Archives, cabled dated 23 July 1937.

27 Telegram from Gray to American Embassy, 30 July 1937, Franklin D. Roosevelt Library, Hyde Park, New York.

28 *New York Times*, 25 July.

29 National Archives, file A4–5 (5).

30 *Ibid.*

31 Welles to McIntyre, 5 August 1937, Franklin D. Roosevelt Library.

32 Memo sent from National Geographic Society to GP dated 7 September 1937, Schlesinger Library files.

33 *Ibid.*

34 GP to AOE, 29 July 1937. Schlesenger Library.

35 Cable signed 'Grey' to American Embassy, London, 2 August 1937, Purdue Special Collections Library.

36 National Archives File A4–5(5), 361030–3.

37 *Ibid.*

38 *Ibid.*, File A4–5(5), 361030–5.

39 GP to AOE, 9 May 1939. Schlesinger Library.

40 GP to AOE, 3 December 1940. Schlesinger Library.

41 GP to AOE, 9 May 1939. Schlesinger Library.

42 Author's interview with Mr Albert Bresnik in Los Angeles, July 1988.

43 An original page of manuscript, received from Amelia by George after her disappearance. Purdue Special Collections Library.

44 Earhart, *Last Flight*, p. 108.

45 Janet Mabie to AOE, 19 August 1939. Schlesinger Library 83–M69 Box 2. File 61. Janet Mabie to AOE 28 July 1941.

46 *New York Times*, 8, 9 October, p. 21.

47 *Ibid.*, 27 August 1937.

48 *Ibid.*, 5 August 1937, p. 25; 6 August, p. 18.

49 GP to BG, 28 October 1937. Schlesinger Library.

50 Information contained in probate file of Amelia Earhart Putnam: File 181709 Superior Court, Los Angeles, California.

51 Note that after this first sentence the document had been cut and pasted together, obviously to edit material that was either irrelevant to this trip, or perhaps contained material too personal to be included. In an article written by GP in an unidentified newspaper (clipping in Purdue scrapbook 'Amelia always held Self Responsible for Flights') he did include part of the missing message: 'However, I believe my equipment is the best available.'

52 Original (edited) document in Purdue Special Collections Library.

53 GP to AOE 24 December 1937. Schlesinger Library.

54 Letter to the author from Robert E. Lee, December 1987.

55 Janet Mabie to AOE, 28 July 1941, Schlesinger Library 83–M69, Box 2, File 61.

56 *Ibid.*, records of the Amelia Earhart Foundation 'Dimity'.

57 GP to AOE, 20 May 1939. Schlesinger Library.

58 'The Broncho that Would Not be Broken'; Putnam, *Soaring Wings*, p. 23.

59 GP to MEM, 15 September 1938. Schlesinger Library.

60 Putnam, *Soaring Wings*, p. 63.

61 GP to AOE, 28 September 1938. Schlesinger Library.

62 GP to Admiral William D. Leahy. National Archive, file A4–5(5).

63 General: National Archive file A4–5(5).

64 GP to AOE, 1 December 1938. Schlesinger Library.

65 Last will and testament of Amelia Earhart Putnam; made in New York 5 April 1932 and originally filed at Los Angeles Superior Court, 5 January 1939. Probate file 181709.

66 *Ibid.*
    At the first appraisal the Estate was valued as follows:

	$
Cash in Fifth Ave Bank, NY	8,190
Property at Valley Spring Lane	21,000
Tract of land and property inhabited by Helen Earhart	1,500
2 Terraplane automobiles	1,190
1 Cord automobile	900
1 Electric Power Company bond	962
Promissory note from Paul Mantz	4,973
Furniture and effects	350
Contract regarding sale of name Amelia Earhart for promotional purposes	850
Outstanding amount due from publishers for *The Fun of It*	1,000

		$
50% interest in *Last Flight* appraised at		5,000
Clothing including two fur coats		900
Jewellery		75
	Total	46,890
Additions at later date		2,790
Film rights and other royalties		9,429
	Total	59,109

67 Amy had been injured in a car accident in the previous year.
68 The house at Rye was actually sold in December 1938. Reported in the *New York Times*, 6 January 1939, p. 37.
69 GP to AOE, 9 May 1939. Schlesinger Library.
70 Letters from Janet Mabie to AOE. Schlesinger Library, 83–M69, Box 2, File 61.
71 *Ibid.*
72 Letter to the author from Robert E. Lee.
73 *Stunt Girl* and *Hollywood Doctor*.
74 Jerome Lawrence: playright/director who in collaboration with Robert E. Lee created outstanding American theatre productions: *Inherit the Wind, The Night Thoreau Spent in Jail, Auntie Mame*, etc.
75 Robert E. Lee: see previous note. Mr Lee was also co-founder of the Armed Forces Radio Service and the American Playrights Theatre.
76 Letter to the author from Robert E. Lee.
77 *Ibid.*
78 Author's interview with Jean-Marie Asp, San Diego, July 1988.
79 *Ibid.*
80 Author's interview with Muriel E. Morrissey, Medford, June 1987.
81 *New York Times*, 6 January, p. 4; interviews with Jean-Marie Asp and Muriel Morrissey; probate file records AEP, Los Angeles.
82 GP to AOE, 4 May 1939. Schlesinger Library.
83 *Ibid.*
84 Author's interview with Charles Palmer, Los Angeles, July 1988.
85 *Los Angeles Times* also *Los Angeles Examiner*, 20 April 1939.
86 *New York Times*, 21 April 1939.
87 GP to AOE, 15 May 1939. Schlesinger Library.

CHAPTER 22

1 Author's interview with Jean-Marie Asp, San Diego, California, 27 June 1988.
2 *Ibid.*

3 Paul Mantz to AOE, 22 March 1940. Schlesinger Library.

4 GP to Elmer Dimity, 6 April 1949. Schlesinger Library.

5 GPP to AOE, 19 April 1940. Schlesinger Library.

6 *Ibid.*

7 Paul Mantz file: 83–M68 Schlesinger Library.

8 E. Dimity to AOE, 20 May 1940. Schlesinger Library.

9 Paul Mantz to AOE, 20 May 1940. Schlesinger Library.

10 Letter from Captain Irving, 4 June 1940. File 83–M69, Dimity, Schlesinger Library.

11 Letter from Bessie M. Young to E. H. Dimity, 4 August 1940. Schlesinger Library.

12 Bessie Young to AOE. Schlesinger Library.

13 William C. Hollister to AOE, March 1941. Schlesinger Library.

14 AOE to William C. Hollister, 23 March 1941. Schlesinger Library.

15 Josephine Berger died of cancer in New York in March 1941.

16 Author's interview with Margaret 'Peg' Putnam Lewis, Los Angeles, California, 29 June 1988.

17 Jean-Marie Asp interview.

18 Charles Palmer interview.

19 Jean-Marie Asp interview.

20 Interview with David Binney Putnam, Fort Pierce, Florida, 24 June 1988.

21 Elizabeth Hyatt Gregory Collection: UCLA Special Collections Library. Box 6101 L615.

22 Writer of many screenplays, also the novel *They Shoot Horses Don't They?*

23 Academy of Motion Pictures and Sciences; RKO and motion picture subject files.

24 Letter to the author from Charles Palmer, 15 February 1989.

25 *Ibid.*

26 AOE told reporters: 'Amelia told me many things, but there were some things she said she could not tell me. I am convinced she was on some sort of government mission . . . and died in Japan.' *New York Times*, 25 July 1949, p. 17.

George was astonished at Amy's statement, dismissing it as 'nonsense'; Muriel also dissociated herself from Amy's line of thinking, having received personal assurances from Eleanor Roosevelt that Amelia had not been involved in any clandestine arrangement to spy.

27 US Army Diploma, dated 17 October 1942 in possession of Mrs Margaret Putnam Lewis.

28 David Binney Putnam interview.

29 Colonel Harvey H. Holland (Air Corps) to GPP, 9 March 1943, in possession of Mrs Margaret Putnam Lewis.

30 Charles Palmer interview.

31 GPP to Joseph Henry Jackson, undated, Berkeley College Special

Collections Library, Berkeley, California.

32 Jean-Marie Asp interview. She also stated: 'I always hoped, indeed thought, that we *would* get together again . . . I never remarried until after I heard that GP had remarried . . .'

33 Letter to the author and enclosure entitled 'Reminiscences of GP' from Robert E. Lee dated 6 August 1988.

34 Margaret Putnam Lewis interview and subsequent letters to the author.

35 David Binney Putnam interview.

36 Margaret Putnam Lewis interview.

37 George Palmer Putnam, *Up in our Country*, Duell, Sloan and Pearce, New York; pp 17–18. This was George Putnam's last book and was published, posthumously, in 1950.

38 Charles Palmer interview.

39 Putnam, *Up in our Country*, p. 19.

40 Divorce Decree, 2 March 1945, courtesy Mrs Jean-Marie Asp.

41 Charles Palmer interview.

42 Margaret Putnam Lewis interview.

43 *Ibid.*

44 *Ibid.*

45 The fire at Rye in November 1934 and also the fire at the Whitney Portal Lodge, the year after George's death, which destroyed the bulk of his own and Amelia's private papers.

46 Courtesy Margaret Putnam Lewis.

47 Margaret Putnam Lewis interview.

48 Letter to the author and enclosure entitled 'Reminiscences of GP' from Robert E. Lee dated 6 August 1988.

49 David Binney Putnam interview.

50 Putnam, *Up in our Country*.

51 GPP to Margaret 'Peg' Putnam.

52 Charles Palmer interview.

53 Letter to the author from Helen Ogston, October 1988.

54 GPP to Isiah Bowman, Johns Hopkins University Library, Baltimore, MD. Bowman files.

55 Lawrence M. Gould to Margaret Putnam. Margaret Putnam Lewis papers.

56 Rockwell Kent to Margaret Putnam. *Ibid.*

57 George Agnew Chamberlain to Margaret Putnam. *Ibid.*

58 Charles Palmer interview.

59 Letter to the author and enclosure entitled 'Reminiscences of GP' from Robert E. Lee dated 6 August 1988.

60 *Ibid.*

APPENDIX 1

1 Considerable confusion has arisen in reports of Amelia's last flight because many time factors were involved. Greenwich Mean Time has been used as the definitive time for Amelia's flight from Lae to Howland with a conversion to local time at Lae, where appropriate; and to ship's time at Howland Island. The US Navy and Coast Guard subdivide hourly time zones into half hours and it is this 'ship's time' which is referred to as local time in all ship's logs and reports used as source material for chapter 20, and in the appendices to this book.

2 J. Collopy report.

3 *Itasca* report, p. 2, 'Known Facts no. 17'; confirmation of this also appeared in the log of the USS *Lexington*.

4 Cable from Alfred M. Doyle (US Consul in Sydney, Australia) to US State Department; National Archives.

APPENDIX 2

1 On Amelia's charts the distance between Lae and Howland was given as 2556. This was correct information if using the coordinates used by Clarence Williams. These, however, were found to be incorrect as explained later in Appendix 2.

2 Unless otherwise stated all fuel measurements are US gallons: see Collopy report *Amelia Earhart* dated 28 August 1937 to Secretary Civil Aviation Board: 'One tank contained only 50 gallons of its total capacity of 100 gallons . . .'

Note: There was no 100-gallon tank on the Electra but there were two wing tanks which each held 102 gallons. Purdue files X B.9.

3 Author's interview with Elgen and Marie Long, San Mateo, California, 2 July 1987.

4 *Daily Telegraph* Sydney, Australia, 6 July 1937 p. 1: also similar reports in other papers Australia, New Zealand, New Guinea.

5 Unidentified news cutting, believed to be *Herald Tribune*, 20 March 1937.

6 Cable: GP to Jacques de Sibour, 13 February 1937; Public Record Office, Kew, England. Ref: AVIA2/1082.

7 Author Dick Strippel's examination of the so-called Earhart Mystery, *Amelia Earhart, The Myth and the Reality* used calculations from Lockheed, statements by Paul Mantz and the expertise of Bill Polhemus (who flew as navigator on a duplicated commemorative flight to Howland, in a standard Lockheed 10, in 1967) to make these points. My own research bears out his statements.

See also *World Flight*, Anne H. Pellegreno, Iowa University Press, 1971.

8 *The Myth and the Reality*, Dick Strippel, p. 116.

9   *Ibid.*

10   Letter from Amelia Earhart to Sir Francis Shelmerdine dated 13 February 1937: Public Record Office, Kew, London. File no: AVIA 2/1082.

11   Fuel notes and other unidentified notes; Purdue collection.

12   Figures taken from information contained in *The Myth and Reality* op. cit.; article in Lockheed house magazine *Horizons* by Roy Blay, May 1988 issue, pp 23–36; research notes from Schlesinger and Purdue collections.

13   All fuel measures quoted here are US gallons.

14   On a navigation chart a compass bearing (rhumb line) plots as a straight line, intersecting each meridian at the same angle. A Great Circle arc intersects each meridian at a different angle and appears longer, but is actually the shortest distance around the earth's sphere. The Great Circle is the route followed by any radio signal or electromagnetic propagation, and the visual line of sight is also a Great Circle arc.

15   Fred Noonan wrote several articles on navigation; see also his letter to Weems, quoted at length in the source notes to chapter 19 (note 60).

16   Sir Francis Chichester pioneered this system of 'find the island'. It is described fully in his book *The Lonely Sea and the Sky*, Hodder and Stoughton (London) May 1964. The extracts used here appear on pp 119–21.

17   *The Lonely Sea and the Sky, ibid.*, pp 108–41.

18   *Ibid.*

19   An arc from zenith in sky to horizon: an angle is measured to this from a meridian.

20   Line of position: 157–337 ran from north, north-west to south, south-east (through Howland) assuming Noonan's dead reckoning position north of the island was accurate.

21   I am indebted to the staff (especially Mr Tom De Clare) in the US Hydrographer's Archives office, Madison Building, Library of Congress, Washington, DC for this information. Correct co-ordinates for Howland first appeared in *Lippincott* in the 1941 edition.

22   *Itasca* report, p. 106.

23   Muriel E. Morrissey and Carol L. Osborne, *Amelia, My Courageous Sister.* Osborne Publisher Inc, 1987.

24   *Itasca* radio log, 19 June 1937. National Archives, p. 3.

25   *Ibid.*, 12 June 1937, p. 3.

26   *Ibid.*, 23 June 1937, pp 10 & 17.

27   *Ibid.*, 25 June 1937, p. 21.

28   Cable from Amelia Earhart in Lae, to Richard Black aboard *Itasca*, via Radio Manilla 27 June 1937: *Itasca* log, p. 23.

29   *Itasca* radio log: 29 June 1937, p. 29.

30   *Itasca* report p. 25.

31   US Naval Archives: Earhart Files – Microfilm reel B SC A21–5 (25) Nav 327.

32   Report by Lt D. Cooper of Army Air Corp. Dated 27 July 1937. This report was declassified in 1977.
33   *Itasca* report, pp 104–6.
34   Transcript of Earhart Symposium held at Smithsonian Institution in 1983.
35   Department of Commerce Aircraft Inspection Report – F.A.A.
36   *Oakland Herald Tribune,* 7 March, 1937.

APPENDIX 3

1   There are various sources for this, but specifically see books by Goerner, Loomis and Pellegreno in bibliography section. Original statements by Elieu stated only that a woman flyer landed, but later the woman seems to have acquired a male companion.
2   The *American Weekly,* 10 September 1944, p. 9 – other sources too. The album seems to have been lost after this story was released, probably taken by a souvenir hunter, but many early researchers claimed that the album was confiscated by the government as part of their cover-up of the *real* story.
3   Interviews with Cap Palmer and Jean-Marie Asp.
4   Thomas Devine has now written a book, *Eyewitness* (Frederick & Co., 1988). [Author's note: I have not had the opportunity to read *Eyewitness* before finishing *Sound of Wings*].
5   *Stars at Noon.* op. cit., p. 160.
6   *Ibid.,* pp 90–91.
7   *Daughter of the Sky,* Paul Briand.
8   This paragraph is not, however, intended to denigrate a fine book. It remains one of the most readable on the subject.
9   Letter from Billy Burks to Col. John Miller, US Marine Corps, 27 March 1983. NA&SM library, Smithsonian Institution, Washington DC.
10   *Amelia Earhart Returns from Saipan,* Joe Davidson (Davidson Publishing Company, Ohio), 1969. Also letter from Florence Kothera, NA& Smithsonian Library, *Ibid.*
11   *Amelia Earhart Lives,* Joe Klaas (McGraw Hill, NY, 1970).
12   ER to MEM 14 July 1961, Schlesinger Library files. Letter to Mantz is published in *Hollywood Pilot* by Don Dwiggins op. cit.
13   Fred Goerner's speech during Amelia Earhart Symposium at Smithsonian Institution, Washington, DC, 1983.

BIBLIOGRAPHY

Adams, Jean, and Kimball, Margaret, *Heroines of the Sky*, Doubleday, 1942.

Allen, Frederick Lewis, *Only Yesterday*, Harper, 1931.

Babington-Smith, Constance, *Amy Johnson*, Collins, 1967, London.

Backus, Jean, *Letters from Amelia*, Beacon Press, 1982.

Balchen, Bernt, *Come North with Me*, Dutton, 1958.

Batten, Jean, *My Life*, Harrap, 1938.

Beaty, D., *The Water Jump*, Secker & Warburg, 1976.

Bilsten, Roger E., *Flight in America 1900–1983*, Johns Hopkins University Press, 1983.

Boase, Wendy, *The Sky's the Limit*, Macmillan, London, 1979.

Bostok, Peter, *The Great Atlantic Air Race*, Dent, 1979.

Briand, Paul Jr, *Daughter of the Sky*, Duell, Sloan & Pearce, 1960.

Brooks-Pazmany, Kathleen, *United States Women in Aviation 1919–1929*, Smithsonian, 1983.

Bruno, Capt. Harry, *Wings over America*, Robert McBride & Co., 1944.

Burke, John, *Winged Legend – The Story of Amelia Earhart*, Arthur Barker, London, 1970.

Byrd, Richard E., *Skyward*, G. P. Putnam's Sons, 1928.

Cadin, Martin, *Barnstorming*, Duell, Sloan & Pearce, 1965.

Chadwicke, Roxanne, *Amelia Earhart – Daring Flyer*, Lerner, 1986.

Chichester, Sir Francis, *The Lonely Sea and the Sky*, Hodder & Stoughton, 1964.

Cochran, Jacqueline, *The Stars at Noon*, Robert Hale, London, 1955.

Collins, Paul F., *Tales of an Old Air-Faring Man* [publisher unknown], 1957.

Davidson, Joe, *Amelia Earhart Returns from Saipan*, Davidson Publishing Company, 1969.

Davis, Burke, *Amelia Earhart*, G. P. Putnam's Sons, 1972.

Davis, Kenneth S., *The Hero*, Doubleday, 1959.

De la Croiz, Robert, *They Flew the Atlantic*, Muller, 1967.

De Leeuw, Adele Louise, *Story of Amelia Earhart*, Crossett, 1955.

Dixon, Charles, *Conquest of the Atlantic by Air*, Lippincott, 1931.

Dwiggins, Don, *Barnstormers*, Tab, 1986.

——, *Hollywood Pilot*, Doubleday, 1967.

——, *Flying Daredevils of the Roaring Twenties*, Arthur Barker, London, 1969.

Earhart, Amelia, *20 Hrs. 40 Min.*, G. P. Putnam's Sons, 1929.

——, *The Fun of It*, Brewer, Warren & Putnam, 1932.

——, *Last Flight*, Harcourt Brace/Harrap, 1938.

Farmer, *Celluloid Wings*, Tab, 1986.

Ferris, Helen J., *Five Girls Who Dared*, Macmillan, 1931.

Ford, Corey, *The Time for Laughter*, Little, Brown, 1967.

Frazer, Chelsea, *Famous American Flyers*, T. Y. Crowell, New York, 1942.

Gallagher, Desmond, *Shooting Suns and Things*, Kingsford Press, Ireland, 1986.

Garst, Doris Shannon, *Amelia Earhart: Heroine of the Skies*, Messner, 1950.

Gentry, Viola, *Hangar Flying*, privately published.

Gilroy, Shirley Dobson, *Pilot in Pearls*, Link Press, 1985.

Goerner, Fred, *The Search for Amelia Earhart*, Doubleday, 1966.

Gower, Pauline, *Women with Wings*, John Long, 1938.

Gwynn-Jones, Terry, *Aviation's Magnificent Gamblers*, Orbis, 1986.

——, *The Air Racers*, Pelham Books, 1984.

Hawks, Frank, *Once to Every Pilot*, Stackpole, 1936.

——, *Speed*, Brewer, Warren Putnam, 1931.

Heath, Lady, and Murray, Stella Wolfe, *Women and Flying*, John Long, 1929.

Howe, Edward, *The Story of a Country Town*, Holt, Reinhart & Winston, 1928.

Howe, James Moore, *Amelia Earhart – Kansas Girl*, Bobbs Merrill, 1950.

Huxley, Gervase, *Both Hands*, Chatto & Windus, London, 1970.

Ireland, Norma Olin, *Index to Women of the World*, Faxon Company Inc., 1970.

Jablonski, Edward, *Atlantic Fever*, Macmillan, 1972.

——, *Ladybirds – Women in Aviation*, Hawthorne Books, 1968.

Jenkinson, Sir Anthony, *America Comes my Way*, 1941.

Johnson, Amy, *Skyroads of the World*, Chambers, 1939.

——, *Myself when Young*, Muller, 1963.

Klaas, Joe, *Amelia Earhart Lives*, McGraw-Hill, 1970.

Knaggs, Oliver, *Amelia Earhart – Her Last Flight*, Timmins Publishers, South Africa, 1983.

Lauwick, Herve, *Heroines of the Sky*, Muller, 1963.

Lindbergh, Anne Morrow, *North to the Orient*, Harcourt Brace, 1963.

——, *Bring Me A Unicorn*, Chatto, London, 1972.

——, *Hour of Gold – Hour of Lead*, Chatto, London, 1973.

——, *Locked Rooms and Open Doors*, Chatto, London, 1974.

——, *The Flower and the Nettle*, Chatto, London, 1976.

Lindbergh, Charles, *The Spirit of St Louis*, Scribners, 1953.

Lomax, Judy, *Women of the Air*, John Murray, London, 1986.

Loomis, Vincent, *Amelia Earhart*, Random House, 1985.

Mollison, Jim, *Playboy of the Air*, Michael Joseph, 1937.

——, *Death Cometh Soon or Late*, Hutchinson, 1932.

Mondley, David, *Women of The Air*, Wayland Ltd, 1981.

Moolman, Valerie, *Women Aloft*, Time-Life Books, 1981.

Morrissey, Muriel, *Courage is the Price*, McCormick-Armstrong, 1963.

——, *Amelia Earhart*, Bellerophon, 1985.

Morrissey, Muriel and Osborne, Carole, *Amelia, My Courageous Sister*, Osborne Publishers Inc., 1988.

Mosley, Leonard, *Lindbergh – A Biography*, Doubleday, 1976.

Nichols, Ruth, *Wings for Life*, Lippincott, 1958.

Oakes, Claudia, *United States Women in Aviation 1929–39*, Smithsonian Institution Press, 1978.

O'Neill, Paul, *Barnstormers and Speedkings*, Time-Life Books, 1981.

Pellengreno, Ann Holtgren, *World Flight*, Iowa University Press, 1971.

Plank, C., *Women with Wings*, Harper & Bros, 1942.

Putnam, George Palmer, *Soaring Wings*, Harcourt Brace 1939/Harrap, London, 1939.

——, *Wide Margins*, Harcourt Brace, 1939/Harrap, London, 1939.

——, *Up in Our Country*, Duell, Sloane & Pearce, 1950.

Putnam, David Binney, *David Goes to Greenland*, G. P. Putnam's Sons, 1922.

Railey, Hilton Howell, *Touch'd with Madness*, Carrick & Evans, 1938.

Rickenbacker, Eddie, *Rickenbacker*, Hutchinson, London, 1968.

Roseberry, C. R., *The Challenging Skies*, Doubleday, 1966.

Ross, Walter, *The Last Hero*, Manor Books, 1974.

Rowe, Percy, *The Great Atlantic Air Race*, Angus & Robertson, 1977.

Schoneberger, *Californian Wings*, Windsor Publications, 1984.

Smith, Elinor, *Aviatrix*, Harcourt Brace Jovanovich, 1981.

Southern, Neta Snook, *I Taught Amelia to Fly*, Vantage Press, 1974.

St John, Adela Rogers, *Some are Born Great*, Doubleday, 1974.

Strippel, Dick, *Amelia Earhart – The Myth and the Reality*, Exposition Press, 1972.

Tate, Grover Ted, *The Lady who Tamed Pegasus – the Story of Pancho Barnes*, Maverick, 1984.

Thaden, Louise, *High Wide and Frightened*, Stackpole Sons, 1938.

Underwood, John, *Madcaps, Millionaires and 'Mose'*, Heritage Press, 1984.

Veca, Donna and Mazzio, Skip, *Just Plane Crazy*, Osborne Publishers Inc., 1988.

Vidal, Gore, *Armageddon*, André Deutsch, London, 1987.

Voisin, Gabriel, *Men, Women and 10,000 Kites*, Putnam, London, 1960.

GLOSSARY

Altimeter Instrument which indicates the altitude of aeroplane in flight.

Azimuth An arc of the horizon, normally measured clockwise from the north.

Barnstorm Pioneer aviators used to travel around the country, carrying fare-paying passengers on local 'pleasure flight'. Usually they operated out of farm fields. This was known as barnstorming.

Bubble sight A sextant observation in which a bubble floating in liquid is used instead of the horizon.

Dead stick An aeroplane making a landing when the propeller has ceased turning (or when it is still turning but the engine has stopped) is said to be making a dead stick landing.

Dolly A wheeled cart, placed under a tail skid (in the days before tail wheels) to assist in moving the aeroplane on the ground.

Dope A tautening agent used on fabric aeroplane surfaces, which is painted onto the fabric to make it drumskin tight and impenetrable by wind and weather.

Drift The sideways angle of movement of an aeroplane in relation to the ground, caused by cross winds.

Drift Indicator An instrument for determining drift by sighting an object on the ground along the wires of a grid incorporated in the instrument.

Great circle The shortest distance between any two points on a hemisphere.

Ground loop An uncontrollable turn by an aircraft while it is rolling over the ground at a speed too low for the rudder to be effective.

Ground speed The speed of an aeroplane relative to the ground. This will be affected by wind speed to give air speed.

Line of Position A straight line obtained by plotting on a chart a sextant observation of a celestial body. An accurate line of position passes through the point of observation. The intersection of two lines of position, with compensation for the time difference between the first and second sightings, establish a position on the earth's surface.

Pancake To hit the ground too hard after levelling off too high for a proper landing.

Stall The condition of an aeroplane which has lost the airspeed necessary to maintain forward flight or control.

Sun line A line of position obtained from a sextant observation of the sun.

Variation The difference in angle in a compass reading between true north and magnetic north.

ACKNOWLEDGEMENTS

Many organisations provided me with access to collections of documents, materials and facilities and unfailing patience:

American Heritage Center, University of Wyoming (Emmett D. Chisum). Collection: Papers of Eugene Vidal.

Atchison County Library; Atchison, Kansas. Collection: Amelia Earhart.

Butler Library; and Oral History Research Office; Columbia University, New York. Aviation tapes.

Atchison Museum; Atchison, Kansas. (Father Angelus and his team) Collection: Amelia Earhart.

British Library, Newspaper Collection; Colindale, London.

British Library, Reading Room, London.

The Carnegie Library, Pittsburgh, Pennsylvania. (Mrs Ann Lloyd.) Phipps family records.

Amelia Earhart's Home and Museum; Atchison, Kansas.

International Women's Air and Space Museum, Ohio. (Ms Steadman) Amelia Earhart files.

Library of Congress, Map Room: Madison Building; Washington, DC (Tom De Claire). Charts of Howland Island and Pacific Ocean, before and after *Itasca* survey of 1936.

Public Record Office, Kew, England. File: AVIA2–1082 Amelia Earhart.

National Archives & Record Service; Washington, DC (Richard Van Dernhoff, Military Records): Record Group 80 (file A21–5)

US Naval Archives; Navy Yard, Bldg 210, Washington, DC (Janice Beatty, Paula Murphy; reference staff in the Naval history department). Records held on 5 reels of microfilm: NRS246

Ninety-Nines' Resource Center, Oklahoma (Loretta Gragg and Virginia Qualine). Collection: Amelia Earhart.

Purdue University; Lafayette, Indiana:
  Special Collections Library, (Ms Helen Q. Schroyer)
  Publishing Dept (Mr Bob Topping).

Royal Geographical Society, London (Mr Jeremy Smith – Map Room)

Seaver Center, Los Angeles County Museum of Natural History (Janet Evenden) Collection Betty Bowers.

Salisbury Library, Salisbury, Wiltshire.

Arthur and Elizabeth Schlesinger Library, Radcliffe College, Cambridge, Massachusetts. Collections: Amy Otis Earhart; Muriel Morrissey; Amelia Earhart.

Smithsonian Institution, National Air and Space Museum Library, Washington, DC. File: F0171300

UCLA Library and special collections, Los Angeles, California Collection: Elizabeth Hyatt Gregory.

University of California Library, Santa Barbara, California.

University of California, Library and Special Collections, Berkeley, California.

Wellesley College, Wellesley, Massachusetts (Ms Jean Berry) Women's Union and student records; Dorothy Binney Putnam.

I would like to make it very clear that at no time did I meet any resistance to my researches and everyone I met or spoke within what might be called 'official' circles in the USA, was most helpful.

The amount of research material available on the subject of Amelia's disappearance is enormous, amounting to many thousands of original contemporary documents, much of which is on microfilm. In addition much material of a more personal nature exists in private collections. There is inevitably duplication and where I have attributed a source in the book, it may be that I have accessed that particular document in other collections elsewhere as well.

It would be impossible to produce a work of this scope without the assistance and co-operation of a great number of people and so I wish to thank the following:

Richard Sanders Allen; Jean-Marie Asp; Russell E. Belous; Albert Bresnik; Montgomery R. Budd; Sally Putnam Chapman; James LeRoy Crowell; Vera Dunrud; Peggy Erasmus; Les George; Jill Fitzhugh; Lester E. Hopper; Elspeth Huxley; Jerome Lawrence; Shirley Johansen; Robert E. Lee; Margaret Lewis; Elgen and Marie Long; Graeme and Shari Lovell; Cliff Lovell; Sandy MacKenzie; Dorice McKelvy; Greg Mantz; Muriel Earhart Morrissey; Claudia Oakes; Helen Ogston; Carol Osborne; David Putnam; George Palmer and Marie Putnam; Helen Q. Schroyer; Helen B. Schleman; Marion Sharpe; Doris Smart; Laura Stickney; Elinor Smith Sullivan; Richard K. Smith; Peter Stevenson; R. B. Stewart; Ann Cain Tibbets; Robert W. Topping, Cynthia Putnam Trefelner; Bobbi Trout; Gore Vidal; John Underwood.

Although I have mentioned the various members of the Putnam family by name I should like to thank them collectively for their kindness to me, their marvellous co-operation in allowing me to see documents which for so long had been considered very personal, and last – but not least – their hospitality. George Putnam's fourth wife – his widow, Peg – was an unfailing source of information and for a while it seemed that every post brought some new anecdote, photograph or document.

While most of Amelia and George's story lies in the United States, both in archives and in the minds of their many connections, there is also a British connection due to AE's two record-breaking flights across the Atlantic. One of my last research tasks was a visit to Burry Port in South Wales where Amelia and her two male companions landed in June 1928. There I met Les George, a restaurateur, who has made a point of keeping Amelia's name alive in the small town with *The Amelia Dining Room* and the *Friendship Bar*. On the walls are newspaper cuttings, photographs and paintings of the *Friendship*'s landing; menu cards and coasters are also dedicated to the story. And Mr George kindly provided audiotapes of townspeople who actually witnessed the landing over sixty years ago and other memorabilia which have proved helpful.

I wish to thank Katy Belcher who undertook two lengthy research trips with me to the USA, and so halved the time required to delve through the masses of documentation held in various collections there; and Susan Rabiner, who was responsible for reawakening my interest in the subject.,

My editors Tony Whittome and Barbara Anderson have been a source of enormous help, especially during the final stages of the book and I am most grateful for their interest and always constructive advice.

Finally a very special thanks to G.A.H.W., without whose help and encouragement this book would probably have been finished in half the time.

Photographic acknowledgements
The author wishes to thank all those who kindly provided photographs during the course of her research, only a small number of which can be reproduced here. As with original documents, many photographs are duplicated in various collections and in some cases several people have provided me with the same picture. Those that are featured in this book are used with appropriate permission from:

Purdue University; Mrs Margaret Lewis; James Crowell; Albert Bresnik; Geoffrey A. H. Watts; Laura Stickney; BBC Hulton picture library.

INDEX

Also by Mary S. Lovell

THE MITFORD GIRLS

The Biography of an Extraordinary Family

'I am normal, my wife is normal,
but my daughters are each more foolish than the other'
bewailed Lord Redesdale, father of the Mitford girls.

Even if the six daughters, born between 1904 and 1920, of the
charming, eccentric David, Lord Redesdale and his wife Sydney had
been quite ordinary women, the span of their lives – encompassing
the most traumatic century in Britain's history – and the status to
which they were born, would have made their story a fascinating one.
But Nancy, Pamela, Diana, Unity, Decca and Debo, 'the mad, mad
Mitfords', were, and are, far from ordinary.

'The remarkable Mitfords have inspired dozens of books
but this may well be the best' *Independent on Sunday*

'A sensational saga' *Mail on Sunday*

'This is an excellent book' *Daily Telegraph*

ABACUS
978-0-349-11505-4

A RAGE TO LIVE

A Biography of Richard and Isabel Burton

'A splendidly spirited yet sensitive study of that redoubtable pair'
Philip Ziegler, *Daily Telegraph*

Brilliant, charismatic, an incomparable linguist, erudite scholar, famous translator of the *Arabian Nights* and a daring adventurer, Richard Burton was arguably the most eminent of all the 'eminent Victorians'. Yet until now, none of his numerous biographies has fully addressed his relationship with Isabel, his intelligent, striking, and unconventional wife. Her role has hitherto been reduced to one – misinterpreted – event: the burning of many of Burton's papers after his death. Now, drawing on startling new evidence, Mary S. Lovell restores Isabel Burton to her rightful place. The result is an extraordinary, compelling biography of a fascinating, controversial and celebrated couple.

'A monumental biography . . . Mary S. Lovell is the real thing:
a biographer passionately interested in her subjects'
The Times

ABACUS
978-0-349-11016-5

BESS OF HARDWICK

First Lady of Chatsworth

'Lovell has excelled at bringing the Tudor age
to exuberant life. A phenomenal story'
Hugh Massingberd, *Mail on Sunday*

Bess Hardwick, born into the most brutal and turbulent period of England's history, did not have the most auspicious start in life. Widowed for the first time at sixteen, she nonetheless outlived four monarchs, married three more times, and died one of the wealthiest and most powerful women in England's history.

The Tudor Age could not have been more hazardous a time for an ambitious woman; by the time Frances, Bess's first child, was six, three of her illustrious godparents had been beheaded. Plague regularly wiped out entire families, conspiracies and feuds were rife. But through all this Bess Hardwick bore eight children and built an empire of her own; the great houses of Chatsworth and Hardwick.

'Utterly absorbing . . . one of those biographies in which the reader
really doesn't want the subject to die'
Alexander Waugh, *Independent on Sunday*

ABACUS
978-0-349-11589-4

STRAIGHT ON TILL MORNING

The Life of Beryl Markham

'A splendid addition to the tales of Kenya's colonial past'
Daily Mail

Beryl Markham, like Karen Blixen, could only have come out of Africa. Pioneering aviatrix, flamboyant beauty, brilliant race-horse trainer, unscrupulous seducer – her life story is for every reader who was enthralled by Blixen's exotic world, that of Kenya between the wars.

This fully authorised biography, drawn from the author's personal association with Beryl and her family, paints a vivid portrait of a tempestuous and controversial character. It tells of her friendship with Karen Blixen (though she commandeered Blixen's husband Bror and lover Denys Finch Hatton), of her spectacular courage when she became the first person to fly from England to America, and of the mysteries surrounding her highly praised, bestselling book *West with the Night*.

'Filled with revelations, gossip and fascinating details . . . Mary Lovell's superbly researched biography is likely to be definitive'
New York Times

ABACUS
978-0-349-12175-8

Now you can order superb titles directly from Abacus

☐ The Mitford Girls: The Biography   Mary S. Lovell   £10.99
   of an Extraordinary Family

☐ A Rage to Live: A Biography of   Mary S. Lovell   £14.99
   Richard and Isabel Burton

☐ Bess of Hardwick: First Lady   Mary S. Lovell   £10.99
   of Chatsworth

☐ Straight on Till Morning: The Life   Mary S. Lovell   £10.99
   of Beryl Markham

The prices shown above are correct at time of going to press. However, the publishers reserve the right to increase prices on covers from those previously advertised, without further notice.

————————————————— ⬭ABACUS⬭ —————————————————

Please allow for postage and packing: **Free UK delivery.**

Europe: add 25% of retail price; Rest of World: 45% of retail price.

To order any of the above or any other Abacus titles, please call our credit card orderline or fill in this coupon and send/fax it to:

Abacus, PO Box 121, Kettering, Northants NN14 4ZQ

Fax: 01832 733076   Tel: 01832 737526

Email: aspenhouse@FSBDial.co.uk

☐ I enclose a UK bank cheque made payable to Abacus for £ . . . .

☐ Please charge £ . . . . . . to my Visa/Delta/Maestro

☐☐☐☐☐☐☐☐☐☐☐☐☐☐☐☐☐☐

Expiry Date ☐☐☐☐   Maestro Issue No. ☐☐

NAME (BLOCK LETTERS please) . . . .

ADDRESS . . . .

. . . .

. . . .

Postcode . . . . Telephone . . . .

Signature . . . .

Please allow 28 days for delivery within the UK. Offer subject to price and availability.